Tradition and Imagination

Tradition and Imagination
Revelation and Change

DAVID BROWN

OXFORD
UNIVERSITY PRESS

OXFORD
UNIVERSITY PRESS

Great Clarendon Street, Oxford OX2 6DP

Oxford University Press is a department of the University of Oxford.
It furthers the University's objective of excellence in research, scholarship,
and education by publishing worldwide in

Oxford New York

Athens Auckland Bangkok Bogotá Buenos Aires Calcutta
Cape Town Chennai Dar es Salaam Delhi Florence Hong Kong Istanbul
Karachi Kuala Lumpur Madrid Melbourne Mexico City Mumbai
Nairobi Paris São Paulo Singapore Taipei Tokyo Toronto Warsaw

with associated companies in Berlin Ibadan

Oxford is a registered trade mark of Oxford University Press
in the UK and in certain other countries

Published in the United States
by Oxford University Press Inc., New York

British Library Cataloguing in Publication Data

Data available

Library of Congress Cataloging in Publication Data

Tradition and imagination: revelation and change
David Brown.
Includes bibliographical references.
1. Revelation. 2. Tradition (Theology) 3. Bible—Evidences.
authority, etc. I. Title.
BT127.2.B76 1999 231.7′4—dc21 99–12411
ISBN 0-19-826991-9

1 3 5 7 9 10 8 6 4 2

Typeset in Bembo by
Cambrian Typesetters, Frimley, Surrey

Printed in Great Britain
on acid-free paper by
Biddles Ltd., Guildford and King's Lynn

PREFACE

THIS is a book which had its origins in an invitation from the University of Oxford to deliver the Hensley Henson Lectures in the Hilary Term of 1996. I am most grateful for the encouragement offered at the time by those who attended, including erstwhile colleagues and pupils, as well as friends in other subject areas. Particular mention should be made of Basil Mitchell, Richard Swinburne, Keith Ward, and Maurice Wiles. Inevitably, however, my greater debt is to my present context. A number of friends and colleagues have read the manuscript in whole or in part, and offered helpful comments, among them Gregor Duncan, James Dunn, Harold Guite, Michael Ipgrave, Ann Lambton, Walter Moberly, Stephen Pedley, Peter Phillips, Peter Robinson, and Loren Stuckenbruck. Greta Gleeson and Paul Fletcher offered invaluable computer advice and ensured that the manuscript was in the most presentable and accessible form. David Fuller and Ann Loades commented in detail at every stage. David prevented many an infelicity in style and ensured that imaginative issues remained to the fore, while Ann was indefatigable in drawing attention to relevant literature as well as in giving gentle nudges to my prejudices. Without Ann's encouragement and enthusiasm it is doubtful whether the work would ever have been completed. I am also grateful to the readers for the Press for their helpful and encouraging comments.

As every academic knows (sometimes to their great cost) no less important in writing is a suitable environment, and in this respect my debt to the cathedral at Durham and to its dean, my fellow canons, the choir, and congregation, knows no bounds. In an unguarded moment in response to a question of a former Oxford colleague I once used the word 'heaven' to describe my present setting. Exaggeration though it was, I am conscious that without the daily support and prayers of individuals too numerous to mention my life, and this project, would have been hugely impoverished. Yet one more debt remains to be acknowledged. In a book about tradition Durham's glorious living past cannot possibly escape mention. So I end by thanking the cathedral's two saints, Bede for his example of tireless scholarship and Cuthbert for the realism of his engagement with a wider world.

University of Durham

CONTENTS

LIST OF PLATES

INTRODUCTION

ALTHOUGH this is the first of two volumes on the role of tradition
in Christian theology, both are written in such a way that each can
be understood independently of the other, though obviously
complete comprehension of the project as a whole can only be
ascertained by consulting both volumes. My aim is to show that
tradition, so far from being something secondary or reactionary, is
the motor that sustains revelation both within Scripture and
beyond. Indeed, so much is this so that Christians must disabuse
themselves of the habit of contrasting biblical revelation and later
tradition, and instead see the hand of God in a continuing process
that encompasses both. In order to establish that contention, there
is much in what follows about the limitations of biblical insights.
Such remarks could easily be misread. So let me say at the outset
that this is done, not to disparage Scripture, but rather to extricate
it from a burden which in my view it cannot possibly bear. The
incarnation reveals a God who took with maximum seriousness
the limitations of a specific cultural context, and so we only do
that revelation a disservice if we posit as always present in Scripture
the viewpoints now taken by the contemporary Church. Instead,
we need to hear how the story develops, and thus of a God
continuously involved in the history of the community of faith.
The Bible, however, remains an indispensable part of that story,
and so, though in what follows numerous arguments are offered to
justify further development and even talk of the 'correction' of
biblical perspectives, none of this is intended to deny to that earlier
scriptural tradition the power also in its turn to offer a critique of
what came later. The reason why little attention is paid to that
possibility in what follows is not that I do not concede the point,
but rather that I want to persuade readers of the truth of a less
familiar contention, the need for continuing development.

The word 'imagination' occurs in the title of both this work
and its sequel: *Discipleship and Imagination*. This is not because I do
not take doctrinal issues seriously, but because I regard them as

secondary and parasitic on the stories and images that give religious belief its shape and vitality. The form of these stories and images change as a result of complex interactions between existing communitarian assumptions, new cultural contexts and the continuing work of God. Present-day Christianity, it seems to me, will go badly wrong, if it attempts an unmediated dialogue with the biblical text rather than recognizing also the intervening history that has helped shape its present perception of the text's meaning. The second volume focuses more closely on two specific issues: first, on what kind of difference being an involved reader—a disciple—makes; secondly, on the impact of the fact that such discipleship is necessarily constituted by membership of a particular community. It is thus to the second volume that the reader must turn for consideration of issues of authority or more personal questions of discipleship.

Here, however, I am concerned to establish the general structure of the argument. The discussion that follows is divided into three parts. Part One situates my contention in relation to three major features of our contemporary world, current debates between modernism and postmodernism and the resultant competing claims as to how Scripture should be read, dialogue between the religions, and the paradox of Christianity being apparently at its most appealing (in Christmas celebrations) at a point where many a theologian and preacher finds the imaginative details at their most embarrassing. Part Two then examines how religious tradition operated in the ancient world. The degree of change that occurs is held to legitimate my title: 'The Moving Text'. Some may take offence at the parallels drawn between the Greek religious tradition and changes that occur in the presentation of the stories of the patriarchs across Jewish, Christian and Islamic history, but, as will become obvious to the attentive reader, the comparison is intended to reflect to the credit of both, not as a means of undermining the value of the scriptural narratives. Part Three then turns specifically to Christianity, and seeks to illustrate how the appropriation of the message and person of Christ corresponds exactly to the type of pattern exhibited in earlier chapters, but this, so far from undermining a doctrine of incarnation, I argue, actually strengthens its plausibility. Even at his point of greatest contact with humanity, God exposed himself to the limitations of a specific culture and its assumptions, and thus necessitated continuing developments in how Christ would be appropriated in subsequent centuries. Although by way of illustration a chapter specifically devoted to the history of the visual arts occurs at this point, as the reader will discover, throughout both volumes there is repeated reference to the visual and literary imagination as an indispensable constituent of the living and developing dynamic of religious belief.

I write as a committed Christian. Nonetheless, I hope that I have done so in the way that will make the book accessible to those of different perspectives, including those of other faiths or none. What I am attempting to offer is an alternative way of conceptualizing Christian belief, in the light of our changed understanding of the relation between its biblical roots and what came later. Although those without Christian belief might wish to exclude the hand of God, it would still be possible for them to assess and appropriate the argument in terms of how in fact a developing tradition works, and in particular the key role which I have assigned to the imagination.

No bibliography is provided. Instead, complete biographical details are to be found at the first mention *within* any chapter of the particular work concerned.

PART ONE
Tradition as revelation

IN this first part of my discussion I want, as it were, to set the scene for the more specific case studies which follow in Parts Two and Three. These will seek to illustrate my conviction that, so far from Christianity being undermined by post-biblical developments in its self-understanding, it has been hugely enriched by them. Not, of course, that this was always so, but I do want to challenge the view that later reflection that deviates from its scriptural roots must necessarily stand under divine judgement. Instead, it can sometimes, I shall argue, not only be positively enriching but actually act as a critique of the scriptural text. A Christianity that confines God's revelatory acts to the narrow compass of Scripture, even when this is expressed in terms of the effect of that Scripture upon us in the here and now, I find less and less plausible, the more I become aware of the historical situatedness of that text. It seems odd to postulate a God without revelatory impact upon the history of the Church when that history is not significantly different in fallibility and conditionedness from the history of the biblical community itself.

Perhaps the most common motivation for resisting such a high place for later tradition—even more common than anxieties about the apparent undermining of scriptural authority—is to be found in the conviction that the sort of thing offered by tradition is pedantic and boring without any deep religious life to it. Thus the tendency is to think of formal pronouncements by councils and popes, or of such things as liturgical formulae and forms of clerical dress. These do have their place, but only on the periphery of my argument here. Instead, I want to focus the reader's attention upon the way in which even the stories within Scripture itself have not stood still. In very many cases they have been subject to imaginative 'rewriting', both within the canon and beyond, and that 'beyond' needs to be taken with no less seriousness than what

nominally lies on the biblical page. One of the principal ways in
which God speaks to humanity is through the imagination, and, as
we might have expected, the human imagination has not stood
still over a further two thousand years of Christianity. One reason
we fail adequately to appreciate this is because we assume continuity of text means continuity of content, whereas perceived variations in the latter are so extensive that they fully justify on my
view the title of Part Two: 'The Moving Text'.

But here in this Part my aim will be to set such questions in a
contemporary context, both in respect of academic discussion and
the life of the Church, as well as that of the wider world. So we
begin with a chapter on 'Narrative and Enlightenment', where
current academic debates about the relation of theology to
modernism and postmodernism are used to argue for an approach
to the Bible that takes seriously aspects of both. While maintaining that the questions raised by the Enlightenment cannot be side-
stepped and have therefore rightly found their place in the history
of biblical criticism, I shall argue that postmodernism should also
have an impact on us, in forcing proper recognition of a more
complex reality, one in which conflicting communal narratives
cannot easily be weighed against one another. Within modern
theology I find too much parody from both sides of the opposing
perspective, and want instead to find a middle course, not least
because this is where the notion of an open tradition would find
its natural place. Against the Enlightenment and modernism 'tradition' asserts the importance of situatedness: the impossibility of
standing totally outside deep-rooted perspectives that shape who
we are. Against postmodernism 'open' then refuses to draw the
implication, 'arbitrary'. However difficult access to alternative
perspectives may be, not only must they be taken seriously if we
are to lay any pretence to rational inquiry, they also contain the
potential to give new life and fresh vigour to a tradition that might
otherwise grow stale.

The second chapter, 'The hermeneutics of Pentecost and crib',
then tackles matters, as it were, from the pew. It attempts to
implicate contemporary Christian practice in the view I am advocating, by observing how deeply embedded is a narrative that
goes well beyond Scripture in the modern celebration of
Christmas. Most academics and many a preacher find this embarrassing, whereas to my mind it constitutes one of the strengths of

the Christian tradition, and illustrates well how its insights have been deepened by imaginative retelling and adaptation of the original story. The additions are not, of course, historically true, but the same could also be said of much in the narratives of Matthew and Luke. So it would seem odd summarily to dismiss later developments—as so many do—when the same criterion ought then rightly to condemn Scripture also. Instead, therefore, my suggestion is that we take seriously the possibility of applying a different criterion of truth and one more directly related to the operation of the imagination: the truth of imaginative 'fit' rather than literal fact. The point will be given due consideration in that chapter. Here suffice it to note that for a narrative to reflect or be true of someone's significance, it must have secure foundations in reality at some point, but it by no means follows from this that a one-to-one correspondence is required of the narrative; indeed that could be misleading or counterproductive, in failing to indicate the truth as a whole as distinct from its disparate parts.

The third chapter then tackles the question of God's role in all of this. Though our primary focus will be on Christianity, as its title 'Continuing revelation: learning from Judaism and Islam' indicates, this particular chapter is written in the firm conviction that the Enlightenment continues to require of us an open tradition that is willing to learn from approaches beyond the narrow compass of the Christian community itself. It is all but universally assumed, even by Christians critical of Scripture, that the more it is claimed one's religious views are found reflected in the Bible, the higher the view one has of God's revelatory action through its contents. So deeply engrained is this assumption that whatever new ideas begin to emerge within the Church, such as the quest for an improved status for women, the tendency is to project these back upon the text itself, as though otherwise its credit would be undermined. But there is an alternative way of looking at the matter. As Part Three will observe, modern biblical scholarship suggests that the incarnation involved a more radical kenosis than Christianity has assumed throughout most of its history, with Jesus very much conditioned by the culture of which he was part. But if this was true at the point of God's deepest disclosure and involvement with humanity, then *a fortiori* one would expect matters to proceed similarly elsewhere in revelation, and this is in fact what we find as we study the origin of the various biblical ideas. Revelation was thus a matter of God taking seriously our historical situatedness, our dependence on our own particular environment and setting, rather than attempting to override it. That being so, my contention is that the process of revelation had to continue beyond Scripture, since otherwise the tradition would have become stultified through being trapped within one particular epoch and its assumptions. The Christian story has thus acquired new insights not merely through recovery of neglected aspects of its past but also through external stimuli necessitating fresh thought and with it rather different imaginative appropriations of the Christian message from what the primitive community would have envisaged.

But before we reach that point, we begin our discussion by setting the question in the context of current intellectual debates about where humanity in general stands on issues of knowledge and imagination, tradition and communal identity. As we shall discover, much of the debate focuses on the issue of narrative.

I

Narrative and Enlightenment: The challenge of postmodernism

IN later chapters I shall suggest that the Western religious tradition has worked imaginatively, in the main by building upon existing narratives. Quite a few contemporary theologians would see stress on narrative as one of the most important contributions to come from postmodernist thinking, while the Enlightenment and the modernism that it initiated are often characterized as essentially destructive of religious belief. To my mind, though, matters are somewhat more complicated and the contribution of each, as well as their limitations, need to be duly acknowledged. This chapter will be concerned to explore what these are.

'Modernist' and 'postmodernist' are in fact rather slippery terms, used as they are in quite a wide variety of different senses. To some of these ambiguities I shall direct the reader's attention in due course, but as an opening shot a rough characterization will suffice. Indeed this will prove most useful in characterizing one of the most fundamental cleavages in the contemporary intellectual climate, which has had a marked impact also on recent theological writing. On the one hand we have the modernists, those who continue to support the Enlightenment project of the pursuit of universal values and an ever increasing human knowledge that is seen as objectively validated in shared and secure foundations; on the other, the postmodernists, convinced that objectivity is a will-o'-the-wisp and that therefore what can be achieved is at most the celebration of particularism, with no overarching system of assessment available. To some critics this must mean the cult of the instant and superficial. Sometimes the response is given that pragmatic criteria of choice can at least be applied to secure greater permanence, but of particular relevance to theology and our present topic is the position of those who insist that the retreat to particularism should carry with it greater rootedness in a more thorough cultivation of the narratives that define specific groups and communities. On this understanding, what is then at stake is the replacement of the all-embracing metanarrative of the Enlightenment with a plurality of narratives, each to be assessed in terms of its own internal criteria and standards.

To conceive the contrast thus puts quite a number of scholars into a camp of which they would be very reluctant to be seen as part, largely because for them postmodernism is identified with the extremes of the deconstructionism of Derrida or the pragmatism of Rorty, but, as I hope to demonstrate later, however different their recommendations, it can be helpful to note the similar challenges and problems which arise from the rejection of Enlightenment assumptions in major thinkers such as Barth, MacIntyre and Plantinga. At an early stage of his discussion in the *Republic* Plato recommends that if we wish to see an issue clearly we need to focus first on the large scale.[1] Continuing therefore with that advice, we may observe that both contemporary biblical studies and systematic theology display the cleavage of which we speak. So in respect of the former some scholars are still totally wedded to the historical method and the search for assessment firmly based on fact, while others, particularly those employing more recent literary methods, privilege the narrative content above any questions of its external reference. Put at its crudest, the issue becomes 'How does the narrative work and what is it trying to say to us?' rather than 'What foundation does it have in historical fact?' Again, some systematic theologians continue to attempt to build their understanding of God and his world, as Rahner and Tillich had done, on universal elements in human experience, while for others the pessimism of Bonhoeffer was fully justified and so theology must rely on its own internal foundations alone, most obviously on the narrative of the life, death and resurrection of Jesus Christ. Once again putting the contrast this way generates some reluctant bedfellows for postmodernism, but doing so will, I hope, prove illuminating in what follows, by clarifying the key issues at stake in our principal concerns with narrative and tradition.

I shall begin by considering the Enlightenment and modernist

[1] *Republic* 2, 368d 1–7.

side of the divide. So often in theology is the Enlightenment characterized as the source of all our problems that I shall be very much
concerned to highlight its other side, in a real concern for religious
issues and even a commendable engagement with narrative. One
of its principal legacies has been properly researched history.
One may observe that here too in most historical writing an
adequate narrative has been seen as the ultimate aim. That over-
confidence in the objectivity of the process was the result cannot
be denied, but I shall argue that neither in biblical studies nor more
generally does this legitimate us going to the other extreme. What
instead is required is greater awareness of the antecedent assumptions with which we approach any material. This is then used to
introduce what for me is the principal fault of modernism generally, its contempt for tradition. For to my mind, so far from undermining the search for knowledge and understanding, being aware
of the traditions upon which one inevitably draws is what makes
progress possible, provided that these traditions are allowed to
function as open, both towards their past and to the wider context
within which they are set. Since in later chapters almost all my
examples come from religiously inspired literature or art, I shall try
to illustrate this conception here by noting how the same point
applies also to developments in more secular works of a similar
kind. The notion of a 'canon', I shall contend, is no less integral
to understanding how the imagination develops in secular art and
literature than it is in religious.

Then in the second half of the chapter I shall first turn to a
consideration of postmodernism in its own right. Here I shall
observe just how slippery the term in fact is. Five different versions
will be identified, generative of very different attitudes to narrative, some less beneficial to theology than others. Rather,
however, than engage in an excess of negative criticism, I shall try
to draw something positive from each version that will help carry
the argument a little further forward. How this might apply to the
question of hermeneutics is then faced in the final section. Using
the history of the subject as a vehicle for reflection, my conclusion
is that neither the Enlightenment stress on historical criticism nor
postmodern emphasis on the integrity of the narrative is sufficient
of itself. Instead, both require each other, as well as supplementation by a more explicit recognition of the essentially open-ended
character of all texts. Traditions of reading continue to maintain

their imaginative power not by staying the same but by being open to the transforming power of influences beyond themselves. Subsequent chapters will then pursue that point in some detail.

The Enlightenment: challenges and limitations

Enlightenment religion: new narratives

Clearly this is not the place to pursue a general history or analysis of the Enlightenment.[2] My concern here is much more limited. It is to observe that to characterize the movement as a whole as no more than an excess of rationalism and its religion as no more than deism is a complete caricature. Instead, despite its undoubted extremes, we must take seriously the continuing challenge of its inheritance.

It is still common to find the Enlightenment as a whole depicted as hostile to religion, with deism as merely a superficial veneer. Significantly, what is still perhaps the best known book on the subject carries as its sub-title 'The Rise of Modern Paganism', while the entry on religion in a recent *Companion to the Enlightenment* portrays the intention as fundamentally orientated towards the undermining of religious belief.[3] It has also been argued that, by adopting the same methodology as their opponents and arguing for the existence of God, even those sympathetic to Christian belief helped in the advance of atheism since intellectual combat was accepted on terms which Christianity could not possibly win.[4] In a moment I want to consider Voltaire and Lessing as two representative figures, but first some more general remarks.

---

[2] Still less, to examine the claim that the problems raised by Enlightenment rationality are as old as Homer, as claimed by T. Adorno and M. Horkheimer, *Dialectic of Enlightenment* (London: Verso, 2nd edn., 1986), 13–80.

[3] P. Gay, *The Enlightenment: The Rise of Modern Paganism* (1966; current edn., New York: Norton, 1977); J. W. Yolton (ed.), *The Blackwell Companion to the Enlightenment* (Oxford: Blackwell, 1995), 447–52, s. v. *Religion*.

[4] M. J. Buckley, *At the Origins of Modern Atheism* (New Haven: Yale University Press, 1987). Though one cannot fault the erudition of his argument, his concluding appeal to Pascal (363) seems to me misconceived. The fault lay not in the engagement as such, but in the failure to widen the nature of the argument, by drawing attention to the possibility of more than one type of perspective.

Part of the problem is that we see the movement's history in retrospect. This is particularly true of what happened in France, where it is all too easy to read the enthronement of Reason in Notre Dame cathedral as the natural and inevitable conclusion of the French Enlightenment, whereas in fact there were many practising Roman Catholics, including clergy, who had placed their hopes in a combination of Christianity with Enlightenment values.[5] Indeed, had Fénelon rather than Bossuet won the day, the history of the Church in France might have been very different.[6] Moreover, the Frenchman who is often regarded as the first major representative of the Enlightenment, René Descartes, leaves us in no doubt in his private letters that he was actively seeking a reconciliation between faith and the science of his own day.[7] As with many another Enlightenment figure, this was based on the firm conviction that, since God is the source of all truth, all truths, however derived, must be compatible with one another: 'as to theology, as one truth can never be contrary to another truth, it would be a kind of impiety to fear that the truths discovered in philosophy were contrary to those of the true Faith.'[8] Indeed, the dreams that led him to pursue truth in this way were deeply associated in his mind with the piety of a pilgrimage to Loreto.[9] So, while hostility to Christianity was stronger in France than elsewhere, we must be careful not to exaggerate. The general view among professional historians in

[5] The origins of the French Enlightenment have been traced to Catholic thinkers such as De Thou, Sarpi and Berulle: H. R. Trevor-Roper, 'The religious origins of the Enlightenment' in idem, *Religion, Reformation and Social Change* (London: Macmillan, 1967), 193–236, esp. 226 ff.

[6] Of the two major French religious writers at the end of the seventeenth century, though Bossuet did enter into correspondence with Leibniz, his strong alliance of the Church with the crown was to exact a heavy penalty in due course, whereas Fénelon's *Télémaque* (on politics), like his religious writings, suggested a more open mind.

[7] Particularly clear in letter to Mersenne, 31 March 1641: A. Adam and P. Tannery ed., *Oeuvres de Descartes* (Paris: Vrin, 1964), III, 349–50.

[8] Letter to Fr Dinet in E. S. Haldane and G. R. T. Ross, *The Philosophical Works of Descartes* (Cambridge: Cambridge University Press, 1968), II, 360. The letter as a whole (347–76) is invaluable for revealing his underlying religious attitudes.

[9] He had three dreams of this kind in 1619 that led him to vow a pilgrimage to the shrine at Loreto, fulfilled in 1623.

respect of Britain and Germany is that the desire for accommodation was very deep seated.[10] Isaac Newton, for instance, hoped
that his scientific theories would be useful in Christian apologet-
ics,[11] and, however strange it may seem to us, we need to
acknowledge that his scientific studies, his commentary on
Daniel, his Arianism and even his interest in alchemy would have
seemed to him as all of one piece.[12] They were part of the
sustained attempt by one particular committed Christian to integrate all of reality. That search for an overarching metanarrative,[13]
it is important to stress, was not new. It had long been part of the
Christian ideal. What was new was the realization that the change
brought about by the rise of science meant that there could no
longer be any easy integration with Scripture or ecclesiastical
authority.

Few now share the confidence that was once placed in that
search, but in our pessimism we should not discount its religious
motivation, nor its legitimacy as ideal. If God is the source of
the natural world no less than of revelation it seemed plausible
to suppose that the logical or mathematical forms of reasoning
that had proved so successful in gaining deeper understanding of
the former might also help with the latter, particularly if one
supposed, as many did, that it was as reasoner that human beings
reflected the divine image.[14] Indeed, even those worried by
some of the implications drawn nonetheless assumed the parallel, as did Butler in his *Analogy*. Significantly, Butler secured

[10] Already strongly endorsed by E. Cassirer as early as 1951 in his *Philosophy of the Enlightenment* (Princeton NJ: Princeton University Press, 1951), 134, though it has taken longer for the more nuanced picture of France to emerge.

[11] J. Redwood, *Reason, Ridicule and Religion: The Age of the Enlightenment in England: 1660–1750* (London: Thames & Hudson, 1976), 93–115, esp. 95.

[12] Alchemy, like science, spoke of invisible forces deriving from the Creator and at work in the universe: J. Appleby, L. Hunt and M. Jacob, *Telling the Truth about History* (New York: Norton, 1994), 174–80.

[13] Though I follow the conventional terminology, it seems to me a pity that such inclusive accounts are thus implicitly equated as essentially the same sort of thing as the more imaginative exercise that commonly characterizes specific narratives.

[14] For the extent to which this understanding of the image implicitly influenced Enlightenment thinking, E. Craig, *The Mind of God and the Works of Man* (Oxford: Clarendon Press, 1987), esp. 13–68.

England for the Enlightenment by arguing that whatever difficulties revelation might encounter, these are paralleled by
nature itself.[15]

Unfortunately, that very success meant that English thought
was diverted from considering some of the more substantial issues
that were being raised on the continent, particularly by Voltaire.
Though any attempt to portray him as a committed Christian must
be pronounced utterly implausible,[16] it is important to note that
the issues he raised do come from someone with a religious
perspective, and that these issues remain with us to this day. His
overarching theme is the issue of fairness, and his principal object
of attack rather than Scripture as such is the theology of Augustine
(*la tête chaude*), with its arbitrary reward of one individual and
denial of even basic support to another.[17] With ruthless sarcasm he
relentlessly pursues the point as it applies to traditional conceptions
of original sin, grace, the status of other religions and the problem
of evil. Due attention will be given to revelation in other religions
in what follows. On the last issue, his novel *Candide* may appear
to suggest someone devoid of religious sympathies, so trenchant is
his critique, but what his other writings reveal is someone
genuinely concerned to offer some kind of answer. *Candide* was
not in fact his first response to the tragedy of the Lisbon earthquake, but a thoughtful, if inconclusive, poem.[18] Later, stung into
action by Diderot's declaration of atheism, he wrote *Histoire de
Jenni*, where he presents what appear to be his own views through

---

[15] That this was Butler's effect, so R. S. Porter, 'The Enlightenment in
England' in R. S. Porter and M. Teich, *Enlightenment in National Context*
(Cambridge: Cambridge University Press, 1981), 1–18; for its creation of a confi-
dent Church, J. Spurr, *The Restoration Church in England* (New Haven: Yale
University Press, 1991), 384–7.

[16] Such a sustained attempt was made by Alfred Noyes that, though himself
a convert to Roman Catholicism, his huge biography was briefly put in the Index
of prohibited books: A. Noyes, *Voltaire* (1st edn., London: Sheed & Ward, 1936;
2nd edn., London: Faber & Faber, 1938).

[17] Particularly illuminating in his *Dictionnaire Philosophique* are his entries on
Péché originel (where he describes Augustine as 'a hothead') and *Grâce: Dictionnaire
Philosophique* (Paris: Flammarion, 1964), 310–1 and 215–7. Much fun, though, is
had also with biblical inconsistencies.

[18] The earthquake of 1755 is believed to have killed 40,000 people, many of
whom would have been in church, it being All Saints' day. Noyes has some helpful comments on the poem: *Voltaire*, 463–5.

the mouth of an Anglican cleric, Dr Freind.[19] What those views were is less important to note that the style of response he offered on each occasion. Like Diderot with his novel *The Nun*, points are made imaginatively through narrative rather than directly by philosophical argument. So metanarrative was by no means the only response to the new challenges.

In fact, imagination and reason were not at all perceived as necessarily in opposition. The dominance of classical models of philosophy ensured that writers could not possibly suppose that philosophy required of them the abandonment of narrative. Far from it. Plato's use of story and myth in his dialogues or Seneca's working out of his Stoicism through his plays suggested a very different answer. So when Hans Frei and his successors in the Yale school of narrative theology accuse the Enlightenment of being responsible for the abandonment of the Bible as narrative, and its replacement by the search for external referents, it is important to note in what sense this is, and is not, true. 'The great reversal had taken place; interpretation was a matter of fitting the biblical story into another world with another story rather than incorporating that world into the biblical story.'[20] While it is true that the Enlightenment sought external referents, this need not have led of itself to a divorce from the biblical narrative. As we shall observe in a moment, the Enlightenment in fact gave added impetus to the search for appropriate historical narratives, while Voltaire was by no means alone in his use of fictional narrative. The problem was that the Bible turned out to be not quite one thing or the other, and so left one's appropriate response in doubt. Treating it as a single whole thus no longer seemed a viable option. This is an issue to which we shall need to return. Suffice it to note for the moment that it may be no accident that roughly at the same time as this crisis was occurring the novel arose, for it could be that as pure fiction it allowed an easier engagement for self-reflection than the now complex genre that the Bible was discovered to be. At all events, one of the reasons postulated for the popularity of the early English

[19] The advantage of general laws and the guidance of conscience are both defended.
[20] H. W. Frei, *The Eclipse of Biblical Narrative* (New Haven: Yale University Press, 1974), 130.

novel has been that it offered an alternative means of confronting the problem of evil.[21]

Lessing, like Voltaire, also sometimes used fiction as his philosophical method, perhaps most famously in his parable of the ring in his play *Nathan the Wise*. Devised to indicate the status he assigned to the three major monotheistic religions, he suggests we think of a father giving each of his three sons identical rings.[22] This version implies that there is no significant difference accessible to us between the three religions, but there is evidence to suggest that in this last period of his life he was toying with alternative approaches. Thus, the following year saw the publication of his *Education of Mankind* where, in part under the influence of Origen, he appears to see the three revelatory traditions developing their understanding of God and his purposes for humanity at different speeds and all within a story that can be told. Unfortunately, Judaism is viewed very negatively and there is little sense of ups and downs.[23] Worse still, there are some signs that for Lessing such revelation could never be more than a poor substitute for what more enlightened individuals, though few in number, could in any case have discovered by their reason alone.[24] Yet it was a hint of something more, which one also finds even more remarkably reflected in his alleged death-bed conversion to pantheism.[25] His friend Mendelssohn was deeply shocked,[26] but it does illustrate how even at the heart of the Enlightenment there was already contemplation of a more immanent and historically orientated

[21]   J. Lamb, *The Rhetoric of Suffering* (Oxford: Clarendon Press, 1995), 226–73.

[22]   *Nathan der Weise* (1779): Act 3, scene 7. The story is borrowed from Boccaccio, *Decameron* I, 3.

[23]   The Jews are described as 'the roughest and wildest' of peoples who only gradually through revelation overtake more cultivated peoples (21, 39), with Christ 'tearing their exhausted textbook from their hands' (53): *Die Erziehung des Menschengeschlechts* in *Schriften* (Frankfurt: Insel, 1967), II, 544–63 (my trans. with section numbers).

[24]   Ibid., 72.

[25]   For the story and an analysis of the resultant dispute between Jacobi and Mendelssohn, F. C. Beiser, *The Fate of Reason* (Cambridge, Mass.: Harvard University Press, 1987), 44–108.

[26]   As he had been by the historicism of Lessing's *Education*, though this was eventually the direction that nineteenth-century liberal Jewish thought would follow: D. Sorkin, *Moses Mendelssohn and the Religious Enlightenment* (London: Peter Halban, 1996), 154.

God of the type that is so characteristic of Hegel in the following century. So we ought to be hesitant in supposing that his final view would have remained one of unqualified endorsement for his famous 'ugly ditch', the apparently unbridgeable gap between the necessary truths of reason and the contingent uncertainties of history upon which Christianity depends.[27]

Nor was Lessing alone in engaging with the issue of history. Voltaire attempted several historical works, while Hume made his public reputation not so much through his philosophy as by writing a history of England. So it would be quite unfair to claim that the Enlightenment was only concerned with great arching meta-narratives; it engaged equally with specific narratives, and empirical detail. A more legitimate criticism would be the observation that because of its metanarrative of universal values its historical writers more often than not fail to appreciate the importance of context, and so there is no real awareness of how different generations might have had very different values and very different ways of viewing things. Voltaire, for instance, despite being 'a master of narrative',[28] constantly makes judgements entirely from the perspective of eighteenth-century morality and ideas.[29] Nowadays, so aware are we of the difference that context makes that it is tempting to go to the other extreme, and suppose relatively objective historical writing an impossibility. In the case of the Scriptures this is a frequently made complaint, and now increasingly used as justification for retreating from historical questions. Difficulty, however, does not argue for impossibility. I want next to illustrate this by placing the issue in the wider context of historical writing generally.

Historical research and prejudice

The novelist Gore Vidal has one of his narrators declare: 'there is no history, only fictions of varying degrees of plausibility. What

[27] 'Der gastige breite Graben': 'Uber den Bewies des Geistes und der Kraft' in *Schriften* II, 307–12, esp. 311. One notes that Lessing speaks of 'often and earnestly' attempting the leap.

[28] The view of Lytton Strachey; endorsed in A. J. Ayer, *Voltaire* (London: Faber & Faber, 1986), 86–107, esp. 107.

[29] Though in response, it might be observed that Voltaire was only subjecting the Bible to the same objective and unhistorical values as the eighteenth-century Church found within the Scriptures: so J. H. Brumfitt, *The French Enlightenment* (London: Macmillan, 1972), 150.

we think to be history is nothing but fiction.'[30] In similar vein one can find Michel Foucault declaring of his own often profound analyses of the past that 'I am well aware that I have never written anything but fictions,' though significantly going on to add— much as Vidal retreats with his 'degrees of plausibility'—that this does not mean that 'those fictions are beyond truth' (*hors vérité*).[31] The sentiments are typical of much postmodern insecurity about the status of history. That there are some grounds for worry we must concede, for there has probably never been a period at which human beings have been more aware of the extent to which the past is their own creation. For instance, the foundational events of American history, such as the arrival of the Puritans, the formation of the Constitution by its founding fathers, and the Civil War have all been forced into a more complex and troubled light.[32] In similar vein, late twentieth-century Scottish nationalism has the embarrassment of its modern identity having been forged through a romantic history of kilt, ballad, and so forth that is largely fiction.[33] More worrying, though, is the realization that we often seem to prefer the fictions, as when tourists are found objecting to too much historical realism in presentations of the past, or when premature ageing of buildings is used to create a deliberately artificial history.[34] It is almost as though the landmarks are more important to us than reality, in much the same way as the Masai in Africa are reputed to have taken the names of the mountains, rivers, and so forth with them whenever they migrated to a new environment and named the new land accordingly.[35] That is an

[30] G. Vidal, *1876* (London: Heinemann, 1976), 196–7, cf. 194.

[31] Quoted in A. Megill, *Prophets of Extremity* (Berkeley: University of California Press, 1985), 234–5.

[32] J. Appleby, L. Hunt and M. Jacob, *Telling the Truth about History* (New York: Norton, 1994), esp. 91–159. Put crudely, the Puritans were not democrats, the founding fathers were self-interested politicians, and slave-owning attitudes were as deeply entrenched in the North as in the South.

[33] H. Trevor-Roper, 'The invention of tradition: the Highland tradition of Scotland' in E. Hobsbawn and T. Ranger (eds.), *The Invention of Tradition* (Cambridge: Cambridge University Press, 1983), 15–41. In the same book similar points are made about Wales by P. Morgan and about the British monarchy by D. Cannadine.

[34] For examples of the former, D. Lowenthal, *The Past is a Foreign Country* (Cambridge: Cambridge University Press, 1985), 298, 329; for the latter, ibid., 149–63. [35] Ibid., 42.

extreme case, but in a book praised by the postmodernist philosopher Richard Rorty one Cambridge academic has questioned
whether even with the greatest of care it is ever possible to attain
historical knowledge, or only at most a range of possibilities.
Taking three very different case studies (the course of the bubonic
plague, American intervention in Korea, and Duccio's altarpiece
of 1308), he notes how study of the available evidence seems to
open up more and more options rather than directing one to any
overarching explanation.[36]

Turning to the work of famous historians only seems to confirm
such pessimism, as we observe the extent to which their judgements have been conditioned by their own society rather than the
object of their study. To take first two great ancient historians of
the nineteenth century, it is not difficult to discover in Grote's
History of Greece English self-confidence in democracy subsequent
to the passage of the Great Reform Bill of 1832, no less than in
Mommsen's *History of Rome* German pessimism after the 1848
revolutions and the resultant desire for a strong leader.[37] A similar
judgement has been given on the work of great twentieth-century
medievalists. Thus, the inter-war studies of Percy Schramm on
Otto III and Ernst Kantoriwicz on Frederick II have been found
to reflect the chaos of the Weimar republic and German desire for
a strong man, just as, it is suggested, the admiration of C. H.
Haskins and J. R. Strayer for the statecraft of the Norman kings
and their advisors should be traced to their commitment to the
polices of the United States under Woodrow Wilson.[38] That the
Benedictine Dom David Knowles should choose to write on the
history of the religious orders occasions no surprise; that his assessment of St Francis should parallel his own rebellion against authority, however, raises the deeper issue of whether the result is merely
the projection of his own anxieties or whether a deeper understanding has been created through the presence of shared

[36] G. Hawthorn, *Plausible Worlds* (Cambridge: Cambridge University Press,
1991). He repeatedly stresses that 'possibilities increase' (e.g. 156), and so we
'cannot produce knowledge' (187).

[37] E. H. Carr, *What is History?* (Harmondsworth: Penguin, 2nd edn., 1987),
36–7. For some more recent examples, M. I. Finley, *The Use and Abuse of History*
(Harmondsworth: Penguin, 1990), 76–81.

[38] So N. F. Cantor, *Inventing the Middle Ages* (Cambridge: Lutterworth Press,
1991), 79–117, 245–86.

conflicts.[39] Moreover, if anything, the problem intensifies as we get nearer the modern period. In the nineteenth century J. A. Froude's unstinted praise of Henry VIII can in part be explained by his desire to make recompense to the Church of England for the religious doubts with which he was plagued. His very much lower estimate of Elizabeth was to be reversed in the following century by J. E. Neale's eulogizing of her abilities, but he too reflects a contemporary mood, the desire to escape the drabness of the thirties into a glorious past.[40] As a more recent example, one might mention the way in which Sir Geoffrey Elton's failure to take the religious dimension of the Reformation with sufficient seriousness reflected his own lack of religious belief.[41]

In an attempt to circumvent such difficulties, some historians have sought to avoid the inevitable generalities that attach to narrative through alternative forms of presentation, such as the prosopographical that one finds in Sir Lewis Namier[42] or on the Continent the hugely influential sociological, characteristic of the *Annales* school.[43] But there was a penalty to be paid in their inability to account for sudden change brought about by the actions of individuals.[44] More substantially, we need to recall that it is only as narrative that historical writing is likely to be able to engage our imaginations, and thus be truly effective in helping us either to give shape to our identity as members of particular communities or to comprehend what it is that makes others 'tick'. In any case the recognition of distortion in our understanding of the past should not lead us to suppose that no knowledge is at all possible through narrative. Even those who speak of foundational myths in respect of earlier American history are also to be found insisting

[39] Ibid., 296 ff., esp. 315–16.

[40] So J. Kenyon, *The History Men* (London: Weidenfeld & Nicholson, 2nd edn., 1993), 118–29, 215–17. [41] Ibid., 222.

[42] By 'prosopographical' is meant the study of history through study of the privileges, acquisitions, rights, and so forth of key families. There was a parallel movement in ancient history, particularly associated with Sir Ronald Syme.

[43] Though Marc Bloch's *Feudal Society* (London: Routledge, 1989) is the most important text, Braudel's writings are now more widely known. In theology, the most significant examples come from the work of Le Roy Ladurie and Le Goff.

[44] As a criticism of Namier, Kenyon, *History Men*, 278–9; of the Annalists, Cantor, *Inventing*, 144.

that postmodern denials of knowledge to historical narrative are mere 'rhetorical exaggeration'. 'Knowing the past completely' is of course an impossibility, but that does not mean that provisional judgements may not make some claim to truth. There can still be vast differences in degrees of plausibility even if these are often difficult or even impossible to quantify.[45]

Ironically, to refuse to talk of knowledge or truth in such cases because it is open to revision seems to concede to the Enlightenment what ought never to have been conceded, that mathematical truth is the only adequate model of what might constitute knowledge. Postmodern scepticism is thus crucially dependent on what it rejects. One further irony is that such scepticism has emerged at a point at which the amount of information available to us about the past has greatly increased, so much so that one medievalist declares the good college student better informed than all books written before 1895.[46] Much the same might be said in respect of our knowledge of the biblical world. The problem in fact lies not with the amount of facts or information available, but with their interpretation. But even here a couple of cautionary strategies may be employed, to lessen the likelihood of extraneous influences distorting in the way that an earlier paragraph suggested.

First and most obviously, there is the need to make one's underlying assumptions and values explicit both to oneself and to the reader. In a work criticizing those who seemed to write unaware of the way in which their view of the past was influenced by their understanding of the present, Herbert Butterfield makes the interesting observation: 'it is not a sin in a historian to introduce a personal bias that can be recognised and discounted. The sin of historical composition is the organisation of the story in such a way that bias cannot be recognised.'[47] Hopefully, in my case the reader scarcely needs to be told that this book is premised on the assumption of God's active involvement with the history of the Church and its resultant imaginative engagement with the biblical narrative. Secondly, there needs to be constant testing of any narrative interpretation against possible alternatives. Even wrong

---

[45] Appleby, Hunt and Jacob, *Telling the Truth*, 241–70, esp. 258.

[46] Cantor, *Inventing*, 37; cf. 44.

[47] H. Butterfield, *The Whig Interpretation of History* (London: G. Bell, 1931), 41.

grids can help clarify what elements are particularly worth retaining in an earlier version, as proved to be the case with two of the most hotly contested revisionary accounts of early modern English history this century, Elton's Cromwellian revolution under Henry VIII and R. H. Tawney's 'rise of the gentry'.[48] Even when wrong, feminist or Palestinian readings of Scripture can thus exercise a similar corrective function. Modern Palestinians are scarcely continuous with the Canaanites, but being asked to read the Bible from their perspective can be profoundly challenging as well as disconcerting.[49]

Obviously my particular interest here is biblical history, but I have deliberately spread the net this widely, to demonstrate that the problems that confront theology are by no means unique or idiosyncratic. Indeed, in terms of information available the New Testament period is as well off as many another period of early history,[50] nor, as we have seen, are its problems of interpretation without parallel elsewhere. So any retreat from historical questions would seem to me quite mistaken. Of course, sometimes the net result of such investigations will prove thoroughly disappointing, but such consequences should be faced rather than circumvented. So, for example, in Part Two we shall observe the way in which once confident assertions of the historicity of the patriarchal narratives have declined as the alleged sociological parallels disclosed by archaeology have been found to be not unique after all to the early second millennium BC. The first chapter in that Part will, however, have already observed that the same kind of issue confronts the student of Homer, as Schliemann's 'discoveries' at Troy seem now to dissolve in a fog of uncertainty. Perhaps in one or both cases there will be a swing back once more to historicity,

---

[48] Kenyon, *History Men*, 220, 257–61.

[49] Feminist readings are discussed in my second volume, *Discipleship and Imagination*. For a range of Palestinian perspectives, Na'im Ateek, *Justice and Only Justice* (Maryknoll, New York: Orbis, 1989), K. W. Whitelam, *The Invention of Ancient Israel: The Silencing of Palestinian History* (London: Routledge, 1995); C. Chapman, 'One land, two peoples—how many states?', *Miskkan* 26 (1997), 4–15. A moving personal account is given by E. Chacour, *We Belong To The Land* (HarperSanFrancisco, 1990).

[50] 'For the era down to about 1250 almost everything of value in the documentary and literary heritage of the medieval world has been published in modern editions;' so Cantor, *Inventing*, 30.

but our task at the present is surely to confront the knowledge we now have, however provisional it may be, and interpret it.

Similarly, my attempt in Part Three to provide the building blocks for a narrative of the life of Jesus may well prove very wide of the mark, but that does not argue against the attempt being made. Indeed, it is in my view essential that it should be done since, however wrong in detail I may be, what now seems incontrovertible is that the Christian must face a very different narrative of the life of Jesus from the one that was prevalent before the rise of biblical criticism. This is because, as with all history, we are now aware as never before of the otherness of the past, and that Jesus' life cannot therefore plausibly survive as a story pulled out of its own times. Instead, study of the Gospels again and again forces us to the realization that what Jesus did and what he said were very much conditioned by living in one particular time and place rather than any other.

Such distancing does of course raise acute problems about how Christ can then be appropriated for the very different circumstances of our own day. One solution that was tried in the past was to tell narratives of Christ-inspired lives lived under different circumstances, and this was one major reason for the popularity of the saints in the history of Christianity. How that worked out in detail and its relevance, however transformed, for our own day will be considered in the companion volume to this, *Discipleship and Imagination*. But it would be foolish to think this the only response that happened. Rather, it is essential to recognize the generation of a second type of narrative of Christ's life that goes beyond the strictly historical.[51] There is no doubt whatsoever in my mind about how inspiring it can be to hear how far God was willing to go in identification with humanity in all the specificity inevitably implied by a particular culture and context. So that is not the problem. Rather, it is the issue of translation to a different context, as succeeding generations faced significantly different questions and perspectives. Suffering is the example I shall consider in the final chapter, while in the one immediately following this attention is focused on a very different instance, how presentation of the gospel has been affected by new valuations of childhood.

[51] The range of transformations is well indicated in J. Pelikan, *Jesus through the Centuries* (New York: Harper & Row, 1985).

The result, I contend, is significantly different narratives that need to be assessed differently.

Consistency with the historical narrative is important, but not, it seems to me, decisive. For if, as the Christian believes, Jesus is still alive, then the question has ceased to be merely what he did in the past, but how his presence and influence can be appropriated in the here and now. A better imaginative relation between believer and Lord, greater coherence to the story and so forth, all then become relevant questions. The possibility is even there that, because later generations can open up new perspectives undreamed of in the first century, this new, imaginative narrative may provide a critique of key aspects of the historical narrative. What all this entails will become clearer as we proceed, though we may observe here in passing that the process is already at work in the alterations the evangelists make to the words and actions of Jesus which they have inherited. It should also be noted that the point does not just apply to the life of Christ, but to the narratives of Scripture as a whole, including those that are purely fictional. If we accept that new insights can become available to later generations, then all this was to be expected, with the imagination not resting content with the same version of the narrative for all time, and that is exactly what we find both within Scripture and beyond.

As for what stimulates such developments, sometimes the pressure will have come purely from within the tradition in a refocusing of the balance of how the existing narrative is read, but perhaps more commonly it will be a matter of the dynamic of an inherited past interacting with fresh stimuli for change from outside, from the wider surrounding culture. Enlightenment writers such as Diderot could conceive of tradition in no other way than as a mindless inhibitor of change,[52] and, unfortunately, those who responded were often not much better, as with Burke who defends the 'prejudice' of tradition simply for its inherited wisdom and social cohesion.[53] But tradition can be imaginative and innovative. Perhaps nowhere has this proved to be so than in literature

[52] In related vein in the opening sentence of his essay *What is Enlightenment?* of 1784 Kant defines enlightenment as freedom from any form of intellectual dependence on another: *der Ausgang des Menschen aus seiner selbstvershuldeten Unmündigkeit*.

[53] Most obviously in his *Reflections on the Revolution in France* of 1790.

and art. As many of my examples in what follows are drawn from
these areas, what I would like now to do is move the reader slowly
to a rather different view of tradition by beginning there.

Canons and context in literature and art

For most of Christian history biblical revelation has been
conceived of as something like a thunderbolt from heaven, as a
message from beyond our own world that spoke of eternal verities
and so, though applicable to its immediate context, it carried none
of the transience that marked it as a product of its age. This is not
to deny that elements of a progressive revelation were accepted,
and these in fact will be discussed in Chapter 3, but it is to draw
attention to the shock which the Enlightenment and the resultant
rise of biblical criticism brought. However revelation worked, it
now had to be seen as heavily context dependent, with notions
assumed at the time that were later to be abandoned. Nor were
these always minor; a case in point would be the approach to
suffering which the Book of Job has as its main focus of critique.[54]
In my view that forces us towards giving less weight to the image
of dramatic intervention which so often characterizes Scripture, as
in the story of the patriarchs or some of the prophets, and instead
accepting a certain gradualism in what happens. Though this
makes it harder to identify the specific divine contribution, this
does not imply its absence, any more than creativity and original-
ity in the arts are undermined by recognition that these too work
within the context of a developing tradition.

Yet since at least the Renaissance, and particularly with the
advent of the Romantic movement, the artist has commonly been
seen, on the model of the prophet, as an inspired figure[55] who
stands against the currents of his time to draw out daring and new
insights from which we can all learn. One suspects that this is
still the dominant model among the general public, but it also

[54] Discussed in *Discipleship and Imagination*, Chapter 4, though it is important
to note that, as in other cases, the theology criticized is not always earlier but
sometimes continued well beyond the time of the critique.

[55] The Renaissance image revived Plato's famous description of prophecy
and artistic inspiration as two of the four types of 'madness' sent by the gods:
Phaedrus 244A ff. Despite its denial of knowledge to the poet, appeal was also
made to the stress on divine inspiration in the *Ion*.

continues to influence the thinking of some academics. One distinguished example would be the American literary critic, Harold Bloom, who at one point actually describes himself as 'an aged institutional Romantic'.[56] Fighting for the continuance of the existing 'canon' of literature against those who argue for the application of moral and political criteria,[57] he insists that only aesthetic criteria are relevant and constantly speaks of 'strangeness' as 'the quality that, more than any other, makes a work canonical'.[58] Yet in his determination to secure the maximum degree of 'strangeness' and individuality for his authors, some of them end up by being presented as little more than bloated egos, with, for instance, the poetry of Dante, Milton, and Blake reduced to little more than the projection of their wills rather than seen as embodying any reflection of deep commitments to beings and ideas external to themselves.[59] What all this ignores is that, even were this so, such projection would only be impressive if what they rebel against also carried force and conviction; otherwise we would think of them exactly as we think of all who battle against paper tigers. So, for instance, to describe J as the most impressive writer in the Old Testament because he/she is a rebel only makes sense if the alleged portrayal of God that is offered is found seriously to engage with some alternative that might also have succeeded in capturing our imaginations.[60] The trouble with Bloom's whole approach is that, so far from admiring otherness, his canon ends up as little more than self-reflection, with writers pronounced great because they reflect his own views.[61]

We need therefore to look for alternative criteria, if any attempt

---

[56] H. Bloom, *The Western Canon* (London: Macmillan, 1994), 518.

[57] The *Oxford English Dictionary* gives 'Platonic canon' in 1885 as the earliest secular use of the term.

[58] Bloom, *Western Canon*, 336; cf. 4. For his aesthetic stress, e.g. 23, 29.

[59] On Dante, ibid., e.g. 84, 96. For Milton, *Ruin the Sacred Truths* (Cambridge, Mass.: Harvard University Press, 1989), 91–6; for Blake 123. Note 125: 'All strong poets, whether Dante or Milton or Blake, must ruin the sacred truths … precisely because the essential condition for poetic strength is that the new song … must always be a song of one's own self.'

[60] Bloom, *Ruin the Sacred Truths* 3–12; at greater length, *Book of J* (New York: Grove Weidenfeld, 1990). Bloom warms to the possibility that J might have been a woman.

[61] For example, he praises Johnson for a passage that comes nearest to his hero Montaigne: *Western Canon*, 198–9; cf. 155–8.

is to be made to define the secular, literary canon. Quite a number have been suggested. Samuel Johnson, for instance, suggested the communication of 'general and transcendent truths' while Matthew Arnold argued for the ability to conjure up another age in its full significance.[62] What seems most important to me is the insight that is given that can take us beyond where we now are, in particular the ability to perceive matters from perspectives very different from our own natural bent or inclination. Here it is important to distinguish two sorts of imaginative advance. Most relevant to the notion of tradition is the way in which the artist concerned pulls us beyond where as a community of readers or viewers we now understand ourselves to be, by building upon what we already comprehend but going beyond it. But relevant too is what happens to us in the present as we look back over the centuries, because the effective artist then becomes one who enables us to comprehend very different assumptions and values from our own, and that is why the test for inclusion in the secular canon can never simply be our own mindset. The imagination is there to challenge, not to reinforce conformity, however valuable or true we may think our present assumptions to be.

As already noted, it was the Renaissance that first launched us on the notion of the individual genius standing against tradition. In part such a stance was helped by how little we actually know about some artists—Leonardo da Vinci, for instance, easily lending himself not only to the notion of a self-generated genius but one whose precise form could readily be adapted to suit the changing values of subsequent centuries.[63] Yet historical investigation suggests a rather different analysis. As the very title of the movement suggests with its implied recovery of classical norms, the Renaissance's freedom from the past was a matter of degree, not kind, and major historians of the movement have not been slow

[62] Johnson, *Rasselas*, ch. 10, 'A dissertation upon poetry'; cf. 'just representations of general nature' in his Preface to his edition of Shakespeare's plays of 1765; Arnold, 'On the modern element in literature' in *Selected Prose*, ed. P. J. Keating (Harmondsworth: Penguin, 1970), 72.

[63] A. R. Turner in *Inventing Leonardo: The Anatomy of a Legend* (London: Macmillan, 1995) contrasts how little we know about him (e.g. 9, 12, 58) and that little needing a contemporary context (e.g. 180, 192–4) with the widely differing notions of genius that his life has taken on from Vasari onwards.

to acknowledge that debt.[64] Equally, as a later chapter will argue, it would be a mistake to think of the Middle Ages as by contrast a mindless following of convention, for otherwise it would be impossible to explain the extraordinary degree of change that occurred over this period.[65] Nor will it do to think of more recent history any differently. Dynamic interaction with the inheritance of the past remains constant, however apparently new particular ideas or practices may at first sight seem to be. To give some examples at random, Constable may appear like a breath of fresh air and his landscapes quite unlike the figurative scenes of Poussin and Claude, but in fact his apparent naturalism is not only carefully contrived but a painting like *Dedham Vale* is a close reworking of Claude's *Hagar and the Angel*.[66] Again, if we turn to the dawn of modern painting, Cézanne repeatedly made copies of Rubens while van Gogh with equal frequency turned to Rembrandt.[67] This is in no sense to deny their achievement in enabling us to see nature and colour in new ways, but it is to insist that in part that achievement was mediated through a deep knowledge of the inheritance of the past.[68] Equally, the twentieth century was to draw heavily upon African and other early art for its inspiration, something which can be seen very clearly in the cubist paintings of Picasso or in the sculptures of Henry Moore.[69]

Much the same point can be made about literary developments. In an influential book F. R. Leavis argued persuasively for the

[64] In *Renaissance and Renascences* (San Francisco: Harper & Row, 1969) E. Panofsky, while conceding that 'the Renaissance was linked to the Middle Ages by a thousand ties' (6), finds in it the third and decisive period of engagement with classicism in Western art after estrangement: 42 ff.

[65] In Chapter 7 I shall argue that there is innovation by the artists themselves as well as by their clerical patrons.

[66] For Constable, J. A. W. Heffernan, *The Re-creation of Landscape* (Hanover Pa.: University Press of New England, 1984), 22–5.

[67] P. Callow, *Lost Earth: A Life of Cézanne* (London: Allison & Busby, 1995), 176, cf. 101; M. Roskill (ed.), *The Letters of Vincent van Gogh* (London: HarperCollins, 1983), 62, 80, 251.

[68] In his somewhat misleadingly entitled *Art and Illusion* (London: Phaidon, 5th edn., 1977), E. H. Gombrich makes 'schema and correction' within a developing tradition integral to his history of art, e.g. 126–52.

[69] Often noted is the influence of African art on Picasso's *Les Demoiselles d'Avignon*; for Henry Moore on 'primitive art,' P. James (ed.), *Henry Moore on Sculpture* (New York: Da Capo, 1992), 157–66.

decisive influence that Jane Austen had on George Eliot, and she in turn on Henry James, with Austen herself developing out of an already existing tradition.[70] Nor are matters otherwise in the case of poetry. To the uninitiated Milton and the Romantic school of poetry can seem utterly different, whereas the deeper one explores, the greater the debt that is discovered, not least because 'Milton was, for the Romantics, a daring individualist'.[71] For them great poetry has to stem from a great man, and so, though they sought in their own way to move beyond Milton, their debt is acknowledged, whether it be with Shelley's back-handed tribute in his *Defence of Poetry*, Blake's *Milton*, or Wordworth's familiar poem with its opening line: 'Milton! Thou shouldst be living at this hour'.[72] Of course, to establish extensive historical continuities one would need to investigate a much longer time span. Somewhat disarmingly, though, Bloom himself admits that influence must after all be crucial in determining canonicity, and so concedes that by this criterion some writers must be included whom he believes overrated, such as Vergil and Milton.[73] Even amid all the changes wrought by poetry in the twentieth century, T. S. Eliot in a famous essay insisted upon the poet's continued debt to the past,[74] while one influential critic has seen that revolution as only possible in the context of what was received from the earlier tradition.[75]

What I have been seeking to do through these examples is to release the reader from the common prejudice that tradition necessarily implies something static, the mere inheritance of the past. Instead, we need to acknowledge that the resources for

[70] F. R. Leavis, *The Great Tradition* (1948; Harmondsworth: Penguin, 1993), esp.13–26 for outline of argument.

[71] The extent of the debt is explored in J. A. Wittreich, *The Romantics on Milton* (Cleveland, Ohio: Press of Case Western Reserve University, 1970), esp. 11.

[72] Shelley may say that 'Milton's Devil as a moral being is ... far superior to his God', but he also declares that 'nothing can exceed the energy and magnificence of the character of Satan as expressed in *Paradise Lost*'.

[73] Bloom, *Western Canon*, 28, 526.

[74] 'Tradition and the individual talent' (1919) in F. Kermode (ed.), *Selected Prose of T. S. Eliot* (London: Faber & Faber, 1975), 37–44. Polemically, though, he underestimates the role of innovation (e.g. 39).

[75] The argument of the American critic, Cleanth Brooks in *Modern Poetry and the Tradition* (London: Editions Poetry, 1948).

change come in part at least from within tradition itself. Sometimes this can be decisively so, as forgotten aspects of the past are recovered and reapplied in new ways, as with classical art at the Renaissance or 'primitive' in modern times. More often, however, it will be a case of the past interacting with some fresh stimulus from outside the tradition, and responding creatively. For nine-teenth-century art the invention of photography constituted such a powerful challenge towards fresh forms of representation, just as in the second half of the eighteenth century Lowth's discovery of the principles of Hebrew verse released English poetry into new forms of metre.[76] Sometimes, rather than a specific prompt, it may be more a matter of the general current at the time within the culture as a whole. Cultural historians can often surprise us by the extent to which apparently unrelated phenomena find a similar explanation, as, for example, with Milton's reshaping of the Samson legend and Vanbrugh's monumental fireplace at Castle Howard connected through an ecstatic late Baroque spirituality that also leads Rubens to retune classical myths in order to empha-size the element of struggle.[77]

Obviously this is not the place to pursue the details of such a history, but, given our contention that both sacred and secular canons are alike in drawing their inspiration from the imagination, the question inevitably forces itself upon us as to how then they are to be differentiated. Adding to the complexity of the issue is the fact that there has been much interaction between the two, not only with the secular drawing on the sacred for much of its imagery but the sacred in its turn, as subsequent chapters will illus-trate, also being profoundly shaped by the secular. For, though the tendency remains to think of sacred canons as static, this is true only in the trivial sense of the words on the page, not of the inter-pretation to which they have been subject nor, significantly, even the grid or shape of their assumed narrative. Perhaps the most obvious difference between the two can be expressed in terms of there being a different 'threesome'. In secular canons there is

[76] Robert Lowth's *Sacred Poetry of the Hebrews* (Latin, 1753; English, 1793) by identifying parallelism as the basis of Hebrew poetry legitimated escape from strict Augustan rules.

[77] One example of the type of argument employed by Murray Royston in his book: *Changing Perspectives in Literature and the Visual Arts 1650–1820* (Princeton NJ: Princeton University Press, 1990), 13–86, esp. 19, 25, 75–6.

creative interaction between the inheritance of the past, contextual triggers and the standard objects of reflection such as human experience or the natural world, whereas for the religious believer, in the sacred canon the last is seen as subordinate, merely a medium through which imaginative interaction with God himself is presumed. That being so, though subsequent chapters will argue that in practice Christian self-reflection operates with a considerably less static canon than is commonly assumed, even so very different criteria apply in determining relevance in shaping the sacred canon from what determines the secular, and so on this analysis artistic perceptivity is by no means the same thing as religious, even where explicitly Christian categories have been employed.

The claims of modernism thus need to be modified through recognition of plausibility as the norm and not certainty, as also by acknowledgement of the key role played by tradition as the backdrop against which all thought occurs. Nonetheless, the very fact of continuing interaction between two such apparently quite different types of canon, the secular and the religious, does at least indicate one clear reason why any extreme version of postmodernist retreat into an allegedly self-contained tradition cannot hold: Christian history has been quite otherwise. However, this does not mean that there are no elements of truth in postmodernism What these are, I shall now attempt to delineate, as well as the approach's limitations.

Postmodernism

In this part of the chapter I shall first identify five different versions of postmodernism and their likely implications for narrative before going on to consider the history of hermeneutics and the way in which the move away from historical dissection of the text towards stress on its literary unity has led some to find in postmodernism a suitable ally for theology. That, however, I shall contend is a mistake if it ends up by assuming some deeper notion of self-contained unity for Christianity than is in fact either possible or desirable.

Postmodernism and pluralism

Despite my earlier acceptance of a single, simple definition for postmodernism, discussion of the topic inevitably becomes more complicated once due account is taken of the wide variety of different senses in which the term is actually used.[78] With some plausibility one might argue that all such usages have some kind of family resemblance to Lyotard's basic definition as 'incredulity towards metanarratives',[79] but their implications for theology can be quite diverse. What I propose therefore to do here is examine five variant formulations and see how far any of them might be beneficial (or harmful) for the future development of Christian theology. At the same time it will be important not to look at these implications in isolation, since it is an integral part of the argument of this book as a whole that theology (and revelation) always operates in intimate relation with developments within culture as a whole. A brief anticipation of the five variants may be useful at this point, especially as this may help explain why such very different responses are possible to the same umbrella term. In fact, depending on how formulated, diametrically opposed conclusions can be drawn, in particular some pressing towards greater rootedness in tradition and others according positive value to diversity in surface appearance, or again some advocating a return to narrative and others its abandonment. The first two I shall consider, though closely related, should not be treated as identical, since it is one thing to argue for the rejection of all master narratives, quite another to postulate the absence of any adequate criteria for adjudicating between them. A third version focuses upon the collapse of master narratives within particular subject areas, such as history or art, while yet another argues that narrative becomes crucial to the interpretation of texts since criteria can only be generated internally. Finally, brief mention must be made of the most extreme version, characterized as it is by the claim that it is impossible to achieve reference beyond the written page. By examining each in turn we can note points of interconnection, though even at this stage the most obvious should be

---

[78] In an attempt to simplify my task in what follows, I ignore some of the ways in which the term has in fact been employed. Its earliest use in theology in fact seems to have been in association with process theology: J. B. Cobb, 'From crisis theology to the post-modern world', *Centennial Review* 8 (1964), 174–88. For a discussion of this complexity, D. Brown, 'Postmoderne II' in *Theologische Realenzyklopädie* (Berlin: Walter de Gruyter, 1996), 27, 87–9.

[79] J. F. Lyotard, *The Postmodern Condition* (Manchester: Manchester University Press, 1984), xxiv; cf. 31–7.

clear: the decline of confidence in the universal applicability of a shared concept of reason; hence why each version can legitimately be identified as post-Enlightenment and so as postmodern.

(i) *Exclusion of master narratives*   If, to take the first of our variants, postmodernism were to be defined as constituted by the exclusion of all master narratives, then it would seem clear that Christianity could only claim a postmodern identity by radically altering its character, since Christian theology has conventionally sought to provide just such an over-arching narrative, and indeed the term 'systematic theology' is often interpreted to mean just that, the attempt to systematize all of reality under a single Christian frame of reference. It is thus perhaps no accident that what appears to be the first use within theology of the term 'postmodern' involved an appeal for the enlargement of Enlightenment concerns rather than their diminution.[80] Certainly, when postmodernism is presented as the collapse of master narratives such as Cartesianism or Marxism, it is too often forgotten that Christianity was once in the same game, and in the eyes of many should still be so. John Milbank's highly acclaimed *Theology and Social Theory* might be used to illustrate postmodernism in this form; given his desire to defend an alternative universalist perspective that he derives from Augustine, modernism has to be characterized not as universal reason as such but as a particular form of it, as indeed his subtitle indicates: 'Beyond Secular Reason'. Even so, as several critics have noted, his own position fails to escape some of the more obvious features of postmodern instability, most obviously perhaps in his ontology.[81] One difficulty that advocates of any inclusive master narrative inevitably have is explaining why it fails to win general acceptance. Arguably, moderns like Marx and Freud, in identifying reasons in perversions of psychological or social consciousness, have acted no differently from an earlier generation of Christian theologians who spoke of original sin. The nearest

---

[80]   Cobb, 'From Crisis theology to the post-modern world'. This also seems true of many of the volumes in the SUNY series *Constructive Postmodern Thought*, edited by another process theologian, David Griffin.

[81]   Everything, including God, seems to dissolve into relations: 'no things, no substances, only shifting relations': J. Milbank, *Theology and Social Theory* (Oxford: Blackwell, 1990), 423–7, esp. 426. For a critique, C. E. Gunton, *The One, the Three and the Many* (Cambridge: Cambridge University Press, 1993), esp. 193, 195–6; V. White, *Paying Attention to People* (London: SPCK, 1996), 94–107, esp. 97–8.

contemporary equivalent of the latter one finds in the application of the warrant theory of belief to religion in the so-called Reformed epistemology of America's most distinguished philosopher of religion, Alvin Plantinga.[82] This is not the place to discuss the general plausibility of the theory, any more than that of Milbank's proposals. I introduce it here simply to draw attention to the way in which apparently disparate movements in contemporary culture can in fact stem from similar concerns: the collapse of Cartesian foundationalism. Even so, there remains the question of how adequate sin might be as a general explanation, and whether resort might not have to be had instead to inherent limitations to the extent of human knowledge, and if so whether this might apply no less to Christian theology than to secular self-understanding. That is no doubt why it is the second variant that is the more common.

(ii) *No criteria for choice*   Here the contention instead is that there are no adequate criteria for choosing between the various proposed master narratives. Another highly influential book in postmodernist discussion has been Alasdair MacIntyre's *After Virtue* in which the implausibility of presenting much moral discussion as in fact a shared debate (as, for example, over the issue of abortion) is used as a lever for advocating instead the cultivation and practice of virtue within specific communities of shared values.[83] Others have carried the claim of incommensurability further and detected its existence within the same individual.[84] As a remedy, philosophers have been recommended to give closer attention to how such issues are worked through in literary texts.[85] In this

[82] A. Plantinga, *Warrant: The Current Debate* and *Warrant and Proper Function* (both New York: Oxford University Press, 1993). The third volume that applies his ideas to belief in God is still awaited, but his basic idea is that for any belief to have warrant it must have been produced by processes that are functioning properly. For a discussion of the issues, J. L. Kvanvig (ed.), *Warrant in Contemporary Epistemology* (Langham: Rowman & Littlefied, 1996).

[83] A. MacIntyre, *After Virtue* (London: Duckworth, 1981), 6–7.

[84] e.g. T. Nagel, *Mortal Questions* (Cambridge: Cambridge University Press, 1979), esp. 53–74, 128–41.

[85] M. Nussbaum, *Love's Knowledge: Essays on Philosophy and Literature* (New York and Oxford: Oxford University Press, 1990) finds help in Dickens, James, and Proust, among others. In an earlier work, *The Fragility of Goodness* (Cambridge: Cambridge University Press, 1986), she had contrasted Plato's attempts to make all value commensurable with the work of the Greek tragedians.

there is a clear parallel to the course that has been advocated within theology, in cultivation and emulation of the narratives which gave the Christian faith its birth. Stanley Hauerwas, for instance, paints a fine portrait of the ideal Church as a 'peaceable kingdom', inspired by the gospel story to stand as a model community over against the rest of society which others are then enticed to join.[86] As such it fits well with the Barthian image of preaching to the world rather than arguing or dialoguing with it, and this is no doubt one reason why Barth's theology is currently enjoying a major revival of interest, with him seen as in some sense a precursor of postmodernism in his stress on narrative.[87]

The undoubted merit in such approaches is the way in which they turn the Church inwards to reflect more on its own resources, but this does not come without corresponding penalties, in particular in the tendency to think of its own traditions as self-contained. The history of the formulation of Christian doctrine is a history of sustained indebtedness to Greek thought, and for those who would jettison such borrowings, I would add that the same seems to me no less true of the history of Scripture in relation to its surrounding cultures. This is in no way to deny many an original contribution, but even here triggers from outside have often proved necessary before such new ideas could be generated. Examples will be given in later chapters. Here let me focus instead on another danger, in conceding incommensurability too soon. Apparently profound moral differences, for instance, need not necessarily always be seen as so. Refusing Christian burial to suicides and our present compassionate attitude may sound initially like incommensurable behaviour, whereas in fact Christians took the lead in securing the repeal in England in 1961 of the penalties attaching to attempted suicide, not because their morality had fundamentally changed but rather because the act was now seen to stem from depression and not from a wilful attempt to escape one's

---

[86] S. Hauerwas, *The Peaceable Kingdom* (London: SCM Press, 1983). For his narrative and communitarian understanding of Scripture that he locates beyond fundamentalism and biblical criticism, 'Interpreting the Bible as a political act', *Religion and Intellectual Life* 6 (1989), 134–42.

[87] For narrative seen as Barth's principal hermeneutical resource, D. Ford, 'Barth's interpretation of the Bible' in S. Sykes (ed.), *Karl Barth: Studies of his Theological Method* (Oxford: Clarendon Press, 1979), 55–87; idem, *Barth and God's Story* (Frankfurt am Main: Peter Lang, 1981), esp. 33–71.

social responsibilities. Of course, many another conflict is more deeply rooted, but even here discussion need not be at an end. Partly under the impact of Thomas Kuhn's writings on revolutions in scientific thinking, criteria of comparison for conflicting totalities continue to be offered.[88] While their success so far is limited, they do show that rather more than Richard Rorty's purely pragmatic approach is possible. Not only that, their necessity would seem demonstrated by MacIntyre's own contribution to such comparative assessments in his more recent writing.[89] Whatever we call them—communities, totalities, frames of reference—few of us are likely to stand within one alone, and even if we do almost certainly there will remain friends and family there to exhibit attractive features of the alternatives, to tempt or allure. However, important though the search for such criteria undoubtedly is, I want here to draw a rather different lesson for what follows. For, recognizing our embeddedness in competing traditions contains the salutary warning that there is little value in attempting simple one-to-one translations across such opposed frames of reference.[90] Instead what we need to do is look at how any apparently similar elements function within their own particular tradition as a whole, and that may produce very different results. At all events, that is why, though later chapters take seriously the Enlightenment demand to contextualize Christianity in relation to what is happening in other religions, they fulfil that demand by looking at Judaism and Islam as holistic, developing traditions, and not as some arbitrary sum of various discrete elements.

(iii) *Failure of local master-narrative* Sometimes, however, the focus moves inwards and by talk of the collapse of master narratives is meant not some generally applicable frame of reference but what has hitherto applied within one specific area. This appears to

---

[88] e.g. B. Mitchell, *The Justification of Religious Belief* (London: Macmillan, 1973), esp. 75–95; Vincent Brümmer, *Theology and Philosophical Inquiry* (London: Macmillan, 1981), esp. 136–43.

[89] In *Whose Justice? Which Rationality?* (London: Duckworth, 1988) four competing moral traditions are identified, and the necessity of comparative assessment insisted upon: 349–403.

[90] While not denying the seriousness of John Hick's engagement with other religions, it is the absence of such considerations that for me make his case less impressive than it might otherwise have been.

be what is meant when the discussion is of postmodern history or art. Used in this way, the consequence becomes not the rein-forcement of particular narratives but their abandonment in the face of a radical pluralism. Initially, to hear talk of the 'end' of history or art sounds quite paradoxical, since in the most obvious sense they are still both very much alive. In the case of history, what all such contentions share is the conviction that the various interpretative schemes such as Marxism, progress, or growth of the nation state that were once used to give a narrative shape to the march of past events have all lost—for whatever reason—their applicability.[91] Support might be drawn from Christianity itself with the virtual disappearance of the once common providential reading of secular history. Certainly, the absence of common values does make the writing of evaluative narrative history that much more difficult, and that is no doubt one reason why we now find resort to alternative forms of presentation, such as the *Annales* school or the prosopographical approach, but, as we noted earlier, awareness of the imposition of values upon a narrative can, when used with care, make the narrative function more effectively, not less.

That much contemporary art has broken free of the earlier history of art, few would deny. Whether that rift should be assessed positively or negatively is the more difficult question, even for those who, like Arthur Danto and Hans Belting, speak of 'the end of art'.[92] Their contention is that the production of art has undergone a number of decisive changes in its history, two of the most important being the emergence at the Renaissance of the self-conscious artist concerned with imitation, and the move in the nineteenth century to reflection on technique, partly in response to the invention of photography in 1839. Painting was now to be

---

[91] Talk of the 'end' can be justified in terms of fulfilled as well as unfulfilled aims. Contrast F. Fukuyama, *The End of History and the Last Man* (London: Macmillan, 1992) and J. Baudrillard, *The Illusion of the End* (Oxford: Blackwell, 1994). For its impact on professional historians, G. Himmelfarb, *The New History and the Old* (Cambridge, Mass.: Harvard University Press, 1987).

[92] A. C. Danto, *After the End of Art* (Princeton, NJ: Princeton University Press, 1997); H. Belting, *The End of the History of Art* (Chicago: University of Chicago Press, 1987); *Das Ende der Kunstgeschichte* (2nd German edn., Munich: Verlag Beck, 1995).

'looked at, rather than through'.[93] Since the mid-1960s the third
has now been upon us, with the focus on what it is to be a work
of art but without resort to any previously established standards of
assessment, and thus in marked contrast to artists such as Picasso or
Rothko who saw themselves as still developing the canon.[94]
Danto finds such freedom exhilarating, and selects the works of
Julian Schnabel for special praise.[95] But there is no shortage of
others who take the opposing view, even among those prepared
to offer unstinted praise for some contemporary artists. The challenge is raised as to whether in the absence of criteria drawn from
the past postmodern art is not best characterized as the imposition
of artificial values set by the commercial market.[96] It would be all
too easy, though, to exaggerate. However confused the present
situation may be, there are also considerable signs of hope, with
some artists at least trying to root themselves in ways that develop
artistic insights of previous generations.[97]

Though no less commercial, postmodernist architecture has, on
the whole, received a much more welcoming response from the
general public than has postmodernist art.[98] Not only does it
outrage less, it offers quotations from past styles that can help
people feel more at home in a particular environment, and this is
no doubt one reason why it has received such praise from the
Prince of Wales, among others. Yet one should be on one's guard
against too quickly supposing that it is necessarily strongly

[93] Danto, *End of Art* 75. For him the decisive change occurs with Van Gogh
and Gauguin. He also suggests that it marks a move towards consideration of the
conditions of understanding that parallels Descartes in philosophy: 7–8.

[94] 1964 is seen as the decisive date; Ibid., 46–7; for the new canon: 29–30.

[95] Ibid., 104. The postmodern character of his work is also highlighted by
Danilo Eccher who describes it as 'territorio di confine, precaria ed instabile fron-
tiera fra aspetti distanti e contraddittori': D. Eccher (ed.), *Julian Schnabel* (Bologna:
Galleria d'arte moderna, 1996), 30.

[96] So S. Gablik, *Has Modernism Failed?* (London: Thames & Hudson, 1984),
esp. 62–3. Among contemporary artists, Richard Long and Anselm Kiefer are
given high praise: 44, 124–6. Contrast her negative judgement on Julian Schnabel
with Danto's enthusiasm: 88–91.

[97] For the need to be rooted in tradition as a way of giving criteria: Gablik,
Modernism, 30–1, 76–7, 116–17. For a British journal that takes this issue seriously,
Modern Painters, founded by Peter Fuller in 1987.

[98] For a generally favourable survey: C. Jencks, *What is Post-Modernism?*
(London: Academy, 4th edn., 1996).

communitarian simply in virtue of such quotations. For it seems not implausible to maintain that such quotations offer more the patina of depth than the depth itself. So, for instance, the Marxist critic Fredric Jameson talks of 'the random cannibalisation of all the styles of the past', while the geographer David Harvey finds in buildings like Charles Moore's much praised Piazza d'Italia only 'the penchant for fragmentation'.[99] Contemporary art and architecture may thus not be nearly so far apart as they initially appear. Jameson suggests the fault lies in the logic of late capitalism requiring endless innovation. Harvey, more plausibly in my view, points to a profound tension in modern society between the collapse of wider spatial markers in the environment as a whole and the attempt to compensate with at least a nominal assertion of there being some specific place occupied.[100] The irony, though, is that the 'the sign of the success of the anti-universalist language and style of architectural postmodernism is that one can find it *everywhere*' throughout the world,[101] and so it fails after all to offer any real sense of rootedness. That can only be restored by a narrative that takes our various different relations to the past seriously.[102] Central to the argument in what follows will be the contention that the imagination works by building upon tradition. Even revolt only becomes truly significant if it takes seriously the appeal of what it is attempting to supplant. If that is so, then clearly breaking with all tradition or even just random dipping is bound to have dire consequences, in a pervasive superficiality. That, I suggest, is one plausible way in which to interpret the extensive pluralism that currently exists within all the major Christian denominations for, though the resultant freedom in thought is welcome, it seems

[99] F. Jameson, 'Postmodernism, or the cultural logic of late capitalism', *New Left Review* 146 (1984), 53–92, esp. 65–6; D. Harvey, *The Condition of Postmodernity* (Oxford: Blackwell, 1990), 97. The Piazza d'Italia is in New Orleans. Contrast Jencks' praise for James Stirling's pluralism of styles in the Staatsgalerie at Stuttgart: *Postmodernism*, 32–4.

[100] Harvey, *Condition*, Part III, 201–323, esp. 302–3, with its stress on 'the motivational power of tradition'.

[101] S. Connor, *Postmodernist Culture* (Oxford: Blackwell, 2nd edn., 1997), 87; author's italics.

[102] For an argument that uses the Tower of Babel to argue that openness within pluralism is what gives both modernity and postmodernity any strength they may have: G. Rose, *Judaism and Modernity* (Oxford: Blackwell, 1993), 225–40, esp. 230, 233.

to have been bought at the price of most adherents knowing less and less of the faith to which they allegedly belong. Thus, for example, though it is perhaps understandable why 'great' Anglican theologians of the past are no longer read, such attitudes have also resulted in a heavy price being paid in lack of awareness of the wealth of spiritual classics and major literary figures that underpin Anglicanism.

(iv) *Meaning given internally by narrative* Ironically, the end of the local master narrative and the resultant internal pluralism has led in the field most directly concerned with narrative—literary studies— to the reassertion of its importance. Wider narratives of attribution or canon are rejected, but this is only so that greater weight can be given to what appears on the page itself. This is because, with no appeal possible on the postmodernist view to some wider frame, criteria of assessment are forced to come entirely from within the object in question. In the case of music, that might mean a particular composition throwing up its own set of rules, whereas in the case of a literary text this is presumed to entail, where it has a narrative structure, that structure being allowed to determine its meaning rather than any information derived from outside. This amounts to the claim that there is no need to know anything of the context in which the work was written or the author. The text itself is king. Earlier this century such claims had a modernist, objectivist ring, in that the aim was to avoid subjectivism at all costs, as in T. S. Eliot's declaration that 'poetry ... is not the expression of personality, but an escape from personality'.[103] In its more recent, postmodernist form there is no longer the search for a single meaning that transcends the particular passions and prejudices of the author. Instead, a plurality of possible meanings is accepted but they are all to find their rationale from within the text itself. In such attitudes Roland Barthes' 1967 essay 'The Death of the Author' was particularly significant, though Foucault and Derrida were also to launch similar contentions about the same time.[104]

---

[103] 'Tradition and the individual talent' in F. Kermode (ed.), *Selected Prose*, 43.
[104] R. Barthes, *Image–Music–Text* (London: Fontana, 1977), 142–8; J. Derrida, *Of Grammatology* (Baltimore: Johns Hopkins, 1976), 157–64. In Derrida's case, the extreme version is soon rejected explicitly elsewhere, e.g. *Positions* (London: Athlone, 1981), 88.

The positive value in such claims is the recognition that texts can indeed break free of their authors and acquire different forms of significance that are not only intelligible in relation to the narrative as a whole but sometimes more illuminating than the intended meaning. To give a minor example, when schoolchildren first hear Hamlet's injunction to Ophelia, 'Get thee to a nunnery', they take on board a rather different conception of Hamlet's state of mind from what the original audience probably understood, given that 'nunnery' was contemporary slang for a brothel.[105] Yet, arguably, it is the modern reading that the more easily allows us to sympathize and engage imaginatively with Hamlet's condition. Other more substantial cases might include instances where the sympathies of later readers have been drawn to characters whom the authors seem to have intended negatively, such as Satan in Milton's *Paradise Lost*, Anna in Tolstoy's *Anna Karenina* or Gudrun in D. H. Lawrence's *Women in Love*.[106]

On my view there are no shortage of cases where this is also true of Scripture, and in fact quite a number of illustrations will be offered in subsequent chapters. Even so, we need also to protest against the negative side of the more extreme versions of such 'postmodernist' readings. For the fact that the intentions of the author are not necessarily relevant in determining an acceptable meaning should not be taken to imply that questions of authorship have no relevance. As several commentators have observed, advocates were soon tying themselves in knots as they appeared simultaneously to deny the relevance of the author but yet pursued issues that only had significance if the role of the author were also accorded importance.[107] So much would seem to depend on what questions are being addressed. Added to that was the apparent confusion of purely literary and historical concerns. The acceptance of the theory by Paul de Man seemed too much like a convenient ploy for him to escape from moral

[105] *Hamlet* III, 1, 121.

[106] In Gudrun's case she seems to lose Lawrence's argument that runs through the book, but win imaginatively. The fact that none of my examples are from postmodern literature illustrates how the issue of 'against the grain' readings is nothing new.

[107] The critique is pursued in some detail in S. Burke, *The Death and Return of the Author* (Edinburgh: Edinburgh University Press, 1992), 20–153, with Barthes, Foucault and Derrida being considered in turn.

responsibility for his Fascist writings during the Second World War, while, however successful as fiction Thomas Pynchon's postmodern novel *Gravity's Rainbow* might be, his endorsement of the legitimacy of a wide range of explanations for the conduct of that war, none of which includes Hitler, cannot be allowed to stand as historical narrative without fundamentally undermining any notion of moral seriousness.[108] We need therefore to continue to insist that, though authorial meaning is not the only type of meaning, it is one important and legitimate strand. Equally, it is worth observing that new meanings, no less than authorial, cannot escape all questions of context. For one thing, how meanings are received very much depends on the nature of the community to which they are addressed. So, while the people originally intended as recipients of the author's address cannot necessarily be allowed to have the final say, it is emphatically not the case that such a community frame can later legitimately be displaced by some simple, personal preference. Communal frames of reference will continue to remain the controlling reference, and that is clearly a matter of some relevance in determining how the Bible should be read.

(v) *No reference beyond the text* Such remarks already indicate what is wrong with the more extreme version of the claim that meaning must be generated internally: the contention that no reference or meaning can successfully be made beyond the text itself: '*il n'y a pas de hors texte*'.[109] As the quotation indicates, it is an assumption which has come to be especially associated with the name of Jacques Derrida, but he himself has since disowned the position on a number of occasions;[110] and with good reason, since, while, it may not always be necessary to know about the author, without specification of context of use very little can be said at all. Some deconstructionist theologians such as Mark Taylor have sought to make more of the thesis, by stressing the celebration of

---

[108] On Paul de Man, Burke, 1–7; S. Earnshaw, *The Direction of Literary Theory* (Basingstoke: Macmillan, 1996), 23. A critique of *Gravity's Rainbow* (London: Jonathan Cape, 1973) is offered in Earnshaw, 65–70.

[109] *Of Grammatology*, 158.

[110] 'There is nothing beyond language ... and other stupidities of that sort'; quoted in C. Norris, *Derrida* (London: Fontana, 1987), 144.

language that might be entailed.[111] Though the focus on the play of language can be a substitute for more serious concerns, it can also have its positive side in drawing attention to the openness of language, its capacity to be developed in novel and unexpected ways, and that is not without relevance in eliciting a more favourable response to some of the more extraordinary interpretations that have sometimes been imposed upon the biblical narratives.[112]

It is to an assessment of the hermeneutical assumptions underlying treatment of those narratives that we turn next. Current approaches exhibit a marked shift towards a more literary understanding and away from the earlier dominance of historical questions that was so characteristic of Enlightenment assumptions. The question remains, however, whether the latter can be wholly jettisoned, as also whether the former is any more satisfactory if it assumes a stable or unchanging text.

Biblical hermeneutics and the search for method

In effect, the questions raised by modern hermeneutics began with Schleiermacher. In contrast to established confessional interpretations of Scripture he insisted that our aim must be, as with every other kind of text, to get back to the mind and intentions of the author. That means thorough immersion in the text, for which the best analogue is conversation or dialogue with a friend. He insists that speech just as much as writing involves hermeneutical issues,[113] and that 'just as in life we are most successful in understanding our friends, so a skilful interpreter is most successful ... when an author is among those favourites with whom he is best acquainted'.[114] He is also careful to point out that this does not necessarily mean discovering a literal meaning, as though the

---

[111] M. C. Taylor, *Erring* (Chicago: University of Chicago Press, 1984); for more detailed comments on Derrida and Taylor, D. Brown, *Continental Philosophy and Modern Theology* (Oxford: Blackwell, 1987), 33–6.

[112] For some of the ways in which biblical scholars have used Derrida and deconstructionism, A. C. Thistleton, *New Horizons in Hermeneutics* (London: HarperCollins, 1992), 103–32.

[113] F. Schleiermacher, *Hermeneutics: The Handwritten Manuscripts*, H. Kimmerle (ed.), (Missoula, Montana: Scholars Press, 1977), 181 ff.

[114] Ibid., 185.

allegorical is always 'a second and additional meaning'.[115] Wilhelm
Dilthey (1833–1911) was less cautious: 'allegorical interpretation', he
suggests, is best described as 'a skill as necessary as it is pernicious'.[116]
But it was thanks to Dilthey that Schleiermacher's approach became
more generally known, as also one particular complication which
comes with it, the so-called 'hermeneutical circle', the notion that
total objectivity in such a search is impossible because by starting at
one point rather than another we inevitably make certain assumptions about the appropriateness of the starting point; to give one of
Dilthey's own examples, considerable though Schleiermacher's
achievements were in his analysis of Plato's thought, he had
constantly to move back and forth between his assumptions about
Plato and the problems thrown up for those assumptions by particular passages, with the result that one must conclude that with
hermeneutics 'it can only fulfil its task to a degree'.[117]

For those of us who stand at the end of this process of searching for the text's original meaning it is often hard to comprehend
how far we have come in so short a time. Jowett's essay on 'The
Interpretation of Scripture' in *Essays and Reviews* of 1860 was
regarded as controversial at the time, but we would now all
acknowledge we live with an immeasurably more complicated
situation than his view of Jesus as essentially a moral teacher incul-
cating 'universal truth' that 'easily breaks through the accidents of
time and place'.[118] Yet to understand such a remark, it is only
necessary to recall that Wellhausen's work of source criticism on
the Pentateuch (to which we shall allude in Part Two) only dates
from the 1880s, and Bultmann's development of it for application
to the New Testament as form criticism only from the 1920s.[119]

---

[115] Ibid., 213.
[116] 'Necessary' as a means of avoiding the real truth behind religious texts,
which is no doubt how it sometimes functions; cf. W. Dilthey, *Selected Writings*,
ed. H. P. Rickman (Cambridge: Cambridge University Press, 1976), 251.
[117] Ibid., 259. cf. 262, 203.
[118] *Essays and Reviews* (7th edn. London: Longman, 1861), 330–433, esp. 412.
[119] J. Wellhausen, *Die Komposition des Hexateuchs und der historischen Bucher des
Alten Testaments* (1885); R. Bultmann, *Die Geschichte der synoptischen Tradition*
(1921); It was not until 1963 that an English translation was published—by John
Marsh (Oxford: Blackwell)—which is perhaps one indication of the slowness
with which such methods were accepted in England, though Vincent Taylor was
already a moderate advocate by 1933.

Strauss, Renan and others had of course issued earlier challenges,[120] but because their approach was based on prejudice against the miraculous rather than careful scholarly analysis of the text, the ultimate effect was to delay a proper reception of such careful placing of the text in its original historical context.

The invention of source and form criticism had meant that Schleiermacher's original concern with authorial intention had now become considerably more complicated. A still further level of discussion was initiated by Willi Marxsen's invention of the term 'redaction criticism' in 1954 to indicate questions that specifically focused upon what concerns of the author are indicated by the precise way in which he had chosen to 'redact' or edit the material available to him. As such, it continued to presuppose the type of questions raised by the other forms of criticism: the sources available to the author and the way in which their form has been adopted in transmission to suit the interests of the community. Given Dilthey's identification of the problem of the hermeneutical circle so many decades earlier, it is perhaps surprising that such a methodology achieved such unqualified ascendancy for so long, but it had one undoubted advantage, in conveying academic respectability: it seemed that theology could be as rigorous and objective in its approach as any other arts discipline.

However, though many biblical scholars continue to pursue such methods, they are meeting with increasing challenge for at least three reasons. First, there has been a general decline in confidence in objectivity in the arts disciplines generally. How this has affected the study of secular history we noted earlier in this chapter, while more recently its impact on philosophy, literature and the arts has also been noted. Secondly within biblical studies itself, while confidence came with apparent progress, this has declined as apparently assured results have come under attack. Obvious examples would be changing attitudes to the source hypothesis for the Pentateuch or to the existence of Q in gospel criticism. Finally, and most relevant to our concerns here, there was the recognition that such studies seem to be doing little to advance appreciation of the value of Scripture, as scholarly consensus and use in church grew ever wider apart.

---

[120] D. F. Strauss, *Leben Jesu* (1835); translation by George Eliot (1846); J. E. Renan, *La vie de Jesus* (1862).

The more recent response to such worries has been the development of more literary approaches to the Bible, where historical questions are either treated as secondary or bracketed out altogether.[121] We shall look at some examples in due course. As we saw earlier, Karl Barth is quite often treated as an early anticipation of this more literary or narrative approach. The following chapter will briefly address his contribution. Perhaps, however, a more obviously transitional figure to introduce at this point is Rudolph Bultmann. To consider here his writings rather than Barth's has the added advantage that, unlike Barth, he was equally distinguished as a New Testament scholar and as a theologian.

On first reading, Bultmann's concluding thoughts in his *Theology of the New Testament* can sound like the perfect integration of biblical scholarship and theology. The 'reconstruction of past history' is essential, but it is done 'under the presupposition that the New Testament writings have something to say to the present'.[122] What is worrying, though, is his narrow definition of that relevance: 'the expression of an understanding of human existence'. For, though this is explicitly contrasted with 'timeless, general truths', it is hard not to read him as seeking to achieve precisely that, a universal anthropology that thereby escapes the contingency of the historical Jesus. Thus in his more explicitly hermeneutical writings, though he constantly stresses this question of 'life-relation' as an essential additional presupposition to the critical method,[123] it is simply assumed that this is personal, and not also social, historical and transcendent. The result is two major distortions, both the consequence of his search for a secure, unchanging content at the heart of the Christian gospel.

First, the significance of the past is distorted, as history becomes merely the medium for the anthropological message, rather than

---

[121] I should not be taken as implying that the historical and literary are the only two types of approach currently adopted by biblical scholars. There is a great variety; cf., e.g. J. B. Green (ed.), *Hearing the New Testament: Strategies for Interpretation* (Grand Rapids, Michigan: Eerdmans, 1995). I focus on these two only, as the two most relevant to my concerns.

[122] (London: SCM Press, 1955), II, 251.

[123] 'Is exegesis without presuppositions possible?' in *Existence and Faith* (London: Collins, 1964), 342–51, esp. 349; 'The problem of hermeneutics', in *New Testament and Mythology* (Philadelphia: Fortress Press, 1984), 113–33, e.g. 118, 126.

itself the message. Thus notoriously, not only does Bultmann relegate the historical Jesus to the old dispensation, he equates the resurrection with the meaning of the cross.[124] It is no excuse that his fellow existentialist, Paul Tillich, went one stage further in declaring that all that matters is that the New Being has occurred, not whether it has occurred in that particular historical figure.[125] In short, it is not that Bultmann's search for relevance for today was illegitimate, but that this was sought in a way which, so far from taking the past seriously, accepted Lessing's 'ditch' and so ignored the contextual character of Christian truth claims: that it was not merely the form of presentation that was affected by historical context but the content as well and that this therefore could not be elided without reductionism.

The second distortion is not unrelated, in that it makes essentially the same point about our own historical context. Bultmann thought that his programme of translation from the biblical context to our own could proceed without loss, whereas in fact his programme of demythologization involved loss at both ends, our own contemporary context no less than the biblical. Many critics have observed that New Testament 'myth' is about much more than human anthropology.[126] But it is equally true that modern society has its myths, and so to propose elimination rather than development is to fail to engage modern society with sufficient seriousness, far less the biblical community. The French writer, Roland Barthes, for instance, finds the presence of myth everywhere in modern society.[127] Indeed, some would argue that the contrast between history and myth is artificial since so much of the history that shapes our present condition is made up of our myths. 'Humanity cannot understand or know anything without its traditions. Traditions are myths, narratives of the place of the human in time.'[128] Obviously

---

[124] For the former, even his opening sentence in *Theology of New Testament* (London: SCM Press, 1952), I, 3; for the latter: 'Faith in the resurrection is really the same thing as faith in the saving efficacy of the cross': *Kerygma and Myth* (New York: Harper and Row, 1961), 41.

[125] Tillich, *Systematic Theology* (London: SCM Press, 1978), II, 113–17.

[126] Cf. D. Ferguson, *Bultmann* (London: Geoffrey Chapman, 1992), 126–30.

[127] R. Barthes, *Mythologies* (London: Granada, 1973); cf. also D. Brown, *Continental Philosophy*, 62–6.

[128] D. McGaughey, 'Through myth to imagination', *Journal of the American Academy of Religion* (*JAAR*) 56 (1988), 51–76, esp. 73.

much more detailed attention would need to be given to what we understand by myth before the truth of this claim could be determined. But perhaps enough has been said to indicate that Bultmann's failure lies in a narrow rationalism. As subsequent chapters will try to demonstrate, the strength of myth or story lies in its capacity to be appropriated in different sorts of ways over the course of its transmission, not in it having a single meaning reducible to some purely literal, timeless statement.

One more recent writer on hermeneutics who avoids this kind of critique directed against Bultmann is Paul Ricoeur. He shares Bultmann's existentialist concern for the appropriation of the text in our own day, but rejects his understanding of myth. In effect Bultmann had seen myth as dispensable, whereas for Ricoeur its poetic character is essential as the means whereby the message is conveyed.[129] This is not to say that it has to be naïvely accepted as it stands. Though in our 'first *naïveté*' we will inevitably confuse the message with the immediate presuppositions of our surroundings, there is a 'second *naïveté*' beyond this, once we have placed the text in its original context and subjected it to the hermeneutics of suspicion required of those who live in a world that is subsequent to those 'masters of suspicion', Nietzsche, Marx, and Freud; in that 'second *naïveté*' the myth can then hold its own.

This is a great improvement on Bultmann. Even so there remain two major difficulties. The first concerns the question of whether in his desire not to undervalue the mythical Ricoeur does not go to the other extreme. Given that the two biblical expositors he seems most to admire are von Rad on the Old Testament and Moltmann on the New[130] one might have thought his hold on the importance of history secure. Yet so insistent is he upon the indispensability of myth that poetic discourse alone is allowed to be revelatory,[131] while its metaphoric character is declared to be so inescapable that he is even prepared to speak of 'the abolition of reference'.[132] But, as one commentator has observed,[133] down that

[129] Cf. P. Ricoeur, 'Preface to Bultmann' in *Essays on Biblical Interpretation*, ed. L. S. Mudge (London: SPCK, 1981), esp. 65 ff.
[130] So, Mudge, in his introductory essay, ibid., 17, 29.
[131] Ricoeur, 'Preface to Bultmann', 101–3.
[132] *The Rule of Metaphor* (London: Routledge & Kegan Paul, 1978), 224.
[133] G. Ward, 'Biblical narrative and the theology of metonymy', *Modern Theology* 7 (1991), 335–49.

path lies a docetic form of Christianity that radically distorts its origins. It is not that myth must be denied in order to avoid this, but that its metaphorical content needs to be supplemented by clear claims to metonymy, of the imagery being rooted in historical fact.

But, if his corrective to Bultmann's views on mythology is thus carried too far, he also continues Bultmann's mistake in supposing that dialogue with the text is essentially an individual matter. One critic has observed:

A certain analysis of how the mind works, not only individually but also in concert with others, would seem to be a necessary part of any solution. Since this aspect is not sufficiently developed in Ricoeur, it seems to me that he ends up placing too much emphasis on the text itself and to attribute to it a weight of objectivity which it cannot bear on its own.[134]

With that judgement I would agree, but not with the critic's suggestion that adequate supplementation can be provided through appeal to the methodology advocated by Bernard Lonergan.[135] For, though there is much in Lonergan's classic work *Method in Theology* about intersubjectivity and historical contextualization and development, he seems to share a pattern that is common even among those who are willing to stress a communitarian perspective, that it is essentially a matter of the present dialoguing with a distant past or a past as now received. What this fails to take seriously is the value of tradition as a staged process, where the steps on the way might be of as intrinsic interest as the beginning or the end.

Somewhat surprisingly, such privileging of the present is also a fault shared by the philosopher who is normally regarded as the principal defender of the importance of tradition among contemporary writers on hermeneutics, namely Hans-Georg Gadamer. In *Truth and Method* he makes much of the inevitability of 'prejudices', perspectives given to us by a tradition of which we cannot help being part:

[134] R. Moloney, 'Stages in Ricoeur's Hermeneutics', *Irish Theological Quarterly* 58 (1992), 119–28, esp. 126–7.
[135] Ibid., 128, n. 59.

History does not belong to us, but we belong to it. Long before we understand ourselves through the process of self-examination, we understand ourselves in a self-evident way in the family, society and state in which we live ... The self-awareness of the individual is only a flickering in the closed circuits of historical life. That is why the prejudices of the individual, far more than his judgements, constitute the historical reality of his being.[136]

All this is excellent; so too is his explanation of how change occurs, through the 'fusion of horizons' (*Horizonverschmelzung*), with our inherited prejudices, through confrontation with the text, producing a modified tradition which continues to be subject to subsequent developments.[137] But one looks in vain for adequate recognition of the fact that there are in fact potentially (and certainly legitimately) far more than just two dialogue partners, the present community and its prejudices and the past text. For, in so far as we are aware of its history, each stage of the transmission of the tradition, including those aspects that were jettisoned, has the potential to act as a critique of our own present concerns and obsessions.

Taking such a conception on board would make possible a very different configuration to the debate in Germany between Gadamer's own stress on tradition and Jürgen Habermas's classic defence of Enlightenment rationality in his notion of the goal of interpretation as 'the ideal speech situation' totally devoid of our 'interests' or 'prejudices'.[138] If Habermas failed to see the positive value of tradition in helping us to build upon what we already understand and know, Gadamer fails to acknowledge how often it is that what we most need is release from our 'prejudices', not their reinforcement. As the history of Christianity well illustrates, even tradition itself needs first to be undermined before it can acquire a capacity for further development. Here is one way in which the various stages in the process, the very different perspectives of previous generations, can help release us from our present biases, and open up alternative options of interpretation. Though

---

[136] H.-G. Gadamer, *Truth and Method* (London: Sheed & Ward, 1979), 245.
[137] Cf. Ibid., 271.
[138] Cf. J. Habermas, *Knowledge and Human Interests* (London: Heinemann, 1978, 2nd edn.); *The Theory of Communicative Action* (London: Heinemann, 1984, 2 vols.).

even Habermas thinks that what he advocates is only an ideal goal, not one ever capable of complete realization, my comments here are not meant to side wholly with his position. Rather, while conceding postmodernist insistence that all thought involves antecedent presuppositions and also that many of these can be captured in the notion of tradition, what I am denying is that thereby they become exempt from any form of effective critique. Not only are all human beings likely to be members of more than one tradition, each of which will require reconciliation with the other, but also even within that tradition which is held to be most dear radical critiques are possible, provided one takes seriously every stage in its development and not just where it has now reached. Nor do I mean by that only the critique of formal rational argument. No less attention needs to be given to the way in which the thought of our own or earlier generations may have been shaped—for good or ill—by sociological factors, imaginative considerations or even the precise way in which a particular view was presented.[139]

This perhaps already hints at why recent moves towards a more literary approach to biblical studies do not seem to me to provide the complete answer. For inadequate though historical studies are on their own, it will not do to substitute for them the other extreme: instead of the launching pad for a tradition, the point where it has presently reached. Who is appropriately characterized as representative of this approach is a moot question, but there is some advantage in stretching the net widely, and so including among others the canonical criticism of Brevard Childs and the narrative theology of Hans Frei.[140] Childs is himself a biblical scholar, while Frei's narrative theology has received enthusiastic endorsement from quite a number working in that field.[141] Both

---

[139] For an excellent review of the role of rhetoric in the history of philosophy, cf. M. Warner, *Philosophical Finesse* (Oxford: Clarendon Press, 1989); for the application of the point to the Gadamer–Habermas debate, S. E. Shapiro, 'Rhetoric as ideology critique', *JAAR* 62 (1994), 123–50.

[140] B. S. Childs, *Introduction to the Old Testament as Scripture* (London: SCM Press, 1979), and subsequent writings; H. Frei, *The Eclipse of Biblical Theology* (New Haven: Yale University Press, 1974); *Theology and Narrative* (New York: Oxford University Press, 1993).

[141] e.g. F. Watson, 'Literary approaches to the gospels: a theological assessment', *Theology* 99 (1996), 125–33.

adopt what might be called a holistic approach, with the former assigning supreme significance to the final, balanced shape of the canon as a whole and the latter maintaining that the integrated character of its narrative will be destroyed if it is atomized into numerous attempts at reference to the external world.[142]

So strongly has this kind of approach been associated in the United States with Yale that its adherents are sometimes called the Yale school and then contrasted with what emerges from the Chicago Divinity School and in particular the work of David Tracy.[143] Given the latter's talk of 'classics' and 'paradigm shifts' it might be thought that I would find this approach the more congenial, but in fact I find difficulties in both. Admittedly, Tracy has no difficulty in acknowledging a developing tradition, but his language is altogether too externalist for my liking. One cannot as easily stand outside a religious tradition as one can a changing scientific perspective, for it is something within which one lives as giving life and substance to the practice of one's faith, and it is that stress on the living text which is Yale's great strength. But Yale too has its weaknesses. Quite a few have found in the related approach of the literary scholar, Robert Alter, justification for dispensing with historical questions altogether but, as another narrative critic, Meir Sternberg, has wisely observed: 'text requires context.'[144] Historical questions may be difficult and not always capable of adequate resolution, but without the effort something valuable will be lost in understanding not only the genesis but the power of the text. In this connection it is particularly interesting to read the limitations yet another literary critic, Stanley Fish, placed on his conversion to the more internalist approach that is characteristic of Yale.[145] On his own admission he has moved from an approach to literary criticism which assumed that the reader and text were

---

[142] *Eclipse*, 28; The contrast between the Yale/Hans Frei and Chicago/David Tracy approaches to reference is helpfully explored and criticized in G. L. Constock, 'Two types of narrative theology', *JAAR* 55 (1987), 687–717.

[143] D. Tracy, *The Analogical Imagination* (London: SCM Press, 1981), 99 ff.; cf. H. Küng and D. Tracy, *Paradigm Change in Theology* (Edinburgh: T & T Clark, 1989).

[144] A repeated theme in his book, *The Poetics of Biblical Narrative* (Bloomington: Indiana University Press, 1985).

[145] S. Fish, *Is There A Text In This Class?* (Cambridge, Mass.: Harvard University Press, 1980), 1–17.

totally separate entities to 'reader-response' as what shapes interpretation, with reader and text inevitably interacting with one
another to redefine both sides of the equation. Yet he remains
insistent that this need not mean the abandonment of objectivity
altogether, of any tests of applicability that arise beyond the text
itself. For certain standard tests are usually found to be set by the
communities which use the text in question, while even these can
be subject to revision through various forms of persuasion.[146]

Conclusion

In a later chapter I shall seek to identify more clearly how I see
God's role in respect of a developing religious textual tradition,
but here I end my consideration of the debate between modernism
and postmodernism by indicating in summary form why I want to
set myself on both sides of the controversy.

To begin with, difficult though historical questions often can
be, I remain sufficiently a child of the Enlightenment to remain
convinced of the necessity of facing them. There is no easy way of
meshing the significance of the life, death and resurrection of Jesus
Christ into an historical metanarrative that is entirely shared by
secular culture, but that does not mean that Christians cannot go
part of the way. Indeed, they must, if Christianity is to retain its
basic claim to be founded upon an historical revelation. But the
pressure is by no means entirely external. Pertinent also is the way
in which historical investigation can throw up some account of
what factors led to further change in religious perspective. Close
attention to original context can uncover open trajectories as it
were, pressure points that almost demand further development.
What these are for some key biblical narratives will be discussed in
detail in later chapters. Here let me merely throw out a couple of
examples of what I have in mind, almost at random. Some parts of
the Old Testament assume the existence of other gods, just as in
at least one passage the actual existence of the great sea-monster
Leviathan appears to be accepted.[147] Though these are, I think, the
natural reading of the author's intention, the gods can without

---

[146] S. Fish, *Is There A Text In This Class?*, 14–15.
[147] For the former, e.g. Pss. 82, 86, 97; for Leviathan, Ps. 74: 13–14.

much difficulty be reinterpreted as a council of angels, just as Leviathan can become purely a mythical symbol for the future, complete victory of God.[148] But something is lost in our understanding of the history of the tradition if we simply assume the later reading and do not acknowledge the pressures that led to it. To give a rather different example, so prominent is modern Liberation theology's exegesis of the exodus as an act of divine liberation that it is very easy to conceal from ourselves that the focus of the original authors was significantly different. For, while the Israelites groaning under bondage may be the occasion of God hearing them, he responds because 'God remembered his covenant with Abraham, with Isaac and with Jacob' (Exod. 2: 24). In other words, the primary reason is not compassion at all but because God has a nation to establish, and that is presumably why the final redactors of the Pentateuch found no incongruity in retaining an earlier account of a Hebrew mother (Sarah) abusing an Egyptian slave (Hagar) with God's full and explicit endorsement. Likewise, it is surely here that we shall find the explanation for why the Mosaic legislation has no difficulty in assuming that even in the promised land some of the Israelites will continue to be slaves.[149] Respecting the integrity of a text, and its original author and readers, must surely mean at least attempting to discover where their original focus lay, even if we choose to read the text differently.

In such refusal of the final say to history and advocacy in appropriate circumstances of a different reading, there is clearly a major divergence from Enlightenment assumptions, that there is a single, authorial meaning to be discovered. Some versions of postmodernism, as we have seen, allow a riot of individually imposed senses. That is not what is being proposed here, but I am suggesting that, though developing traditions of reading do limit options by imposing some criteria of appropriateness, these are by no means confined to an obvious historical development from the original sense. Matters are much more complicated, and involve considering how the text is situated in relation to other accepted narratives and the assumptions they contain. What the criteria are

[148] As in Isa. 27: 1. At Gen. 1: 26 patristic interpretation went even further than angels in finding a reference to the Trinity.
[149] For former, Gen. 16: 9; for latter, e.g. Exod. 21: 2.

will emerge more clearly as our discussion proceeds. Here suffice
it to say that any temptation to equate non-historical with untrue
must be firmly resisted. Metaphor and fictional discourse remain
no less capable of conveying truth than the literal or historical.[150]
There is now much greater recognition among biblical scholars
than there would once have been of the key role played by
symbolism in the Gospels, and that, whether a particular incident
happened or not is really from the evangelists' perspective less
important than the significance implied by what they describe.[151]
Herein lies one of the major strengths of postmodernist
approaches: narratives succeed by conveying significance and
values rather than by one to one correspondence with historical
fact. This is a matter which will particularly engage our attention
when we consider the life of Jesus and what has been made of his
significance in Part Three.

But if continuing concern with historical objectivity and narrative integrity are to my mind the two main positive contributions
of modernism and postmodernism respectively that need to be
brought into effective relation with one another, there is also a
downside. So let me end this chapter by noting one element in
each which seems to me to require correction, taking
Enlightenment assumptions first. Here one may note the failure to
acknowledge the conditioned character of all thought. This is not
to adopt historical determinism, but it is to insist that even in our
shrinking modern world there are few universally shared assumptions, and we can only think otherwise because the high profile for
tolerance masks what is in fact little more than an agreement to
differ. But, if that is true even of our own world of high speed
communications, the point applies still more so to earlier cultures.
What is seen as an issue cannot be completely independent of the
culture in which the individual is set. The consequence, however,
is not complete cultural relativism since not only can our own age
learn through study of the different agendas of previous generations,

---

[150] For metaphor as truth, cf. J. M. Soskice, *Metaphor and Religious Language*
(Oxford: Clarendon Press, 1985); for fictional discourse as truth, G. D. Martin,
'A new look at fictional reference', *Philosophy* 57 (1982), 223–36.

[151] e.g. M. Hooker on Mark's view of miracle as 'acted parable' in *The Gospel
according to St. Mark* (London: A & C Black, 1991), 197–8, 252. For a more obvious example (John 2: 1–11), cf. D. Brown, *The Word to Set You Free* (London:
SPCK, 1995), 128–31.

it is also the case that there is no such thing as a cultural totality. Apparently minor changes can generate large upheavals, as can wider changes in economic or social conditions. As an example of the former, consider what has happened since the decriminalization of homosexual practice; of the latter, the migrations that led to the collapse of the Roman empire, or the rise of science and its impact on human self-understanding. One of my aims in what follows will be to identify some of the triggers that have led to changes in religious perception. The extensive use of insights from the social sciences by scholars of the stature of Gerd Theissen and Wayne Meeks illustrate how much more sophisticated the search for such triggers can be, but that they existed I have no doubt. It is hard, for instance, not to think that the move of the New Testament away from the deontological, rule-bound approach of the Old Testament towards a teleological or goal-orientated morality was unconnected with expectation of the imminence of a new order in the kingdom of God.[152] What we therefore seem to have is a community of faith in continual process of change as fresh contexts trigger fresh handlings of inherited traditions. Only thus can we explain the huge transformations which take place, for instance within the Old Testament in respect of the importance of law, personal responsibility and the afterlife, or in the New on the status of Christ or expectation of the end.

To speak in this way of such triggers is, however, already to undermine any postmodernist view of texts which claims that they can function in a self-contained way. The reason why narratives retain their power in different circumstances is because readers either give new prominence to hitherto neglected aspects of the text or because they resolve to tell the story in a new way. One type of biblical criticism applied to the Old Testament has commonly been known in English as the traditio-critical method. Though a cumbersome expression, it at least indicates the need to see narrative in a continuing process of re-presentation, as also to examine why this should be so. If the division of the Pentateuch between J, E, D, and P has become less fashionable in recent years,

---

[152] This is not to advocate revival of the notion of Jesus' ethics being an *Interimsethik* as in A. Schweitzer, *The Quest of the Historical Jesus* (1910). For a more moderate version of the connection, T. W. Ogletree, *The Use of the Bible in Christian Ethics* (Philadelphia: Fortress Press, 1983), 87 ff., esp. 90.

even without any delving beneath the biblical text there remains for all to see an example like Chronicles' rewriting of Kings. Equally, in the New Testament we have the alterations made by Matthew and Luke to Mark, and John's radical rewriting, whether or not in conscious awareness of the details of the narratives of the other evangelists.

Of course, not all such developments need be seen as positive. But, if historical fact is not the only form of truth, there is no reason in principle why they could not be, and charity would seem to demand that we at least take seriously the motives under which such changes have been wrought. Moreover, if all thought is conditioned, it would seem inevitable that certain issues will not have been faced adequately by the scriptural writers. That being so, it would seem scarcely credible that the last significant change that required a fresh imaginative application of the tradition occurred in the first century of our era. To endorse the plausibility of this contention one need only think for a moment of the rise of individualism, the emergence of capitalism, the changes in human self-understanding wrought by science, declarations of human rights, and the numerous other changes that have taken place in the succeeding two thousand years. This is why the Yale approach seem to me so inadequate, with Childs in effect suggesting that the canonical text already has all the necessary checks and balances for subsequent reflection, or Hans Frei that the existing, unaltered narrative has the power in itself to shape the life of the Christian in any age. In support, George Lindbeck talks of 'texts projecting imaginatively and practically habitable worlds'.[153] But in practice, they have seldom been able to do so over the centuries unaltered, and that is why almost all biblical narratives have been subject to huge transformations over the course of the Church's history.

There are signs that biblical scholars are now beginning to take that history with increasing seriousness.[154] The methodology has even acquired its own characteristic German name

---

[153] 'Scripture, consensus and community' in *This World: Journal of Religion and Public Life* 23 (1988), 5–24, esp. 21. His stress on imagination and engagement is welcome, but not that on cultural totalities (e.g. 20).

[154] One distinguished example is the work of Ulrich Luz: *Matthew 1–7: A Commentary* (Minneapolis: Augsburg, 1989); *Matthew in History* (Minneapolis: Fortress Press, 1994).

Wirkungsgeschichte, but the task is not the biblical scholar's alone.[155] There is also work for the historian, systematician and philosopher. For what is at stake is nothing less than the nature of Christian identity and its capacity to accept further change under God's direction in its self-understanding. I am no prophet; so I shall refrain from commenting here on future directions. But I do want to stress that in the contemporary Church change is often resisted for very bad reasons, whereas the capacity for narrative identity to change has been precisely one of the great strengths of the community of faith in the past. To illustrate this, the following chapter will take changes in the way the story of Christmas has been told, though I shall begin with my first attempt to link the Spirit with such change, a more developed account of revelation being offered in the subsequent chapter. That the New Testament could be improved will seem to some readers an outrageous claim. But that in effect has been what tradition has done, and rightly demanded, as new social triggers required fresh resolutions. Narratives must engage the imagination, and to do this they must relate to the readers' own life situations and dilemmas, not simply to the past.

[155] Though the advantage of the methodology in identifying alternative meanings is acknowledged by the Pontifical Biblical Commission, it ignores what seems to me the main issue, whether it might be a means of God disclosing new understandings to his Church that are not in any sense already embedded in the text: J. L. Houlden (ed.), *The Interpretation of the Bible in the Church* (London: SCM Press, 1995), 31–2.

2

The hermeneutics of Pentecost and crib

BEFORE seeking to set this attempt to mediate between modernism and postmodernism in the context of a specific understanding of revelation, I want first to anticipate the argument of Parts Two and Three, by offering a specific example of what I have in mind. It is commonplace to find both preacher and professional theologian decrying the form taken by contemporary celebrations of Christmas: that they owe more to myth and sentiment than to serious engagement with the significance of Jesus Christ. The more conservative demands a return to the simplicity of the biblical narrative; the more radical a complete jettisoning of its equally mythological content. It is that wide consensus which I wish to challenge. So far from the accumulation of the centuries representing a decline, I shall contend that in important ways this improves upon and even corrects the content of Scripture. As such, the present practice of the Church will be found to embody an implicit acknowledgement of what subsequent chapters will argue constitutes a much wider pattern of divine disclosure, even if our own age seems peculiarly resistant to such a recognition. But first let me set such adaptation and elaboration of Scripture within the framework of what we find within the Bible itself. I shall argue that the liberties John takes in his treatment of Pentecost implies an openness of narrative structure that neither ancient nor modern hermeneutics has as yet taken with sufficient seriousness. The imaginative reappropriation of the past in tradition emphatically does not mean simply accepting it as it once was.

Pentecost as critique of hermeneutics, ancient and modern

In current usage the word 'tradition' more often than not carries with it negative overtones. 'The dead weight of tradition' perhaps expresses best its most common connotation, of something inherited from the past that now constrains and restricts the present. Even when spoken of more positively, we find an apologetic tone; tradition helps to indicate a long established institution such as the University of Oxford and its colleges, or, as with traditions associated with the monarchy, such as the Opening of Parliament or Trooping of the Colour, it is observed that such ceremonial helps cement society or at least is good for the tourist trade.

Even in the case of the Church an appeal to tradition is judged a weak argument. Scripture, reason and experience are all commonly regarded as much more powerful cards to play, and, despite the advocacy of an independent role for tradition once favoured at the Council of Trent, this is now no less true of Roman Catholic thought.[1] As one might expect, the phenomenon is even more marked in the more Protestant denominations. Anglican identity, for instance, is currently seen almost entirely in contemporary and not historical terms, with much vaunting of the idea of the Anglican Communion, through the Lambeth Conference and other means, and, more specifically within the Church of England, much effort expended upon reaching a common mind through decisions of General Synod and the work of its delegated bodies, such as the Doctrine Commission. Yet this is pursued almost entirely without serious engagement with the denomination's own past. Intending ordinands now emerge from theological college with almost no acquaintance with those who would have once been regarded as Anglicanism's principal theologians, spiritual writers and poets. No doubt many factors are involved in such a downplaying of tradition, but almost certainly the most significant is the conviction that tradition can add nothing of importance to Christian identity; instead it brings only divisiveness and resistance to change.

That tradition can, and often does, imply reactionary and unthinking conservatism I would not wish for a moment to deny. However, what I shall seek to demonstrate in the chapters that follow is that, when rightly understood, so far from being peripheral to the nature of the Christian religion, it lies at its very heart.

---

[1] I discuss the contrast between Trent and Vatican II later in this section. One might also contrast the frequency of appeal to Scripture in John Paul II's encyclicals with those of a century earlier.

Over the past three centuries our understanding of the other three major resources for Christian reflection have all been transformed—the Bible through the critical method, reason through the critiques of Hume and Kant and all that came in their wake, and experience through Schleiermacher and his influence as much on Roman Catholic as on Protestant thinking.[2] Amidst these transformations, however, tradition has remained largely out in the cold. For, though Newman liberated the Church from the notion that everything arrived either explicitly or through logical implication with the initial revelation,[3] because he continued to accept a very sharp contrast between revelation and tradition he left it as very much the weaker sister. It is that status which I wish to begin to challenge, by considering the very different way in which the matter has been treated by the Fourth Evangelist.

The promise of the Spirit as 'another Paraclete' who will guide us into all truth plays a central role in his Gospel (John 14: 16; 16: 13). Not only that, but the promised gift after Jesus is glorified seems to be shown as in some sense already fulfilled in the context of his resurrection, as the risen Christ breathes on his disciples and promises them the power to forgive sins (John 21: 22–23, anticipated at 7: 39). How this relates to Luke's account of Pentecost in Acts 2 we shall consider in a moment, but more immediately pertinent is that this gift of the Spirit may have been symbolically anticipated in John's account of Jesus' death, and in a way that tells us something about the nature of tradition. For the words used by John to record Jesus' death employ the same verbal form as the Greek word for 'tradition', (*paradosis*) a pattern repeated by the Vulgate, where the very same word is used from which our own English term is derived: '*Et inclinato capite tradidit spiritum*' (John 19: 30). While this could be no more than a linguistic accident, the Latin in fact retained an ambiguity in the Greek which English translations uniformly fail to capture. The RSV reflects the normal pattern: 'He bowed his head and gave up his spirit.' But 'gave up' as a translation is certainly inaccurate, since 'give up' does not imply an indirect object, whereas the Greek compound verb used does; so the basic meaning is more like 'gave over', which the

[2] Particularly evident in Küng, Rahner and Schillebeeckx.
[3] For the contrast with earlier views, O. Chadwick, *From Bossuet to Newman: The idea of doctrinal development* (Cambridge: Cambridge University Press, 1957).

Latin reflects. So the question inevitably arises whether we have here a hint of Christ handing over his Spirit to his disciples and thus to the subsequent Church. Among New Testament scholars, C. H. Dodd finds the secondary meaning 'just possible', though feels 'unable to decide';[4] C. K. Barrett concedes this other meaning 'possible', though rules it out on the grounds that 'there is no room for an earlier giving of the Spirit'.[5] Similar worries about the incongruity of two allusions to the giving of the Spirit have likewise constrained most other commentators from giving the matter any further attention, but one major recent book on John does take a contrary view. Here we find mention of 'a notable instance of that fruitful ambiguity which makes it possible for two different meanings to be conveyed in a single phrase'. John Ashton's view is that such a reading allows John to bind passion, resurrection and Pentecost into a single reality.[6]

Even though it too has its heavy symbolic content in its suggestion of a reversal of the Tower of Babel and a parallel with the giving of the Law on Mount Sinai,[7] nevertheless there would seem to me good grounds for supposing that it is in Luke's account of Pentecost in Acts 2 that we approach nearer to the historical foundations of the Church's nascent belief in the distinct identity of the Spirit.[8] The action of John's Risen Christ would hardly be enough of itself to generate the importance attached to the notion by the early Church, still less the highly allusive phrase that is our present concern. Luke had the advantage of a two-stage account, to indicate the much more gradual way in which the belief arose. Not so, with John; here the resurrection could so easily have come across

---

[4] C. H. Dodd, *The Interpretation of the Fourth Gospel* (Cambridge: Cambridge University Press, 1968 edn.), 223, 428.

[5] C. K. Barrett, *The Gospel According to St. John* (London: SPCK, 2nd edn., 1978), 554. The better known giving of the Spirit in John is at 20: 22.

[6] J. Ashton, *Understanding the Fourth Gospel* (Oxford: Clarendon Press, 1991), 424–5.

[7] F. Jackson and K. Lake, *The Beginnings of Christianity* (London: Macmillan, 1933), V, 114–16.

[8] Jackson and Lake accept the basic historicity of the event (ibid., 120), unlike Ernst Haenchen who uses John to deny a common tradition: *The Acts of the Apostles* (Oxford: Blackwell, 1971), 173. But, if not on the occasion that Luke describes, one would still need to postulate an analogous experience to make sense of early insistence upon experience of the Spirit being distinct from that of Christ.

as an end rather than a new beginning. So he duly moves the giving of the Spirit into his account of the resurrection appearances, with Jesus breathing on his disciples. Yet not content with this hint alone, he carries his presentation one stage further, to connect the gift directly with the deepest core of his theology, and so marks the cross as the true source from which all new resurrection life comes, in the shape of our present verse.

In making this suggestion I do not intend to imply that John's concern was also directly with the notion of tradition. At most he was claiming that the Spirit as the new form of Jesus' presence in our midst is primarily conveyed to the community of faith through identification with his crucifixion. But that emphatically does not mean that we may not draw larger conclusions from the way in which he handles here the stories and teaching that he has inherited. There is a freedom implied that refuses to be content with what has come down from the past, and a resultant willingness to rewrite the story so that some truths may be told more effectively. Of course it is irritating for us today that such behaviour makes it more difficult to discover the underlying historical core, but on the other side two important qualifications need to be noted. First, John is following a common pattern in the Scriptures as a whole that even applies to his 'rival' on this question of the dating of Pentecost. For instance, in his determination to downplay eschatology, Luke does not hesitate to alter substantially Mark's version of Christ's words before the High Priest,[9] while, depending on whether the ending of his Gospel comes from his own hand or not, it looks as though he was even prepared to give two very different accounts of the ascension.[10] Secondly, it is often forgotten that the evangelists did not write in isolation. The communities for whom they wrote already knew something, and indeed in the case of John it is sometimes thought that he wrote with Luke's Gospel before him.[11] Though we cannot prove it, the

[9] Luke turns Mark's 'you will see the Son of Man seated at the right hand of power' into a present reality: 'From now on the Son of Man shall be seated ...' (Mark 14: 62; Luke 22: 69 RSV).

[10] Acts 1: 6–11; Luke 24: 51: 'and was carried up into heaven.' Acts 1: 1–2 seems to imply that allusion had already been made to the Ascension in the Gospel.

[11] For the arguments that John had read Luke, J. M. Creed, *The Gospel according to St Luke* (London; Macmillan, 1930), 318–21; for evidence of a more general debt to the synoptics, Barrett, *St John*, 42–54.

aim may often have been to supplement rather than to supplant, but, even if not so, this is in fact the scenario that has been bequeathed to the Church, with the survival of more than one Gospel.

So far, then, from tradition being the mere endorsement of the dead hand of the past, I would argue that we may use John to think anew, and thus recognize the way in which tradition can be seen as biblically constituted by the imaginative reappropriation of the past, and not its slavish copying. In a moment I shall consider in some detail how such creative rewriting functioned in respect of the Christmas story both within Scripture and beyond, but first let me try to carry the comments in the previous chapter on hermeneutics one stage further. What I want to do is locate more accurately why the account of tradition I am proposing will not be wholly satisfied either with the new interest in literary approaches or with any proposed return to pre-critical hermeneutical rules. I shall take modern approaches first.

Hermeneutics of the present

In the previous chapter we observed how present-day biblical criticism exhibits a wide variety of different techniques, with some scholars still favouring the more conventional historical approaches but quite a number of others now wanting to privilege the question of contemporary intelligibility and relevance through more literary strategies. There my response was to insist on the importance of both types of question, historical context as well as spiritual meaning for today. However, the very positive value accorded here to John's treatment of Pentecost could very easily mislead some readers into supposing that my real preference is very much for the latter approach. This is in fact not so, as there remains in my view insufficient attention in most such literary methods to the open-ended character of the narrative and what this entails. Not only can it offer a plurality of meanings but these help generate the possibility of a second narrative that also needs to be told, the narrative of developing patterns of interpretation over the centuries, in relation to which even our own present concerns should not necessarily take priority. Let me illustrate what I mean by noting some remarks of the theologian most commonly credited with launching the modern stress on narrative.

In his preface to the second edition of his famous *Epistle to the Romans* Barth launches a resounding indictment of the work of biblical scholars. While insisting that he has 'nothing whatever to say against historical criticism',[12] he objects that they fail to reveal the Word in the words, producing parallels in thinking and actions of the time instead of wrestling with, and appropriating, 'scandals to modern thought'. Modern scholars are contrasted unfavourably with Calvin: 'how energetically Calvin, having first established what stands in the text, sets himself to re-think the whole material and to wrestle with it, till the walls which separate the sixteenth century from the first become transparent!' But the problem is whether a meaning for today can be extracted that simply through close attention to the words; whether in attempting thus to bypass historical criticism Barth does not in fact distort the range of meanings which can be derived from the biblical text and thus how it may best be appropriated for today. Thus, suppose that scholars such as Stendahl and Sanders are right that the real thrust of this epistle for Paul was other than justification by faith,[13] do we not need some argument from Barth or his successors that the way in which the Reformation appropriated the epistle to such a view was a legitimate development? In other words, my point is not that Barth's readings of Scripture are necessarily wrong or unhelpful, but that we need some justification of how the Church came to read the text in a rather different way, and that would seem to raise acutely the whole question of tradition. This makes it all the more surprising that having chosen to emphasize his ecclesial perspective in the very title of his *Church Dogmatics* he offers us only a brief, dismissive reference to tradition, especially when his own reading of Scripture has been clearly so formed. Thinking of tradition in exclusively oral terms he declares that 'since it does not have written form it obviously cannot have the character of an authority irremovably confronting the Church'.[14]

The sense of the otherness of God being encountered through Scripture is undoubtedly Barth's great strength, but his approach

---

[12] (Oxford: Oxford University Press, 6th edn., 1968), 4 ff., esp. 6, 12 and 7.

[13] K. Stendahl, *Paul Among the Jews and Gentiles* (London: SCM Press, 1977), 2–4 and 28–9; E. P. Sanders, *Paul and Palestinian Judaism* (London: SCM Press, 1977), 442–7 and 474 ff.

[14] *Church Dogmatics* I, I (trans. G. W. Bromiley, Edinburgh: T & T Clark, 1975), 99–111, esp. 105.

carries with it its own inherent weaknesses. Though acknowledging that some help can be given by biblical criticism, he is insistent that the biblical text can only properly speak to us today when it operates by analogy with its first witness: the Word speaking through the words as we approach the text humbly with our membership of the Church as Christ's body made explicit.[15] That in so doing we might discover something of more significance for the contemporary Church than Paul's original intention seems to me quite possible. What worries me, though, is the assumption that openness to the otherness of the text in another sense, to the possibility that it might run counter to an acceptable faith for today, must necessarily prove destructive rather than valuable in understanding the way in which God speaks to us through specific contexts.[16] The types of meaning found by Barth were themselves heavily influenced by the wider social and intellectual environment in which he was writing,[17] and this is no less true of Paul. Neither could wholly escape their context. So in assessing the truth of their claims we need to be as aware as possible of those contexts, and their possible obfuscating as well as illuminating implications. By far the best way of ensuring that we are thus suitably on our guard will be if we take seriously the history of a passage's interpretation, that the text has had a continuing life, and do not just confine ourselves to our own present dialogue with it, as though it had a distant past and a lively present but no story in between. Initially, earlier interpretations can often sound bizarre, but, once we become familiar with their very different rules, I would suggest that they will seem many a time no more idiosyncratic than some of the approaches of our own generation.

It is a recurring temptation to place all our emphasis on the foundations or the conclusions of a story, but integral to a proper

[15] For a helpful exposition of Barth's position, B. McCormack, 'Historical criticism and dogmatic interest in Karl Barth's theological exegesis' in M. S. Burrows and P. Rorem (eds.), *Biblical Hermeneutics in Historical Perspective* (Grand Rapids, Michigan: Eerdmans, 1991), 322–38.

[16] Barth seems to suppose that once a particular perspective is adopted, it must necessarily be determining; for a critique, W. Jeanrond, *Theological Hermeneutics* (London: SCM Press, 1991), 133–7.

[17] For a brilliant analysis of Barth's theology as a reflection of the secular culture of his own time: K. J. Kuschel, *Born Before All Time?* (London: SCM Press, 1992), 67–89.

understanding is that we consider the development as a whole. Within Scripture we would not dream of declaring, for instance, Chronicles 'inferior' to Kings or John an 'advance' on the Synoptics without offering clear criteria upon which such judgements were based, which means detailed attention to how the one might have developed into the other.[18] Yet regularly post-biblical retellings are summarily dismissed without comparable care. It is only once we show ourselves willing to hear that story of development that we will begin to take seriously the present shape of our Nativity celebrations.

Hermeneutics of the past

If, with conspicuous exceptions such as Bultmann, modern hermeneutics has tended either to face firmly towards explication of the text in its historical setting or resolutely towards present relevance and so—either way—ignore what lies in between, pre-critical exegesis presents us with a rather different problem, in its effective denial of there being a history altogether. Instead, the search seems to have been for what might be regarded as the text's eternal meaning. The most obvious advantage in such a search for 'spiritual meanings' was the way in which the impact of the text upon one's life was seen as of primary importance. Yet that emphasis was bought at a high price, and is still so bought today whenever any simple return to such principles is advocated.[19] For effectively we have a form of escapism when such exegesis is used to discount the importance of historical issues or, still more seriously, when inadequate recognition is given to the reasons why the text had to change or be reinterpreted. More often than not this was because of some perceived doctrinal inadequacy or even sometimes because of a sensed moral turpitude.

---

[18] For an example of the former judgement, G. von Rad, *Old Testament Theology* (Edinburgh: Oliver & Boyd, 1962), I, 347–54; for the latter, R. Bultmann, *Gospel of John* (Oxford: Blackwell, 1971) and *Theology of the New Testament* (London: SCM Press, 1952), II, 3–92. For an impressive challenge to Von Rad's view, S. Japhet, *I & II Chronicles* (London; SCM Press, 1993).

[19] For modern attempts to defend 'spiritual' readings: A. Louth, *Discerning the Mystery* (Oxford: Clarendon Press, 1983), 96–131; D. C. Steinmetz, 'The superiority of pre-critical exegesis', *Ex Auditu* 1 (1985), 74–82; R. Swinburne, 'Meaning in the Bible' in S. R. Sutherland and T. A. Roberts (eds.), *Religion, Reason and The Self* (Cardiff: University of Wales Press, 1989), 1–33, esp. 16 ff.

In assessing such situations earlier writers were often much more aware of the need for criteria than is conceded by many a modern critic. Aquinas, for instance, declares that 'nothing is contained under the spiritual sense that is necessary for faith that Scripture does not hand down openly elsewhere through the literal sense'.[20] That could easily lead to the view that nothing valuable was ever communicated through application of the two or three other senses,[21] but that would be to ignore the role of the imagination which cannot always be satisfactorily expressed in the alternative language of doctrine or 'fact'. It is also to ignore the way in which allegory might be used as a form of critique, to advocate alternative approaches to those dominant within the culture within which the author finds himself.[22] So any wholesale dismissal of the use of the spiritual sense as wholly derivative will not do. As in other uses of Scripture, there were reasons both good and bad.

Nonetheless, even when the reasons might be judged good, there were still limitations, most particularly in some distortion of the truth, through failure to acknowledge deficiencies within the text itself. For though theologians of the stature of Origen and Gregory of Nyssa acknowledged that it was 'stumbling blocks and impossibilities' that forced them towards an allegorical reading,[23] for them this betokened no deficiency in the text itself, but rather the necessity of assuming that God himself intended a different level of meaning, whereas what I suggest is required of us today is full and frank acknowledgement of the limitations within the text

[20] *Summa Theologiae* 1a, 1, 10 (my trans.). For some careful reflections on what was meant by 'the literal sense': R. Williams, 'The literal sense of Scripture', *Modern Theology* 7 (1991), 121–34.

[21] Origen's three senses (literal, spiritual and moral) were expanded by Cassian into the four that became normative for the Middle Ages: literal, allegorical, tropological or moral, and anagogical: *Collationes* 14.8. There is a danger, though, that such classifications oversimplify how in practice classical exegesis operated: cf. F. M. Young, *Biblical Exegesis and the Formation of Christian Culture* (Cambridge: Cambridge University Press, 1997).

[22] The contention of D. Dawson, *Allegorical Readers and Cultural Revision in Ancient Alexandria* (Berkeley: University of California Press, 1992), with Valentinus and Clement as his Christian examples.

[23] Origen, *De Principiis* 4. 1–3; the quotation comes from 2.9. Gregory of Nyssa, *Life of Moses* 2. 74–6 and 90–2; the morality of hardening Pharaoh's heart and punishing the first born are both questioned.

itself: that the Bible contains that from which we may now legitimately recoil. Taking the Book of Joshua's description of the
destruction of the native population as a symbol of the defeat of
evil by another and greater 'Joshua',[24] or the end of Psalm 137 as
indicative of our own hopes in this respect, fortunately considerably lessened the impact of the morality they conceal, but the only
sure-fire way of guaranteeing the elimination of such sentiments
from Christianity would be proper recognition of the fact that the
texts were, after all, intended literally and as such significantly fail
as acceptable religious expression.

The temptation even today is to suppose that the ultimate
control over such alternative readings, if they are to be acceptable,
must come from elsewhere within the Bible itself. So, for instance,
though F. F. Bruce is happy to endorse the reading of the familiar
Old Testament verse, 'Is it nothing to you, all you who pass by?'
(Lam. 1: 12 RSV) as a reference to the crucifixion, he is careful to
add that we 'cannot get more out of Scripture than is already
there—implicitly, if not explicitly'.[25] Again, though Richard
Bauckham shows willingness to concede a much larger role to
tradition, in terms of which it can be 'really creative of the fresh
meaning which is generated in the encounter between Scripture
and each new context in which the message is heard', yet he too
is careful to add that such treatment of the Bible 'must remain
subject to the apostolic account of its meaning'.[26] More surprisingly, similar sentiments are also to be found among contemporary
Roman Catholic theologians. The majority at Trent seemed to
have thought of tradition as a valid, additional authoritative
resource for the Church.[27] However, the ambiguity in the final
version of the decree has allowed modern Roman Catholic

---

[24] The Fathers made much use of the fact that Joshua is the Hebrew version
of Jesus, and that he too was charged with leading the people of God into a
promised land.

[25] 'Scripture in relation to tradition and reason' in B. Drewery and R. J.
Bauckham (eds.) *Scripture, Tradition and Reason* (Edinburgh: T & T Clark, 1988),
35–64, esp. 52–4.

[26] R. Bauckham, 'Tradition in relation to scripture and reason' in ibid.,
117–45, esp. 128, his italics.

[27] Y. Congar, *Tradition and Traditions* (London: Burns & Oates, 1966), 164–7;
G. H. Tavard, 'Tradition in early post-Tridentine theology', *Theological Studies* 23
(1962), 377–405.

theologians, even while accepting Newman's views about development in doctrine, also to insist that Scripture remains determinative,[28] and we find a similar view within modern Orthodoxy.[29]

But will this do? In the previous chapter we noted how the range and reference of all human thinking is heavily dependent on the context within which such thinking is done, and that increasingly recognition is also now being given to this fact by studies of the sociology behind the biblical narratives. Against such a backdrop I argued that it would be foolish to suppose that the Bible covered the complete gamut of social conditions, and it was therefore reasonable to expect that exposure to new conditions might generate new insights. That suggests to me that such triggers are themselves part of the revelatory process, and that the text cannot of itself be said to be the exclusive generator of new meanings. If that is so, then it will not be a case of simply always imposing already existing criteria, but rather, sometimes at least, of new criteria emerging as a result of interaction between trigger and text.

More detailed examples will follow shortly, but first a brief word on how this might apply to John's treatment of Pentecost. As we saw earlier, in one sense John's references to the giving of the Spirit are unintelligible without reference to the more historically based account that we find in Luke. At the same time John builds upon those historical origins in a way that can even be seen as their own critique, for on John's reading the Spirit is available to any follower of Christ, whereas on Luke's the gift of tongues could be seen as indispensable. A narrowly charismatic understanding of the Spirit has thereby been very effectively undermined. Not all readers will agree with my assumptions about the relation between Luke and John. It is the principle, though, that matters not the specific example. Descriptions of, or early reflections upon, events within Scripture can, I suggest, establish trajectories that, though in some sense controlled by their initial historical location, nonetheless have the power not only to go

---

[28] Cf. e.g. K. Rahner, 'Scripture and tradition' in *Theological Investigations* Vol. 6 (Darton, Longman & Todd, 1969), 98–112, esp. 106–8.

[29] Cf. G. Florevesky, *Bible, Church, Tradition: An Eastern Orthodox View* (Belmont, Mass.: Norland, 1972), and his rejection of a two sources view in Basil, ibid., 85–9.

considerably beyond them but even, as it were, to turn back upon them and in the process offer a critique of those earlier interpretations. In Luke's case the critique of course comes from elsewhere in Scripture, but what if the point of reflection is still later?

Where both modern and ancient hermeneutics to my mind err is thus in not taking with sufficient seriousness the conditioned character of all human thought, and therefore the necessity for tradition to keep meanings alive not simply by preserving them but by allowing their constant adaptation as—if a mix of metaphors may be allowed—the trajectories from the past meet fresh triggers in new situations and thereby help generate new meanings. This happened again and again, to the profit of the community of faith, within Scripture. As we turn to consider the Nativity, it will be my contention that the same applies no less to what happens beyond its confines.

Crib: reflective truth in a changing narrative

Complaints against the celebration of Christmas have had a long history. In England during the fourteenth century Wycliffe had uttered many a protest, while in the seventeenth under the Commonwealth even services were banned, and those who disregarded the regulations fined or imprisoned.[30] Such attitudes continued into the nineteenth, and are hilariously parodied by the incident Edmund Gosse narrates of his childhood violation of the day's proper solemnity in eating some Christmas pudding and his father's furious response.[31] Nowadays, suspicions are less extreme and even those denominations which once frowned on Christmas Day services have for the most part yielded.[32] Even so, it is not uncommon to find committed Christians displaying a disdainful attitude towards the many who flock to the churches at this time. Sometimes, no doubt, there is adequate justification in the heavy degree of commercialism and sentimentality associated with the

---

[30] John Evelyn's *Diary* for 25 December 1657 records one such incident.

[31] E. Gosse, *Father and Son* (1907; Oxford: Oxford University Press, 1974), reporting on Christmas, 1857.

[32] As has the presbyterian Church of Scotland, most of whose parishes would not have celebrated Christmas even as late as 1960.

feast, but all too often such attitudes are engendered by superficial evaluations of the point behind later developments or 'legendary' accretions. Ships sailing into land-locked Bethlehem may sound like nonsense,[33] but to dismiss the matter that quickly would be wrongly to assume that the only important type of truth is narrowly historical.

Take the common contention that Renaissance depictions of the nativity represent a marked decline in religious art. 'By the time we come to Raphael … they don't on the whole prompt us to kneel.'[34] As a reflection of twentieth-century attitudes that may well be true, but it by no means follows from this that this is how someone in the early sixteenth century would also have responded. In other words, the truth in the painting is relative, in part at least, to the assumptions which we bring to any particular work of art, and our contemporaries seem peculiarly unable to read any coded language except the most explicit. So Raphael is read as an exercise in pure naturalism, whereas each of his paintings of Madonna and Child or of the Holy Family have delicate prompts to make us think further. Several, for instance, use the device of the equilateral triangle surrounding the figures to suggest the presence of the divine, or a curtain drawn back to indicate a theophany, as in his most famous painting on this theme, the *Sistine Madonna*.[35] Again, the Child may be given an interrogating gaze far beyond his years, or gently play with a goldfinch to remind us of his future destiny and significance for us.[36]

Medieval and Eastern painting had made the point much more explicitly by having the child lie on a flat altar-like surface rather than in a crib, but, as we shall see, the concern arose that such

---

[33] As in 'I saw three ships come sailing in'; though much older, the carol was first printed in 1666. The imagery seems to assume a journey from western Europe, and so one with which singers could more easily identify.

[34] R. Harries, *A Gallery of Reflections: The Nativity of Christ* (Oxford: Lion, 1995), 10.

[35] Now in Dresden: illustrated in J. H. Beck, *Raphael* (New York: Abrams, 1976), 144. The device of an equilateral triangle is particularly obvious in the *Canigiani Holy Family*: Munich; ibid., 102.

[36] For the former, the *Madonna of the Granduca*: Pitti, Florence; ibid., 100. For the latter, *Madonna of the Goldfinch*: Uffizi, Florence; ibid., 106. Goldfinch are particularly partial to the seeds of thistles: hence their alternative name, 'the thistle-finch'.

representations failed adequately to safeguard the humanity and so our own ability to identify with the child. The incarnation was about more than the divine coming to die; it was also equally about being able to live a full, human life. That is a complaint which could also be made against some of Barth's earlier treatments of Christmas, as, for instance, when he tells us that 'except we see the Cross of Golgotha, we cannot hear the Gospel at the crib of Bethlehem' or again when he interprets the primary message of Christmas to be God entering 'into the whole seriousness of the perversion of human likeness'.[37] This effectively turns a developing narrative into a single dogmatic point.

Doctrinal theologians can sometimes be very suspicious of the imagination and this can at times even extend to poets, when too heavily influenced by them. Although in his long Christmas poem *For The Time Being* W. H. Auden declares that through the incarnation 'Imagination is redeemed from promiscuous fornication with her own images',[38] elsewhere he questions the legitimacy of any visual art for the Christian: 'It is impossible to represent Christ on the stage ... nor is it really possible to represent him in the visual arts for, if he were visually recognisable, he would be a god of the pagan kind.'[39] In that latter essay Kierkegaard's stress on the complete otherness of God is very much to the fore, but, while caution is necessary, equally there is a desperate need for something to be said on the other side. Stories, including the biblical story, will only engage the reader if they are allowed to function as very much more than the sum of a series of historical facts. We need in some sense to be allowed to be present, if their full impact upon us is to be felt, and this is precisely what the imagination makes possible, including of course visual representations. It is this insight which provides much of the rationale for what happened in the later history of the Church, in what was in effect a substantial rewriting of the biblical narrative.

On my view that rewriting succeeds better than does Scripture

[37] K. Barth, *Christmas* (Edinburgh: Oliver & Boyd, 1959), esp. 11 and 13. The contents were written between 1926 and 1933.

[38] From the section, 'The Meditation of Simeon', *Collected Longer Poems* (London: Faber & Faber, 1974 edn.), 182.

[39] W. H. Auden, 'Postscript: Christianity and Art' in *The Dyer's Hand* (London: Faber & Faber, 1963), 456–61, esp. 457.

itself, and in that I include both its effectiveness as narrative and, more importantly, its claims to truth. To see why, I propose to examine the various changes under two main headings: the new focus on the child that achieves increasing prominence as the Middle Ages advance, and, secondly, developments in the treatment of the surrounding figures (Magi, shepherds, and animals).[40] As we shall see, the two elements functioned rather differently: in the former case in allowing closer identification with Christ, in the latter a more powerful self-critique of the society in which later generations were set. Though my focus in what follows will be almost exclusively on positive developments, this should not be taken to deny the existence of many negative creations. Almost wholly bad, for example, was what followed from the invention of the midwife Salome who was punished with a withered hand for doubting Mary's virginity,[41] but even here it is as well to remember that the nastiness of this punishment is no worse than that accorded to Zechariah within the biblical narrative for himself doubting that his wife would bear him a son in her old age (Luke: 1: 20).

Identifying with the child in the crib

Much attention is devoted in Part Three to consideration of the relation between historicity and doctrinal assessment, as this applies to the life, death, and resurrection of Christ. In Chapter 6 particular stress is placed on the way in which not only the narrative of John but that of all the evangelists has been fundamentally shaped and altered by the experience of the resurrection. If this is accepted, much added weight is given to the commonly

[40] The treatment of Mary and how this developed is considered in *Discipleship and Imagination*, ch. 5.

[41] Already in the second-century *Protevangelium of James*. Though this story of the testing of Mary's virginity by one of the midwives presumed to be present is scarcely illuminating, even it could incidentally be put to more positive uses. Thus at Assisi the midwives allow Giotto to suggest the presence of ordinary women at the nativity scene, while in Gentile da Fabriano they function as a means of stressing the relevance of the infant to sinful humanity, as they greedily examine the Magi's gifts. For the former, E. Lungi, *The Basilica of St Francis of Assisi* (London: Thames & Hudson, 1996), 120; for the latter, A. P. Tofani (ed.), *The Uffizi Gallery* (Florence: Bonechi, 1995), 57.

acknowledged difficulties in reconciling the infancy narratives of Matthew and Luke.[42] For the overall impression gained from study of the Gospels as a whole would then be that these early chapters are at root incompatible as they stand with the gradualism in the growth of Jesus' own consciousness of his mission (as well as that of his disciples) which we find implied elsewhere. This of course does not preclude the presence of some historical elements in the two narratives,[43] but it does imply that historical record was not their primary aim. It would be rash, though, to infer from this that they cannot therefore be bearers of serious truth claims. For, if one is happy to find the historical foundations for such claims elsewhere (as I am),[44] the discovery that much of the narrative is 'fictional' need only suggest that truth is here being conveyed through other means. Nor should we think, as we shall see, that such truth is reducible to purely historical claims: the narrative not merely reinforces the history, it enlarges upon it.

However, to say this is one thing; it is quite another to say that the two evangelists were as successful as they could possibly have been in securing those theological intentions, whether measured against the standards of their own theology or the final position adopted by the Church on the significance of Christ as this is reflected in its various credal and related formulae. What I shall argue is that, just as the story of Jesus' birth was rewritten towards the end of the first century by the evangelists to reflect the significance now found in Jesus, so the later Church continued this process, and in so doing improved upon the contents of

---

[42] The various difficulties in the narratives are discussed at length in R. Brown, *The Birth of the Messiah* (London: Geoffrey Chapman, 1993 edn.). For a brief analysis of the difficulties in Luke's account: J. A. Fitzmeyer, *Luke the Theologian* (London: Geoffrey Chapman, 1989), 27–56. An obvious difficulty is reconciling Luke's assumption that immediately after the presentation in the Temple the family return to Nazareth (2: 39) with Matthew's massacre of the innocents and flight into Egypt.

[43] In Chapter 5 of *Discipleship and Imagination* I say something in favour of the historicity of the Virgin Birth.

[44] For my argument for the view that the full divinity of Christ is a legitimate development from earlier less explicit claims: D. Brown, *The Divine Trinity* (London: Duckworth, 1985), 101–58. Part Three of this work draws attention to the importance of non-biblical factors.

the original narratives.[45] That is, of course, an evaluative judgement, but amply justified in my view once we allow the trajectory
of incarnational belief to feed back upon the narratives offered to
us by Matthew and Luke. To demonstrate that this is so, I shall
begin by considering the infant itself.

For a start we need to disabuse ourselves of any notion that the
two evangelists involved were at all interested in the child as such,
rather than what he became, for the kind of significance we now
accord to Jesus' childhood is in fact something we owe almost
entirely to the medieval period. As we shall see, attaching individuality to children was a very slow notion to develop, and it would
be quite anachronistic to attribute this to the Bible. What our two
evangelists were concerned to assert was something quite different,
that God's providential plan operated right from the beginning of
Jesus' life, and the two narratives are thus there less in their own
right and very much more as a means of anticipating such significance as the adult Christ will have. So, for instance, Raymond
Brown insists that 'one thing is certain' in respect of the first two
chapters of Matthew, that they are intended to 'anticipate the
theology of the rest of the Gospel', with the child already the future
Moses (in Egypt) and already subject to a passion and rejection (the
treatment by Herod).[46] Similarly, for Luke's first two chapters he
eventually adopts the analogy of the prologue to a Greek play,
where the action takes place on a different plane but still with the
primary intention of anticipating what is to come. Inevitably, with
his explicit use of scriptural quotation Matthew's intention is much
the more obvious. Luke achieves the same effect more allusively,
but thereby 'the spirit of expectancy which pervades the whole of
the Old Testament' is brought to life, as the framework is provided
within which the child's future life should be read.[47]

---

[45] It is puzzling to find biblical commentators accepting that Matthew's
midrash 'was suited to the needs of the church ... at the time,' but then insisting
that any further developments can only be 'expository and applicative rather than
creative': R. H. Grundy, *Matthew* (Grand Rapids, Michigan: Eerdmans, 2nd
edn., 1994), 599–640, esp. 639–40

[46] *Birth of the Messiah*, 585–6; for his views on Luke, 620.

[47] G. B. Caird, *Saint Luke* (Harmondsworth: Penguin, 1963), 48. In similar
terms C. F. Evans speaks of the intention being to anticipate the eventual confession of Jesus as 'son of David' and 'son of God': *Saint Luke* (Philadelphia: Trinity
Press International, 1990), 137–8.

As noted above, that future reference is also what essentially characterizes earlier pictorial representations of the nativity, with the child more often than not lying on an altar-like slab.[48] But slowly this changes. Instead of the child due as an adult to pay the penalty of our sins and in that sense 'save us',[49] gradually an additional focus emerges, one in which God becoming a child has value in its own right. In making this claim, my intention is not to lay any blame against the biblical presentations. It has taken the long march of the centuries to generate a different perception of children. To the ancient world, Jewish no less than pagan, children were largely without rights, and in some senses dispensable. A later chapter, for instance, will observe how much easier it is to comprehend the story of the sacrifice of Isaac if such attitudes are taken into account—God could provide a substitute child. But, even if that were not so, the focus of Christ's significance had to widen before his being a child as such could come to prominence. Redemption from sin, the concern of Matthew and Luke, is one thing; the endorsement of the value of every aspect of our humanity quite another. Such an implication was very much further down the line, and had first to await a more full-blooded doctrine of incarnation than either Matthew or Luke allow: not merely Spirit filled, but unqualifiedly God himself. Gospel imagery of becoming like a little child could then be reinterpreted to mean rather more than uncomplicated trust in God:

> For he is our childhood's pattern
> Day by day like us he grew;
> He was little, weak and helpless,
> Tears and smiles like us he knew;
> And he feeleth for our sadness,
> And he shareth in our gladness.[50]

Almost certainly Matthew and Luke would have found this nineteenth-century hymn incomprehensible, and not simply

---

[48] In part conditioned by the ancient form of the manger as 'a flat tray' (Evans, *Saint Luke*, 199), but soon adapted as an altar. There is a very explicit example at Chartres: illustrated in M. Vloberg, *La Vierge et L'enfant dans l'art français* (Paris: Arthaud, 1955), 25.

[49] Matthew, unlike Luke, uses the presumed derivation of Jesus' name also to anticipate his eventual destiny: Matt. 1: 21.

[50] Verse 4 of Frances Alexander's hymn of 1848: 'Once in royal David's city'.

because of its sentimentality. What led to such huge changes in the way in which the child was perceived is hard to say. No doubt it was the result of a number of factors rather than one single cause. Although scholars have sometimes detected major alterations in perspective very much earlier in history,[51] visually the decisive change seems to occur about 1280, and this has been attributed to a much more empirical and thus much more observant age.[52] One need only think of the experimental interests of Aquinas' teacher, Albert the Great, or the still more radical changes introduced into Christian philosophy by Aquinas himself, though, to be fair, an openness to new ideas was already emerging in the previous century.[53] Another factor which undoubtedly helped was the desire for closer involvement in the story. Though this was initially primarily mediated through the Virgin, as in the Cistercian spirituality of St Bernard, the more interactive the relation portrayed between her and her child, the more interest came to be focused directly upon the child himself. The mother's adoration and care legitimated interaction and so turned the spotlight elsewhere.

Caution is therefore necessary in interpreting Francis' famous act in establishing a Christmas crib at Greccio in 1223. Not only was he probably not the first to do so,[54] the absence of any stories concerning children from his own legend suggests that he may have been closer to biblical attitudes than that act might initially incline us to believe. Though a live ox and ass were used,[55]

---

[51] That there was any significant change during the Hellenistic period is challenged in M. Golden, 'Change or continuity? Children and childhood in Hellenistic historiography' in M. Golden and P. Toohey (ed.), *Inventing Ancient Culture* (London: Routledge, 1997), 176–91. Likewise patristic attitudes seem to have brought little change: G. Clark, 'The fathers and the children' in D. Wood (ed.), *The Church and Childhood* (Oxford: Blackwell, 1994), 1–27.

[52] A. Martindale, 'The child in the picture' in Wood (ed.), *Childhood*, 197–232, esp. 206 and 227–8.

[53] Against the conservatism of the majority needs to be set the *sic et non* approach of Abelard and the attacks of the Victorines on hostility to innovation: M.-D. Chenu, *Nature, Man and Society in the Twelfth Century* (Chicago: University of Chicago Press, 1968), 310–30.

[54] There was a crib in Santa Maria Maggiore in Rome from the sixth century, while it is sometimes believed that Francis was anticipated in the precise form of his devotions by a Beguine, Marie de Oignies (d. 1213).

[55] Bonaventure, *Life of St Francis* 10.7.

unwillingness to allow a real child to represent Christ would also have delayed any appreciation of the child in its own right.[56] Two works written within half of a century of one another, both profoundly influential in their own ways, may be used to illustrate the extent of the change that finally came, as well as its gradual emergence. The later and more conservative of the two, dating from the middle of the fourteenth century, are the writings of St Birgitta of Sweden. In her key revelation describing the birth,[57] it is clearly still awe and wonder that is at the forefront of her vision rather than engagement. The painlessness of the birth is particularly stressed and, of great significance for subsequent artistic work, there emanates from the infant a supernatural light so strong that it extinguishes the candle Joseph has placed nearby.[58] By contrast, half a century earlier the anonymous Franciscan work once attributed to Bonaventure and called *Meditations on the Life of Christ*, though also displaying awe, has already as its central concern that we all should experience ourselves as participants in the scene before us.

The author tells us that his intention is to describe events in the life of Christ 'as they occurred or as they might have occurred according to the devout belief of the imagination'.[59] Again, the reader is told that 'you must learn all the things said and done as though you were present'.[60] Some quite marvellous images are the result, such as Joseph as master carpenter working to close the cave, the ox and ass breathing on the infant to keep him warm, Joseph laughing and playing with the child, and so on.[61] Perhaps the best example of the author's urge to get us involved is when he exhorts: 'Pick him up and hold him in your arms. Gaze on his

---

[56] Though no dolls have survived specifically for this purpose, alabaster representations were common in the mystery plays: W. L. Hildburgh, 'English alabaster carvings as records of the medieval religious drama', *Archaeologia* 93 (1947), 51–101, esp. 61.

[57] *Revelations* 7. 21–2; ed. M. T. Harris, *Birgitta of Sweden: Life and Selected Revelations* (New York: Paulist Press, 1990), 202–6.

[58] There is a fine example by Correggio in Dresden: A. Bevilacqua (ed.), *L'opera completa del Correggio* (Milan: Rizzoli, 1970), ill. 57.

[59] I. and R. B. Green (eds.), *Meditations on the Life of Christ* (Princeton, NJ: Princeton University Press, 1961), 5. Similar explicit references to the imagination also occur in the infancy section at 9, 16 and 49.

[60] Ibid., 15.

[61] Ibid., 32–4, 55. In the last case he acknowledges his debt to Bernard.

face with devotion and reverently kiss him and delight in him. You may freely do this, because he came to sinners to deliver them.'[62] That more imaginative appropriation was to have the more powerful influence than Birgitta's vision, as can be seen, for instance, in Margery Kempe's own visions from the early fifteenth century. She sees herself arranging for lodging and bedding for Mary and helps at the birth, swaddling Jesus, while after the crucifixion she makes his mother 'a good hot drink of gruel and spiced wine'.[63] In the sixteenth century St Ignatius Loyola is more restrained, but the message remains essentially the same: 'Represent to yourself in imagination ...'[64]

One way of putting the contrast in attitudes would be to observe how the Church moves from dogmatic fact or anticipated type to the notion of engaged, relational action. This is not to say that the Gospels exhibit none of the latter; most obviously they do, though it is more hidden than what comes later.[65] But it is to insist that that pattern of engaged, relational action is something almost wholly new with respect to the infancy stories. Matthew's story of the sojourn in Egypt is intended to recall the principal Old Testament story of liberation in the exodus from Egypt and thus to hint at what is to come. Again, even the Virgin Birth's primary import is not to tell us anything about Mary, but rather to indicate the absolute priority of God's action and thus that the Spirit-filled child will become a Spirit-empowered adult, with all that implies. When therefore the incident of Salome the midwife is invented, we are not yet in another world: the attitudes and assumptions are fundamentally the same. It is merely one way of giving added emphasis to the idea of the supernatural power of God totally directing all that is still to come, and that seems to me so even with respect to the legends of Mary's childhood and marriage. The interest, at least to begin with, is not with her in her own right, but in reinforcing the sense of anticipation: Mary's presumed holiness adds to the wonder of what is yet to come.

---

[62] Ibid., 38–9.

[63] *The Book of Margery Kempe*, I, 6 and 81; (Harmondsworth: Penguin, 1985), 52–4 and 235–8, esp. 236.

[64] Ignatius Loyola, *Spiritual Exercises*, 112: First day of second week, second contemplation, second preliminary.

[65] My *Discipleship and Imagination* illustrates how this operates in respect of the evangelists' treatment of the male disciples, the Virgin Mary and Mary Magdalene.

However, as subsequent chapters will emphasize, texts can have a life of their own. The introduction of the midwives not only allowed interest to be taken in Jesus being bathed, it also appeared to legitimate ordinary humanity touching the child rather than carefully standing at a distance to adore. From that conclusion it was but a small distance to reflect on the ordinariness of the child's own humanity, and so think of oneself touching and bathing the child, or even of the bathing taking the form of a baptism like one's own.[66] Again, the Gospel genealogies appear to have been introduced to locate more precisely Christ's future significance, and it is that same approach that one finds adopted in earlier centuries, though sometimes in surprising ways and places. Thus, it looks as though the figurative decoration surrounding the Lucan genealogy in *The Book of Kells* was intended to anticipate Christ's future baptismal and eucharistic significance.[67] Much attention has also been devoted to Matthew's reasons for including four women in his genealogy. The two most common explanations identify them as sinners or Gentiles;[68] either way, their presence would once more be by way of anticipation, in terms of the infant's future role. Yet an alternative approach was possible, and this seems to have been exactly what happened in the role given to Anne as Jesus' grandmother. In the later Middle Ages she was used not only to endorse the extended family of the time, but more importantly to legitimate the full relational involvement of the elderly in the life of the growing child. The women of Jesus' past now had significance in their own right, rather than as pointers elsewhere. As a final example, consider the way in which the child's circumcision was transformed. For Luke it was a means of locating Jesus in relation to his destiny: it reinforces the notion of him as Son of David and so as legitimately the Messiah. Once more, initially we find ecclesial reflection repeating that pattern of anticipation, by focusing on the

---

[66] P. J. Nordhagen, 'The origin of the washing of the child', *Byzantinische Zeitschrift* 54 (1961), 333–7; P. A. Patton, '*Ex Partu fontis exceptum:* the typology of birth and baptism', *Gesta* 33 (1994), 79–92.

[67] J. O'Reilly, 'Exegesis and the Book of Kells: the Lucan genealogy' in T. Finan and V. Twomey (eds.), *Scriptural Interpretation in the Fathers* (Portland, Oregon: Four Courts Press, 1995), 315–55.

[68] Gentiles is the more popular explanation because literature of the time treated them as honoured converts rather than as sinners.

notion that the act heralds the greater shedding of his blood upon
the cross. But one notes that in the *Meditations* the author has
Mary perform the deed, and he uses the act as a means of engaging us in reflection on its immediate significance: 'The child cries
today because of the pain he felt in his soft and delicate flesh, like
that of all other children, for he had real and susceptible flesh like
all other humans.'[69]

It is against this wider background that we need to consider the
increasing focus given to the nakedness of Christ. Birgitta has the
shepherds uncertain of the sexuality of the child, and his masculin-
ity being demonstrated to them.[70] In a controversial book Leo
Steinberg has argued that with the Renaissance came a strong
interest in the sexuality of Christ and this seems confirmed by the
prevalence of numerous works of art which give a prominent
place to nudity in the infant.[71] Despite the lack of any substantial
confirmation from sermons or other related literature, plausible
too is his suggested explanation that this was the artists' way of
powerfully asserting the complete reality of the incarnation, that
the child took on our sexuality, thereby both endorsing its value
and overcoming its problems. Much less convincing is his claim
that the hint of an erection was sometimes used to suggest the new
life of the resurrection. Acceptable though such an image was to
the classical thought to which the Renaissance owed so much, the
symbolism is too far distant from anything that would make easy
sense in a Christian context. It seems to me therefore much more
likely that the bulges of the loincloth are used to underline the
tautness and inner strength of the male figure rather than offer a
sexual reference.[72] Similarly, I think he goes wrong in suggesting
that artists sometimes intended the worshipful gaze of the wise
men to focus upon the child's exposed penis. In understanding the

---

[69] Green (eds.), *Meditations*, 44.

[70] *Revelations*, 7.22; Harris, *Birgitta of Sweden*, 205.

[71] L. Steinberg, *The Sexuality of Christ in Renaissance Art and Modern Oblivion*
(Chicago: University of Chicago, 2nd edn., 1996). He traces the beginning of the
change to c. 1310 and notes its decline under Counter-Reformation objections:
ibid., 28, 30.

[72] Ibid., 81–94, 298–325. Unless warned to think in sexual terms, the first
thought of the viewer on seeing the problematic paintings is likely to be either
of the cloth giving the look of added strength to Christ's body, or when it is
flying unfurled in the wind as the banner of a victory already achieved.

apparent direction of their gaze what one needs to recall is the
tradition of the *Meditations* that the wise men bowed to kiss the
child's feet and the resultant necessity of a humility of gaze that
could not look directly upon the child's face but became averted
almost to the ground (but not quite, since then the eyes would
look shut).[73]

Despite these qualifications, however, such artistic representations do show how far Christian thought had travelled over the
centuries, in wrestling with what it meant to claim that God in
becoming incarnate had taken upon himself every aspect of our
humanity. It is only in this wider frame that we can begin to
understand such an initially strange notion as that of Catherine of
Siena choosing the cut foreskin as the symbol of her spiritual
marriage to Christ:[74] certainly it spoke of the blood of the cross
and so of the first offering of Jesus' humanity, but also of the full
reality of that humanity, including an ordered and fruitful sexuality.[75] Such questions would never have occurred to Matthew and
Luke in writing their narratives, but that does not make them any
less important.

More generally, through reflection on the incarnation childhood had now acquired a significance that would have been totally
new to the evangelists. Their narrative was transformed as the
Church read it in a new way, hearing as it did within it the
complete endorsement by God of the value of childhood, with
Mary's pregnancy described as 'Immensity cloistered in thy dear
womb', and the nativity itself

[73]   Green (eds.), *Meditations*, 64–70. Not all versions of the Latin manuscript
have a reference to the infant's feet: for the quotation of one that does, J. Wood,
The Nativity (London: Scala, 1992), 57. Steinberg fails to include any illustrations
where the reference to the feet is clear, but cf. Gentile da Fabriano (Uffizi,
Florence) or Filippo Lippi (National Gallery, Washington).

[74]   N. Tommaseo (ed.), *Le Lettere di S. Caterina da Siena* (Florence: Giunti,
1940): letters 50 and 221; cf. 143.

[75]   For a sustained argument that the Old Testament similarly thought of
circumcision as no mere arbitrary sign but as an image of fruitfulness: H. Eilberg-
Schwatz, *The Savage in Judaism* (Bloomington: Indiana University Press, 1990),
141–76. For a contrary view, that the practice had its origins in notions of self-
sacrifice and that it constitutes a severe limitation on the possibilities of sexual
pleasure: C. Price, 'Male circumcision: an ethical and legal affront', *Bulletin of
Medical Ethics* 128 (1997), 13–19.

> God all-bounteous, all creative,
> ... a native
> Of the very world he made.[76]

This is not to say that the right conclusions were always drawn. The celebratory idea of boy bishops was soon running out of control,[77] while on the other side the use of images of the Christ child as a means of disciplining children seems to have begun early and of course continues into our own day,[78] as each year our children are encouraged to sing:

> Christian children all must be
> Mild, obedient, good as he.[79]

That will not do. Instead we need to think anew about the implications for our treatment of children's vulnerability, as also about what being fully human might mean for them. As we shall observe in Part Three, the treatment of Christ in modern film and drama shows that the issue of Christ's sexuality also still awaits a satisfactory agreed solution, and so any final version of how the story of Jesus' growth to manhood might be told as yet lies in the future.[80] But the Christian centuries have already taken us a long way along that path.

[76] The first quotation constitutes the last line of John Donne's poem 'Annunciation', 'Salvation to all that will is nigh'; the second, part of the last verse of Christopher Smart's poem, 'The Nativity of our Lord and Saviour Jesus Christ', 'Where is this stupendous stranger?'.

[77] Celebrated on Holy Innocents' Day, 28 December. For history and problems, articles by Dudley and Shahar in Wood, *Nativity*, 233–60.

[78] Giovanni Dominic's *Rule for the Management of Family Care* of 1403 was already advocating the use of images of the infant Christ as a means of educating children. The relevant passage is quoted in D. Freedberg, *The Power of Images* (Chicago: University of Chicago Press, 1989), 4.

[79] From the third verse of the original version of 'Once in royal David's city'. Though retained in the New Standard version of *Hymns Ancient and Modern* (1983), the sentiments were clearly too much for the editors of the *New English Hymnal* (1986) where verses 3 and 4 are combined so as to omit them: No. 34.

[80] Whether there will ever be a 'final version' on my argument is a moot point, since cultural change is likely to continue until the Parousia, but some developments may be seen as more definitive than others.

Self-criticism and the crib's spectators

Probably the most obvious criticism to make of my argument thus
far would be to observe that Matthew and Luke do in fact each
offer one group of people through whom the involvement of
which we have spoken is made possible: the Magi in the case of
Matthew, and the shepherds in the case of Luke. Matters are,
however, not quite that simple. For the intention in neither case
seems to have been that we should delay over the infant, but rather
that we should use these two visits once more to mediate future
significance. It is the later Church which gives the rather different
thrust with which we are so familiar, but also an element of self-
critique largely absent from the narratives themselves. To demonstrate this, I shall consider Magi and shepherds in turn, before
looking more widely to the role of nature in later versions of the
narrative, from animals to Christmas trees. That will enable us to
conclude with some reflections upon the 'paganism' of Christmas
celebrations and their alleged shallowness when compared with
the real heart of the narrative, in the crucifixion.

The Magi   Though unanimous in interpreting the Magi as indicative of Christ as the fulfilment of pagan or Gentile hopes, commentators demonstrate much less agreement regarding the genesis of
Matthew's narrative or how the Magi should be conceived. It is
widely acknowledged that it is virtually impossible to reconcile
their visit with the Lucan version of events.[81] Where disagreement
emerges most strongly is over the extent to which Matthew has
created a midrash out of Old Testament material. Some are
prepared to state dogmatically that his source of ideas is a combination of the Chaldean magicians of Daniel and the reference to the
star of Jacob in Numbers, interpreted in messianic terms within
contemporary Judaism (Dan. 2: 2, 10; Num. 24: 17–19).[82] But
against is not only the failure of Matthew to make explicit the fulfilment of Scripture to which he is so fond of pointing elsewhere, but

[81]   Instead of a flight to Egypt, on Luke's account we have the child taken to
Jerusalem after forty days, and the family then heading straight for Nazareth.
Brown comments: 'even the most determined harmonizer should be foiled' (*Birth
of the Messiah*, 189).
[82]   Emphatically asserted in R. H. Gundry, *Matthew* (Grand Rapids,
Michigan: Eerdmans, 2nd edn., 1994), 26–7.

also the fact that the Numbers passage represents the Messiah as himself the star rather than what is discovered through its agency.[83] It seems better therefore to interpret the passage as generated by reflection upon the common pattern of the ancient, pagan world in finding in the stars the destinies of great men. Certainly, the earliest interpretation of the narrative that we possess—from Ignatius at the beginning of the second century— assumes that the intention was to mark the end of all pagan magic.[84] This the passage would do if Matthew is seen as claiming that all attempts to read and control the future through the stars have now come to an end in that pattern of hope finding its proper and complete realization in Christ.[85] So, just as the explicit quota- tion of Old Testament prophecy has been used to indicate that Jewish expectations will find their fulfilment in Christ, so Matthew's Gentile readers are being told through their character- istic form of expectation that the same is no less true of pagan longings.

Calvin agrees that they were astrologers, but speaks of it as 'a childish error' to think of them as three, and 'more than laughable' to make them out to be kings.[86] By contrast, Raymond Brown thinks that Matthew may even have had in mind the passage from which the idea of them as kings is principally derived, but this seems to me highly improbable, since if so Matthew would surely have identified them as such. More plausible, though, is his contention that later developments do have some continuity with Matthew's intention.[87] Of course we can only smile when we hear of the discovery of the tombs of the Wise Men and their subse- quent removal from Constantinople to Milan and thence in 1164

---

[83] The leader of the Jewish revolt in 132, Simon ben Kosibah, reflects that literal reading in his popular name, Bar Cochba—'son of the star'.

[84] Ignatius, *Letter to the Ephesians*, 19.3.

[85] That in appealing to pagan astrology Matthew is prepared to conceive of revelation operating through the shadier side of pagan religion is stressed in G. W. H. Lampe, 'Athens and Jerusalem: joint witness to Christ?', in B. Hebblethwaite and S. Sutherland (eds.), *The Philosophical Frontiers of Christian Theology* (Cambridge: Cambridge University Press, 1982), 12–38, esp. 26 ff.

[86] *Harmony of the Gospels*, trans. A. W. Morrison (Grand Rapids, Michigan: Eerdmans, 1972), 82, 83.

[87] 'Not too far from Matthew's intent': Brown, *Birth of the Messiah*, 199. For Ps. 72: 10–11 as 'implicit citation': ibid., 187.

to their present magnificent shrine in Cologne Cathedral,[88] but are such stories any worse or more misconceived than the many attempts to elaborate upon and justify the historicity of Matthew's narrative? Even as distinguished an astronomer as Kepler had in the end to conclude that the only way of making scientific sense of the narrative was to presume that the star had been specially created and allowed to behave like no other star.[89]

But quite a different judgement I think emerges if we ask for the reason behind the rewriting of the story. One of the most significant alterations was the move away from the pagan analogue of prophecy and expectation to concrete realization in the present. It is one thing to say that the past history of the Gentiles has now reached its climax in Christ, quite another that the world of one's own day should have its focus in the living Christ; not of course that Matthew would have denied the latter, but it is not, I suggest, his principal point at this stage in his narrative. For Matthew the Magi primarily function as pointers from a past way of doing things (astrology) to a future significance still as yet to be related by the narrative, whereas what we discover in later treatments is that in place of such an idea comes the substitution of a story that could be experienced as contemporary with the reader's own world. The way this was done was by transforming the astrologers into kings who then became symbolic of the world as it was then known. Matthew almost certainly had Persian astrologers in mind, which is why they come from the east. Reflection on Psalm 72, however, allowed them in due course to encompass all the then known world.[90]

Inevitably some attempts were more successful than others. The

[88] The remains were found in 1158 during a siege by the emperor Frederick Barbarossa, and transferred to Cologne by its archbishop, Renaud de Dassel, although he personally expressed doubts about their veracity. For further details, M. Élissagaray, *La légende des rois mages* (Paris: Éditions du Seuil, 1965), 42–59. For the move to Constantinople and thence Milan, John of Hildesheim (d. 1375), *Historia trium regum*, ch. 40.

[89] For references and quotation, M. A. Screech, 'The Magi and the star' in *Histoire de l'exégèse au XVIe siècle*, ed. O. Fatio and P. Fraenkel (Geneva: Librairie Droz, 1978), 399–401.

[90] Though their identification as kings is early (e.g. Tertullian *Adversus Judaeos* 9), it is the symbolism of the gifts that seems first to attract interest: Irenaeus, *Adversus Haereses* 3.9; Origen, *Contra Celsum* 1.60. But the obscurity of the places listed in Ps. 72: 10 did lend itself to a symbolic interpretation.

magnificent eighth-century Franks Casket seems to me still basically consonant with Matthew's intention, though developing considerably beyond it. The artist remains close in still seeing the visit of the Magi as a culmination of pagan expectations; where he develops the theme is in integrating those expectations with a universal history that includes the foundation of Rome, the fall of Jerusalem and some legends of Anglo-Saxon 'history'.[91] By contrast, two centuries earlier under the Arian emperor Theodoric the basilica of St Apollinare at Ravenna had already been decorated in a way that suggested their timeless significance.[92] Balancing a procession of martyrs on the other side of the church, they head one of twenty-two female saints, marching in single file towards adoration of the Christ child. Significantly, they are also made to represent the characteristic three ages of our nature: young, middle-aged, and old. In this case there is no attempt made to hint at different races, but eventually, especially through linking of them with the three sons of Noah, this also came and helped to secure a similar universality on this issue as well. That one of them should be black dates from at least the twelfth century,[93] and hence the established pattern of one of them commonly being an Oriental, one a European and one an African. The result, among numerous others examples, is Dürer's powerful statement in the Uffizi Gallery in Florence: that painting, like many a more humble nativity scene, leaves us in no doubt about Christ's universal significance.[94] Two centuries later Handel sought to make the same point by his use of Haggai's 'desire of *all* nations'.[95] It is an image which has even gripped the film industry, as in its highly

[91] D. M. Wilson, *Anglo-Saxon Art* (London: Thames & Hudson, 1984), 46–7, 85–6.

[92] The fusion of the centuries was originally still more powerfully portrayed through representations of Theodoric and his court observing the procession from above, but these were removed by orthodox successors.

[93] As in the text *Excerptiones Patrum*, the influence of which was considerable because of its false attribution to Bede.

[94] For the relation between Dürer's five versions of the scene and his debt to predecessors: H. Keher, *Die heilige drei Könige in Literatur und Kunst* (Leipiz: Seemann, 1908), vol. 2, esp. 290–8.

[95] *Messiah*, Pt. I, reinforced by several other related quotations. His librettist, Charles Jennens, sought to make a similar point on the cover, by quoting both Paul and Virgil: D. Burrows, *Handel's Messiah* (Cambridge: Cambridge University Press, 1991), 16.

effective use in the 1927 version of *Ben-Hur*.[96] The intention is to speak of a child relevant to every age of humanity and every race. Astrological anticipations and the contrast with Judaism have now entirely receded over the horizon, and in their place has come a symbol of Christ's universal significance, whatever one's race and whatever one's age. All of human society was now required to bow before the infant God.

To such a defence of the developing tradition it may be objected that having kings thus present at the nativity undermines any critique there might have been from the gospel of established positions of power. No doubt this may sometimes have been the result, but it would be quite unfair to say that this was generally the case. Part of the problem is the way in which paintings of the scene have been read by later generations, often quite contrary to the intentions of the time. This applies even to the most magnificent of them all, with its procession of unparalleled splendour, that by Benozzo Gozzoli in Florence.[97] It used to be thought by art historians that it was intended primarily as a way of glorifying the Medicis but we now know that it was quite otherwise. Integral to Florentine society of the time was the annual procession of the Magi together with the related activities of the confraternity known as the Compagnia de' Magi,[98] and this seems to have played its part in how the family regarded its wealth. Cosimo began a balance sheet with God in which he carefully recorded how his profits were returned to God, in building programmes and so forth, and symptomatic of such an attitude was the way in which he had the story of the Magi painted in the cell that he had personally assigned to himself in the monastery of San Marco.[99] It was his son Piero who commissioned Gozzoli's painting for the private chapel of the Palazzo Medici. Though less fervid in his devotions than his father,

---

[96] In this case a Hindu, a Greek and an Egyptian, with the last mentioned used as the indispensable link between the first and second halves of the story.

[97] For illustrations and detailed discussion, D. C. Ahl, *Benozzo Gozzoli* (New Haven: Yale University Press, 1996), 81–112.

[98] R. Hatfield, 'The Compagnia de' Magi', *Journal of Warburg and Courtauld Institutes* 33 (1970), 107–61; for sermons of the time, S. M. Buhler, 'Marsilio Ficino's *De stella magorum* and Renaissance views of the Magi', *Renaissance Quarterly* 43 (1990), 348–71.

[99] Illustrated in Ahl, 18. Also by Gozzoli, it was painted twenty years earlier *c.*1440 and is by comparison an extraordinarily feeble effort.

nonetheless he was still careful to allot a properly subordinate role
to his own family in the procession, and there seems little doubt
that his intention like his father's was to acknowledge where ultimate value lay, however wealthy one might be.[100] So far from
undermining the gospel, attributing power and wealth to the Magi
could thus add to its potential for social critique.[101]

In our own day the imagery of kings may not seem particularly
appropriate.[102] Yet Christmas cards of the kings far outnumber sales
of the shepherds' adoration. Might this not be because, however
remote experience of kingship might be from most people, it can still
perform its essential role of hinting at the possibility of the transformation of all values in a way that the shepherds cannot? Ultimate
worth, it is implied, does not in the end lie with power as the world
now assesses it. Certainly in its twentieth-century appropriation
through poetry, disenchantment with wealth as a significant measure
is a common theme. In his familiar 'Journey of the Magi' Eliot plays
on the contrast between the wise men missing the luxury of their
summer palaces on the hard journey and them 'no longer at ease
here, in the old dispensation' on their return home. It is also a recurring theme in a number of George Mackay Brown's Christmas
poems, with the dissonance of life and poetic image recently reinforced by them being set to the music of Sir Peter Maxwell Davies:

> We stand, three vagrants at the last door.
> A black fist
> Lingers, a star on withered wood.[103]

[100] For an excellent account of this family's attitudes, E. H. Gombrich, *Norm and Form* (London; Phaedon, 4th edn., 1985), 35–57. He describes the family portraits as 'not in the centre, but on the margin' (49).

[101] This is to take issue with those who continue to find in such practices only 'a legitimating icon' for monarchy and power: R. C. Trexler, *The Journey of the Magi* (Princeton, NJ: Princeton University Press, 1997), 89–92, esp. 90. It is not, however, to deny that it may have played its part.

[102] To solve the problem, occasionally, their story is even identified with a poverty as great as that of the shepherds, as in Wolfgang Borchert's story of three destitute soldiers: 'Die drei dunklen Könige' in B. Von Heiseler (ed.), *Die heilige Zeit* (Stuttgart: Steinkopf Verlag, 3rd edn., 1962), 320–2.

[103] The words of 'the third king' towards the end of 'Stars: A Christmas Patchwork' in George Mackay Brown, *Selected Poems* (London: John Murray, 1991), 126. Peter Maxwell Davies sets kings and orchestra in a different key in his *Christmas Cantata*.

With that last line we observe one way in which the language of transformation implicit in the retelling of the story of the Magi can be made to connect with imagery of crucifixion and resurrection.[104] Rather than borrowed imagery, however, resort has sometimes been had to integrating nativity and crucifixion within the same story, through the tale of a fourth wise man, absent from the nativity but present at the crucifixion. Because Psalm 72 can be taken to refer to four rather than three kings, the notion of such a fourth king had in any case never quite died out. One finds him present, for instance, in Piero Della Francesca's famous painting of Christ's baptism. A particularly powerful version of this tale is to be found among the novels of the French writer, Michel Tournier, in which even the crucifixion is missed but not the experience of the Eucharist.[105]

In Piero de Francesa's painting, following long liturgical precedent, he links together three of the principal epiphanies of the Gospel: Jesus' baptism, the miracle at Cana and the visit of the wise men.[106] Because of its apparent eucharistic imagery, Cana no less than the baptism has for long been allowed to speak of transformation. Later legend insisted upon no less marked an effect in respect of the wise men, with them baptized by St Thomas as he journeyed east, and the rest of their lives devoted to prayer.[107] There is no need in our own day slavishly to repeat such legends, but there is the need to hear in them the transformation of the biblical story into a deeper social critique than Matthew himself offers. Through the use of his imagination the evangelist set the Church on a particular path, but what arose was no mere straightforward deduction or implication, but itself a creative reworking in the light of later, more developed, Christian self-perception.

---

[104] Eliot does much the same thing, particularly in the second stanza.

[105] M. Tournier, *The Four Wise Men* (London: Methuen, 1982). Other twentieth-century versions came from the Englishman R. B. Cunninghame Graham, the American H. L. Van Dyke (d. 1933) and the German Eduard Schaper (b. 1908). One might also note the related tale of the old peasant woman, Baboushka, who tries to follow the wise men on their pilgrimage: e.g. T. Goldsmith, *Christmas* (Poole, Dorset: Blandford, 1978), 148–51.

[106] For illustration and commentary, M. A. Lavin, *Piero Della Francesca* (London: Thames & Hudson, 1992), 62–7.

[107] The story is told in John of Hildesheim, *Historia trium regum*. For commentary, Élissagaray, *La Légende*, 88 ff.

The shepherds   The role of the shepherds may initially seem a less complex issue. After all, it may be said, they are there, and have always been there, to indicate God's concern for the poor. But matters are not quite that straightforward. Raymond Brown, for instance, detects a complex allusion to the prophet Micah, the intention of which is to remind us of David the shepherd and the messianic hopes associated with him.[108] More commonly, much is made of the evidence that in later Judaism shepherds were regarded as disreputable characters, but none of the evidence is contemporary, and in any case it would be one thing to suggest that the intention was to indicate good news for those regarded as 'sinners', quite another to draw an inference for the poor.[109] The long and hallowed associations of the imagery of shepherding with God and the monarchy surely invite rather different conclusions.[110] At most, we might talk confidently of a message for all humanity, as shepherding was such a common occupation of the time, with perhaps just a hint of the dignity potentially conveyed by the role in the first shepherd who became king at Bethlehem (1 Sam. 16: 1–13; Ps. 78: 70–72). Equally, caution is necessary in any conclusions one may draw from biblical or patristic declarations that speak of him who was rich becoming poor for our sake, since more often than not the poverty that the author has in mind is by contrast with Christ's past exalted state: in other words, there was no intention to address ordinary human poverty as such, and one needs to bear this possibility in mind also when reflecting upon how the shepherds were viewed.

That tension in how Christ's lowly birth should be interpreted one finds reflected in the history of artistic representation. In earlier art a simple dignity rather than any obvious signs of poverty is the chosen image. It is only under Franciscan influence that marked changes begin to occur in the later Middle Ages but then not without some resistance. One might, for instance, contrast the *Meditations'* repeated insistence on the poverty of the Holy Family

---

[108]   R. Brown: *Birth of the Messiah*, 420–4.

[109]   As one example of the speed with which commentators can move from 'despised class' to 'poor': L. Boff, *Jesus Christ Liberator* (London: SPCK, 1984), 170–1.

[110]   e.g. Ps: 23; Ezek: 34. Though the latter passage is critical of those in authority, the way the imagery is handled suggests that kings and shepherds were often compared and so shepherding held in honour.

with the assumption in Ignatius Loyola that they had a servant girl.[111] Despite our present familiarity with the adoration of the shepherds, astonishingly it was not until the fifteenth century that they established themselves there instead of always being portrayed receiving the message of the angels.[112] The delay was partly because of biblical precedent (Luke focuses on the former scene).[113] Ironically, one indirect result was that it inhibited greater stress on God's association with the poor, for the message of the angels was essentially an otherworldly scene whereas the conjunction of a child in a barn with shepherds immediately invited notions of identification with the poor in a way that would only sound incongruous, so long as the only visitors to be portrayed were kings or even wise men with their rich gifts.

So a sometimes elaborately costumed Mary slowly begins to give place to simple dignity,[114] and occasionally conspicuous poverty. The contemporary objections to the dirty feet of the peasants adoring Caravaggio's *Madonna di Loreto* are well known. One finds no less stress on the Holy Family's involvement in poverty in his *Adoration of the Shepherds* of 1609, where Joseph's carpentry tools are to the forefront of the picture and Mary is in the centre on the floor of the barn cradling the child, while bare-footed shepherds look down adoringly on them.[115] Only one of them makes his response explicit in hands enfolded in prayer, and here we encounter another key role for the shepherds, in their exploration of ordinary human reactions to the Christian claim that God has a special concern for the poor. So, for instance, Hugo van der Goes in his *Portinari Altarpiece* of 1475 uses the three of

---

[111] Rather surprisingly, despite the *Meditations'* repeated insistence on the poverty of the Holy Family (e.g. 26, 36), only a single line is devoted to the annunciation to the shepherds (38).

[112] E. Mâle notes an Italian example from 1340 by Taddeo Gaddi, but no French instances until the fifteenth century: *Religious Art in France: Late Middle Ages* (Princeton, NJ: Princeton University Press, 1986), 49–51. He notes the influence of drama.

[113] One example of where respect for the biblical past arrested or slowed down a potenitally creative development within tradition.

[114] One of the finest early examples comes from Giorgone: P. Zampetti, *Giorgone* (London: Weidenfeld & Nicholson, 1970), pl. 13–16.

[115] For detailed commentary on the two pictures, H. Hibbard, *Caravaggio* (London: Thames & Hudson, 1983), 184–91, 245–7; for coloured illustrations, A. Moir, *Caravaggio* (London: Thames & Hudson, 1989), 98, 126.

them to explore various possible stages in human response to the infant, from unbelief to prayerful conviction.[116] Indeed, precisely because of their ordinariness they became a highly effective avenue for such forms of reflection. This is particularly evident in some of the mystery plays, themselves the likely source for that fifteenth-century move towards depicting the adoration of which we spoke a moment ago.

Debate continues regarding the evolution of the mystery plays and their presentation of the nativity. For some they emerge naturally out of liturgical drama, whereas for others their impetus comes overwhelmingly from Franciscan preaching and teaching methods.[117] Certainly, nothing of comparable signifi-cance happened in Eastern Christendom. The institution of Corpus Christi and guild plays also offered another focus.[118] In England four important cycles survive, which vary widely in their presentation and approach.[119] Certain events are to be found in some and not others, for instance, the dramatization of Bernard's account of the debate between Mercy and Justice prior to the incarnation, or the parallel discussion between Augustus and the Sybil.[120] Again, characterization can vary widely, Joseph receiving warm and sympathetic treatment in the relevant Towneley play but surprising hostility from the Coventry dramatist. Yet all agree in giving the shepherds a lively role that includes much banter. They complain of their wives, make rude references, fail to understand the angels' Latin and so forth, and even in one case have among their number a petty

[116] The point is made in J. Dillenberger, *Style and Content in Christian Art* (London: SCM Press, 1965), 135–43, esp. 140.

[117] For the former view, L. R. Muir, *The Biblical Drama of Medieval Europe* (Cambridge: Cambridge University Press, 1995), esp. 13–44; for the latter, D. L. Jeffrey, 'Franciscan spirituality and the rise of early English drama', *Mosaic* 8 (1975), 17–46.

[118] Though formally established by Urban IV in 1264, his death in the follow-ing year delayed matters, and so it was not until 1317 that it was finally established as a universal feast of the Church.

[119] York, Chester, Coventry and Towneley (commonly associated with Wakefield). For a critical edition: S. B. Hemingway ed., *English Nativity Plays* (New York: Russell & Russell, 1964).

[120] For the former (based ultimately on Ps. 85 esp. 10–11), Coventry I, 1: ibid., 71–9; for latter, Chester I, 1–4; ibid., 5–20. For Bernard's annunciation sermon: Migne, *PL* 183, 383–90.

thief, the notorious Mak.[121] Clearly the aim here was not simply to amuse but also, more importantly, to engage. Ordinary people like themselves, the audience was being told, were also present at the nativity, and this the plays express powerfully and effectively. In art likewise, though Mak fails to appear, women do begin to accompany the shepherds, and are found adoring the child.[122]

In early Christian art and literature Christ and the shepherds had to some degree been set quite apart, with the former idealized as Good Shepherd and the latter sometimes criticized for their failure to bring any gifts to the crib.[123] Whether the uniform practice of the plays in having the shepherds present simple gifts was intended in part to answer that criticism we do not know. What, however, we can say is that such actions did make possible a deeper relation with the child.[124] The pipes that were given were, for instance, regularly used as an excuse in Italy to play tunes for the child and mother, and of course such presents could quickly become symbolic of a more spiritual commitment, as in the German sixteenth-century carol which moves from the shepherd having the child by his side to having it in his heart,[125] or more familiarly in the words of Christina Rossetti's poem:

---

[121] e.g. a Chester shepherd worries about getting a clout from his wife (ibid., 40), another engages in vulgar jokes (48), while there is a lively exchange expressing their incomprehension of the angels' Latin (53–4). In Towneley there is similar puzzlement (180) and complaints about wives (173, 196), as well as the incident with Mak. York has croaking voices (149), with Coventry the most serious.

[122] For examples, including paintings by Murillo and Tintoretto: F. J. S. Cantón, *Naciemiento e Infancia de Cristo* (Madrid: Biblioteca de Autores Cristianos, 1948), illus. 55, 65, 82, 85–7. Presumably, the thought was that the shepherds could easily have brought their wives or other women along, whereas the Magi must have travelled alone because of the arduous journey.

[123] Taking ram-bearing Hermes as the model for images of the Good Shepherd inevitably tended to place Christ apart from ordinary life.

[124] Even here humour was not absent as in the Chester inclusion of the offer of 'a payre of my wyves ould hose,' though the promise of 'my good harte' is suitably added: Hemingway, *Nativity Plays*, 63.

[125] 'Als ich bei meinen Schafen wacht' ': H. Keyt and A. Parrott, *New Oxford Book of Carols* (Oxford: Oxford University Press, 1993), no. 31.

> What can I give him,
> Poor as I am?
> If I were a shepherd
> I would bring a lamb,
> ...
> Yet what I can I give him,
> Give my heart.[126]

The lurking danger is of course sentimentality. One sees this in another nineteenth-century composition, Berlioz' *Shepherds' Farewell*.[127] Though meant sincerely, the tribute is perhaps too unqualifiedly lyrical to be acceptable. A similar objection could be made to the common explanation given for Zinzendorf's naming of Bethlehem in Pennsylvania.[128] That was a temptation which the medieval plays at least avoided not only with their earthy realism but also equally in their frequent allusions to judgement, the second advent of judgement in some ways merging with the first.[129] Despite the likely, much more limited intention of Luke's narrative, there seems no good reason why we should not hear today in the involvement of the shepherds in the nativity God's judgement on our failure to value adequately the poor and marginalized, and indeed that message would accord well with the import of his Gospel as a whole. The advantage later tradition affords, however, is in making that point explicit not only right from the beginning of the story but also where Christ is at his most vulnerable, as a child. Yet we should also not forget the other side of the developing tradition, as the Middle Ages received it: God's involvement in the ordinariness of our lives. The shepherds had

---

[126] From her poem 'In the bleak mid-winter', not originally intended to be sung.

[127] In *L'enfance du Christ* (1854), Part 2. Though Berlioz was without any serious religious commitment, he appears to have been sincere in his suspense of judgement, in order to return, momentarily at least, to the Catholicism of his own childhood.

[128] Bleating sheep were supposed to have warmed the Pietist's heart with their reminder of the message to the angels. For the true and subtler explanation, H. Renkewitz, 'Das amerikanische Bethlehem' in W. Freytag and H. J. Schultz (eds.), *Evangelische Weihnacht* (Hamburg: Im Furche Velag, 9th edn., 1956), 128–36.

[129] For an exploration of the theme: T. P. Campbell, 'Eschatology and the nativity in English mystery plays', *American Benedictine Revue* 27 (1976), 297–320.

become quintessentially ordinary folk, and so, if kings already speak of the transformation of worldly values, perhaps the shepherds, rather than merely always repeating the same message, should also sometimes be allowed to speak of divine engagement with even the most ordinary of our concerns.

Animals The third and final group of spectators at the crib—the animals—find no mention in Matthew and Luke. Instead, they owe their origin to reflection on the Old Testament, and to two verses in particular. An early verse of Isaiah declares that 'the ox knows its owner, and the ass its master's crib' (Isa. 1: 3 RSV), while Pseudo-Matthew helped mediate the Septuagint's mistranslation of a verse from Habakkuk: 'you will be made known in the midst of two animals' (Hab. 3: 2 my trans.).[130] Unfortunately, the second half of the verse from Isaiah continues by declaring 'but Israel does not know, my people does not understand', and thus it was that the animals began their life in the nativity story more as symbols for Jew and Gentile than as actual participants. Occasionally, it is the Gentiles who are portrayed more negatively, but more commonly it is the Jews, with them identified with the ass,[131] and this is how we find them in many a medieval painting, and indeed sometimes later. So, for instance, to give two examples from the late fifteenth century, in both Hugo van der Goes' *Portinari Triptych* and Botticelli's *Mystical Nativity*, whereas the Gentile ox holds its head upright, the Jewish ass bends its head in shame.[132]

But this was by no means the only symbolic current. In the second-century *Protevangelium of James* we find all of nature standing still as it awaits the Saviour's birth (18: 2).[133] Presumably, the motivation here is similar to what dictated that the sky should be darkened as Jesus hung on the cross (Mark 15: 33, supplemented

---

[130] The continuing influence of Pseudo-Matthew is all the more surprising in view of the fact that the Vulgate has 'in the midst of the years': *in medio annorum*.

[131] The contrast is as early as Origen. Gregory of Nazianzus is a rare example of someone who puts the emphasis on the idolatory of the Gentiles: Migne, *PG* 45, 1138.

[132] The latter is in the National Gallery, London, the former in the Uffizi: illustrated in Tofani (ed.), *The Uffizi Gallery*, 102–3.

[133] W. Schneemelcher, *New Testament Apocrypha* (Cambridge: James Clarke, 1991), I, 433.

in Matt. by an earthquake: 27: 45 and 51), in other words the appropriateness of all nature participating in the decisive events of world history. The participation, however, in both cases is essentially passive. It is what the Creator decides should happen, and this is so even in later variants such as Milton's where personification occurs:

> Nature, in awe of him,
> Had doffed her gaudy trim,
> With her great master so to sympathise:

And that is why she hides 'her guilty front with innocent snow'.[134]
    A poet from the same century offers what I think will be judged in the long run a more valuable emphasis. George Herbert pleads:

> To Man of all beasts be not thou a stranger.[135]

Implicitly here a value is assigned to the animals in their own right: they are beasts like ourselves. Already in the *Meditations* we find ox and ass assigned a specific role in keeping the infant warm through their breath, actions performed 'as though they possessed reason'.[136] It is that desire to give the animal creation an active, if intuitive role that becomes more pronounced as we reach our own age. Familiar from the opening scene of *Hamlet* are the words of Marcellus about the cock's song:

> Some say that ever 'gainst that season comes
> Wherein our Saviour's birth is celebrated,
> The bird of dawning singeth all night long;
> ...
> So hallowed and so gracious is the time. (I, sc. 1, 158–64)

Many a passing allusion could be quoted from poetry of subsequent centuries, but it is really only with the late nineteenth and twentieth century that the image begins to occupy centre stage.

[134] 'On the Morning of Christ's Nativity' in *The Poems of John Milton* (Oxford: Oxford University Press, 1958), 396.
[135] 'Christmas,' line 12 in *George Herbert: The Complete English Poems* (Harmondsworth: Penguin, 1991), 74.
[136] Green (eds.), *Meditations*, 33–4.

One thinks of Kilvert's diary entry recording the worship of the animals,[137] Kipling's poem 'Eddi's Service' with the animals there alone to celebrate a Saxon Christmas, or in similar vein Kenneth Grahame's insistence that it was the animals who were the very first to celebrate Christ's birth.[138]

It would be altogether too simple to dismiss all of this as mere sentimentality. Even after his loss of faith, Thomas Hardy, recalling in his poem 'The Oxen' the legend of the kneeling oxen told to him in his childhood, does not hesitate to end his poem with a sense of something lost: 'Hoping it might be so.' What I think such sentiments succeed in expressing, in a way that the earlier, more passive participation does not, is not only that the non-human creation has a value in its own right but also that it too as part of that value can share in the salvation that Christ brings. Initially, it might seem as though this does no more than repeat already existing biblical themes, but it needs to be recalled that there is only one brief New Testament passage that speaks of the non-human creation actively looking forward to a new order (Rom. 8: 19–22),[139] while the familiar words of Isaiah that speak of the reconciliation of lion and lamb had virtually no influence until modern times (Isa. 11: 6–9).[140] In the eighteenth century it was to become the central theme of Telemann's *Christmas Oratorio*,[141] in the nineteenth the American painter Edward Hicks was to give the image a further great surge in popularity, while in the twentieth the reference was, at it were, canonized with its inclusion in the service of nine lessons and carols, adopted by King's College, Cambridge in 1918.[142]

[137] One of his parishioners reports the animals kneeling on 'old Christmas eve': entry for 5 January 1878: W. Plomer (ed.), *Kilvert's Diary* (Harmondsworth: Penguin, 1977), 346. Beatrix Potter in *The Tailor of Gloucester* goes one stage further and has the animals speak.

[138] Last verse of the carol in Chapter 5 of K. Grahame, *The Wind in the Willows* (London: Methuen, 21st edn., 1926), 93.

[139] Even then the likely meaning is that its present state is due to the Fall of Adam, and likewise its restoration is made to depend on 'the revealing of the sons of God' (v. 19 RSV). Col. 1: 15–20 makes nature even more passive.

[140] For its lack of influence till modern times, and for the role of Hicks, J. F. A. Sawyer, *The Fifth Gospel* (Cambridge: Cambridge University Press, 1996), 234–9.

[141] To give the work its official title, *Die Hirten an der Krippe zu Bethlehem* uses the poetic expansion of the poet Karl Wilhelm Ramler (d. 1798).

[142] Though based on E. W. Benson's proposals of 1880.

Each Christmas when we sing of 'The ox and the ass and the camel/Which adore'[143] it is very easy to fall into supposing that our sentiments are the same as other Christians over the past two thousand years, whereas it seems to me that a subtle shift has been occurring, from the animals reflecting purely human concerns to a focus directly on their own inherent value. One way the earlier symbolic reference was undermined in the Middle Ages was through the notion of Joseph being too poor to pay the tax without taking an ox to sell to raise the money,[144] but even then the focus remains entirely human. In recent years a lively debate has been engendered by the accusation that the Judaeo-Christian inheritance is largely responsible for our present environmental crisis by its acceptance of Genesis' apparent view that man was given 'dominion' over the earth. How fair such complaints are need not concern us here.[145] What, however, can be asserted is that Christian and non-Christian alike now have a rather different sense of the rights of animals and with that of humanity's responsibility towards them. As spectators at the crib the animals now assert not only their right to be there but also implicitly a critique of their fellow (human) spectators, especially in a world in which sentimentality about animals remains combined with cruelty, not least in modern inventions such as factory farming.

This integrated narrative of kings, shepherds and animals all worshipping a child has thus travelled a long way from the more limited intentions of Matthew and Luke. In effect, a new 'text' has been created, partly through the development of biblical insights and partly through the stimulus of new ideas that emerged in later centuries. In insisting on speaking of a better text, my argument has relied heavily on assuming the truth of the incarnation. The nature of that dependence will be examined in Part Three, but I

[143] Conclusion of the third verse of 'In the bleak mid-winter'. Camels are included on the basis of Isaiah 60, esp. v. 6. Occasionally, the camel is given a very prominent position, as in Jordaens' *Adoration of the Kings*: National Gallery, Dublin.

[144] As in the fourteenth-century sermon manual *Mirk's Festial*, ed. T. Erbe (London: Oxford University Press, Early English Texts Society, 1905), 22.

[145] Gen. 1.28. For the key original article by L. White and some Christian responses, R. S. Gottlieb (ed.), *This Sacred Earth* (London: Routledge, 1996), esp. 184 ff.

want to end this chapter with some brief remarks on the alleged paganism of Christmas festivities.

A pagan Christmas?

Complaints about the pagan character of Christmas are almost as old as the institution itself.[146] Debate continues about how the date was chosen. A minority of scholars continue to argue that it was as result of computation backwards from 25 March as the date of the crucifixion,[147] the majority that it was to combat celebration of the feast of Sol Invictus. The most recent survey of the issue observes that we lack definitive evidence either way.[148] More importantly, the author observes that, even if the latter view is right, this should not be allowed to count against the appropriateness of such accommodation to the wider culture, and she draws a helpful parallel with our own day. So far from being embarrassed by the greater popularity of Christmas, the Church might take note of the fact that the infant provides a more easily accessible symbol of new life than the resurrection of Easter Sunday; again, unlike Good Friday, the themes of Christmas can engage and affirm the personality without immediately raising problems of guilt.[149] To endorse these comments is not to deny the indispensable contribution of cross and resurrection to the proper shape of Christian belief, only to suggest that they are generally not the best point of access for those brought up in a culture whose assumptions stand so distant from many of the basic assumptions of the Christian faith.

It may be objected that such a response ignores how deeply paganism has in fact penetrated into the way in which Christmas is currently celebrated. That there is much that is wrong cannot be

---

[146] The feast may have been established by Pope Liberius in 354; by the end of the century Asterius of Amasea was already complaining of abuses: *Homilies* 38.

[147] The date of the crucifixion having been determined as 25 March, the argument goes that Jewish conventions about the patriarchs were then followed, and so this also assumed to be the date of his conception.

[148] S. K. Roll, *Toward the Origins of Christmas* (Kampen, Netherlands: Kok Pharos, 1995), 57–164, esp. 90–1, 150. Duchesne, Engberding, and Talley offer variants of the former view; Botte, Frank, and Cullmann the latter.

[149] Ibid., 235–6, 239–40.

denied, most obviously perhaps the excessive commercialism. But there is also something to be said on the other side. Consider first pre-Christian borrowings, such as mistletoe and Yule log from Druid practice or holly and ivy from Greek and Roman. Quite a number of these play on the time of year at which the feast is celebrated, and so hint at possibilities of joy in new life even in the darkest moments of winter.[150] Their imagery thus chimes well with the message of Christmas, and it would therefore seem odd to condemn them simply because the invention of the imagery predates Christianity. One might argue that even if Jesus had been born in the summertime, at least for the northern hemisphere December would remain more imaginatively appropriate, as then it can more easily speak of new life coming to the deadness of our nature.

Equally, if we turn to those secular features which have assumed prominence in modern times, the question needs to be raised whether the fault does not lie, at least in part, with the Church, and its unwillingness to engage with the wider society's existing imaginative sensibilities. Perhaps the point can be made most effectively by observing that many modern features derive from earlier, more explicit religious practice, but the Church, so far from building upon such developments, retreated in hostile critique. So, for instance, earlier we observed the once intimate connection between nativity and drama. Yet, though many of the themes in contemporary renderings of Christmas pantomime imply a reversal of values, seldom is any connection made with its sacred counterpart. Again, though in some countries such as Britain Christmas trees have virtually lost any religious association, elsewhere the lighting of candles to place on them remains an integral part of the annual ritual. Moreover, there is some evidence to suggest that they only migrated to the home at the Reformation. The medieval practice was to use fir trees in

---

[150] Mistletoe and Yule log were used to suggest drawing strength from outside oneself in difficult times (the mistletoe grows on the oak that provided the log which was kept for this special winter use). Holly as a sign of happiness was borrowed from the Roman feast of Saturnalia, but given added significance through its prickly character being taken as a reminder of the crown of thorns. Evergreen ivy, used in the cult of Dionysus to suggest immortality, was now taken to imply the eternal life which Christ promises us.

churches on Christmas Eve to represent the apple tree from which Adam had plucked the fatal fruit, but hostility to plays being performed in church meant that they needed a new location, and hence the gradual change in the way in which they were treated.[151] Even the custom of kissing under the mistletoe, surprising as it may seem, was once associated with explicit Christian symbolism. In fourteenth-century England it was the custom to embrace anyone visiting one's home at Christmas under the Holy Bough, a nativity scene placed in the shape of a bough hanging inside the front door and surrounded by mistletoe.[152] Better known is the story of how Saint Nicholas was transmogrified via the Dutch 'Sinterklaas' into Santa Claus. Less familiar is the key role played by a Christian minister.[153] More importantly, at least in the country where all this first happened (the United States), there remains, despite the rampant commercialization, a sustained attempt to link the myth with the underlying rationale of Christmas through continued insistence on charitable giving at this time. Sometimes the most appropriate response is to turn the stream in a better direction, rather than attempt the impossible and stop its course altogether.

My examples have deliberately been somewhat random, because my objective has been a simple one: to challenge the common assumption that the power of revelation is necessarily undermined if external material from the surrounding culture is used to illuminate or even to rewrite its story. That can happen, but need not if due care is taken to integrate what appeals to the pagan or secular imagination into an appropriate underlying Christian framework. Criteria will of course be required, but it is

---

[151] Their introduction into England by Prince Albert in the nineteenth century needs therefore to be set against this wider background. The legend of St Boniface cutting down a sacred oak and identifying a fir tree instead as the *Christbaum* might possibly imply even earlier origins for its use than those indicated in the text.

[152] D. Morris, *Christmas Watching* (London: Jonathan Cape, 1992), 67–8.

[153] The first person to introduce a reindeer-drawn sleigh was Clement Clarke Moore in his hugely popular poem: 'A Visit from St. Nicholas' of 1822. Given his occupation and his authorship of several theological works, the omission of any reference to the nativity in the poem is very surprising. For the growth of the cult in the United States: J. H. Barnett, *The American Christmas* (New York: Macmillan, 1954), 24–48.

hard to see what any could be which would legitimately exclude in principle all such attempts at emendation. To demonstrate how hard it is to isolate revelation in this way I turn now to the question of revelation itself and how best to analyse this notion in the light of contemporary understandings of the various ways in which Scripture came to be written.

3
Continuing revelation: Learning from Judaism and Islam

IN the previous two chapters I sought to offer a wider context in which to place our present discussion of the notion of revelation and how it should be understood. In the first, 'Narrative and Enlightenment', my concern was to steer a middle path between two common contemporary extremes: on the one hand, unqualified advocacy of the virtues of Enlightenment objectivity, and on the other the fashionable retreat of so many theologians from its challenges into allegedly self-validating claims for Christianity. Though undoubtedly part of the strength of any particular tradition does lie in its internal structure and foundations, to give these the last word as well as the first would be to court disaster. A tradition flourishes not only through a healthy respect for its roots, but equally in lively confrontation with external pressures and influences whereby it is forced to think itself anew. That phenomenon I sought to illustrate in the second chapter, with changing understandings through two millennia of the significance of Christ's nativity. I argued that, so far from the Church being embarrassed by the 'legendary' material which has accrued to contemporary celebrations of Christmas, this sometimes deserves to be seen not merely as illuminating but even as corrective of the original biblical narrative. Where the Enlightenment, therefore, erred was not in looking more widely than any particular tradition, but in supposing that this spelt the death of tradition rather than its enrichment. The 'prejudice' of antecedent assumptions and perspectives is inescapable, but traditions grow through interaction with alternatives, and not always in opposition to them.

These contentions I now want to take a stage further in this chapter. It is Enlightenment values that force us towards the recognition of the historically conditioned character of Scripture,

Enlightenment values too that require us to take seriously religions other than Christianity. But that is only one side of the coin. For, though the implications drawn from these values have generally been reductive, leading either to the dismissal of religion or to the assertion of some lowest common denominator, this is by no means the only alternative. Instead, the conditioned character of religious truth can open up to us two important, alternative perspectives, both of which I wish to pursue here. First, it would seem to entail that surface conflicts between religions are not necessarily deep contradictions since the perception of truth now becomes relative to context and so the way in which any truth is presented will vary depending on how the assumptions of any particular religion have developed up to that point. Of course, not all conflicts can necessarily be resolved in this way, but at least the possibility is there. A number of examples, both small and large, will be offered to illustrate the point in the second half of this chapter. In that same section I shall also attempt to give my approach a wider framework. Judaism and Islam, I shall contend, should be seen as operating within developing traditions, in relation to which it inevitably becomes misleading to draw particular verses from the Hebrew Bible or Talmud on the one hand, or from the Qur'an or Hadith on the other, out of context and immediately into conflict with Christianity. That second section, however, will be preceded by consideration of a still more fundamental claim, that, so far from undermining the notion of revelation, these Enlightenment considerations enable us to develop a more profound understanding of how God relates to humanity than is allowed by the 'deposit' view of revelation which has so dominated most of the history of Christianity. Instead, we may view God as constantly interacting with his people throughout history, and in a way which takes their humanity and their conditionedness with maximum seriousness. While within Christianity the primary focus of reflection on that interaction must remain the Bible,[1] it would be on my view a huge mistake to assume that any interaction thereafter is mediated through an unchanging text. Rather, the text becomes part of a living tradition that is constantly subject to change, and that includes change in the perceived

---

[1] Primarily because at root Christianity rests upon an historical claim, that God became incarnate in Jesus Christ.

content of the biblical narratives: new insights are generated as different social conditions open up new possibilities and perspectives.

In a moment I shall offer three arguments for such an account of revelation as a process that continues well beyond the closure of the canon, but first some more general comments about what happens within the canon itself. Philosophers prefer that arguments run in only one direction, but, unfortunately for them, the life of ideas is seldom that simple. Thus in this case, how one understands revelation will undoubtedly affect how one understands the incarnation, but so equally will one's understanding of the latter have an effect on the former. This might seem to generate a circular argument, and in one sense it does, but it does not follow from this that it is viciously circular, and to my mind it is more a matter of mutual reinforcement and enrichment.

Chapter 6 will sketch arguments for the acceptance of certain, specific historical conclusions regarding Jesus' life and significance. Here, however, let me anticipate a little, in order to illustrate how a particular understanding of incarnation might help in our approach towards revelation. As I understand matters, modern biblical scholarship has forced upon us a very different understanding of the nature of the incarnation from that which prevailed through most of Christianity's history. Gone is the incarnate Lord who remained transcendent to the ambiguities of history and in his place has come someone so thoroughly shaped by the social setting in which he found himself that in retrospect we must declare some at least of his beliefs false. It is not just a matter of easily containable error such as the three-decker universe or the authorship of the Pentateuch and Psalms but also some beliefs which helped profoundly to shape the very substance of his message. Probably he thought that the end of the world as we now know it was imminent, and as a corollary he may well have died disappointed or in despair. Perhaps also he presumed continuing obedience to Jewish law.[2] Most significantly of all, the human Jesus had no consciousness of his own divinity. Such admissions are often thought to carry with them the automatic demise of orthodox Christian belief. But in that later chapter it will be my contention that, so far from this being so, such discoveries can instead be very effectively

---

[2] These are some of the issues considered in Chapter 6.

employed towards the actual strengthening of incarnational doctrine. The incarnation has now become a total identification with our humanity and its limitations. Though such extensive accommodation to the human condition inevitably generates major problems concerning the adequate translation of some aspects of Jesus' teaching from his world to our own, the benefits in my view far outweigh the losses. We now have a fellow-human being with whom we can unqualifiedly identify, with all that implies for our understanding of 'salvation'. However, more relevant here are the implications such a picture can have for the way in which we understand revelation.

To put the matter at its simplest, if God was willing to subject himself to such restraints at the point of his most concrete and definitive engagement with the world, it seems probable that *a fortiori* this is how in general his relation with that world should be characterized. At the point of the greatest risk of human misunderstanding he showed the maximum degree of accommodation to the human condition that was possible (without compromising his divinity);[3] so, surely, that must also be how he treats his human creation elsewhere. Revelation was mediated through the very particular social matrix in which Jesus found himself; elsewhere the matrices will differ, but not the necessity of their mediation. As I have argued in another context,[4] God valued something more than the immediate perception of truth: that the truth should be freely received, freely comprehended and freely embraced, and that is clearly a matter of the particular social context within which the community of faith happens to find itself. Deeply embedded socially established patterns of thought make it very hard for any particular individual to step too far outside his or her existing culture; still harder for that person to persuade their community as a whole so to move. To place the issue in a wider frame, models of rationality can also vary from century to century, with the influences that affect their underlying assumptions hidden even from the most outstanding intellects of the time.[5]

---

[3] The qualification is added to take account of the issue of Christ's sinlessness. What might be meant by that claim is discussed in Chapter 6.

[4] D. Brown, *The Divine Trinity* (London: Duckworth, 1985), 52–98, esp. 71 ff.

[5] For an excellent treatment of the way in which contemporary concepts of God exercised a largely hidden influence on philosophical models of reason, cf. E. Craig, *The Mind of God and the Works of Man* (Oxford: Oxford University Press, 1987).

None of this is intended to deny the possibility of objective truth, but it is to insist that its discovery is very much harder than was once supposed. More sensible, therefore, is it to begin by considering questions of coherence with immediate context and particular conceptual systems. Even then, as the previous chapter sought to illustrate, contexts and systems are both constantly in process of change; so it becomes one thing to ask about 'cognitive fit' in relation to a certain period of the Church's history, quite another to ask how that measures in relation to the assumptions of our own day. That last comment could easily be read as acceptance of complete relativism. It is not. Rather, thereby due acknowledgement is made of the extent to which it is the case that what is accepted as true from past tradition has to be measured anew in each generation. Nor will that 'new' for the Christian be merely the triggers to fresh thought that inevitably occur as circumstances change; of greater significance will be God's own role in imaginatively engaging the community to reflect upon the appropriate relation between those triggers and the community of faith's existing assumptions. In other words, the change is by no means passive, or one way, as the triggers themselves become subject to assessment and analysis.

In an earlier book I defined revelation as 'a process whereby God progressively unveils the truth about himself and his purposes to a community of believers, but always in such a manner that their freedom of response is respected'.[6] Yet, though thus already acknowledging the considerable role played by social conditioning and human fallibility, my implicit assumption remained that revelation ended with the closure of the canon of Scripture. While insisting that the contribution of the early ecumenical Councils of the Church were indispensable, I had assumed that this was simply a matter of drawing out what was already in some sense there in the New Testament writings. The Church's role was thus to clarify the contents of revelation rather than to add to them, even if my argument had carried with it the implication that considerably more clarification was now required than the Church had thought throughout most of its history! Here, however, I want to challenge that assumption, and that is why the view of revelation I propose here may be said to be radical in its implications.

---

[6] Brown, *Divine Trinity*, 70.

With the retreat of the Roman Catholic Church from the Tridentine position that revelation and tradition constitute two distinct sources of authority, one of the main points of modern ecumenical consensus has become the view that Scripture has supreme authority within the Church.[7] Such a change of perspective has been greeted with welcome approval by many a Protestant writer, and this finds apt illustration in some remarks by one distinguished biblical scholar. Reflecting upon recent official pronouncements from Rome as well as some remarks by Cardinal Ratzinger, he gives warm endorsement to the direction he now finds being pursued:

> This definitional role of scripture has become increasingly important within Roman Catholicism since Vatican II. Recent years have seen an increasing recognition that within the twofold norm of scripture and tradition primacy must be given to scripture, that the canon must be allowed to function as norm within the twofold norm, that scripture must be recognised to have a critical function vis-à-vis tradition.[8]

It is, however, that very consensus which I wish to challenge. While not denying the right of Scripture to offer a critique of later elements in the tradition, there is also in my view an equal right of later tradition to critique Scripture, and this is what makes it inappropriate to speak of one always acting as the norm for the other. Instead, a dialogue must take place, with now one yielding, now the other.

In what follows our discussion will proceed by two stages. First, I shall offer three types of consideration which seem to me to point decisively towards abolishing the sharp distinction that is still so widely assumed between tradition within Scripture and tradition beyond its confines. My contention will be that they are part of a single, ongoing process of revelation. Thereafter, we shall turn to consider what we may learn from the role of tradition within the other two major monotheistic religions, Judaism and Islam,

---

[7] The retreat is presumably to be explained by difficulty of defence, as an independent oral tradition no longer looks plausible, while further revelations unconnected with Scripture seem like special pleading.

[8] J. D. G. Dunn, 'The Bible in the Church' in D. F. Ford and D. L. Stamps (eds.), *Essentials of Christian Community* (Edinburgh: T & T Clark, 1996), 117–30, esp. 126 n. 29.

though in significantly different ways. Both have suffered from Christianity's own besetting sin, of trying to project everything that is deemed worthwhile back to a definitive early canon. Yet lurking only just beneath the surface are rather different assumptions. Orthodox Judaism has a very lively notion of tradition, and this was of course eventually to lead to the widening of its canon to include the Talmud, and also for some the *Zohar.* Although Islam's very high respect for the Qur'an means that any attempt to engage with critical analysis of the text will inevitably prove even more traumatic than has biblical criticism for Christianity, and there is much less explicit recognition of development than within Judaism, even so already present internally are powerful analytic tools which could be given wider application and thus generate a very fruitful concept of its own developing tradition. Though I write as a Christian, it seems to me not implausible that sometimes at least God might have spoken more effectively through the history of faiths other than one's own, and if that is so, it becomes no less important to offer some conception of how revelation might operate in these instances as well.

Tradition as revelation

In essence my argument is that to describe one period of the community of faith's history as revelation and the rest as mere tradition generates a contrast which cannot be sustained. This is not to deny the existence of important differences, most notably the indispensability of the Gospels for understanding the significance of Jesus, but, however important, such differences are still, in my view, better seen as differences of degree rather than kind. To suppose otherwise not only conceals the real continuities which undoubtedly exist but also distorts the full range of justifications available for later forms of Christian expression and self-understanding. Three general forms of argument may be advanced.[9] While only with the third will our focus be first and

[9] The first and third are improved versions, with a number of objections answered, of what I labelled the 'analogical' and 'providential' arguments in my article, 'Did Revelation Cease?' in A. G. Padgett (ed.), *Reason and the Christian Religion* (Oxford: Clarendon Press, 1994), 121–41; the middle argument is wholly new.

foremost on what God does, implicitly that will be our concern throughout.

A continuing pattern

Though the precise extent of its occurrence may be disputed, no biblical scholar could now possibly deny how deeply a developing tradition has helped shape the thinking of the biblical writers. Not only John, but also the synoptics do not simply pass on such material as they have inherited but creatively adapt it to address new circumstances. Likewise, even though the source theory for the origins of the Pentateuch has come under attack in recent years, there is no shortage of other illustrations from the Old Testament that could be supplied to indicate a similar pattern, from the various layers of additions to the prophetical books to even the adaptation of traditions from outside the community of faith, such as the Canaanite creation myth.[10] Even material that might initially be thought not to exhibit such patterns, such as the Pauline corpus, is not immune. The pseudo-Pauline epistles such as Ephesians and Colossians build creatively upon earlier thinking of Paul, subtly altering it, while even Paul himself seems to put to his own distinctive use earlier credal formulae and hymns.[11] Add to that the extent to which the thought of the biblical writers is reliant on earlier assumptions, and the case for a cumulative tradition appears overwhelming. The question with which we are faced is thus whether it is essentially the same pattern that continues in the post-biblical period, and what assessment should be made of that fact. Clearly the elaboration of earlier patterns of thinking occurs, but, as the

[10] The more likely source for adaptation in Gen. 1 is now thought to have been Canaanite rather than Babylonian myth. For a prophetic example, note how the addition of Amos 9 transforms the unrelieved stress on judgement and doom in the original prophet's message; cf. B. S. Childs, *Introduction to the Old Testament as Scripture* (London: SCM Press, 1979), 397 ff., esp. 405–8.

[11] e.g. contrast the different treatment of the head of the body in 1 Cor. 12: 21 and Col. 1: 18/Eph. 1: 22. Again, in 1 Cor. 15: 3–8 Paul makes his own experience of Christ equivalent to earlier resurrection appearances, while in Phil. 2: 6–11 he may be adapting to his own pre-existent Christology one that spoke only of the new Adam and made no such reference. For that earlier Christology: J. D. G. Dunn, *Christology in the Making* (London: SCM Press, 1980), 114–21.

previous chapter sought to illustrate, so also does the retelling of stories in ways held to be more significant for one's own day. More examples will follow in subsequent chapters.[12] So my argument here is that to freeze the running film at one particular point would be substantially to distort what was in fact happening. From the purely human perspective it distorts by suggesting the instantaneous creation of an authoritative text, whereas process was integral to the formation of the canonical version of the narrative, and it is exactly the same kind of process which we find continuing long after in theory a definitive canon has been officially acknowledged.

Two obvious objections to such a line of argument, however, must be faced: first that, though the pattern continues, its significance does not and so the closure of the canon remains of central importance; secondly, and perhaps more fundamentally, one finds the pattern stopping once, in the intertestamental period, so why not again? We shall now examine each of these objections in turn.

Perhaps the most obvious defence to make of a sharp distinction between canonical and post-canonical reflection is to appeal to the importance of history. What is earlier, it may be said, brings us closer to the historical, and the historical is necessarily of more worth than the imaginative or fictional, precisely because it brings us to the heart of divine revelatory action. Particularly in the nineteenth century, such considerations seem to have been a major factor driving the search for the historical Jesus: the pursuit of what could then be unconditionally endorsed as sound both historically and theologically, at the very heart of divine action in the world. But both judgements, historical as much as theological, need to be challenged. The historical can be faulted on its own terms. It is simply not true that by discovering contemporary judgements one thereby necessarily gains the best assessment of what was in fact the case. History is littered with examples of those closest to a situation subsequently being seen to have totally misperceived their situation. Great artists have been consigned by their contemporaries to oblivion and may have to wait for centuries before their

---

[12] Mainly from the lives of the patriarchs and the adult life of Christ. Among others considered in *Discipleship and Imagination* are the apostles, Mary Magdalene, and Job.

proper worth is appreciated;[13] or again, 'the war to end all wars' is discovered to be merely transitional to the next. Likewise, then, with the incarnation. Christ's earthly life, Part Three will argue, acquired a totally different significance in the light of his resurrection and what flowed from it. Theologically, the judgement is thus equally mistaken. Even if something is shown definitively to have been on the lips of Jesus himself, that cannot of itself establish its irreducible authority. The resurrection may cast his words into an altogether different light. The evangelists saw this, and so felt compelled often to rewrite incidents in his life, in order to bring that full significance out. The fact that what they wrote in consequence was often imaginative, with an element of 'fiction', rather than purely historical does not therefore mean that it was without justification either historically or theologically.

The historical and theological relations between earlier and later do of course still require to be critically explored. But at the same time we must insist that there can be no inevitable triumph for what is earlier, as though it were necessarily 'better' because closer to what actually happened. This seems to me the most important way of appropriating the common German distinction between history as bare facts or annals—*historisch*—and history as a question of meaning and significance—*geschichtlich*. Nowadays we normally express the latter by separately identifiable reflections, whereas the evangelists (following the practice of their day) did so by creative rewriting. Likewise, much the same can be said of the way in which in later history the lives of the patriarchs or the story of Mary Magdalene were retold. The concern was with imaginative questions of spiritual significance rather than the straight recording of events. We need therefore first to be clear about what sort of question we are asking before we jump too readily to pronounce later versions of a tradition necessarily inferior to the earlier. Otherwise, we will soon find our criteria condemning the Bible no less severely than later strands in the tradition.

[13] Perhaps the best known example is the delivery of Bach from oblivion by Mendelssohn. The artist, Georges de La Tour (d. 1652), had to wait even longer, until the twentieth century: C. Wright, *Georges de La Tour* (Oxford: Phaidon, 1977), 3–4. Still more recently, one might consider the transformation wrought in the reputation of Italian Baroque painting by Sir Denis Mahon: *Modern Painters* 10 (1997), 78–82.

My intention in all of this is not to advocate the other extreme, that later necessarily implies better. Even within the canon decline is also possible, and indeed commonly accepted in respect of, for instance, an excessive legalism in some post-exilic writing or undue preoccupation with formal structures of authority in the Catholic epistles.[14] What I am suggesting is partly that there can be no automatic triumph either way and partly that continuing change is inevitable, precisely because circumstances change and by no means always will there be an appropriate analogue in earlier material. It is utterly implausible to suggest that God built into the biblical narratives the ability to deal with all possible future scenarios,[15] and so fresh imaginative adaptations that go well beyond the letter of the text will constantly be sought. Some will be appropriate and others not, but there can be no ruling out of such change in advance.

The second objection to the notion of revelation as a continuous stream of tradition of which we said we would take note is that the stream seemed to stop once for several centuries with the closure of the Old Testament and so, if once, why not again? Here the most obvious reply is that, while such a response might have once seemed plausible (through most of Christian history), modern biblical scholarship has made it quite untenable. As a Christian it is tempting to suppose a natural continuity between the Old Testament and the New, but, if Old Testament scholarship has shown one thing, it is that that continuity is very much weaker than commonly supposed. An excellent illustration of this fact is the way in which the attempt which the New Testament writers make to forge the link through Old Testament 'prophecies' has been shown, more often than not, to be creative misreadings rather than anything to do with the original meaning of the passages concerned. This is particularly true of Matthew's Gospel. One can of course still use them (as we still do at Carol services) to witness to our conviction of the hand of God working through both Testaments towards some ultimate goal (with the incarnation in no sense an afterthought), but one does so more out of a

---

[14] e.g. Ezra 9–10 insisting upon the divorcing of non-Jewish wives, and worries about obedience to ecclesial authority in 1 Pet. 5: 1–5 and 3 John 9–12.
[15] Yet theologians often come close to making such claims: e.g. A. M. Ramsey, *Jesus and the Living Past* (Oxford: Oxford University Press, 1980), 23.

conviction of faith than because of any historically demonstrable connection.[16] That, however, is but one instance of a larger phenomenon, for it would nowadays be widely acknowledged that no adequate comprehension of the New Testament is possible without some understanding of what went on in the intertestamental period. That of course does not necessarily make that intervening stream of itself revelatory, but it does mean that it contributes at the very least to the formation of revelation in much the same way as for many a modern Christian great tracts of the Old Testament contribute towards the intelligibility of the New rather than themselves being revelatory.

Whether that parallel is accepted or not, there can be little doubt of the extent of the New Testament's debt to intertestamental reflection. Eschatology (and with it apocalyptic) plays a major role in the New Testament but only a peripheral one in the Old. The Book of Daniel or Trito-Isaiah hardly prepare us for the kind of connection drawn in the Gospels between the kingdom of God and a new, imminent age, far less for the Book of Revelation, but the numerous apocalyptic intertestamental writings certainly do.[17] Again, the very occasional references to an 'anointed' one in the Old Testament would radically mislead if taken on their own as a guide to messianic expectations, whereas a better comprehension emerges if we turn to the writings of Qumran or to Pharisaic literature such as the *Psalms of Solomon* (most obviously *Ps. Sol.* 17). Much the same might be said of the use to which the title 'Son of Man' is put, and the light thrown on this by 1 Enoch.[18] Again, in quoting from the Old Testament the New Testament writers use the Septuagint, the later Greek translation of the Hebrew Scriptures and not the Hebrew Scriptures themselves, even where

[16] For a more detailed argument to this effect, D. Brown, *The Word to Set You Free* (London: SPCK Press, 1995), 17–21.

[17] In one recent, authoritative collection of intertestamental literature in two fat volumes, one of them is entirely devoted to such material: J. H. Charlesworth (ed.), *The Old Testament Pseudepigrapha* Vol. I: 'Apocalyptic Literature and Testaments' (London: Darton, Longman & Todd, 1983).

[18] Cf. e.g., G. W. E. Nickelsburg, *Jewish Literature Between the Bible and the Mishnah* (London: SCM Press, 1981), 214–5, 221–3; 1 Enoch 62–63 may also be behind Matt. 25: 31–46 with its parable of the sheep and the goats; cf. D. Catchpole, 'The poor on earth and the Son of Man in heaven', *Bulletin of the John Rylands Library of Manchester* 61 (1979), 378–83.

this differs significantly from the original (as in Isa. 7: 14).[19] The
Septuagint contains those books written in Greek which we now
call the Apocrypha. Significantly, two of these, the Book of
Wisdom and Ecclesiasticus (or Sirach) have exercised a marked
influence on the christology of the New Testament, particularly in
Paul and Matthew.[20] Certainly their language is a trajectory of
imagery found in Proverbs 8–9, but that passage of itself does little
to explain the prominence of the New Testament imagery, nor
the presence of various other parallels.[21]

Then to this we must add the way in which some intertestamental literature is implicitly treated within the New Testament as
no less authoritative than the books we currently describe as
canonical. Attempts to prove that these works existed only on the
margins of society have proved unconvincing, and increasingly
due recognition is being given to the fact that both the incipient
Christian community and other Jews of the time operated with a
rather flexible notion of canon.[22] Certainly at Qumran the Book
of *Jubilees* seems to have been treated as Scripture, a practice which
continues to this day in the Ethiopian church not only with
respect to that book but also *1 Enoch* and the *Ascension of Isaiah*.[23]
Within the New Testament, perhaps the most obvious example of
such openness is the Epistle of James which speaks of 'the patience
of Job' (5: 11 AV); in the biblical book Job is anything but patient,
whereas that description corresponds exactly to what emerges
from the intertestamental rewriting, *The Testament of Job*. But this
is by no means the only instance, with James' view of Abraham's
sacrifice of Isaac almost certainly reflecting the influence of *Jubilees*,

---

[19] Only the Septuagint requires one to speak of a 'virgin'; the Hebrew has
'young woman' (*'almah*).

[20] Particularly marked with Wisd. 7–8 and Sir. 24.

[21] Cf. e.g. J. D. G. Dunn, *Christology*, 176–209; Nickelsburg, *Jewish Literature*,
184–5.

[22] For a defence of the traditional view, R. Beckwith, *The Old Testament
Canon of the New Testament Church and its Background in Early Judaism* (Grand
Rapids, Michigan: Eerdmans, 1985); for what to my mind are more plausible
views, J. Barr, *Holy Scripture: Canon, Authority, Criticism* (Philadelphia:
Westminster Press, 1983), esp. 49–74; J. Barton, *Oracles of God: Perceptions of
Ancient Prophecy in Israel after the Exile* (Oxford: Oxford University Press, 1986),
1–95.

[23] Like Irenaeus and Clement of Alexandria, the apocryphal New Testament
writing *The Shepherd of Hermas* is also treated as Scripture.

while the obscure reference in 1 Peter to Christ preaching to 'the spirits in prison' (3: 19) could well refer to the treatment of the fallen angels in *1 Enoch*.[24] Again, to understand the Epistle to the Hebrews' description of the fate of the prophets (11: 37) one must turn to the *Ascension of Isaiah*, which speaks of the prophet being sawn in two (5: 1–14).

Once we go beyond content to questions of style of presentation, the influence is seen to be even more pervasive. The strange use to which Melchizedek is put in Hebrews (6: 19 ff.) or Abraham's two wives in Galatians (4: 21 ff.) can only be described as quite ridiculous for so long as one fails to note their proper context in the style of reading of earlier texts that by New Testament times had become fashionable.[25] Likewise, though the way in which some of the prophetic books are now seen as stemming from more than one hand provides some parallel in explaining pseudonymous writings in the New Testament, once again it is the profusion of intertestamental writing that offers the fuller background, as one reflects upon works stemming from the Johannine community of the beloved disciple, or the development of Paul's thought in Ephesians and the Pastorals, or the letters bearing Peter's name. It was a shared conviction of carrying the mantle of the past into the present. A particular striking instance is the opening of *1 Enoch*, where an initial third person reference to Enoch quickly moves to the first person.[26] So the fact that a minor epistle directly quotes *1 Enoch* as Scripture—'prophesied'—cannot just be dismissed as a wild aberration (Jude 14 AV, quoting 1 Enoch 1.9).

While sympathetic to the restoration of former Protestant practice in including the Apocrypha within the covers of Protestant Bibles,[27] despite the general thrust of my argument I should not be

[24] For the arguments, cf. J. H. Charlesworth and C. A. Evans (eds.), *The Pseudepigrapha and Early Biblical Interpretation* (Sheffield: Sheffield Academic Press, 1993), 228–45.
[25] For the treatment of Abraham, see Ch. 5 of this book; for Melchizedek, B. Lindars, *The Theology of the Letter to the Hebrews* (Cambridge: Cambridge University Press, 1991), 72–7, where, though specific influence from Qumran is discounted, the influence of contemporary principles of exegesis is stressed.
[26] Cf. D. S. Russell's comments in *The Old Testament Pseudepigrapha* (London: SCM Press, 1987), 10.
[27] In England it was only lost gradually from 1826 under the influence of the British and Foreign Bible society: F. F. Bruce, *History of the Bible in English* (Cambridge: Lutterworth Press, 3rd edn., 1979), 110–11.

interpreted as canvassing for a still wider casting of the net. Admittedly, there are precedents. Augustine thought so highly of the wider canon of the Septuagint that he put its inspiration on a par with the prophets, even insisting on its inspiration where it differed from Hebrew originals.[28] Again, like the Ethiopian church, Eastern Orthodoxy in general operates with a wider canon than the western Apocrypha, including 3 and 4 Maccabees and an additional psalm. Though the *New Oxford Annotated Bible* of 1977 prints this wider canon, the possibility of ever achieving consensus on the matter may well be past. So, rather than advocating such an expansion, what I am arguing for here is more sympathetic consideration of this intertestamental literature, whether or not it finally achieved canonical status. If the Greek additions to the Book of Esther make it a more profound book which at least secures a reference to God within its pages, or the alternative title for Sirach—Ecclesiasticus ('The Book of the Church')[29]—indicates how much more spiritually rewarding it is than the canonical Book of Proverbs, there is surely nothing to be lost in going further and conceding the presence of insights in the intertestamental literature that on occasion advance upon the canonical text. Indeed, such a conclusion would seem forced upon the Christian, where those insights appear to have decisively shaped similar perspectives within the New Testament itself. Quite a number of examples will be given in the chapters which follow.

By reading these books more sympathetically Christians will also gain a better understanding of their own communal identity. Books like *1 Enoch* and *Jubilees* were engaged in the task of reinterpreting earlier Scripture in a similar way to Chronicles' treatment of Kings or Deuteronomy's of Exodus.[30] The fact that they sometimes wildly erred does not mean that they could not also sometimes improve upon what they read, just as the later

[28] Augustine, *City of God* 18.43. For a modern expression of similar sentiments, based in part on the creative character of tradition: M. Müller, *The First Bible of the Church: A Plea for the Septuagint* (Sheffield: Sheffield Academic Press, 1996), e.g. 102 ff.

[29] Cf. Box and Oesterley in R. H. Charles, *Apocrypha and Pseudepigrapha of the Old Testament* (Oxford: Clarendon Press, 1912), Vol. I, 270–1 and 298–303.

[30] For a sympathetic treatment of the process, cf. J. C. Vanderkam, 'Biblical Interpretation in 1 Enoch and Jubilees' in Charlesworth & Evans, *Pseudepigrapha and Biblical Interpretation*, 96–125.

canonical writings are a similar mixture of bettering and worsening.[31] So, in short, what consideration of that intertestamental literature suggests is that, so far from there being any break in the pattern, present day Christians, if they are properly to understand themselves, must see that period also, no less than the later Church, as part of a continuing pattern of developing tradition.

A changing post-canonical real text

The second main type of argument which I want to adduce for breaking down the standard contrast between revelation and tradition focuses exclusively on what happened subsequent to the formation of the canon.[32] It is often thought to be a decisive, knock-down argument to what I am proposing here that with the closure of the canon the definitive text was set in concrete, and the source of any possible revelatory content thereby finally fixed. What happens thereafter, it will be said, should be described more accurately as changes in interpretation rather than changes in the text itself, and so one clear difference remains from earlier forms of tradition. Indeed, the attempt may be made to strengthen the objection by observing that it is precisely the power of the text which generates these new interpretations, not forces external to it. One way such change could be explained is through the work of canonical critics in identifying the various checks and balances that exist once one starts looking at the canon as a whole.[33] These, it might be contended, play against each other to generate new emphases. Undoubtedly, this does sometimes happen, and so it would be foolish to discount the power of neglected aspects of a text to reassert themselves. Yet this cannot suffice as a complete explanation, as the previous chapter has hopefully illustrated. There was nothing in the text itself to force the new

---

[31] For a possible bettering, the grounds given for the fourth commandment in Exod. 20: 8–11 and Deut. 5: 12–15; for a definite worsening, Exod. 23: 4–5 and Deut. 22: 1–4.

[32] Though I am less sanguine than Metzger that the canon was essentially self-selecting, my argument here should not be taken to imply, and does not require, any undermining of the written canon as such: B. M. Metzger, *The Canon of the New Testament* (Oxford: Clarendon Press, 1987), esp. 286–8.

[33] Especially, for example, if the distinct identity of the Old Testament is respected or the differing emphases of Matthew and Paul: B. S. Childs, *Biblical Theology of the Old and New Testaments* (London: SCM Press, 1992), 77–9; 556–7.

recognition of the value of childhood nor anything which required the substantial retelling of the narrative which we in fact found. Instead, fresh applications of biblical trajectories were made, and in the process the nature of the text itself so substantially transformed as if a completely new narrative had been written.

Nor does this point apply merely to former ways of reading Scripture. Equally, it is the case today that what appears on the page is seldom what directly enters hearts and minds. Instead, for most Christians the interpretation of any passage newly presented to them will be heavily conditioned by what they have already learnt through the liturgy and sermons. Most obviously perhaps, the Gospel accounts are harmonized, and large chunks of the Old Testament in particular remain permanently closed. The 'real' text which has been in use within the community in the generations that followed the formation of the canon is thus an extremely slippery concept. It has been shaped by external factors to a degree that is quite untrue of any other book. Teachers and our own reading do of course help condition us to receive a play or novel in a particular way, but this affords only a remote analogy to the great 'canon' of assumptions with which most Christians would approach the Scriptures. Such a point would, I am sure, now in general terms be very widely conceded, but seldom are its implications fully drawn: that in so far as God can be conceived of as speaking through the Scriptures, he speaks not through an open text, but one that comes already context laden and considerably 'rewritten'. For, though many a theologian is happy to speak of the Bible as 'the Church's book', what is not acknowledged is the extent to which the written text is not itself the final control.

So, to begin with it certainly needs to be conceded that, whatever form of criticism the biblical scholar uses, his or her demonstration of a particular meaning remains largely secular until and unless it becomes appropriated by the believing community. Indeed, one way of viewing the situation is to say that it has not become part of the 'real' text until such infiltration has taken place. So, for instance, arguably the Song of Songs only acquired a reference to ordinary human love in the modern period,[34] while

---

[34] For a rare attempt to integrate modern and traditional approaches within the same commentary, R. E. Murphy, _The Song of Songs_ (Minneapolis: Fortress Press, 1990), esp. 91–105.

Liberation theology's treatment of the exodus could be read as the attempt to recover that story for the canon, as it began to slip from the community's self-perception and understanding as doubts about its miracles and the harshness of God's actions grew. But serious note also needs to be taken of the more contentious sense in which there is a variable or moving text. Perhaps where this is literally the case can be used to make the point most plain. Though continued resistance within the context of worship to the use of more accurate modern translations is sometimes generated by mere conservatism, often the worry is more significant, that thereby a rich vein of spirituality will be lost. So, for instance, the 1963 Revised Psalter of the Church of England abandoned on grounds of accuracy Psalm 23's allusion to death, speaking instead only of 'the darkest valley'; as a consequence much of its appropriateness for funerals was also lost, and that no doubt in part explains the 1980 Alternative Service Book's restoration of 'the valley of the shadow of death'.[35] The same point applies to many another psalm. Can anyone doubt, for instance, that the Prayer Book's phrase about those 'who going through the vale of misery use it for a well' is far more spiritually profound than flat-footed modern translations that return us to the banality of the original text?[36]

To my mind it is thus a delusion to suppose that the Church, having acquired a fixed canon, thereby lost the pattern of development which characterized the earlier community. The canon of interpretation continued to develop, even if this ceased to be by the simple creation of wholly new texts. Sometimes this involved creative mistranslation; sometimes a new grid being imposed upon an existing story; sometimes lacunae being filled and thus indirectly an almost wholly new story generated. Sometimes even what is constitutive of this real canon is not written text at all but a narrative controlled by visual image. In effect, this is what I suggested in the last chapter happened with the combination of

[35] For a sustained attack from a biblical scholar on 'accuracy' in texts for worship, cf. H. F. D. Sparks, *On Translations of the Bible* (London: Athlone Press, 1973), esp. 16–20; for a specific case in detail, Brown, *Word*, 58–62.

[36] Ps. 84: 6. Contrast, e.g. NEB: 'As they pass through the thirsty valley they find water from a spring.' The ASB also translates literally, but at least in a way that is open to the possibility of the Coverdale meaning.

shepherds and wise men worshipping the infant Jesus, as we find the scene depicted in numerous nativity scenes, and continues to happen in our own day, however much biblical scholars may protest about the difficulty of reconciling the narratives of Matthew and Luke. The real narrative text that controls the Christian imagination of today is not the various biblical stories as such, but an amalgam created over the centuries, and in particular more often than not mediated through nativity plays, art and hymns rather than the details of the biblical narratives.

Dramatic and musical analogies for the role of Scripture in the contemporary Church have become quite prominent in recent years.[37] To my mind, though, the image is still too weak to convey the extent of the changes involved. There is only a limited range of interpretation possible before a particular performance of Bach or Mozart would cease to be an expression of such composers' work, whereas what we seem to have is something more like the option allowed by some modern dramatists and composers of certain elements in a piece being provided by the performers themselves.[38] Among those who use the artistic analogy perhaps the most impressive is Sandra Schneiders' writing where it functions as part of a general strategy to get beyond the customary preoccupation of the biblical scholar with the narrowly historical.[39] But though her attempt to reinstate the primary importance of Scripture as a means of conveying spiritual values is welcome and on the whole well argued, it still suffers on my view from too fixed a view of what the text is, with a resultant tendency to undervalue both its past and its future. Thus, on the one hand it can only weaken her case for spiritual readings if this is bought at the cost of denying the importance or accessibility of the history from which they took their inspiration.[40] On the other, her

---

[37] e.g. N. Lash, *Theology on the Way to Emmaus* (London: SCM Press, 1986), ch. 3; F. Young, *The Art of Performance: Towards a Theology of Holy Scripture* (London: Darton, Longman & Todd, 1990).

[38] As in some of the theatrical work of Antonin Artaud or the music of John Cage. For this as a feature of postmodernist performance, S. Connor, *Postmodernist Culture* (Oxford: Blackwell, 2nd edn., 1997), 141–81.

[39] S. M. Schneiders, *The Revelatory Text* (HarperSanFrancisco, 1991); for the artistic analogy, e.g. 149, 173.

[40] For her rejection of the quest of the historical Jesus, cf. ibid., 49–50, 107, and of authorial intention, 162; yet contrast 116.

repeated emphasis on the 'normative' character of the text,[41] as though any new ideas had to be generated from within it, belies the power of a spiritual perception that is no longer restrained by reference to the specifics of historical detail, even where this is biblical.

Perhaps the difficulties in her position can be made clearer by considering her own 'worked example' with which her book ends.[42] In her interpretation of the incident at the well (John 4: 1–42) Schneiders sees herself as releasing the Samaritan woman from any assessment of her in terms of her loose ways into a symbol of the female equality which she believes Christ preached.[43] Yet the irony of all this is that the more the woman is taken as a symbol of acceptance of the Samaritan mission despite that people's former apostasy, the less relevant does her sex become: like the traditional symbolism of Israel as female, she will then in reality become as much male as female. So, though Schneiders' exposition is plausible, it fails to deliver the very thing she seeks, and for that we would need to look beyond the specific text, and so into the question of whether there is any wider historical basis for declaring that Jesus in fact believed in the equality of the sexes. Equally, even if the 'fallen' character of the woman were central to the passage, it would by no means follow that this prevented her from being accorded high esteem. Much modern commentary assumes that the identification of Mary Magdalene in this way meant her degradation, but there is much evidence to suggest that the very reverse was the case.[44] So, although it remains important to establish intended meaning, Schneiders is wrong in so far as she implies that what is thereby discovered must therefore be taken as definitive or normative. Both earlier history and later application alike have the power to undermine any particular position as definitive.

It must not, however, be supposed that the distinction I have been drawing between 'written' and 'real' canon is only applicable to parts of the text, and not to the Bible as a whole; otherwise we will miss an important dynamic of Christian history, the way in which a new whole is able to generate profound criticisms of

[41] e.g. ibid., 65, 78.   [42] Ibid., 180–99.
[43] e.g. ibid., 182.
[44] I argue the point at length in Chapter 1 of *Discipleship and Imagination*.

earlier parts, including sometimes what is the clear historical meaning. That is to say, recognition of how a new entity comes into existence that is larger than the sum of its parts is vital if we are properly to understand how some forms of doctrinal and moral change occur. In effect, the community acquires a holistic framework that generates new insights that cannot simply be seen as derivative from what has gone before. Moreover, it is a changing holistic framework, not one simply to be equated with a once-and-for-all closure of the canon, whether identified with the completion of the New Testament writings or some time thereafter.

The point may be illustrated from the changing character of Christian art which is the topic of Chapter 7. There much stress is placed on the various social and cultural stimuli that enabled Christian art to develop in specific directions at definite points in time. But, important as these external stimuli undoubtedly were (for example, the passing of the millennium or the Black Death), even more important was the coming into existence of a 'real' canon where Christ as equally divine and human had ceased to be a point of contention. The Bible had been deeply suspicious of all forms of representational art. Even with incarnation established as foundational of the canon, the Bible's hostility continued to exercise a restraining, indeed almost destructive, influence, as the iconoclastic controversy well illustrates. Even so, art found its major place within the Christian tradition, not because of what the Bible taught or what could easily be derived from it, but because the new holistic canon was seen as offering a 'definition' of God in the incarnation and so as legitimating other 'definitions' of God's creation. Scripture itself could now be read with a new, visual eye.

Much the same can be said of the move to a more compassionate and suffering Christ during the Gothic period. The New Testament exhibits considerable restraint on the question of Christ's suffering and indeed even some degree of embarrassment, as the suppression of the cry of dereliction in Luke and John demonstrates. Such restraint and embarrassment were inevitable in a period during which a struggle to establish Christ's exalted status was still underway. It was really only once his divinity was absolutely secure that writers and artists could turn once more to his humanity to bring out the full implications of the suffering which he must have endured. Even then, it required some external stimuli to help the process on its way. More importantly, however, note once again the way in which a new 'real' or holistic text was required before this became possible, one in which his divinity had become totally uncontested, with various titles and verses now read in ways antithetical to their original meaning (e.g. 'Son of God' or the punctuation of Rom. 9: 5).[45] To think that a suffering God can be derived solely from biblical presentations of his humanity would be to throw the Church once more into the uncertainties of whether too explicit a presentation of such suffering does not after all undermine the presence of divinity, as clearly John must have felt.[46]

Assessment of the plausibility of these contentions must await the detailed discussion of later chapters. For the moment let me repeat once more that my argument here is not that the views of the later Church should necessarily be given greater weight than what came earlier with the written canon, but rather that the issue cannot be prejudged in advance, precisely because any adequate model of revelation must take account of the fact that the vehicle of its mediation throughout Christian history has never been some pure notion of text, but rather a shifting real text whose actual content at any particular moment could only be determined by careful analysis of its social setting. Of course, that makes the search for criteria for truth in revelation more difficult, but even so we must not use that as an excuse for not facing the more complex reality which we find: that Scripture has only ever had authority in the history of the Church as a moving stream, not a changeless deposit.

A continuing personal dialogue

Hitherto my arguments have been very much based on the human processes at work, but much the same sort of conclusion seems

---

[45] 'Son of God' is now taken to imply uniqueness and divinity, whereas the original sense only indicated favoured status (seen in Luke's substitution of 'good man': Luke 23: 47; Mark 15: 39). On Rom. 9: 5 contrast AV with most modern translations where 'God' begins a new sentence.

[46] Though accusations of docetism go too far, there is little in John to suggest the acuteness of human suffering. 'Suffering God' is not quite how the medieval world would have put it, but it does indicate well its unqualifed assertion in Christ of both divinity and the extremes of human suffering.

required if we make the divine contribution explicit, and speak of revelation. For if we conceive of God waiting upon a free response, that also requires him to wait for certain social settings where the response becomes both intelligible and possible. To take an extreme case, God could hardly speak of his concern for the inhabitants of other worlds before the very idea of such beings existing became conceivable, and that would mean moving well beyond a three-decker universe. But the point is equally applicable to what has actually occurred within the history of Christian thought. Perhaps the pre-eminent example is the Trinity. For it was only once monotheism was secure that plurality within the godhead could be revealed without the danger of revertion to pagan polytheism. Again, the assigning of value beyond one's tribal or national identity is dependent upon some non-threatening contact beyond that identity,[47] just as the idea of a value attaching to the individual independent of the social whole requires some degree of social mobility and change in society for its perception to be generated.[48] In none of this am I saying that we are trapped by the particular society in which we find ourselves, only stressing how difficult change is without such additional supports. So, not surprisingly, many further pressures towards change in a changing society are indicated in succeeding chapters. The idea that one can only speak of divine involvement if God acts through the narrow base that is constituted by Scripture seems very odd, the more examination of its contents is found to indicate that its ideas are no less context-bound than any other text. It is new contexts that generate new challenges and these must often require fresh responses for which the Bible offers no immediate application.

Though such an analysis with its stress on human response preserves a thoroughly personal account of divine action, on the

[47] The greater interest of Second Isaiah in the fate of other peoples could have been due in part to the discovery that Israel's conquerors were less awful than feared. Certainly, the more widespread post-biblical Diaspora did generate much more positive sentiments, as the second part of this chapter will indicate.

[48] This is, for instance, how the origin of Buddhism out of Hinduism is explained by R. Gombrich, *Theravada Buddhism* (London: Routledge & Kegan Paul, 1988), chs. 1–3. Significantly, the move to greater stress on the individual in the Old Testament also occurs during a period of great social change: cf. Ezek. 18: 19–20.

model of perhaps the teacher or parent,[49] for others it will seem excessively anthropomorphic, with all the mystery and majesty of the divine otherness gone. Here I think that I erred in my earlier account in *The Divine Trinity*. For, as Basil Mitchell rightly observes when discussing this objection,[50] God's presence can certainly sometimes be felt as threatening and disquietening. But the answer is not to abandon the model. It is to recognize that even in those circumstances, to succeed, such experiences need to retain their personal dimension. Fear, for instance, is a very different emotion from awe, or an overwhelming burden of guilt from a sense of release through divine forgiveness. My earlier presentation did indeed suggest too cosy a relationship between God and the recipient of revelation, but that is no reason to abandon the model altogether. Painful, traumatic disclosure is sometimes necessary also in purely human relationships, but it remains possible (and preferable) that the friend or spouse does this in a way that preserves the other's self-identity and integrity rather than destroying it.[51]

The model of revelation towards which such a personalist, interactionist account points must, I think, therefore include further development of the notion of divine accommodation. Such an application to revelation is by no means a new idea. As one recent survey demonstrates,[52] it has been a popular idea throughout Christian and (to a lesser degree) Jewish history. Unfortunately, in the Christian case it has been predominantly used in a negative way, particularly to explain the introduction of the Mosaic law and its subsequent suspension under the Christian dispensation. Here Paul's argument in Galatians 3 undoubtedly played its part, but this was supplemented by the conviction that sacrifice was introduced as a remedy against idolatry, perhaps specifically to counter worship of the animals concerned.[53] But a

---

[49] Cf. D. Brown, *Word*, 7–11.

[50] B. Mitchell, 'Revelation Revisted' in S. Coakley and D. A. Pailin (eds.), *The Making and Remaking of Christian Doctrine* (Oxford: Clarendon Press, 1993), 177–91, esp. 185 ff.

[51] Much modern counselling, e.g. by the Samaritans, is premised on such an assumption. It should be non-directive, so that any decisions made remain fully the client's own.

[52] S. D. Benin, *The Footprints of God* (Albany, New York: SUNY, 1993).

[53] Cf. Benin on Athanasius, 28, on Aphrahat, 79.

more positive notion of education can be traced from Origen through Augustine to Lessing,[54] though even here it retains a somewhat patronizing attitude. More impressive is Maimonides' exploration of the dangers of too much knowledge, or Hugh of St Victor's notion of gradualism in forms of sacramentality running from natural through Mosaic to Christian.[55] Most relevant to our present purposes, though, is the repeated implicit acknowledgement of God's willingness to adapt himself to the present position of his community, however wayward it may be. Perhaps nowhere is our own suggested combination of the restraint imposed by culture and God's desire to act by persuasion better expressed than in Gregory of Nazianzus' Fifth Theological Oration:

> The two Testaments are alike in this way, namely, that the change was not made all at once, nor at the first movement of the undertaking. Why not, we ask, for it is necessary to know? It was in order that we might not be compelled, but persuaded. For what is involuntary never endures, like plants or streams held back by force. It is the voluntary which is the more stable and more secure. The one is characteristic of the justice and goodness of God, the other of tyrannical power ... Accordingly, like a teacher or a doctor God partly curtails and partly condones ancestral practices ... For not at all easy is the change from assumptions honoured by custom and long usage.[56]

If accommodation is a pattern which exists throughout the entire process, then it must also find its place at the very start, as Hugh of St Victor suggested, and that, it seems to me, must mean taking seriously the notion of natural symbols.[57] For the first social matrix within which humanity found itself was the created order and the building blocks which it provided for theological reflection. It is surely no accident, for instance, that eating, water and blood find some place in all religions. Eating until modern times has always been an essentially social activity and that has profoundly affected the religious meaning attached to it,[58] while

---

54 Benin, *The Footprints of God*, 13, 111, 203.
55 Ibid., 147–55; 113–21.   56 Oration 31.25; my trans.
57 This is an issue which I first raised in respect of revelation in 'God and symbolic action' in B. Hebblethwaite and E. Henderson (eds.), *Divine Action* (Edinburgh: T & T Clark, 1990), 103–22.
58 Here I am thinking of the way in which individual 'TV dinners' have become such a feature of modern life.

its negation in fasting has been parasitic upon it, in the sense that the fast is commonly seen as training for some more ultimate 'feast'. Again, although water can sometimes act, and be seen as, threatening, its two basic roles in sustaining life and cleansing have meant that it has had no difficulty in securing a firm place in religious rituals. Likewise, though modern scientific knowledge might incline us to denote DNA rather than blood as the basic symbol for life, that cannot alter the intuitive appeal that blood has as a matter of fact exercised in assuming this role over the course of history. Although the origins of sacrifice continue to be debated, few scholars think that it was a simple matter of feeding the gods. At root lay the conviction that all taking of life (and thus its blood) needed a divine endorsement, and this way the gods were made complicit.[59]

Thereafter, as particular written traditions begin to shape subsequent developments, it is important that we continue to keep in mind the principle of accommodation and envisage God constantly responding to changed circumstances rather than implanting hidden meanings that are only subsequently brought to light. For much of Christian history this was indeed the interpretative key that was applied in particular to the Old Testament, but modern scholarship has very definitely rendered any such view implausible. Indeed, the exegesis of Matthew or Paul sometimes distorts the original meaning so badly (with total disregard to original context) that there is no naturalness whatsoever once this forced meaning is translated back to its original context. It does not always happen, but it often does, and it is important to concede that fact. This is where I would take issue with those philosophers prepared to talk of the subsequent 'discovery' of divinely intended, latent meanings within Scripture.[60] Can we, for

[59] For three scholars coming from different starting points to similar conclusions, cf. F. C. N. Hicks, *The Fullness of Sacrifice* (London: SPCK, 1953), 25–41; W. Burkert, *Homo Necans: The Anthropology of Ancient Greek Sacrificial Ritual and Myth* (Berkeley: University of California Press, 1983), 12–22, 35–48; L. Schele and M. E. Miller, *The Blood of Kings: Dynasty and Ritual in Maya Art* (London: Thames & Hudson, 1992), 175–240.

[60] Cf. R. Swinburne, *Revelation* (Oxford: Clarendon Press, 1992), e.g. 221; A. Plantinga, 'Two (or more) kinds of scripture scholarship', *Modern Theology* 14 (1998), 243–78, esp. 249–50; for an expanded critique of such attitudes, D. Brown, 'Did Revelation Cease?' in A. Padgett (ed.), *Reason*, 121–41. In a subsequent,

example, really claim that it was part of the divine intention that
in inspiring Zechariah to write of a contemporary, promising
leader as valued by the people at only thirty shekels of silver he
intended that his Son should be betrayed for this amount and that
Matthew confuse the passage with another from Jeremiah? (Zech
11: 12; Matt. 27: 9; Jer. 32: 6–15; 18: 2) Or, in inspiring Habbakuk
God intended that he write sufficiently ambiguously for Paul to
derive from him a doctrine of justification by faith diametrically
opposed to the most natural reading of the passage (which we find
reflected in Qumran)?[61] It suggests such a degree of divine manip-
ulation as to call into question the sort of personal interaction
which we have stressed must be central to any plausible account of
revelation in our own day. What therefore we need to say is not
that later generations 'discovered' the true meaning but that under
the providence of God the well-established conventional patterns
of exegesis of the time were used to make general claims which
the Christian continues to believe to be true: that the Old
Testament was not an aberration but an important part of the story
that was to culminate in the life of Christ.[62]

Similarly, care needs to be exercised in describing what happens
in the post-biblical period. Many modern writers assume it an easy
matter to endorse christological readings of difficult Old
Testament passages such as the notorious ending to Psalm 137,[63]
but, however sanctified by past practice, this surely needs testing
against the ease with which this can be done. To move abruptly
from a literal (and moving) understanding of the first part of the
psalm to a strained metaphor of hostility to all things opposed to
Christian vocation in the second part is a hard requirement, and
suggests to me more the desire to save the text at all costs rather

---

personal letter, Swinburne has suggested that all he is committed to is the view
that ' God inspired Paul … to get at what was important in Habbakuk,' but even
that more limited contention still does not seem quite right, since what Paul takes
to be important is contrary to Habbakuk's own view.

[61]   Hab. 2: 4; Rom. 1: 17; Qumran Commentary on Habbakuk in G.
Vermes, *The Dead Sea Scrolls in English* (Harmondsworth: Penguin, 1962), 239.

[62]   For some conservative scholars wrestling with this issue of the imposition
of meaning by the New Testament, W. W. Klein, C. l. Blomberg and R. L.
Hubbaard, *Introduction to Biblical Interpretation* (Dallas: Word, 1993), 117–51.

[63]   As modern examples, Swinburne, *Revelation*, 189; N. Wolterstorff, *Divine
Discourse* (Cambridge: Cambridge University Press, 1995), 212.

than serious imaginative engagement with its possible use. The attempt to conceal from the worshipper how truly dreadful the Bible can sometimes be is well illustrated by the coyness of the translation offered in one Scottish Paraphrase:

> O happy shall that trooper be
> Who riding on his naggie
> Shall take thy wee bairns by the toes
> And ding them on the craggie.

By contrast, Galatians 3: 28 reads very naturally as an assertion of the equality of the sexes, even if (probably) Paul intended no such implication.[64] So, rather than always searching for retrospective applications that somehow save appearances, I would suggest that present-day Christians need honestly to face the limitations of the canonical text: sometimes in respect of original meaning; sometimes, whatever meaning we try to apply to it. Either way, if it does succeed in speaking to us now, it will not be because of some eternal purpose of God, but because the language is sufficiently open either to allow retention of the existing meaning, or, through God's grace, the imposition of a new sense. Both scenarios should equally be seen as vehicles of God's action, and equally relevant in determining where revelation occurs in the here and now.

Conclusion

Some readers will no doubt have been surprised that at no point in this discussion have I attempted to give a precise location to where revelation occurs. In fact, that seems to me one of the great mistakes of past discussions of the topic, including my own. To identify divine act, divine speech, experience of the divine, or scriptural text as the precise moment all have their faults,[65] precisely for the sorts of reasons I have been trying to characterize

---

[64] For the reasons and an alternative defence of the equality of the sexes, *Discipleship and Imagination*, ch. 1.

[65] For an excellent survey of some of the main models, A. Dulles, *Models of Revelation* (Dublin: Gill & Macmillan, 1983); for an attempt to see some of the competing models (Barth, Henry, Rahner, Tillich) as in fact complementary, G. Fackre, *The Doctrine of Revelation* (Edinburgh: Edinburgh University Press, 1997).

in this discussion. There is no doubt whatsoever in my mind that God has revealed himself under all these scenarios, but even to say this much fails to deal with the limitations of what has then been said. For, to allude to each of our three arguments, the pattern continues, the real text changes, and the dialogue advances or retreats. It is thus the whole that needs to be valued and assessed: the running film, not the mime artist momentarily frozen before he keels over.

Even if we confine ourselves to the canon, identifying precisely when and through what causal processes a particular idea entered the consciousness of the community of faith is no easy matter, and indeed more often than not is incapable of any precise answer. This is true of major no less than of minor matters, as for example, life after death or the doctrine of the Trinity. What matters more is their emergence as part of a growing tradition, and the way in which through their emergence the tradition's past is reshaped. Among those who still cling to some notion of divine speech operating through Scripture, increasingly subtle models are now being offered. A conspicuous case in point is that of Nicholas Wolterstorff, who urges us to interpret the text in terms of two main categories—'deputised' or 'appropriated' discourse, with helpful analogies drawn with the relations between secretaries and employers on the one hand or ambassadors and presidents on the other, to remove any hint of a one-to-one correspondence between particular words and the divine will.[66] Even so, what this model still ignores is the need for Christians sometimes to acknowledge the past as the past, that a particular text will speak to us precisely because it witnesses as failed communication, representing options now rightly closed to the community of faith.[67]

This is not to say that revelation should only be identified with the final result. My point is quite different. It is that any adequate account must always take seriously the process itself, as much as the community's present experience and understanding, and it is the entire stream that needs to be seen as part of God's action, failures and all. This will mean taking with equal seriousness questions of cognitive and imaginative fit both with respect to the original

---

[66] Wolterstorff, *Divine Discourse*, 37–57.
[67] Some further examples and their implications will be considered in Parts Two and Three.

context and in relation to our own day. Sometimes a passage or story will be as true for its own day as for ours; sometimes true then, but incapable of application now; and sometimes incapable of any form of truth, since even by the likely measures of its own day it fails. Yet again, sometimes what is under dispute will have for long been judged wholly untrue, simply because it was being measured against the wrong conceptual frame. That in essence was my claim in the last chapter. The Magi as kings cannot be judged as other than nonsense when assessed as history, but that in my view is entirely the wrong frame against which to set them. Change the frame, and they emerge as more profoundly true than even Scripture itself. All this is to place heavy reliance on coherence theories of truth, not because I disbelieve in the possibility of any test for correspondence with the way things ultimately are. Rather, it is to acknowledge the difficulty of that ultimate aim, as well as the extent to which applying it too soon can profoundly distort our judgements.[68]

In effect, that Enlightenment demand for simple correspondence ruined the ability of the Gospel to be received imaginatively, as it became reduced to a crude correspondence with bare historical fact. Facts are indispensable to a religion like Christianity that lays claim to historical foundations, but they are not ultimately what gives it life. Christians need a pattern to be followed, and that pattern must change, as new questions force themselves on to the agenda. What that meant over the centuries to the way in which the life of Christ was told will be considered in detail in Part Three. The other two major monotheistic religions, however, faced not dissimilar difficulties. What, therefore, I want to consider in the remainder of this chapter is the nature of the dynamic that exists in Judaism and Islam between revelation and tradition. Both can, I think, illumine Christian self-understanding, provided we attempt to approach their past with the same sympathy that we have canvassed for the past history of the Church. We must seek to identify first their frames of reference, not ours.

---

[68] Coherence is easier to apply because the test will then be conformity or fit with existing Christian doctrine. This is not to deny the necessity of asking at some stage the more fundamental but more difficult question of correspondence with reality, the way in which God has in fact acted across history.

Learning from Judaism and Islam

It is obviously altogether too large an issue to consider here what degree of truth Christianity might accept within these two religions. Nevertheless, precisely because of the conditioned character of all thought, it would seem reasonable to expect that God might have interacted with more than one religious tradition over the course of the centuries. If that is so, then we ought to approach these other religions, not as at most pale reflections of Christianity, but with the real possibility of actually learning something from them. That at any rate is my hope here, as I investigate how Judaism and Islam have handled the issue of tradition as a possible medium of revelation, and ask what insights might be gained from the various interpretative strategies employed. We begin with Judaism.

Judaism: haggadah, halakhah and kabbalah

The most common way of viewing Judaism among contemporary Christians is still to think of it in essentially past terms, as the religion of the Old Testament which Christianity replaced. But whether we look to Jewish history or take the Orthodox or Reform Judaism of today, what we discover is a very different pattern: a religion which, like Christianity, has been in a continuous process of development, but which, unlike Christianity, has made that development much more explicit by acknowledging a canon beyond the biblical. Sometimes Jews themselves have distorted the extent of this wider authority by the kind of analogies they draw with Christianity.[69] Talk of 'a dual Torah', one written and the other initially oral and only subsequently written down, often seems to have been intended to challenge any notion of development, as was the suggestion that the function of the oral Torah was eternally planned by God to be the distinguishing mark

---

[69] Maccoby suggests an analogy to the status which Aquinas has within the Roman Catholic church, whereas Neusner, more realistically, asks us to envisage the Bible growing to include Aquinas; H. Maccoby, *Early Rabbinic Writings* (Cambridge: Cambridge University Press, 1988), 7; J. Neusner, *The Classics of Judaism* (Louisville, Kentucky: Westminster John Knox Press, 1995), xii.

of the Jew over against heretical Christians.[70] Yet, as with Christianity, the form of biblical exegesis that held sway through most of Judaism's history generated a very different 'real' text from its historical meaning, and there is thus no shortage of reflections that belie such talk of an unchanging Torah. This is obviously not the place to give a detailed history of how such changes occurred, but it will be useful to draw attention to a number of salient features that characterize the three principal means used to initiate further developments: haggadah, halakhah, and kabbalah.

But before doing so, let me first give an example of the general point with which I began: that recognizing God active in traditions other than one's own need not be seen as necessarily destructive of the value of one's own. Earlier in this chapter I argued that, if God is to speak to humanity at all and be persuasive, he must speak within the particular restraints of specific social contexts. That being so, it would seem inevitable that different insights will be attained by different traditions at different times in their respective histories. As a specific example, consider one element of central importance to Jewish tradition, the privileged place it assigns to the Jewish people. How is this to be interpreted? Is it an unconditional gift that marginalizes other nations, or a privilege that also constitutes a summons to service on behalf of the wider world? Though works such as Second Isaiah, Jonah and Ruth do represent a more cosmopolitan spirit, it is arguable that the Old Testament canon as a whole closes with the issue still not fully resolved, especially with the inclusion on the other side of Esther and Ezra, as also Third Isaiah's implicit corrective to Second Isaiah whereby the other nations are portrayed as subject peoples bringing tribute to Jerusalem (Isa. 61: 5–7; 66: 8–10). It is not surprising therefore that sentiments of narrow nationalism continued,[71] or even that the book of Ruth could be given such an interpretation: in *Ruth Rabbah* (post AD 500) she is seen, not as a reprimand to narrow exclusivism, but rather as the model Moabite convert, responding to the injunction, 'not to glean in another field', and

---

[70] B. T. Shabbat 31a, Tanhuma 58b, Pesikta Rabbati 14b; for relevant quotations, F. E. Peters, *Judaism, Christianity and Islam* (Princeton, NJ: Princeton University Press, 1990), Vol. 2, 157–8.

[71] e.g. Pseudo-Jonathan on Numbers 23–4, quoted in P. Grelot (ed.), *What are the Targums?* (Collegeville, Minnesota: Michael Glazier, 1992), 60–1.

rightly incorporated into Israel (the Law only forbade the inclusion of Moabite men).[72]

However, with the Diaspora also went increasing challenge to the idea that the Law should have been offered uniquely to Israel, alongside continuing discussion of why this might have been so. If the answer normally given was that other nations had been found wanting,[73] intense focus was thereby at least fixed on Israel's continuing responsibilities to the wider world in a way that is not characteristic of Old Testament writing. To give but one example of this, Jonah was reinterpreted as a rebuke to Israel, a warning that her privilege might be forfeited:

You know why Jonah fled and sought to suppress his mission of prophecy to Nineveh. It was, as rabbis said, because the Gentiles are readily disposed to repent, and their example would have roused greater anger against Israel, which is stubbornly reluctant to change its ways. Therefore Jonah was prepared to sacrifice his life out of love for Israel.[74]

Thus, while the conviction that 'the land ... and its temple was instituted for the benefit of the whole world' hardly represents the uniform consensus within early rabbinic thought,[75] there is no doubt that this is the view which was to win through, and it would be foolish to pretend that the written Torah or even the Hebrew canon as a whole accomplished this on its own.

Not all readers are likely to be happy with the example chosen. But the important issue is in any case not the illustration, but the principle: that a new social setting (in this case, increasing marginalization through conquest and Diaspora) can force the community of faith towards new insights and emphases (in this case, a greater sense of responsibility to the wider world), and that there need be no conflict in Christians, no less than Jews, seeing the hand of God in such a development. Later we shall note some

---

[72] For not gleaning: Ruth 2: 8; for the law against Moabite men, Deut. 23: 3–4; for Ruth Rabbah, Neusner, *Classics*, 346–66.
[73] Mekilta, Sifré to Deuteronomy, Leviticus Rabbah; Neusner, *Classics*, 110–1, 160, 245.
[74] From an eighteenth-century sermon by Jonathan Eybeschütz in M. Saperstein (ed.), *Jewish Preaching: 1200–1800* (New Haven: Yale University Press, 1989), 338; based on Lamentations Rabbah (c. AD 550) 1.9.36.
[75] Maccoby's view, *Writings*, 47.

cases where we can go further, and observe the ability of another religious tradition to offer a critique of our own. First, however, we must make some progress in understanding how Jewish tradition develops. Integral to the process are three forms of exegesis which almost invariably strike the modern mind as entirely arbitrary. For so long as that attitude prevails, they are likely to fail to win respect, far less be seen as potential bearers of revelation. So it is important that we carefully consider each in turn, to see what can be said on the other side. Inevitably, our discussion must be all too brief, especially as I have the additional aim of wanting to draw some more general conclusions about how the process of tradition works.

Haggadah and new insights Haggadah—'telling' or 'story'—is still quite commonly derided as an arbitrary imposition on earlier material, whose radical retelling and elaboration of the biblical story is held to bear little constructive relation to the original. From such suppositions it is but a short step to the belief that all that is happening is a 'reading in' to the text of what it is already desired one should hear. The element of challenge, of a voice from elsewhere, so central to the notion of revelation, would thus be entirely absent. Though sympathetic to midrash (commentaries that incorporate the biblical text into their expansion of it), Jacob Neusner comes close to seeing it in just such terms, as a purely personal creation: 'Commonly, we read Scripture for its message to us. We do not read ourselves and our circumstances as a means for making sense of Scripture. But that is precisely what in midrash-exegesis the sages accomplish.'[76] No doubt, as with the contents of Scripture, this did sometimes happen, but there is also evidence to consider on the other side, especially once the more complicated nature of the process is taken into account, as a number of Jewish scholars have recently been at pains to stress.

Particularly impressive is Irving Jacobs' successful identification of traditions of interpretation in relation to which the midrash is then seen as a natural further development. So, for instance, the interpretation of Job 21 and 24 in connection with the Flood makes no sense unless put in the context of the widespread belief that Moses wrote both Job and Genesis, or, to take a still more

---

[76] J. Neusner, *A Midrash Reader* (Minneapolis: Fortress Press, 1990), 139.

obscure example, the surprising description of Abraham as the 'daughter' of Psalm 45 and the 'little sister' of the Song of Songs likewise evokes incomprehension until one enters into traditions which assume Abraham as priest-king and sage.[77] In contrast to an earlier generation of scholars who had envisaged complete freedom of association in the commentator or preacher, what in fact one discovers is a lively dynamic in which the speaker or writer can certainly be innovative but always within the context of a tradition of associations shared with his audience.[78] New readings were thus by no means arbitrary self-creations, but evocative, imaginative responses to already existing patterns of thought. A very similar picture emerges from studies of later Jewish thought, such as Marc Saperstein's pioneering investigation of Jewish preaching between 1200 and 1800. Inevitably, there were changes. From the mid-fifteenth century onwards, the starting point was now always a passage from the Torah (called the *nosê*) rather than the Prophets or Writings, itself interpreted by a passage of rabbinic haggadah (known as the *ma'amar*).[79] Yet, whatever changes in formal structure occurred, the pattern of building creatively on existing assumptions continued.

However, even if such an imposition of a framework from tradition considerably lessens the sense of arbitrariness, the protest may still be made that it far from removes it altogether. For the issue remains whether within this framework it was really the questions that determined the answers, or predetermined answers the questions. Obviously, there is no need for us to assume that it is all of one, or all of the other, but there does seem to me good reason for supposing that it was in fact more often than not the former. Take, for instance, an example we shall consider in Chapter 5, post-biblical treatments of Abraham's sacrifice of Isaac. If one accepts the oft iterated demand for a close reading of Scripture (with nothing accidental and all from the hand of God), then there is surely a puzzle about why Sarah's death should be recorded immediately after the attempted sacrifice. The answer given was shock at Isaac's

[77] Ps. 45: 11; S. of S. 8: 8; I. Jacobs, *The Midrashic Process* (Cambridge: Cambridge University Press, 1995), 26–42, 79–144. Abraham becomes the royal bride of Ps. 45 because of the depth of his intimacy with God.
[78] Jacobs, e.g. xi, 14, 21–22, 80, 169–70.
[79] M. Saperstein, *Preaching*, 63–79.

near-death, and the incidental turning of him into an adult of thirty-seven.[80] The moral insight of the appropriateness of Isaac being an adult who could thus offer himself in sacrifice would therefore follow, rather than be a consequence of the desire to escape at all costs the apparent implications of the narrative in accepting child sacrifice. Similarly, when a fifteenth-century preacher declares that 'the resurrection of the dead is one of the fundamental principles of the Torah',[81] he is alluding to a belief that continues to be central to modern Judaism. As such it would seem odd to ascribe its justification to reason; yet, given modern scholarly recognition of its absence from the original meaning of the Torah, that would seem the only option, unless due weight is given to later reflection upon that writing. In this particular case, the preacher appeals to part of Jacob's blessing on his sons, the verse: 'I wait for thy salvation, O Lord' (Gen. 49: 18 RSV). Jacob is prophesying the future of his children, and in this instance—Dan—his most famous descendant was Samson. But how, the argument runs, could Samson have waited for the Lord, when he took action in his own hands by pulling down the Philistine temple upon himself? The answer, the preacher suggests, must be in waiting for salvation beyond the grave.[82] Once more, the answer would seem to have followed the question rather than preceded it. Similarly, it seems to have been the puzzle of why Jacob should have buried his beloved Rachel by the roadside that led to her becoming the great intercessor for Israel that she still is (hundreds still visit her tomb daily at Bethlehem to seek her prayers), rather than a cult producing the retrospective explanation.[83]

At the other extreme, although there is much in *Leviticus Rabbah* that speaks of a profound concern for the holiness of the nation, the way in which it treats the dietary laws as symbolic of the ultimate fate of other nations (the pig, for example, is Rome) is hard not to read as narrowly vindictive, with the answers well set in advance.[84] But equally there is much in between. A good

[80] Gen. 23: 1–2. Sarah dies at age 127, which would make Isaac 37 at her death, since she gave birth to him when aged ninety (Gen. 17: 17).
[81] Saperstein, *Preaching*, 197.
[82] My expansion of the argument; for the denser original, Saperstein, *Preaching*, 189 ff., for a different version of the connection, Genesis Rabbah 99.11.
[83] Gen. 48: 7; Jer. 31: 15; Genesis Rabbah 82.10; Saperstein, *Preaching*, 145–6.
[84] For some relevant extracts, cf. Neusner, *Classics*, 243–55.

example is the continual wrestling that takes place over theodicy.
At its simplest, we find Job's guilt or Joseph's arrogance reasserted,
while more complex theories include a delayed theory of punishment, as in the trials of Joseph's brothers in Egypt long after they
have mistreated him, and a typological reading of the patriarchs in
which they are seen as anticipating Israel's sufferings and thus as
declaring what is really important.[85]
Most of our examples hitherto have been drawn from the
midrashic commentaries which were written between AD 200 and
600, or from medieval sermons, inspired by them. But just before
we pass to consideration of halakhah (law), it is worth observing
that the definitive work on oral Jewish Law, the Babylonian
Talmud (*c.* 600), according to some estimates, is of its enormous
length one quarter haggadah.[86] It is to such haggadah that the
French philosopher, Emmanuel Levinas, has been attracted.[87] His
meditations are full of deep spiritual insights (sometimes his own,
sometimes the text's), but for our purposes here the point to note
is that such insights can sometimes happen even where the answer
seems to have preceded the question! So, for example, the meaning of 1 Samuel 2: 25 is emended by the Talmud to deny that
God's grace is sufficient of itself to effect human reconciliation; a
concrete expression of apology is required, even if it is only an
appropriate debt of words.[88] Levinas comments: 'one cannot be
less attached to the letter and more enamoured of the spirit!'[89]
One might of course disagree with the conclusions drawn in the
particular case, but the possibility it opens up is surely clear: that it
is not only when the interpretation is a response to a question that
revelation might be said to occur, but sometimes also when an
existing assumption (in this case from the second century
Mishnah) is brought into creative tension with the earlier biblical
canon, and its content thereby deepened.
To think of God speaking to the Jewish people through such
methods of exegesis is thus much less absurd than it might initially

[85] Saperstein, *Preaching*, 173–6, 133–4, 169 and 172, 242 ff.
[86] Two and a half million words; so A. Steinsalz, *The Essential Talmud*
(Northvale, New Jersey: Jason Aronson, 1992), 74; cf. 251.
[87] E. Levinas, *Nine Talmudic Readings* (Bloomington: Indiana University
Press, 1990), xxix.
[88] Ibid., 12–29, esp. 18–21; this is seen as an extension of the meaning of
Prov. 6: 1–3.   [89] Ibid., 19.

appear. The approach was premised on a very close reading of the original text, itself premised on the religious assumption that in a text of such importance God would speak in the interstices no less than on the surface. The result is that its suggestions can by no means always be summarily dismissed as merely the arbitrary imposition of a meaning that had already been decided. Yet, even where this was the case, the capacity was still there to generate new insights as past text and present expectations were brought into creative and fruitful tension with one another.

Halakhah and unfolding law   One of the great puzzles of Jewish history is the surprising contrast that appears to exist between the two great Law collections, Mishnah and Talmud. For whatever reason, the former is sparing in its quotation of biblical precedents to justify its own legislation, whereas the scholars of the Talmud see one of their principal tasks to be the reintegration of the two types of law.[90] One explanation has it that the Mishnah had its origins in hostility to Christianity: the existence of an independent oral tradition was therefore intended as a powerful means of asserting that the new faith could not plausibly claim to have inherited the full Jewish tradition, despite its obvious proprietary claim in its use of the term 'Old Testament'.[91] However, this kind of explanation has been challenged by numerous scholars, and indeed it does seem implausible.[92] A continuous process of development of Law can be detected, even within Scripture itself, and while the degree of interrelation between the two types of Law (oral and written) continues to remain a serious source of dispute, there is much evidence to the contrary (even from within the New Testament itself) to suggest that it did not need the destruction of Jerusalem and the growth of Christianity to require the acceptance of even further additions as also authoritative.

The growth of Law as response to questions can be illustrated

[90] A polemic against the Mishnah's non-biblical classifications had already begun in the third century; for examples, cf. Sifra and Sifré to Numbers in Neusner, *Classics of Judaism*, 127–49.

[91] J. Neusner, *Judaism in the Matrix of Christianity* (Philadelphia: Fortress Press, 1986), esp. 120–3.

[92] For a brief resumé of the arguments against, Maccoby, *Writings*, 12–14, though he seems to me to go too far in also claiming total subordination in the Mishnah itself, 27–9.

from Scripture itself. The Ten Commandments forbid work on the Sabbath, but leave open what precisely should be understood by work. The allusions to lighting fires and gathering food later in Exodus itself look like later explanatory expansions (Exod. 20: 18–21; 35: 1–3; 16: 4–27), but, whether so or not, we can certainly see the process at work elsewhere within the canon. Thus Jeremiah seems consciously to rewrite the Deuteronomic version of the prohibition to exclude any form of commerce, while the Septuagint, in order to close a possible loophole, adds a clause prohibiting travel out of Jerusalem as much as towards the city (Jer. 17: 21–22; cf. Deut. 5: 12–14). By the time of the Talmud thirty-nine basic creative labours have been distinguished, all of which were prohibited, to match the divine cessation from creativity on the seventh day. Significantly, in consequence no condemnation attaches to unintentional creativity, nor to purely destructive action, provided it has no further purpose, as, for example, pulling down a building to make way for a new one.[93]

Christians are too quick to see such developments as no more than the growth of legalism. The real heart of Sabbath legislation has been described as *imitatio Dei*, while the insistence upon three meals as part of *Oneg Shabbat* ('Sabbath delight') indicates its essentially celebratory character.[94] Christians tend to forget that when the Law is fully accepted as a framework for life and internalized as no mere external, burdensome imposition, it can be truly liberating. The difference in attitude can already be seen in Scripture (e.g. Pss. 19: 7–8; 119 *passim*). It is still more evident in Targum Neofiti's treatment of the Tree of Life in Genesis as itself the Law,[95] or the elaboration of the *Song of Songs Rabbah* into a love affair between God and Israel in which the Law is what gives Israel her comeliness.[96] To such positive qualities must also be added the way in which Law functioned as the means of securing Israel's survival over the centuries, for without Law and the distinctiveness which it maintained it is debatable whether communal identity would have survived the numerous shocks to which it was subject over more than two millennia. Indeed, given the heavy

93   Steinsalz, *Essential Talmud*, 108–15.
94   Ibid., 108, 112; cf. Maccoby, *Writings*, 65.
95   Quoted in P. Grelot, *Targums*, 21.
96   Neusner, *Classics of Judaism*, 383–401, esp. 397, 399.

contemporary inroads that secularism has wrought (even within Israel's borders three-quarters of its Jews are secular), some would argue that there remains an equally strong need for its preservation today. That is not a debate into which a Christian can reasonably enter. What, however, needs to be stressed is that there is no necessary incompatibility between Christians endorsing their own tradition and at the same time viewing the development of the Jewish tradition in this way as also part of divine providence and revelation. The Jewish ideal has never been that the same pattern of Law should also be followed by other nations,[97] while that there be a community witnessing to the positive value of Law provides a useful corrective to antinomian tendencies within Christianity, often themselves claiming explicit support from the Pauline epistles.

That there was growth and development in the halakhic, as much as the haggadic tradition, is beyond doubt. As with Christianity, however, such growth has not always been acknowledged. Instead, it has been projected back to a more authoritative, original source. In the Jewish case this has been seen as a chain of transmission going back to Moses himself, a position that one finds in Tractate Aboth in the Mishnah. The passage opens with the declaration that 'Moses received the Law from Sinai and committed it to Joshua, and Joshua to the elders, and the elders to the Prophets, and the Prophets committed it to the men of the Great Synagogue' and thereafter follows a long list of *aboth* ('fathers') who lived between 300 BC and AD 200, interspersed by sayings in praise of the Law attributed to them.[98] Such backward projection has not been without its inevitable penalties. Consider the case of marriage. On the one hand, we find the presumption that the patriarchs must themselves have been monogamous, since that is where the present tradition now stands;[99] on the other, when development is recognized, the temptation is to regress, and suppose that, if the Torah endorses polygamy, it thereby enshrines

---

[97] They are required simply to follow natural revelation as this expresses itself in the so-called Noahide laws; cf. D. Novak, *The Image of the Non-Jew in Judaism: An Historical and Constructive Study of the Noahide Laws* (New York: E. Mellon Press, 1983).

[98] H. Danby trans., *The Mishnah* (Oxford: Oxford University Press, 1933), 446–58; the final section is a later addition.

[99] For a sixteenth-century example, Saperstein, *Preaching*, 247.

an eternal value for relations between the sexes.[100] Yet there are also more hopeful signs as contemporary Judaism wrestles with the question of change. Because Reform Judaism has moved so decisively away from Law and towards the prophetic tradition, some of the more interesting comments emerge from within the Orthodox community or those sympathetic to it. David Halivni tries to reconcile the obvious conflicts which modern scholarship has brought to light between *peshat* (plain meaning) and *derash* (derived or applied meaning) by suggesting that *derash* restores the original meaning of what had become a corrupt text.[101] While the notion itself may not be very plausible, the wider framework in which he sets this view does carry with it considerable potential.

Rejecting the maximalist view of the oral Torah according to which all was revealed at Sinai, he suggests that God performed an act of 'withdrawal' (*Tzimtzum*), in order to allow the community of faith to exercise their freedom within the framework of the Sinai revelation, and unfortunately that meant that the community had to face the consequences of its own sins, with the Torah 'exposed to human frailties and constraints' and 'man's corruptive capacities'.[102] The result was that it was only properly appropriated in the time of Ezra and even then difficulties required further explication through *derash*.[103] In that development, the recording of two opposing opinions, he maintains, needs to be taken seriously: though the majority was to prevail, the minority was also part of the creative process.[104] Ironically, though, the text used by the rabbis to justify the rule of the majority has as its *peshat* exactly the opposite meaning in its original context.[105] The extent of human freedom is often illustrated by the story of the way in which even God allowed himself to be overruled when in the minority,[106] but for Halivni the most important reason for preserving the minority view is that one day it may prevail, and be

[100] Cf. Steinsalz, *Essential Talmud*, 133.
[101] D. W. Halivni, *Peshat and Derash* (New York: Oxford University Press, 1991), 126–53, esp. 132–3, 138.
[102] Ibid., 150; for the argument in general, 112 ff.
[103] Because Israel sinned so grievously during the early period, this 'strips the First Temple period of normative halakhic authority'; ibid., 148.
[104] For a similar view in Steinsalz, *Essential Talmud*, cf. 6–7.
[105] Ibid., 104–5; the verse in question is Exod. 23: 2.
[106] For Halivni's own interpretation, *Peshat and Derash*, 108–9, 118.

proved right.[107] Although he wants the security of a fixed, authoritative *derash* in the present (unsurprising in a community based on law), what is particularly encouraging in Halivni's analysis is his full acceptance of the necessity to tell a story of his own tradition that takes three key elements with equal seriousness: the divine initiative, communal shaping, and human fallibility. Michael Fishbane's comment on the Jewish tradition in general is apposite: 'The well-known Talmudic image of God studying and interpreting his own Torah is nothing if not that tradition's realisation that there is no authoritative teaching which is not also the source of its own renewal.'[108]

Kabbalah and interdependence   Though Jewish mysticism is now known to have had a long history in its two main forms, *Ma'aseb Bereshit* (Act of Creation) and *Ma'aseb Merkavah* (Divine Chariot), it was really only with its classic work of the thirteenth century, the *Zohar*, that its own distinctive form of exegesis emerged in any detail. Thanks to the Lurianic movement of the sixteenth century and the Hasidic of the eighteenth, within both of which the *Zohar* acquired something approaching canonical status, some of its theological assumptions were to spread deeply within Judaism as a whole, even where its basic methodology continued to be regarded with suspicion.[109] Kabbalah literally means 'tradition' and, as if to reinforce this fact, the *Zohar* is portrayed as coming as a revelation from Elijah to a second-century rabbi Shim'on.[110] In actual fact, it may be seen as an attempt to revitalize Judaism in reaction to what was seen as the excessive rationalism which philosophy had introduced, through searching for a reasoned justification for all Israel's laws.[111] Yet philosophy's search for reasons is not abandoned. Instead, in their place comes a type which it is

---

[107]   Ibid., 120–1.

[108]   M. Fishbane, *The Garments of Torah* (Bloomington: Indiana University Press, 1992), 3.

[109]   Most obviously in the acceptance of mysticism as a legitimate element within Judaism.

[110]   *Zohar* 1.1b–2a; 3.221a; 231a. Contemporary revelations through Elijah were also claimed: G. Scholem, *Origins of the Kabbalah* (Princeton, NJ: Princeton University Press, 1987), 35–9.

[111]   Seen as early as Philo: e.g. *Letter of Aristeas* 142–7. Maimonides (d. 1204) is the obvious medieval contrast.

held will deepen a sense of intimacy with God. A good example of this is the two approaches' different attitude to sacrifice. Whereas for the philosopher it is an expedient to avoid worse, for the kabbalist it becomes a means of more intimate communion with God.[112] The latter interpretation is partly argued on the basis of the alleged root meaning of the Hebrew word.[113]

The kabbalah's major theme of the *Sefiroth* or emanations from God and our part in identifying with them is equally derived from a close reading of Genesis' opening verses, with, for instance, the Hebrew order in the opening verse used to argue for the emergence of the God of revelation from an unknowable Ground.[114] So far does this depart from the conventional interpretation, it is easy to think of any further developments as nothing but an alien, external imposition, but there is another way to look at matters. Much would seem to depend on what parts of Scripture should act as interpretative controls on others. The Deuteronomic injunction to cleave to God had been downplayed in subsequent Judaism,[115] whereas for kabbalah the possibility of intimacy with God of which it seemed to speak became central. Creation had therefore to become a sharing of the divine nature rather than a *creatio ex nihilo*. Similarly, for the Lurianic version the divine work of creation had to speak of God's own participation in the deep sense of exile experienced by Jews of the time, and so also involve even God in some sort of *Tzimtzum* and need for return.[116] Although, as with Christianity and other versions of Judaism, the pretence is still made of claiming early roots for these ideas, such

---

[112]   The contrast is explored by D. C. Matt, 'The mystic and the mizvot' in A. Green (ed.), *Jewish Spirituality* (London: SCM Press, 1985) I, 367–404, esp. 370–2, 380–5. Maimonides had suggested that it was a way of avoiding idolatry.

[113]   In the twelfth-century *Bahir* (109) *qorban* is derived form *meqarev*: 'draw near'.

[114]   The Hebrew order translates literally as 'in the beginning created God', with 'God' as apparent object.

[115]   In the *Talmud* (b. Ket. 111b; b. Sot. 14a) Deut. 4: 24 ('The Lord thy God is a consuming fire': AV) is used to argue against the author's frequent apparent references elsewhere to the possibility of real intimacy with God: Deut. 10: 20; 11: 22; 13: 5; 30: 20.

[116]   Well argued for by G. G. Scholem in his essay 'Kabbalah and myth' in his book *On the Kabbalah and its Symbolism* (London: Routledge & Kegan Paul, 1965), 87–117, esp. 100 ff. Luria's version is seen as a reaction to the expulsion of Jews from Spain (110).

developments do provide once more a good illustration of how tradition, far from being reactionary, is instead best characterized as thoroughly innovative, as it attempts through rereading of its classic texts to give them new life.

To what extent the concept on which kabbalah places so much reliance, that of divine emanation, ultimately derived from some version of Gnosticism need not concern us here. That, while striving to remain loyal to Judaism, it did exhibit an openness to the ideas of other religions, cannot be denied. A rather startling example is the way in which the possibility of reincarnation is opened up through the notion of levirate marriage.[117] What kabbalah also well illustrates is how false it is to suppose that once Christianity and Judaism had gone their separate ways there was little constructive interaction thereafter. On the contrary, kabbalah was to exercise a major influence on Christian thought in the fifteenth and sixteenth centuries in the writings of Reuchlin and Paracelsus among others,[118] while its influence on Jacob Boehme (largely mediated through Paracelsus) means that we can trace its continuing influence upon Christianity into the eighteenth century with William Law and John Wesley. But the influence was by no means one way. Later parts of the *Zohar* identify four senses to Scripture through the mnemonic *Pardes* (Paradise); added to the two mentioned above, *Peshat* and *Derash*, comes *Remez* (allusions) and *Sod* (a secret sense). Though formally they seem different from the traditional four senses within Christianity, in actual practice they work out very similarly, and many scholars postulate a direct influence from Christianity.

Nor is kabbalah by any means the only instance where such cross-fertilization can be observed. One Jewish rabbi has recently devoted a whole book to illustrations of the influence of the newer faith upon the older. As Michael Hilton observes, 'it is hardly surprising that Jewish communities living for centuries in Christian society should be influenced by the surrounding culture'.[119] The examples he offers,

---

[117] *Zohar* 3.215b. The widow by marrying the brother is held to allow for the possibility of the dead husband being reincarnated in the child of the new union.

[118] Reuchlin showed himself particularly open and sympathetic in his *De arte cabalistica* of 1517: *On the Art of the Kabbalah* (Lincoln: University of Nebraska Press, 1983).

[119] M. Hilton, *The Christian Effect on Jewish Life* (London: SCM Press, 1994), 2.

too numerous even to summarize here, range from the modern modelling of Chanukkah on Christmas to the medieval borrowing of Psalm 23 for funerals.[120] One irony of history is that it is only thanks to the early Church and not Jewish tradition that there survives the most ancient reference to Chanukkah that we possess (in 2 Macc. 10: 1–8). But of more general importance is the corrective given to the still widely prevalent assumption regarding the beginnings of the relations between the two faiths: that anything significant in common during this period must first have occurred in Judaism, even if our only evidence for the Jewish version comes much later than the Christian. Hyam Maccoby's commentary on *Early Rabbinic Writings* is a case in point. Despite the fact that he is dealing with Jewish writings later than AD 200, his natural tendency (found also in many Christian scholars, though for rather different reasons) is to assume a common Jewish source when parallels exist with the New Testament rather than any influence from Christianity itself. So, for instance, of a declaration found in a third-century midrash that 'to you the sabbath is handed over, but you are not handed over to the sabbath', he comments that the likelihood is that both it and Jesus' similar remark derive from a common Pharisaic tradition.[121] While this is possible, as Hilton observes,[122] it is just as likely that Jesus was responsible for it entering into the general Jewish stream of consciousness, though of course without any explicit acknowledgement.

Inevitably, given Christian treatment of Jews, reaction on the Jewish side was often purely negative, particularly in its treatment of disputed passages from the Hebrew Bible,[123] but with that could also go positive attempts at 'improvements' to counter the rival faith's claims, ranging from a new centrality for messianic expectations to the 'churching' of women.[124] Medieval preachers could even use explicitly Christian stories in their sermons without embarrassment.[125] None of this is noted to demote the worth or significance of Judaism. Rather, my point is that the more we acknowledge our interdependence, the more possible does it become to learn from

[120] M. Hilton, *The Christian Effect on Jewish Life*, 15–23, 172.
[121] Maccoby, *Writings*, 170; Mark 2: 27. The midrash is Mekilta.
[122] Hilton, *Christian Effect*, 208–9.
[123] For examples, ibid., 93, 99–100, 105–6, 110, 126.
[124] Ibid., 63–84, 163.   [125] Saperstein, *Preaching*, 97–9.

each other's traditions and admit their revelatory quality without feeling that we are thereby being disloyal to our own. To give one last example, whereas Maccoby merely excludes Paul's use of Deuteronomy's 'cursed be everyone who hangs on a tree' from any conceivable foundation in the Jewish tradition, another Jewish scholar, Michael Fishbane, not only acknowledges it as one possibility but also, more importantly, identifies a traditional reading which could be regarded as more profound by both religions: one in which the 'curse' becomes the 'pain' of God.[126] This is by no means to suggest that all disputes across religious frontiers are easy of resolution, but it is to claim that taking seriously the location of us all within particular, developing traditions releases us from supposing that all apparent contradiction is necessarily deep seated.

Islam: sunna, *Qur'an and Hadith*

Initially, Islam might seem not a very profitable object of study for any one wishing to reflect on the notion of creative tradition, still less so for a Christian for whom the definitive revelation came prior to the inauguration of Islam. But, as I have already tried to indicate with Judaism, even what comes later than Christ in another religion can still illuminate and inform one's own. More problematic, rather, is the present lack within Islam of much internal serious critical study of its own origins. Though in an earlier generation the writings of Muhammad Abduh in Egypt and Sir Muhammad Iqbal in India did represent serious attempts to wrestle with the possibility of change in the modern world, they did not attempt a historical critique as such.[127] More recently one might point to the work of Fazlur Rahman[128] or, among Shi'is,

---

[126] H. Maccoby, *Writings*, 195–7; M. Fishbane, *Garments*, 29–30; Deut. 21: 23; Gal. 3: 13.

[127] M. Iqbal, *The Reconstruction of Religious Thought in Islam* (2nd edn., London: Oxford University Press, 1934; repr. Lahore: M. Ashraf, 1982); for a critical assessment of both Abduh and Iqbal, H. A. R. Gibb, *Modern Trends in Islam* (Chicago: University of Chicago Press, 1947).

[128] F. Rahman (1919–88). In *Islam and Modernity: Transformation of an Intellectual System* (Chicago: University of Chicago Press, 1984) he argues for the need to distinguish Quranic principles from their application in specific historical settings. In *Major Themes of the Qur'an* (Minneapolis: Bibliotheca Islamica, 2nd edn., 1989), this leads him to deny the universal applicability of the prohibition of usury, and to insist on the moral superiority of monogamy (41, 47–8).

Sayyid Hossein Modaressi Tabataba'i.[129] Significant too is the
work of the French Muslim, Mohammed Arkoun.[130] Even so, the
overwhelming tendency remains to see the raising of any such
questions as alien impositions from Western culture. The result is
that in terms of its own self-perception Islam in general does not
regard itself as at all facing the same kind of issues as confront the
two older faiths. Its situation is thus in many ways most analogous
to religious attitudes prior to the Enlightenment. For those
Christians who believe that Christianity itself ought to return to
pre-Enlightenment values, this at least gives some grounds for
sympathetic consideration. Our argument, though, in our first
chapter was that any straightforward return was impossible. What
I want therefore to do here is investigate an alternative strategy,
and note what resources Islam might draw upon, should attitudes
eventually change.

The interest such an investigation holds for the argument of the
book as a whole is that Islam in fact already has built into its structures various formal distinctions and techniques of analysis which,
when Christianity faced similar issues, were either lacking or much
less explicit. So from a Christian perspective there is the possibility of learning, even if for the moment Muslims themselves would
in the great mass reject the precise applications to which we are
about to put those principles. Admittedly, this is hardly the easiest
or most respectful form of dialogue, since our discussion is not
premised on where Muslims now believe themselves to be. On
the other hand, precisely because most Western scholarship fails to
provide any alternative religious frame of reference, its conclusions
would be found even more alien. The advantage in what follows
is thus that an analysis is offered which would allow Islam at least
in principle to continue to claim greater fullness for its revelation
than what exists through Christianity even while accepting the

---

[129] *An Introduction to Shi'i Law: a bibliographical study* (London: Ithaca Press,
1984). The work shows how the present legal system of Shi'i *fiqh* has developed
and been in due course reformed and elaborated. Modaressi should not be
confused with another much more conservative Shi'i of similar name, A. S. M. H.
Tabataba'i whose works include *The Qur'an in Islam* (London: Zahra Publ.,
1987).
[130] M. Arkoun, *Lectures du Coran* (Paris: Maisonneuve & Larose, 1982). A
direct parallel is drawn with the difficulties faced by Christianity and Judaism:
e.g. 2.

implications of historical criticism and contingency. Inevitably, as a Christian I do not as a matter of fact accept such greater fullness, but, as will become obvious, this by no means precludes the possibility of the Christian learning from Islam. I shall indicate how, both in respect of general principles of development as well as some specific instances. Our attention to begin with will focus on Islam's own perception of change in the modern world and in particular how this affects the key concept of *sunna* or 'tradition'. Thereafter I shall consider how the already existing notions of *naskh* or abrogation as applied to the Qur'an and *isnad* or chain of authorities as applied to the oral traditions of the Hadith might be expanded and developed to admit critical investigation of the early period without this necessarily undermining Islam's claims as such.

Sunna, ijma and qiyas   The name by which the great majority of Muslims in the world today are known, Sunnis, derives from the Arabic word for tradition or custom, *sunna*. Sunna had already a clear role prior to the coming of Muhammad, with the tribes of the Arabian peninsula priding themselves on the custom of their ancestors. The Qur'an, however, speaks of the unchanging *sunna* of Allah, and contrasts this with the practice of the Meccans in clinging to the *sunna* of their fathers.[131] Eventually, however, partly under the influence of the jurist al-Shafi'i (d. 820), the term came to be seen as the essential complement to the Qur'an and identified with what could be modelled on the teaching or practice of Muhammad himself, as represented in Qur'an or Hadith, or through principles derived from that conduct.[132] Much of the *sunna* thus established is formally enshrined in the *shari'a* or 'law'. That must not, however, be too narrowly conceived. As for Judaism, so also for Islam, law is more a way of life rather than the minimum necessary to ensure the flourishing of the State. Indeed for the Muslim, State and religion are almost inseparable, and so *shari'a* assumes a much larger importance than it could ever have for the Christian. Muslim means someone who has 'surrendered' or submitted in obedience to God's will, and this is expressed

[131] H. A. R. Gibb, *Muhammadism* (Oxford: Oxford University Press, 1954), 73.

[132] For the key role of al-Shafi'i, N. J. Coulson, *A History of Islamic Law* (Edinburgh: Edinburgh University Press, 1964), 53–61.

through the *shari'a*, which embodies both Qur'an and *sunna*, alike seen as divinely inspired.

Once viewed in this way as a holistic system, it was almost inevitable that innovation or change would come to be seen as necessarily a bad thing, since it was most naturally read as a turning way from the eternal will of God and so as incompatible with submission. The result was what not a few commentators have described as centuries of stagnation, before the challenges thrown up by the impact of the modern world forced fresh reflection.[133] That reflection was not, however, entirely bereft of help from past principles. Two in particular may be noted: argument from analogy (*qiyas*) and appeal to consensus (*ijma*). A trivial example may be used to illustrate both. When coffee was first introduced, it was argued that as a drug it should be treated like alcohol and so banned, but because the general mind thought otherwise a different view was eventually taken. Consensus in this case thus overruled what in theory had been deduced by analogy.[134] Lack of analogy can also be used as an argument for change. A case in point was the Tunisian prohibition of polygamy in 1957, where the justification given was the impracticality of treating all wives equally, as the Qur'an had required if polygamy was to be practised.[135] Again, precisely because the four major schools of law are not thought to be in serious disagreement and thus in some sense already to exhibit consensus, this has been used in modern times to legitimate a certain policy of pick and choose between them.[136] Thus, while it is true that the notion of an eternal deposit continues to be the dominant view, even among the most conservative this is receiving some modification, as new circumstances in the modern world are seen as necessitating fresh applications of analogy. More difficult is any suggestion that this might represent a real growth in understanding of the significance of the original revelation. It is that alternative analysis which I want to consider as we turn back in history to consider the origins of Islam.

---

[133]   E.g. Coulson talks of 'rigor mortis'. Gibb, while noting the common view, also points to continuing signs of vitality: *Modern Trends*, 1–2.

[134]   This seventeenth-century argument is noted in Gibb, ibid., 11.

[135]   In effect, the acceptance of Muhammad Abduh's arguments of fifty years earlier; for this and related arguments, Coulson, *Islamic Law*, 207–15, esp. 210.

[136]   Used in twentieth-century legislation as a means of improving the lot of women: Coulson, *Islamic Law*, 182–91.

Qur'an and naskh   With the Hebrew Scriptures developing through numerous authors across a millennium, and Christianity adding a century more, the contrast with the Qur'an could scarcely seem more marked, with Muhammad its single human recipient and its entirety revealed within a mere twenty-three years. Then to this one must add that, unlike the Bible for modern Christianity, the Qur'an is seen as perfect in every way and indeed formally spoken of as eternal and uncreated.[137] Yet such apparent simplicity is complicated by a number of factors, not least by the fact that it was left to others to gather these separate revelations into a single book. Some non-Muslim scholars envisage this having been done relatively quickly within about eighteen years after Muhammad's death, in AD 650 under the caliph Uthman, while others postulate a gradual process, perhaps even only reaching completion a couple of centuries later.[138] In support of such a lengthy development, not only are negative arguments employed (the absence of sufficiently clear, external attestation), but also appeal made to the type of material within the Qur'an itself: the frequency of formulae suggesting a pattern of oral transmission, the presence of doublets and internal contradictions.[139] However, it is the last (internal contradictions) that is of most interest in comparing the faiths on the subject of revelation as a developing tradition, since this is an issue (and strategy of interpretation) that has been extensively discussed within Islam itself.

While by no means all resolution was supposed to proceed in this way, a significant role was assigned to the phenomenon known as *naskh* (abrogation). Admittedly, in modern times some Muslim scholars have denied its legitimacy,[140] but this remains

---

[137] A view made explicit in the ninth century in response to the rationalism of the Mu'tazilites who insisted upon speaking of a created Qur'an.

[138] For former view, W. M. Watt, *Companion to the Qur'an* (Oxford: Oneworld Publications, 1994), 9; for the latter, more controversial approach, J. Wansbrough, *Quranic Studies* (Oxford: Oxford University Press, 1967), esp. 44–52. Yet more hostile to Muslim claims is P. Crone and M. Cook, *Hagarism* (Cambridge: Cambridge University Press, 1977). They postulate, on what seems to me insubstantial evidence, the origins of the Qur'an in the forging of an identity distinctive from Judaism among Arab immigrants to Palestine: esp. 3–20.

[139] For a clear setting out of the parallels and relations between three passages that repeat essentially the same material, Wansbrough, *Studies*, 21–3.

[140] For typical arguments for such rejection, though coming from a member of a heterodox sect, the Ahmadiyyah, M. M. Ali, *The Religion of Islam* (Columbus, Ohio: Ahmadiyya Anjuman Isha'at Islam, 6th edn., 1990), 28–36.

very much the exception, and in any case its use would seem supported by two verses within the Qur'an itself.[141] The notion became firmly rooted at an early stage for application to both Qur'an and Hadith: by the eleventh century as many as 248 Qur'anic verses were identified as abrogated.[142] A particularly good example of progressive abrogation is the Qur'an's attitude to wine. It moves from viewing it as a mixed blessing, to forbidding the intoxicated from prayer, to, finally, calling drink an 'abomination' as bad as idol worship.[143] The praise of *sakar* at 16.67 is more problematic. One Muslim translator of the Qur'an suggests that it should be taken as 'wholesome drink': 'non-alcoholic drinks ... from the grape ... If *sakar* must be taken in the sense of fermented wine, it refers to the time before intoxicants were prohibited: this is a Meccan Sura and the prohibition came in Medina.'[144] Abrogation was possible thus not only because of the order in which the text was arranged, but also because of the presumed order in which the revelations were received. The verse for which the largest number of abrogations is claimed is the so-called sword verse.[145] It has been held to rescind no less than one hundred and twenty-four other verses which, unlike it, advocate less than an all-out assault on non-believers, though even it in turn is modified by the clause which follows with its requirement for a more lenient policy if repentance is shown.

From a non-Muslim point of view, undoubtedly the best-known case of abrogation concerns the verse which the early Islamic historians, al-Waqidi and al-Tabari, tell us once occurred at 53.19; speaking of three Arabian goddesses, Muhammad declared that 'these are the exalted ones, whose intercession is to be hoped for', only to have his words abrogated later by 22.52:

---

[141] Sura 2.106 and 16.101. Those who deny the need for *naskh* interpret the two verses as rescinding earlier Jewish revelation.

[142] D. S. Powers, 'The exegetical genre *nasikh al-Qur'an wa mansukhuhu*' in A. Rippin (ed.), *Approaches to the History of Interpretation of the Qur'an* (Oxford: Clarendon Press, 1988) 117–38, esp. 122.

[143] Contrast 2.219; 4.43; 5.90.

[144] A. Y. Ali, *The Holy Qur'an* (Leicester: Islamic Foundation, 1975), 673, esp. n. 2096.

[145] Sura 9.5. The most common view is given in the text. Some jurists, though, increase the number of abrogations to 140, while a few question whether *naskh* is even appropriately applied to the verse.

'God will cancel anything vain that Satan throws in'; hence the title of the deleted line, 'the Satanic verses'. From the perspective of the orthodox Islam of today, however, this would not be seen as a legitimate instance of *naskh*, since the view would be taken that the verses could never have formed a true part of the perfect revelation that is the Qur'an.[146] This was one of the many reasons which made Salman Rushdie's novel of the same name so shocking. Though Christian polemic has made much of these verses in the past, there is no reason, however, why their presumed existence, if genuine, should not be treated sympathetically, either as part of Muhammad's growing consciousness of his vocation or as a satirical way of making his audience more aware of new possibilities.[147]

Both explanations, however, would be equally unacceptable to contemporary Muslim opinion, so deeply ingrained are claims to complete perfection for the Qur'an and its Messenger. For *naskh* is not seen as representing any change of mind on the part of Muhammad, far less that of God. Instead, it is a matter of 'ever-changing circumstances' over the twenty-three years of Muhammad's ministry, and some of what he said being of a more 'temporary or limited nature'.[148] Nevertheless, for so long as some notion of abrogation is acceptable, there would seem to be a powerful tool already within Islam for coming to terms with critical scholarship in a way that need not prejudice its fundamental claims. For it offers the possibility of continuing to speak of the perfection of the final product (whether of book or prophet), even while development over the course of Muhammad's ministry is accepted. *Naskh* would then be the way of determining that final result. Certainly, it is possible to view Muhammad as himself growing within a tradition, since Muslim commentators themselves acknowledge Muhammad's debt to prior Jewish and Christian tradition. For instance, the influential Pakistani

---

[146] Many Western scholars would also accept that they were 'later forgeries': e.g, I. R. Netton, *A Popular Dictionary of Islam* (Richmond, Surrey: Curzon Press, 1992), 226.

[147] For the latter, cf. K. Cragg, *The Event of the Qur'an* (Oxford: Oneworld Publications, 1994), 139–46. If so, the satire has a gentle edge that his modern detractor altogether lacks: S. Rushdie, *The Satanic Verses* (Harmondsworth: Penguin, 1988).

[148] A. S. M. H. Tabataba'i, *Qur'an in Islam*, 45.

commentator, A. Mawdudi (d. 1979) quotes from the Bible on numerous occasions, sometimes even whole chapters. In the case of John the Baptist he explicitly admits that a more rounded portrait is possible only through detailed study of the Gospels as well as the Qur'an.[149] In fact, because of Muhammad's allusive style most of the stories to which he refers are difficult in themselves to comprehend without assuming further information from elsewhere. This is true even of the most sustained narrative in the Qur'an, the story of Joseph that occupies the whole of Sura 12. Thus, significantly, one modern English edition of the Qur'an speaks of the story being 'recapitulated rather than told' and adds; 'for the story it is necessary to set down a few more details.'[150] Most of these details are biblical, but occasionally Jewish tradition in the wider sense also helps.[151]

Yet one heavy qualification has to be entered. Though the fact of Muhammad standing within a tradition would be readily accepted, as would indeed the Jewish and Christian Scriptures as revelation, their texts would be regarded as highly defective, and so in desperate need of supplementation and correction from the Qur'an. The Jewish Scriptures are seen as often in need of moral improvement, while modern biblical criticism with its suggestion of alterations to earlier versions of the text, Old and New, is taken to imply a decline from pristine purity.[152] Yet the acceptance of such corruptions befalling earlier revelations does create a problem for the Muslim of how a consistent story can be told of God's action in the world: why should God preserve the purity of one of his revelations and no other? Very occasionally, we find this problem taken up by Muslim writers themselves, particularly those in the Shi'i tradition.[153] Normally, the authority of their first Iman or leader, Ali, is drawn from controversial interpretations of certain key verses, but others, such as Al-Kashani in eighteenth-century Iran, have argued that the absence of appropriate reference is to be

---

[149] So C. J. Adams, '*Abu'l-A'la Mawdudi's Tafhim al-Qur'an*', in A. Rippin (ed.), op. cit., 307–23, esp. 318.

[150] A. Y. Ali, *Holy Qur'an*, 548 and 550, n. 1632.

[151] e.g. cf. v. 24 and Genesis Rabbah 87.9; or v. 67 and the Jewish tradition of the evil eye; only the latter is mentioned by Ali, *Holy Qur'an*, 575, n. 1730.

[152] For an example of the argument, M. M. Ali, *Religion*, 159–62.

[153] Though the minority tradition in Islam as a whole (c. 10%), in some parts of the world, e.g. Iran, they constitute a decisive majority.

explained by verses being 'altered', 'changed', or 'deleted'.[154] Admittedly, such reasons have nothing to do with critical evaluation of the text, but that might one day come, as the conditioned character of all human thinking gains wider acceptance.

To apply that insight to growth in Muhammad's consciousness of his mission will not of course come easy, but the same is also true of what has happened in Christian thinking since the Enlightenment, and in that case there was the added problem that for Christ, unlike Muhammad, the perfection of divinity was claimed. Yet in some ways the problem runs still deeper for Islam, in that certain forms of relation between God and humanity are thought unbecoming, particularly divine exposure to human weakness. So, for instance, God is not thought to have abandoned the prophet Jesus to death on the cross,[155] while it is even sometimes argued that David as a prophet could not possibly have had adulterous relations with Bathsheba.[156] The difficulties in changing perspective must thus not be underestimated. Nor must the range of continuing disagreement with Christianity, even if such a change is eventually forthcoming. Even the most liberal of Christians is likely to balk at any claim for finality in Muhammad's message, though the verse which makes this claim could be regarded as simply placing him as last in a long line of prophets,[157] while in a number of places Muhammad himself appears to concede the equality of his own role with those who have gone before.[158] Also not to be forgotten is my underlying contention that, even while Islam continues to reject historical criticism, recognition of such a pattern of conditioned growth by the Christian in Islam no less than in his own faith allows, at least in principle, acceptance of the idea that God's revelatory action might also have been at work within the other faith as well. But before hazarding some examples, I want first to place Islam in the

[154] M. Ayoub, 'The speaking Qur'an and the silent Qur'an' in A. Rippin, *Approaches*, 177–98, esp. 190.

[155] Sura 4.157; for history of interpretation, N. Robinson, *Christ in Islam and Christianity* (Albany, New York: SUNY, 1991), 107–41.

[156] Gibb, *Modern Trends*, 73–4.

[157] Sura 33.40: he is called 'the Apostle of God and the Seal of the Prophets'.

[158] With Mohammad compared with Abraham, Moses, and Jesus, he is told, 'We make no difference between one and another of them': Sura 2.136; cf. 2.136; 2.285; though contrast 2.253.

fuller context of its revelatory claims and so mention also the phenomenon of Hadith.

Hadith, isnad and matn Naskh as it is employed today is by no means confined to verses within the Qur'an. It is applied equally to the oral traditions, believed to derive from Muhammad's Companions, that tell us more of the Prophet's actions and utterances. Known as Hadith ('news' or 'report'), these are available in six standard collections, the two best-known having been arranged by Al-Bukhari (d. 870) and Muslim (d. 875). Muslim was apparently the more cautious scholar, but Bukhari's collection continues to hold pre-eminent place. Nowadays for most Muslims Hadith are only allowed to correct Hadith, but this has not always been so, and the key role played by them is well illustrated by Ibn Qutayba (d. 889) who stated that 'the Hadith of the Prophet prevails over the Book and constitutes a commentary on it'.[159] The nature of the justification is well indicated by some words of the medieval philosopher and theologian, Al-Ghazali: 'Both are mediated by the Prophet. In each case the abrogator is God alone who indicates the abrogation by means of his Prophet … Thus none other but the Prophet is capable of manifesting; none other but God of initiating.'[160] Perhaps, however, the classical position is best expressed by al-Shafi'i who, while acknowledging the superiority of the Qur'an, nonetheless insisted that it could not contradict Hadith, correctly understood, since the latter were there to explicate the former.[161] Even so, occasional examples of Hadith apparently overriding the Qur'an are to be found to this day, such as the five set times for daily prayer.[162] The main point to note, however, is the motivation behind assigning them such importance, in the desire to have a detailed model in Muhammad's life to imitate. Ibn Hanbal (d. 855),

---

[159] Quoted in A. K. S. Lambton, *State and Government in Medieval Islam* (Oxford: Oxford University Press, 1981), 7.

[160] Quoted in F. E. Peters, *A Reader in Classical Islam* (Princeton, NJ: Princeton University Press, 1994), 245.

[161] Coulson, *Islamic Law*, 56–8.

[162] The Qur'an refers to only three daily prayers: 24.58; 11.116. But another way of reading the evidence would be to say that a supplement is provided to the Qur'an rather than a corrective, with Hadith 'concretising some rather fluid and fluctuating Qur'anic references': the interpretation offered by I. R. Netton in some personal correspondence.

editor of one collection of Hadith and defender under persecution of the uncreated character of the Qur'an, is alleged never to have eaten watermelon, because he could find no record of the Prophet having done so. The instance is extreme, but underlines how deep seated is their role in providing a comprehensive guide to living. All Muslims accept that some Hadith are spurious, and enormous effort has been expended in trying to determine which. At the same time it is contested whether Bukhari was really faced with choosing his four thousand out of a total of six hundred thousand then existing; it is suggested that this is rather to be explained by multiple attestation.[163] In terms of their historical plausibility, non-Muslim scholars have varied from the thoroughly sceptical to the moderately sympathetic.[164] Some were probably invented for political reasons.[165] Muslim commentators themselves identify two key elements in determining the genuineness of any particular tradition, *isnad*, the chain of authorities, and *matn*, the content. The latter includes not only compatibility with the Qur'an but also detection of invention motivated by factors such as pride in one's local town, personal advancement, or the ascription of general wisdom to the Prophet.[166] But most stress has been placed on *isnad*. Here numerous tests have been employed in the attempt to identify those whose reports can be relied upon.[167] Not only the

---

[163] Contrast A. Guillaume, *The Traditions of Islam* (Oxford: Clarendon Press, 1924), 29; S. H. A. Ghaffer, *Criticism of Hadith among Muslims* (London: Ta-Ha Publishers, 1986), 24.

[164] I. Goldziher, *Muhammedanische Studien* (Halle, 1892) also available in *Gesammelte Schriften*, 1–2 (Hildesheim: Georgorius Verlagsbuchhandlung, 1968) for long remained the definitive study, as is witnessed by its translation into French as late as 1952. It has now been largely superseded by the work of J. Schacht, *The Origins of Muhammadan Jurisprudence* (Oxford: Oxford University Press, 1950). Though advocating instead 'healthy caution rather than outright scepticism', Schacht is found 'unassailably scientific and sound in method' by Fazlur Rahman: *Islam* (Chicago: University of Chicago Press, 2nd edn., 1979), 44–9. For a more hostile critique by another Muslim, M. M. Al-Azami, *On Schacht's Origins of Muhammadan Jurisprudence* (New York: John Wiley, 1985); for a sympathetic approach from a non-Muslim, F. Sezgin, *Geschichte des arabischen Schrifttums* (Leiden: E. J. Brill, 1967–86), esp. vol. 1.

[165] By the Umayyads of Damascus to bolster the status of Jerusalem as compared with Mecca and Medina when these were lost; by the Abbasids of Baghdad to argue for the legitimacy of their hereditary kingship. So Guillaume, *Tradition*, 37–76.   [166] For a list, Ghaffer, *Criticism*, 31–46.

[167] Ghaffer, *Criticism*, 59–108, *passim*.

existence of a chain is seen as relevant but its quality, that there should be no links consisting of those known to have been dishonest under other circumstances.

There is no doubt about the considerable care devoted to the entire process.[168] Even so, the parallel with the role of Tractate Aboth within Judaism cannot but cause disquiet. There is clearly the shared desire to demonstrate an unchanging, continuous transmission, whereas, as the history of both Judaism and Christianity illustrates, the natural tendency before the rise of the modern concern for historical accuracy was to assume the mantle of the past, not in order to deceive, but rather to convey what is seen as the past's message for one's own day. In any case, serious discussion of *isnad* apparently did not begin until the late 690s, while even then no account was apparently taken of the possibility of the wholesale invention of appropriate *isnad* to justify particular practices.[169]

The most hopeful way forward would therefore seem to be in terms of *matn* rather than *isnad*: what constitutes an appropriate development of Muhammad's teaching, what not. Whether it is necessary in the process to insist that each development goes back to the Prophet himself, though no doubt some do, seems quite another matter. The Shi'is ('the party of Ali') have always sharply distinguished between *tanzil*, what came down in the revelation, and its *tafsir*, its interpretation or human unveiling, with the successive leaders of the community, the imams, charged with a continuing task of reapplication.[170] So the recognition of a tradition evolving for new circumstances is not unknown to Islam. It would of course be a huge shock to the practice of contemporary Muslims to be told that the Hadith are what Muhammad would have enjoined in those circumstances rather than being what he actually did, but Christianity seems to have successfully undergone a comparable revolution. Intriguingly, one does occasionally already find Muslims prepared to reckon with just such a possibility. So, for

[168] For an illustration, see the detailed analysis of ten Hadith preserved by Sunan Ibn Maja with which Ghaffer's book ends, ibid., 137–247. Only three are pronounced veridical.

[169] Note the pertinent points made by G. H. A. Juynboll, *Muslim Tradition* (Cambridge: Cambridge University Press, 1983), esp. 75.

[170] M. Ayoub, 'Speaking Qur'an', esp. 178–9, 186–7, 197–8.

instance, one distinguished American Muslim comments: 'A Hadith may be false in the sense that the Prophet never spoke the words, but nevertheless true in that it is wholly consistent with his message.'[171]

The most obvious role of Hadith has been to give greater precision to Qur'anic injunctions, such as fasting during Ramadan or the limitation of the Qur'anic injunction to cut off 'the hands' of a thief to one hand.[172] Particularly illuminating is Maulana M. Ali's modern collection of Hadith, mainly from Bukhari.[173] Carefully annotated, each section is also prefaced by an introduction which quotes the relevant verses from the Qur'an; so it is quite easy to detect the kinds of developments that are occurring (otherwise a difficult process given the length of the original collections and uncertainty about which Hadith are regarded as spurious, which not). The consistency of the developments with Qur'anic teaching seems for the most part unproblematic: what is given is greater detail or a deepening of spiritual content.

Occasionally, however, one detects developing lines of thought which might in the long term pull Islam in a different direction from current Western conceptions of its attitudes. Thus, for example, there are a surprising number of positive statements about the status of women, in particular their right to education and a proper position in the mosque;[174] in addition, though a Hadith about wearing a veil is quoted, numerous others discouraging its use are also noted.[175] It is also to a Hadith that we owe the declaration of the Prophet that 'with Allah, the most hateful of all things permitted is divorce',[176] which, when combined with the modern tendency to take Qur'an 4.3 as only a reluctant concession to polygamy,[177] would seem to bode well for a better status for women within marriage. Sometimes, as was only to be expected, the tendency is in the opposite direction, as with the reinforcement of the sword-verse

---

[171] C. Glassé, *Concise Encyclopaedia of Islam* (London: Stacey International, 2nd edn., 1991), 141.

[172] For the development of Ramadan, Peters, *Classical Islam*, 252–6; for treatment of the thief, Qur'an 5.41 and R. Marston Speight, 'The function of Hadith' in A. Rippin, op. cit., 63–81, esp. 72.

[173] M. M. Ali, *A Manual of Hadith* (London: Curzon Press, 1944).

[174] Ibid., e.g. 33–4, 81, 106–7, 160.   [175] Ibid., 391–2.

[176] Ibid., 284.

[177] Ibid., 267; cf. also A. Y. Ali, *Holy Qur'an*, 179 n. 509.

mentioned earlier. Here might be a case, as is sometimes also true of
Judaism and Christianity, of the need for earlier strands in the tradition to critique later, perhaps by applying more widely the injunction: 'let there be no compulsion in religion.'[178]

While it is possible to envisage Hadith in this way encouraging
further developments in Islam, even if they are not all necessarily to
be ascribed to the time of Muhammad himself, much further down
the road would be any recognition of continuing revelation in later
centuries. Yet as a matter of fact *ijma* or consensus has on occasion
been used to overthrow what had once been taken to be the clear
view of both the Qur'an and the early *sunna*. Two examples would
be the admission of the cult of saints and acceptance of the infalli-
bility of the Prophet.[179] So it is not true that no further change
happened after the ninth century once the two principal sources of
Islam, Qur'an and Hadith, had both achieved their canonical form.
Rather than speaking of fresh revelation, though, a more likely way
of interpreting what is happening, as with Christianity, would be a
rereading of the significance of earlier sources. Indeed, this appears
to be precisely what happened in respect of one particularly
contentious issue, the rise of the Sufi or mystical tradition, and its
practice of living in communities that bore a suspicious resemblance to Christian monasteries. One Hadith ('no monasticism in
Islam') had unequivocally condemned such a practice,[180] and this
was reinforced by the most common way of reading the most relevant Qur'anic verse. Yet, the grammar of that verse was sufficiently
ambiguous to allow a very different interpretation, one in which
Muhammad could be taken as granting approval to the practice,
and so, because of this and because elsewhere he is found offering
occasional praise of monks,[181] the movement survived and
produced writings that were to generate some of the earliest positive responses to Islam from non-Muslims in the modern period.[182]

---

[178] Qur'an 2.256.
[179] G. E. von Grunebaum, *Medieval Islam* (Chicago: University of Chicago
Press, 2nd edn., 1953), 149–52, esp. 151.
[180] Its *isnad*, though, could be challenged as weak, and so the Hadith be
regarded as apocryphal.
[181] e.g. 5.85; for the ambiguous, negative verse, 57.27, and F. E. Peters'
commentary, *Classical Islam*, 321–2.
[182] For a helpful discussion of some of its mystical poetry, A. Schimmel, *As
Through A Veil* (New York: Columbia University Press, 1982).

Development continues into the present. Admittedly for some, such as President Gaddafy of Libya, real change is possible only if the entire scheme of tradition is jettisoned and authority confined to the Qur'an alone.[183] Such fundamentalism has led to a very different Muslim north Africa from the society which existed at the beginning of this century.[184] Perhaps this was the only way to undermine the authority that marabouts (traditional holy men) and scholars had acquired there, and return Islam to its traditional egalitarianism. But the trouble is that without tradition key parts of Muslim practice become reduced in significance. A case in point is the *hajj*, the pilgrimage to Mecca. It has become replete with symbolism only marginally connected with the Qur'an.[185] One example would be the rushing back and forth that is taken to represent the Muslim's identification with Hagar's readiness to act for others; another the stoning of the three pillars used as a reminder of Ishmael's fight against temptation before his sacrifice, and thus of the need for a similar struggle on the part of the contemporary Muslim.[186]

The capacity that the traditions of Islam have for continued development in our own day is well illustrated by Richard Antoun's detailed study of contemporary Muslim preaching. He listened to sixty-five sermons, mostly from a local preacher in a Jordanian village of about two thousand inhabitants, and the result makes fascinating reading. They are thoroughly traditional in the sense that Hadith feature as prominently as the Qur'an (distinguished in the text by italics as distinct from the latter's heavy print). But they are also innovative in their own way. Throughout they display a high ethical tone, as in the beautiful Hadith story used to illustrate the true point of pilgrimage,[187] and it is this high

---

[183] For fundamentalism as a search for identity in an uncertain world, A. S. Ahmed, *Postmodernism and Islam* (London: Routledge, 1992).

[184] See further, E. Gellner, *Muslim Society* (Cambridge: Cambridge University Press, 1981), esp. 62–3.

[185] Though still intimately linked of course with a major Qur'anic figure, Ibrahim (Abraham), and his family.

[186] So the best-selling Shi'i writer, A. Shariati in *Hajj* (Houston: Free Islamic Literature, 1980). Jesus' reference to the 'corner stone'—Matt. 21: 42—has even been taken to refer to the Ka'ba; *A Manual of Hadith*, 242, n. 10.

[187] R. T. Antoun, *Muslim Preacher in the Modern World* (Princeton, NJ: Princeton University Press, 1989), 169–70; ch. 6, 154–82 is entirely devoted to the topic of *hajj* in the modern world.

ethical tone that leads the preacher to insist upon the rights of women, and the importance of education.[188] He also uses by implication feminine imagery of God, connecting the Arabic words for 'womb' and 'kinship' with the adjective used to describe God as 'compassionate'.[189] Though the Jordanian was more predictable in interpreting Muhammad's famous night journey to Jerusalem as a call to *jihad*, Antoun is nonetheless able to point to a nearby preacher at Acre who resisted such an interpretation and insisted upon an entirely spiritual, non-literal reading of the legend.[190]

So, however remote the possibility may seem at the present, I would conclude that Islam does have within itself the resources to come to terms with the challenges of the Enlightenment and not be overwhelmed by them. Indeed, the phenomenon of abrogation already draws attention to the way in which new circumstances must generate new principles, while the deeply embedded character of the Hadith remind the believer that such criteria must never be applied simply on the basis of enlightenment rationalism (the mistake so often made by Christianity) but with the need in mind to integrate such conclusions firmly into the imaginative daily practice of one's faith.

Though there is not the space to argue the issue further here, the analysis I have offered would also allow us to see Islam as exhibiting a similar pattern of creative development through tradition as was suggested applies in respect of Judaism and Christianity. As Muslims themselves would recognize, the insights to be found in the Qur'an were built upon the work of earlier prophets, among them Moses and Jesus, while any detailed investigation of Hadith would force the conclusion of continued developments subsequent to Muhammad's death, and, as I have noted, still more were to come in subsequent centuries and continue into our own day. Nor should Christians be dismissive of what Islam has achieved. In his immediate context, Muhammad transformed the attitudes of the tribesmen of the Arabian desert, firmly establishing

---

[188] Antoun, *Muslim Preacher in the Modern World*, 100, cf. 62, 104 for dowries for daughters—*mahr*—and living allowances for mothers—*nafaqa*; and 130, for his role in securing a school for the village.

[189] Ibid., 110; cf. 118.   [190] Ibid., 223–4.

monotheism,[191] and the substitute of retribution for blood-revenge, to mention only two important changes.[192] Women also acquired certain property rights that were in advance of what was practised by either Judaism or Christianity. Again, although Christianity too has its egalitarian streak, Islam seems to me, on the whole, to have been better at preserving that insight. For, despite occasional pointers in the Qur'an in the opposite direction (e.g. 43.32), it was the sentiment of the Hadith that 'people are equal as the teeth of a comb' that prevailed, and received such powerful endorsement through the form taken by Islam's worship in the absence of a hierarchically conceived priesthood. Then, finally as a small example, consider Luke 1: 20. There Zechariah is punished for disbelieving the angel's promise that his wife Elizabeth would bear him a son (John the Baptist). By contrast, in the Qur'an (19.10), the version Muhammad reports is of a three-day dumb-ness specifically requested by Zechariah as an immediate sign that God would indeed do as he promised. Is the Qur'an not, here at least, morally superior to a Christian Gospel?

Because of all the prominence given to adverse publicity about Muslim fundamentalism, it is all too easy for Christians to be dismissive of Islam. But not only is its history of tolerance of other faiths on the whole better than that of Christianity, even today Muslims display a willingness to pray in Christian churches that is seldom reciprocated by Christians.[193] Syncretism is not of course the answer, but the only way forward towards meaningful dialogue is surely through the recognition that Christians can also learn, as well as give. Part of that learning could be expressed in a willingness to hear God also speak through the traditions of Islam, not least the Qur'an itself.

[191] The Nestorian *Chronicle of 'Amr* implies Christian contacts as early as the first century, while some ephemeral conversions to Christianity occurred in central Arabia in the mid-fourth century. Even so, real change was first effected by Muhammad.

[192] For retribution, Coulson, *Islamic Law*, 18; for the bride receiving the dowry in her own right, Ibid., 14.

[193] For some examples from the Middle East, W. Dalrymple, *From the Holy Mountain* (London: HarperCollins, 1998), 45–7, 230–1, 187–91. Commenting on sixth-century Byzantine Christianity, he also observes that 'if John Moschos were to come back today it is likely that he would find much more that was familiar in the practices of a modern Muslim Sufi than he would with those of, say, a contemporary American Evangelical': 168.

PART TWO
The Moving Text

IN the first Part of this book I argued for a much less sharp distinction between revelation and tradition than that to which modern Christianity has become accustomed, even in its more Catholic forms. Instead of thinking of tradition as purely human reflection added on to an original and unchanging divine disclosure, or even of it as small, but significant, divinely added supplements, we need to see that continuing human reflection as itself an indispensable part of the process of divine disclosure. Revelation is mediated to the community of faith through a continuous stream of developing tradition. By way of illustration I noted how, so far from there being any reason for embarrassment at the form now taken by contemporary celebrations of Christmas, sufficient justification can be given for them. Indeed, in my view they speak more effectively of Christ's ultimate significance than would any simple return to the infancy narratives unadorned. That was intended only as a small preparatory instance, with more substantial examples to follow in subsequent chapters, and in particular Part Three will examine in some detail how the argument might be applied to the imaginative development of Christology, both within the canon and beyond. That 'beyond' is important, for in talking about an imaginative, developing tradition I am concerned with a pattern that applies equally within Scripture and in the subsequent history of the Church, and that is why in the second half of Chapter Three I used developments and criteria from within both Judaism and Islam to argue for a similar understanding of their own history.

Hitherto, however, Christian examples have been largely confined to what happened subsequent to the closure of the canon, while even non-Christian illustrations were also mainly drawn from the period since Christ's birth. Before therefore directly tackling the Gospels themselves, I want to set a wider context of the world, both Jewish and pagan, into which Christ entered. Here I shall argue that we find the same phenomenon of a developing, imaginative tradition, that continues with both Jewish and pagan elements alike eventually incorporated into the Christian tradition itself. As my Jewish examples I have taken the way in which the patriarchs, Abraham, Isaac and Joseph are treated, partly because their stories are more manageable than the admittedly more central figure of Moses, and partly because some analogies can be drawn in respect of the issues they raise and the way in which they are handled from within the classical tradition itself. Some of my fellow Christians may find it puzzling or even offensive that the comparison should be drawn at all. So in much of what follows I shall be attempting to dispel what I regard as a number of serious misconceptions about the religion of the classical world, among them that it had no notion of revelation and that its myths were static and without serious religious content. However, in both cases what I shall be most concerned to advance is the idea of a 'moving text', that both in classical and Jewish religion what gives their stories power is not a static content but the ability of the narrative to be adapted through rewriting or rehearing as changing social circumstances help generate fresh insights.

4
Heroic transformations in the classical world

By first focusing here upon the classical world, I shall in effect be continuing a little longer the wider framework with which the last chapter ended. Given the view stated there that it is inappropriate to pursue questions of revelation without reference to the status of other religions, some consideration of the religions of the Indian subcontinent might have been expected in addition to what we have already said about Judaism and Islam. My difficulty, however, is that, though points of importance could no doubt be made about a developing tradition, most obviously perhaps within Hinduism, I lack the requisite degree of knowledge to form independent judgements. In addition, most Western comment tends to focus upon intellectual ideas rather than on lived practice and so ignores how the myths and the various ways in which they are told might impact upon the religious self-understanding of the community.[1]

I therefore turn to what is for me the more familiar classical world. To some this may seem second-best, but the move has in fact a number of positive advantages. Perhaps most fundamental is the way in which it brings together the two major traditions that have shaped Western civilization: biblical and classical. Both have survived creatively by developing and adapting, and it will be interesting to see how far the same points can be made of both traditions. In addition, since it is (very roughly) over the same period of time and in the same part of the world (the Eastern Mediterranean) that they develop in parallel, the classical world

---

[1] But note the different approach of the new series *Princeton Readings in Religions*, as in the volume *Religions of India in Practice*, ed. D. S. Lopez (Princeton, NJ: Princeton University Press, 1995).

can be used (with due caution) as a yardstick against which to measure some of the claims we might wish to make about the biblical tradition. To give an obvious example, to the modern mind the rewriting or invention of history is most naturally read as evidence of a deep malaise and dishonesty, whereas, though bad motives also of course existed in the ancient world, the primary intention in both classical and biblical traditions was, as we shall see, quite different: to ensure the continuing relevance of the past to the present. The story must continue to speak to its present context.

Even so, for some the general parallel will still seem too remote, especially among those who doubt the strength of religious commitment in the Greek context. So I shall begin by observing the extent to which it is also a religious tradition that is at stake here. Thereafter I shall attempt to demonstrate how within the classical word its particular form of story—myth—functioned as a vehicle for serious reflection and as such is entitled to assessment in terms of its truth content, even though, more often than not, such myths are bereft of any historical value. Imaginative truth thus demands our serious attention. A third section then explores the extent to which changes in these myths might legitimate talk of a developing tradition, and, if so, what kind of factors contributed to such change. Finally, the chapter ends by suggesting some classical parallels for the three patriarchs whose stories the following chapter will investigate. What historical content the latter have is, as we shall see, a matter of some dispute, but that is not the point of drawing the parallel. The fascination for me lies in the fact that classical and Jewish traditions, different though they are in numerous ways, nonetheless seem to be alike in this: they both use key stories in their tradition as handles for a kind of imaginative reflection that necessitates that these stories to be retold in new ways.

A religious self-understanding

While from the time of the Enlightenment and indeed well into the twentieth century much writing on the classics was dominated by the assumption that the gods were there to give little more than literary colour to underlying rationalist assumptions, in more recent scholarship the reality of the religious dimension has been taken much more seriously.[2] It was a pervasive fact of communal life, so much so in fact that Greek has no separate word for 'religion' and thus no clear demarcation between sacred and secular.[3] Not only did the performance of tragedy take place in a religious context, so too did comedy. Even the occasional jokes against the gods in the latter context, it has been argued, point to strength of religious conviction not its weakness, as in the parallel mixture of awe and blasphemous humour in medieval religion.[4] The performance of sacrifice was also subject to careful, detailed legislation.[5]

This is not to deny major differences from biblical religion, but it is to challenge the view that we are now attempting to compare two wholly unlike entities. Both biblical and classical scholars are guilty of exaggerating the contrast. We are told, for instance, that Greek religion had 'no revelation, no creed' and lacked 'a ruling class' of priests like those of ancient Israel.[6] Certainly, this is in part true. But the danger for classicist and Christian alike is that the situation of the Christian Church from the Council of Nicaea onwards is projected backwards into a very different cultural context. While it is true that priests had considerably greater authority in Israel than in Greece, they were just as part-time as their pagan counterparts.[7] Again, the great variety of positions

---

[2] As also its irrational side, as in E. R. Dodds' influential *The Greeks and the Irrational* (Berkeley: University of California Press, 1951).

[3] J. N. Bremmer, *Greek Religion* (*Greece and Rome*: New Surveys in the Classics, 24, Oxford University Press, 1994), 2 ff. The point, though, can of course be exaggerated. On the one hand, it is still possible to identify a religious vocabulary; on the other, one notes that some Greek city states had one calendar for political business, another for festivals.

[4] H. Lloyd-Jones, *The Justice of Zeus* (Berkeley: University of California Press, 2nd edn., 1983), 133, 221–2, n. 24; Cf. P. E. Easterling, 'Greek poetry and religion' in P. E. Easterling and J. V. Muir (eds.), *Greek Religion and Society* (Cambridge: Cambridge University Press, 1985), 34–49, esp. 35–9.

[5] R. Parker, *Athenian Religion: A History* (Oxford: Clarendon Press, 1996), 43 ff., 218 ff.

[6] Easterling and Muir, *Greek Religion*, 'Foreword', xiv–v; Bremmer, *Greek Religion*, 28.

[7] Jewish priests were only required to serve one week out of every twenty four in the Temple. How far they dominated society is disputed. Jeremias believes that many of their wider roles had been taken over by lay Pharisees and scribes; Sanders disagrees. J. Jeremias, *Jerusalem in the Time of Jesus* (London: SCM Press, 1969) 147–267; E. P. Sanders, *Judaism: Practice & Belief* (London: SCM Press, 1992), 170–89.

within Judaism and Christianity in the centuries round the birth of
Christ surely paint a rather different picture from the firm orthodoxy of later generations. Moreover, as I tried to indicate in the
previous chapter, even the notion of immovable, fixed canonical
texts is seriously open to question. The biblical books of
Chronicles are a theological rewriting of earlier regal history in
Kings, as is *Jubilees* of Genesis. Examples could easily be multiplied,
even from within the New Testament canon itself with Matthew
and Luke clearly modifying and correcting Mark, and John probably all three. Likewise, if we examine the classical side of the
comparison, later Greek writing does not operate in a vacuum, as
though it had total freedom, since for better or worse Homer was
the standard against which almost all Greek thought felt it incum-
bent to measure itself.

Certainly, huge differences remain. My point is not to deny the
contrasts, but rather to question whether they are so fundamental
that interesting comparisons may not be drawn. Even what is
thought to be the most basic contrast of all can be overdone, when
Greek and Roman religion are presented as exclusively social and
entirely lacking in the element of personal devotion so characteristic of the two Semitic religions. Often quoted is Aristotle's claim
that 'it would be absurd if someone were to say that he loves
Zeus', but the favourite Hellenistic description of him as 'Saviour'
suggests that such devotion did eventually develop, while earlier
Euripides' portrayal of Hippolytus' love for Artemis and Ion's for
Apollo surely implies a similar relationship.[8] So the attitude was
not unknown, and indeed might well have been judged quite
common, had we a better knowledge of the more fervent forms of
religion such as the mystery cults. Likewise, the notion that revelation lacks any classical parallel only holds for so long as we insist
that it must be thought of in narrowly propositional terms. Myths
were told as a way of revealing or 'disclosing' how human beings
stood *vis-à-vis* the gods, and must often have been experienced as

[8] For Aristotle, *Magna Moralia*, 1208b 30; for Euripides, his plays *Hippolytus*
and *Ion*. Even though the decision to use 'Saviour' normally reflected public
rather than private events, its use is another indication that notions of gratitude
to the gods were not alien to Greek religion; cf. Parker, *Athenian Religion*, 186.
It is also from Hellenistic times that we have Cleanthes' magnificent Hymn to
Zeus: e.g. in C. A. Trypanis (ed.), *Penguin Book of Greek Verse* (Harmondsworth:
Penguin, 1971), 283–5.

such. To say this does nothing to establish their objectivity as revelation, but it surely at least opens up the possibility that this could sometimes have been so. Personal revelation was of course also claimed by the priestess at the influential shrine of Delphi, while archaeological evidence has recently demonstrated the truth of the claim that Pan's worship was introduced to Athens as a consequence of a putative revelation.[9]

Because most classical gods can easily be made to correspond to specific aspects of the human psyche it is very tempting to suppose that that is all there was to them. Aphrodite then becomes no more than a means of making sexuality and nakedness acceptable without fear of pollution or violation of taboo, or Hera a way of exploring the oppressiveness of the mother–son relation in the Greek family.[10] All that can be true, but need by no means be the end of the story. Admittedly, the ancient world did sometimes offer sacrifice to what we could scarcely regard as any more than an abstract idea,[11] but on the other side needs to be set the impossibility of any Greek recognizing, for example, the purely internalist account of Dionysus which Nietzsche provides.[12] Dionysus was without doubt experienced as an objective reality, a power greater than oneself. Indeed, so concerned was the mythology associated with him to stress that otherness (which we associate with objectivity) that it even resorted to a claim which we now know not to have been historically true. For, though portrayed as a foreign god, he was in fact as native as the rest of the pantheon.[13] As in any other

---

[9] Parker, *Athenian Religion*, 163–8, where a naturalistic explanation is offered. For a more extensive discussion of the role of Pan, P. Borgeaud, *The Cult of Pan in Ancient Greece* (Chicago: University of Chicago Press, 1988).

[10] Cf. P. Friedrich, *The Meaning of Aphrodite* (Chicago: University of Chicago Press, 1978), esp. 129–48; P. E. Slater, *The Glory of Hera* (Princeton, NJ: Princeton University Press, 1968), esp. 3–74.

[11] Including Democracy; so Parker, *Athenian Religion*, 228–9; but note his comment about such personifications already existing in the Archaic period (235).

[12] The opposition between Apollonian and Dionysian as contrasted mental states runs through Nietzsche's *The Birth of Tragedy*. For a powerful challenge to the view that this is all that needs to be said, A. Henrichs, ' "He has a God in him": Human and divine in the modern perception of Dionysus' in T. H. Carpenter and C. A. Faraone (ed.), *Masks of Dionysus* (Ithaca: Cornell University Press, 1993), 13–43.

[13] As his mention on a Linear B tablet of *c.* 1250 BC appears to demonstrate; ibid., 1.

religion, the gods were used to make sense of reality as a whole and not just our subjective response to it,[14] and if this produced a greater sense of unresolved conflict than one would expect in a monotheistic religion, one needs to recall that Christianity too has at times experienced similar problems as, for instance, in reconciling divine love and justice in some theories of atonement, or the rationality of the Logos and the exuberance of the Spirit.

Yet, however uncanny or inexplicable at times was its experience of the divine, at the heart of classical religion still remained the claim, expressed in the pre-eminence given to Zeus, that order was dominant. Whether or not it also functioned as a sign of supreme authority, the presence of Zeus was (like that of Yahweh) associated with mountain-tops.[15] So the analogies are closer than may initially appear. More importantly, just as the Old Testament world wrestled with how divine justice and human suffering should be reconciled, so also there was a developing discussion of how the justice of Zeus should be understood. Rejecting any notion of a simple progression from a shame to a guilt culture, one distinguished Greek scholar nonetheless insists on a marked contrast between *Iliad* and *Odyssey*, with divine responsibility for evil only rejected in the latter and that rejection still more strongly affirmed in Aeschylus. Yet Herodotus is found closer to the *Iliad*; so development is not inevitable, and indeed little progress is detected in the two later tragedians, Sophocles and Euripides, with the earlier notions of corporate guilt and responsibility continuing in use.[16] It is now almost a commonplace to acknowledge that Euripides was much less the rationalist than he was once commonly portrayed.[17] Even so, there are not wanting scholars

[14] For an excellent and sympathetic account, J. Gould, 'On making sense of Greek religion' in Easterling and Muir, *Greek Religion*, 1–33.

[15] A. B. Cook, *Zeus: A Study in Ancient Religion* Vol. II, (Cambridge: Cambridge University Press, 1940), 869–97.

[16] These are H. Lloyd-Jones' views in outline, from his *The Justice of Zeus* (Berkeley: University of California Press, 2nd edn., 1983). The idea of a simple progression from a shame to guilt culture is argued in A. W. H. Adkins, *Merit and Responsibility* (Oxford: Clarendon Press, 1960).

[17] For a particularly strong assertion of the modern, revisionist reading of Euripides, cf. J. D. Mikalson, *Honour Thy Gods* (Chapel Hill: University of North Carolina Press, 1991), who argues that of all the tragedians it was Euripides who remained closest to popular, conventional religion (esp. 225–36).

who would argue that long before Plato's ringing declaration of individual responsibility Sophocles had already made the move in his *Oedipus Rex*.[18] This is not the place to enter into such a debate. My point simply is that, just as the precise form in which Old Testament stories were told could be used as a means of resolving questions of divine responsibility for evil or the issue of individual versus corporate guilt,[19] so too parallel developments can be observed in the classical tradition of story-telling.[20] It is therefore to a closer examination of its particular form of story-telling that I now turn.

Reflective myth and imaginative truth

To an earlier generation of classical scholars and anthropologists the very title of this section would have seemed a glaring misnomer. Myths were seen as merely 'primitive' and prior to the clear light of rational thinking. For the classical scholar, Francis Cornford, their importance lay solely in their gradual rationalization into the earliest ideas of philosophy, while the anthropologist, Bronislaw Malinowski, partly in his anxiety to protect them from patronizing analysis as being no more than a primitive attempt at scientific explanation, left them without any consciously self-imposed meaning at all.[21] Claude Lévi-Strauss at least offered a meaning with his notion of underlying 'binary opposites' the contradiction between which myths seek to resolve, but it was a meaning largely imposed by the anthropologist from outside rather

---

[18] Plato, *Republic* 617E: 'it is not God who is to blame, but the person who made the choice'. For Sophocles, M. Bowra, *Sophoclean Tragedy* (Oxford: Clarendon Press, 1944), 162 ff; 88.

[19] In 1 Chron. 21: 1–5 the same evil act (a census) is attributed to the promptings of Satan which in 2 Sam. 24: 1–9 had been ascribed to God. In Josh. 7 two different manuscript traditions exist, one of which assumes that Achan alone is punished for his sin, the other his entire family (esp. v. 25).

[20] This is not to say that the focus was always the same. Though the point can be exaggerated, in his retelling of Greek myth Roberto Calasso rightly stresses that the main interest is in psychological powers rather than in morality: *The Marriage of Cadmus and Harmony* (London: Jonathan Cape, 1993), esp. 242–3.

[21] F. C. Cornford, *From Religion to Philosophy* (London: Edward Arnold, 1912; Princeton, NJ: Princeton University Press, 1991); B. K. Malinowski, *Myth in Primitive Psychology* (London: Kegan Paul, 1926).

than one easily seen from within.[22] Given the continuing influence of the massive scholarship of the Swede Martin Nilsson, classicists have still not entirely escaped from the view of myth as 'pre-logical', to use Lévy-Bruhl's famous phrase.[23] There also remains the continued temptation to seek their meaning purely externally, in what they tell us about the practice of Greek religion, particularly its origins. In nineteenth-century Oxford the fashion was to seek explanation in terms of an original primitive awe before natural phenomena.[24] In the late twentieth century, there is much stress on rootedness in ritual practice.[25] Both theories no doubt contain elements of truth. Yet what they miss is why myths continued to have power, even when divorced from such contexts.

More promising, therefore, is the work of those scholars who accept myth as an alternative way of thinking, through narrative and images rather than abstract thought. Among English scholars G. S. Kirk represented an important landmark. Not only is the role of tradition stressed, but also the imagination; indeed, regret is expressed that Greek myth, in contrast to some Near-Eastern mythology, suffers from too little 'fantasy' rather than too much.[26] Likewise, the Paris school of J.-P. Vernant and Marcel Detienne is

---

[22] C. Lévi-Strauss, *Mythologiques*, esp. Vol. I: *Le cru et le cuit* (Paris: Plon, 1964). The value seems to lie in their decoding, rather than as experienced reality.

[23] Still true of a more mature work such as M. Nilsson, *Die Geschichte der griechischen Religion* (3rd edn., Munich: C. H. Beck'sche Verlagsbuchhandlung, 1967) Vol. I, 13–35. Strictly speaking, Lévy-Bruhl is even further removed from sympathy than Lévi-Strauss, since for the former myth-makers even lack any sense of the law of contradiction. Contrast Lévy Bruhl's *Les fonctions mentales dans les sociétés inférieures* (Paris: Alcan, 1910) and Lévi-Strauss's *La pensée sauvage* (Paris: Plon, 1962).

[24] F. M. Müller, 'Comparative Mythology' (1858), in *Chips from a German Workshop* (London: Longmans, Green & Co., 1867), IV, 1–154.

[25] As in the writings of Walter Burkert. But, while a work like *Homo Necans* (Berkeley: University of California Press, 1983) may well demonstrate that sacrifice had its origins in ritualistic attempts to make the killing of animals for food acceptable, it fails to engage with how subsequently sacrifice might have been perceived.

[26] G. S. Kirk, *Myth* (Cambridge: Cambridge University Press, 1970), esp. 282–3, 244. For a more recent comparison, and investigation of near-east influence on classical myth, C. Penglase, *Greek Myths and Mesopotamia* (London: Routledge, 1994).

much less dogmatic than its predecessors and correspondingly more concerned with myth as the imaginative exploration of issues. Detienne speaks of 'the practices of tradition based on memory' that 'escape all attempts at classification',[27] while Vernant concedes the plausibility of Lévi-Strauss only when dealing with his own fieldwork, and instead finds acceptable the basic assumption of writers such as Eliade and Ricoeur that myth is a multifaceted search for understanding that has its own logic and intelligibility, distinctive but comparable to rational modes of thought.[28]

To theologians familiar with Bultmann, let alone Eliade and Ricoeur, this will seem so obvious a point as scarcely to require mention. But the wider scholarly world, including the classical, has been slow to come to such a recognition, while theology itself has not been without fault. For it will not do to treat biblical mythology as profound, while continuing to be dismissive of myth in all other contexts. The situation is much eased if we acknowledge myth to be a phenomenon of the present, no less than of the past. One recent book on classical myth opens by taking the Battle of Britain as an example, where the victory may have been due less to the superior courage and skill of the airmen involved than to successful breaking of enemy codes,[29] while in an earlier book I supported Roland Barthes' stress on twentieth-century myth-making and raised the question of the extent to which the British monarchy might once have functioned in this way.[30]

One difficulty with Barthes' analysis is that he might at first sight seem more concerned with images than with stories, and it may be thought that without a story-line what we have is at most a symbol and not a myth, but matters are not that simple. Certainly, definitions commonly assume explicit mention of a story, as in these two definitions from classical scholars: 'A Greek myth is a narrative about the deeds of gods and heroes and their interrelations with ordinary mortals, handed on as a tradition

[27] M. Detienne, *The Creation of Mythology* (Chicago: University of Chicago Press, 1986), esp. 91.
[28] J.-P. Vernant, 'The Reason of Myth' in *Myth and Society in Ancient Greece* (London: Methuen, 1980), 186–242, esp. 215 ff.
[29] K. Dowden, *The Uses of Greek Mythology* (London: Routledge, 1992), 3–4.
[30] R. Barthes, *Mythologies* (London: Granada, 1973); D. Brown, *Continental Philosophy and Modern Theology* (Oxford: Blackwell, 1987), 62–6, 179–84.

within the ancient Greek world, and of collective significance to a
particular social group or groups;' 'A classical myth is a story that,
through its classical form, has attained a kind of immortality
because its inherent archetypal beauty, profundity and power have
inspired rewarding renewal and transformation by successive
generations.'[31] Though Barthes shows little interest in the element
of tradition which both stress, it is quite otherwise with their
requirement for concentrated imaginative power. Though the
element of story may seem often to be absent from his examples,
as in his selection of a wrestling match or Negro soldier saluting
the French flag, this is too superficial a response. For each can be
expanded into a story: of how empire was nobly acquired or how
in a unequal battle between good and evil good triumphed (the
normal wrestling match pattern, with exaggerated contrasts
between the two opponents). Similarly, in the classical case myth
was often transmitted by visual reminder, in a focused image on
vase and sculpture, rather than by explicit retelling. Inevitably, the
alternative mode of communication sometimes resulted in different perceptions, just as, for instance, with the story of the Garden
of Eden the focus in Christian art moved almost entirely towards
the theme of disobedience and away from the nature of the
knowledge offered by the tree, far less what the presence of a
second tree in the garden might mean.[32]

What factors lead to changes in perception is an issue which we
shall consider further in a moment, but first something needs to be
said on a still more basic issue, the question of truth in myth.
Myths can be vehicles of truth in quite a number of different ways.
They can contain historical truth; they can express truth of particular relevance to the society of which they are part; and they can
embody universal truths of morality or religion. Perhaps the most
neglected element is their relation to history and historical context,
and so we shall begin there.

Nowadays, 'myth' is commonly taken to imply the absence of
all historical truth, but not only is this unnecessarily restrictive, it

[31] R. Buxton, *Imaginary Greece* (Cambridge: Cambridge University Press,
1994), 15; M. P. O. Morford and R. J. Lenardon, *Classical Mythology* (5th edn.,
New York: Longman, 1995), 18.
[32] Gen. 2: 9 mentions a 'tree of life' as well as 'the tree of the knowledge of
good and evil', but almost never in art is this second tree represented or given
any interesting characteristics.

ignores the complex relationship which has always existed and continues to exist between myth and history. Though Greek thought did attempt to distinguish between myth and history, it is surprising how interconnected they remained. So, for instance, the historian Herodotus still sees the role of history in terms of recording (like myth) what is worth remembering,[33] just as the *Legenda* of the saints from which we get our word 'legends' originally meant 'worth reading'. Again Thucydides, despite his dismissal of myth, assumes the eponymous ancestor of the Greeks to be historical,[34] and in fact the taking of myth as literal truth is be found as late as Pausanias, for whom Theseus and numerous other heroes were real persons.[35] Sometimes claims to territory or particular forms of alliance were at stake, as in the postulated rewriting of the *Iliad* to reflect Athenian claims over the island of Salamis or the historical transfer of Orestes' 'bones' to Sparta as a means of establishing entitlement to leadership of the Peloponnese.[36] But perhaps, as with the Bible even in the present day, people had difficulty in seeing how a claim to truth could be preserved except literally. Notoriously, Schliemann in his archaeological investigations at Troy and elsewhere took the substance of the *Iliad* literally, and many a twentieth-century historian can be mentioned who showed a similar lack of reserve over other early myths.[37] Much more recent writing goes to the other extreme in declaring the absence of all historical content. But why should myths not be

[33] The opening paragraph of his *Histories* declares his objective as being to ensure that 'great and marvellous deeds do not pass from the memory'.

[34] Contrast Thucydides' attack on myth in *Peloponnesian War* 2. 22.4 with his acceptance of the historicity of 'Hellen' (Greek) at 1.3.2.

[35] Pausanias (*fl. c.* AD 150), *Periegesis of Greece* 5.10.8. He also regularly informs us that he has seen actual statues by Daedalus, particularly in the remoter parts of the Peloponnese. An inscribed Parian marble, the *Marmor Parium*, provides a powerful illustration of the continuity which the Greeks perceived between their myths and history. Major events are listed from the mythical *c.*1500 BC to the death of Alexander the Great without any sense of break: Dowden, *Uses*, 51–2.

[36] For Athens' contest with Megara over Salamis, J. M. Wickersham, 'Myth and identity in the archaic *polis*' in D. C. Pozzi and J. M. Wickersham (ed.), *Myth and the Polis* (Ithaca: Cornell University Press, 1991), 16–31; for Orestes' bones, Dowden, *Uses*, 89–92, esp. 91.

[37] For two more recent examples: F. H. Stubbings on *Seven against Thebes* in *Cambridge Ancient History* (3rd edn., Cambridge: Cambridge University Press, 1970), II.2, 167–9; N. G. L. Hammond on Heraclidae, *Migrations and Invasions in Greece* (Park Ridge, NJ: Noyes Press, 1976), 141.

commonly, or perhaps even normally, rather than pure fantasy, an intricate combination of fact and imagination which it is extremely difficult for us now to unravel? Thus, the fact that most of Rome's early history lacks historical plausibility need not mean that Rome's earliest form of government was not monarchical, as the myths claim;[38] nor need the fact that the names of Oedipus' sons sounds suspiciously as though they were invented to reflect their supposed actions mean that no elements in the myth reflect history.[39] Indeed, it has been argued that early forms of fosterage and acquisition of a throne through marriage continued as part of the Oedipus story, even though these had ceased to reflect any actual practice in the time for which the myth is best known to us: fifth-century Athens.[40] When one recalls that Gilgamesh was an historical person despite the huge transformations that occurred in his story,[41] it is surely not altogether impossible that Oedipus had likewise an historical identity, even though almost certainly this must have been much nearer the Homeric version (in its simplicity) rather than the Sophoclean.[42]

I mention all this not because I think the question of historicity important in itself, but because myths can only arise from contexts, and that inevitably means historical contexts. Myths are imaginative attempts to reflect on one's experience, and if factual examples are to hand, these are the most likely to have been used. So, if we turn to present times, the Battle of Britain was used to strengthen the need for patriotic reassurance in a difficult hour, whether or not its depiction accurately reflects the facts, in much the same way as the United States' perception of itself today as

[38] The combination of fact and fiction is well illustrated by M. Grant, *Myths of the Greeks and Romans* (Rev. edn., London: Weidenfeld & Nicholson, 1989), 349–72, esp. 363 ff, where the continuing use of *rex* for state offices is noted.

[39] The one who held the city of Thebes is known as Eteocles ('True Glory'), while the one who attacks is called Polyneices ('Much Strife').

[40] C. Brillante, 'History and the historical interpretation of myth' in L. Edmonds (ed.), *Approaches to Greek Myth* (Baltimore: Johns Hopkins University Press, 1990), 93–138, esp. 117–18; J. Bremmer, 'Oedipus and the Greek Oedipus Complex' in J. Bremmer (ed.), *Interpretations of Greek Mythology* (London: Croom Helm, 1987), 41–59, esp. 45–8.

[41] Kirk offers an excellent interpretation of the myth, while also accepting that Gilgamesh was originally an historical Sumerian king of the third millennium BC: *Myth*, 132–52, esp. 133.

[42] He is referred to at *Iliad* 23. 677–80 and *Odyssey* 11. 271–80.

defender of world democracy has some basis in fact, however much it may also be clouded by action to protect American business interests. In a similar way, then, on the Acropolis the fictional battle of the Lapiths and Centaurs and the historical battle of Marathon are alike treated mythically, as part of a common artistic programme to celebrate Athens' victory over the invading Persians. The half-horse Centaurs are identified with the barbarian other, and Marathon given a decisive significance that ignores the historical embarrassment of the greater role played by later victories at Salamis and Plataea.[43]

To the modern mind it can be decidedly irritating that no sharp distinction is thus drawn between fact and fiction, but that is to adopt an unengaged attitude to the 'facts'. For as soon as we ask questions about relevance to ourselves, the narrowly historical recedes and gives place to questions of significance that open up more intangible forms of truth. What then matters in deciding whether the facts are of any interest in determining how we live our lives is not so much the facts themselves as how they are presented. Our modern attitude (in theory at least) is that where the facts do not fit we should turn our attention elsewhere, but in practice, as I have tried to indicate, both as individuals and as communities we sometimes still behave in the same way as the ancients. Nor need this necessarily be seen as a bad thing. It all depends on what question one is addressing. Gilgamesh and Oedipus have proved to be bearers of far more profound truth than would ever have been possible had they remained at the level of their purely historical reality, while Churchill's use of the airmen in his famous speech embodied and helped to realize a larger truth—the few islanders heroically united in battle against a hostile Continent—that a more literal reading would have denied.

---

[43] For a detailed argument to this effect, N. Spivey, *Understanding Greek Sculpture* (London: Thames & Hudson, 1996), 123–51. Nowhere does the sculptural programme make any reference to the role of Athens' allies nor to the significance of the sea battle of Salamis, and indeed seems almost to deny the latter with its celebration of the defeat of the sea-god Poseidon by Athena in the contest to determine which of them should be patron of Athens. Even the number of heroic figures on the frieze is apparently made to correspond to the number (192) who fell at Marathon: Ibid., 148.

Developing tradition and cultural change

At this point I want to attempt a necessarily all too brief survey of
the way in which, in general, myth has developed within the classical tradition from the earliest Greek period through Roman
times until the Renaissance. Both in its narrative and its visual
form myth has been continually subject to change. Determining
what initiates that change is no easy matter. Here I can only hazard
some guesses, but that it is change that helps to sustain the life of
the myth would seem to me not in doubt. Such changes could of
course be taken to imply that myth cannot in itself be the bearer
of truth, since it lacks consistency in its content. Yet I would argue
that it is precisely its capacity for change in this way that ensures a
continuing truth content, for thereby, as cultural change initiates
the possibility of fresh insights, so the myth continues to sustain
the capacity to communicate them.

Though it is possible immediately to universalize the truth
content of some myths, the primary relevance of many, if not
most, is likely to be culture-specific, precisely because they are
seeking to address specific situations within the society in which
they are set. Indeed, that is one obvious reason why the way in
which myths are told has of necessity to change, if they are to
retain their power, as the culture about them changes. The
majority of Greek myths will perhaps on analysis prove to be of
this type. As we shall see, in the late classical period many do in
fact tend to acquire universal characteristics, but, though this
ensures longer life, it often brings with it a degree of artificiality
and therefore a corresponding diminution of power (though there
are conspicuous exceptions). One sign of that underlying capacity for adaptation is the way in which some details seem there
only for colour and can quite happily be told indifferently in one
way or another.[44] In other cases, the change may be more a
matter of a differing emphasis or perspective from within the
same contemporary context, as in Hesiod's depiction of the age
of Kronos as a golden age in his *Works and Days*, but not in the

---

[44] For examples, Buxton, *Imaginary Greece*, 74–5; T. H. Carpenter, *Art and
Myth in Ancient Greece* (London: Thames & Hudson, 1991), 79.

Theogony.[45] One helpful way of looking at this phenomenon invites us to think of some apparently incompatible myths as complementary rather than contradictory, in much the same way as in the modern world we can regard two apparently incompatible proverbs as both pointers to the truth.[46]

Among those Greek myths which have a strong culture-specific flavour, much examined of late have been those which explore the borders between society and what is beyond, through notions such as metamorphosis, strange religious behaviour in the countryside and attitudes to the foreigner. They seem to speak of a society uncertain or insecure in the value it places on city life. The symbolic resonance of Centaurs has already been noted, while the length of Ovid's poem *Metamorphoses*, irrespective of how seriously Ovid himself took the issue, still indicates how deeply this particular metaphor for otherness ran through Greek myth. The feeling that poetry and religion alike lay at the boundaries of social existence is well illustrated by the Orpheus myth.[47] Orpheus was also commonly presented as a foreigner (a Thracian), and so like Medea, who came from Colchis on the Caucasian side of the Black Sea.[48] Yet otherness did not necessarily mean rejection. A sympathetic portrayal of Medea is offered by Euripides in the play of the same name, while the myth of Narcissus warns of the heavy penalty to be paid by those who neglect the proper respect that is due to otherness.[49] Indeed, Orpheus himself became the subject of a major mystery cult. The attempt to get the balance right is also

---

[45] M. Grant (*Myths*, 108–9) thinks factors such as these sufficient to necessitate difference in authorship, but more plausible is one of perspective. It matters whether one's primary point is divine order or the present hard lot of humanity. One observes a similar difference in stress between the P and J creation narratives in the opening chapters of Genesis, where two authors were involved but have been combined into a single narrative without any sense of tension.

[46] Buxton (*Imaginary Greece*, 164) illustrates with 'too many cooks spoil the broth' and 'many hands make light work'.

[47] F. Graf, 'Orpheus: A poet among men' in J. Bremmer (ed.), *Greek Mythology*, 80–106.

[48] Medea could also be used multivalently, to speak of the threat both from foreigner and mother, as in the relation of Theseus to his stepmother, Medea: C. Sourvinou-Inwood, 'Myths in images: Theseus and Medea as a case study' in L. Edmonds, *Approaches*, 393–445.

[49] E. Pellizer, 'Reflections, echoes and amorous receptivity: on reading the Narcissus story' in J. Bremmer, *Greek Religion*, 107–20.

probably reflected in the story of Prometheus stealing fire from the gods to give it to men, for that way human beings are placed midway between animal and god.[50] Likewise, *hubris* or arrogance in the face of the divine is a recurring theme for exploration in a way that it is not for us, and indeed this can be seen in the often misinterpreted injunction from Delphi: 'Know yourself.'[51]

As a further example of culture specificity consider the Oedipus myth. Though Freud sought to give Oedipus universal significance, his importance for people of the time must have been quite different since the only woman of whom he had any real knowledge as a child was not his real mother, as Freud's version would require.[52] For the Greeks the power of this myth is therefore likely to have lain elsewhere, in the claustrophobic relation between boy and mother and the total legal dependence of sons on fathers from which the young adult male had to try to escape. Yet we must also guard against dismissing any myth too easily as merely symptomatic of a past age. The way in which a back to nature movement and Gaia religion have revived in our own day shows that even in the late twentieth century very similar concerns to those of the Greeks over the value of culture versus nature can reassert themselves.

While we have no reason to think cultural determinism true, it would be foolish to deny that the perception of truth and the form of its presentation are made much easier in some cultural contexts than others. Given our temporal distance it is not always possible to pinpoint such factors. Why, for instance, did details in the Heracles myth undergo such ups and downs in popularity?[53] Again, sometimes the factors may be so complex and multiple that it is hard to be more precise. Thus the moral changes that the lyric poet Pindar (515–438 BC) makes to earlier myths should perhaps

[50] J.-P. Vernant, '*The Reason of Myth*', 168–85, esp. 182–3.

[51] For us it speaks of the importance of self-knowledge; to the Greeks of the need to know the limitations of one's station in life: M. P. Nilsson, *Greek Piety* (New York: W. W. Norton, 1969), 47–8.

[52] J.-P. Vernant, 'Oedipe sans complexe' in J.-P. Vernant and P. Vidal-Naquet, *Mythe et tragédie en Grèce ancienne* (Paris: F. Maspero, 1972), 75–98. A more political thrust to Freud's reading is given in J. Moltmann, *The Crucified God* (London: SCM Press, 1974), 303–7.

[53] T. H. Carpenter, *Art and Myth*, 117–34 charts the changes, without offering any explanation.

simply be set in the general pattern of critique which runs from the sixth-century philosopher Xenophanes onwards. So he rejects as unfitting to the gods the story that Tantalus's punishment was due to his abuse of their hospitality by serving up, unknown to them, his own son, Pelops, while also omitted is any suggestion that Pelops won the famous race for the hand of Hippodamia by suborning the charioteer Myrtilos.[54] A strong general moral critique is thus present. Yet that same poem also contains another change of perspective that is likely to be strongly culture specific, his introduction of a homosexual relation between Pelops and the god Poseidon, almost certainly deriving from the athletic context within which Pindar's poetry was written. Similarly, we know that with the rise of democracy went corresponding changes in the administration of religious rites,[55] and with those changes appear also to have gone corresponding changes in the way some myths were presented on stage.[56] Some versions plausibly lend themselves to interpretation in terms of definite historical contexts. One illustration of this is Sophocles' play *Ajax*, with its plea for a more humanitarian handling of leadership and war. For it has been argued that, just as Aeschylus' trilogy the *Oresteia* of 458 was intended to endorse reforms as a way of ending a cycle of conflict, so this play of the 440s was designed as an implicit critique of unyielding imperialist expansion by someone who had actually served in 443 as treasurer of the Delian League, the alliance upon which Athenian power was based.[57]

My point should not be misunderstood. It is certainly no part of my intention to claim that the presence of detectable cultural pressures undermines the value of any changes made; to revert to the examples give above, homosexuality or a more humanitarian approach to political leadership are not necessarily worse (or better) simply because we can point to specific factors that have helped create changes in perspective. Rather, my point is that the limitations of the human imagination are such that, more often

---

[54] Pindar, *Olympian Odes* I, esp. 35–58. The Ode was written in 476 BC.

[55] R. Parker, *Athenian Religion*, e.g. 125–33.

[56] For numerous examples, Buxton, *Imaginary Greece*, 32–3. Dowden, with his simple contrast between mythic kingship and democracy (*Uses*, 150), therefore needs heavy qualification.

[57] D. J. Bradshaw, 'The Ajax myth and the polis: old values and new' in D. C. Pozzi and J. M. Wickersham, *Myth and the Polis*, 99–125.

than not, new perspectives only emerge when they are given some external prod. That major changes did occur long before the more allegorical readings of later classicism cannot, I think, be doubted. The gods become less arbitrary (from the *Odyssey* onwards); there is more stress on individual responsibility (as in the more individualistic reading of Sophocles' *Oedipus Rex* noted earlier); and there is more sympathy for the other, whether stranger, foreigner or woman (as in Euripides' *Bacchae* and *Medea*).[58] Most classicists speak of a great decline after the fourth century, but there seems to me something to be said on the other side. First, however, we need to note the parallel but distinct developments that had been taking place in artistic representation.

Since the history of Greek art is often spoken of with little mention of its specific religious context, it is salutary to be reminded that overwhelmingly it was of a religious character, with most statues, including the famous male *kouroi*, intended as votive offerings of various kinds.[59] In the case of the *kouroi* this would be consequent on victory in the games, and their nudity expresses a religious, heroic ideal rather than mere representation.[60] Though art historians once associated the portrayal of the human figure with developments towards democracy, this is apparently not correct. The move from a more apotropaic form of religious art had other causes, perhaps purely practical.[61] Whatever the reason, it also allowed greater engagement for the viewer; though initially the human figure began in as confrontational a pose as its predecessor, it soon acquired a more engaged tone, something which one finds reflected in architectural style as well, with the move from Doric (best seen from a distance) to the more interior style of Ionic.[62]

---

[58] Euripides' attitude is in marked contrast to the way in which Aeschylus resolves the curse on Orestes for the killing of his mother, Clytemnestra. The mother, it is argued, is not the real parent of the child, only the father: *Eumenides* 658–61.   [59] Spivey, *Greek Sculpture*, 84–95.

[60] Ibid., 111–13.

[61] The famous eighteenth century German critic, Winckelmann, made the association with democracy. For other, more plausible factors, Spivey, 22–9. Those mentioned include the greater flexibility allowed by the development of hollow casting of bronze in the sixth century compared to the solidity of marble. Apotropaic sculpture would include such figures as Medusa with her famous stare.

[62] For a detailed study of the move to Ionic as part of an innovating tradition, R. F. Rhodes, *Architecture and Meaning on the Athenian Acropolis* (Cambridge: Cambridge University Press, 1995), *passim*, esp. 53–60.

Making for still more engagement was also (as noted earlier) the necessity for art to concentrate on a more focused image to act as a reminder of the myth's narrative.

One important, indirect consequence was the way in which this generated powerful new stresses in the myth. So, for instance, the origins of Aphrodite are shorn of their narrative crudity and already prepare the way for Botticelli.[63] Of course, such changes were sometimes only made for dramatic effect, as with the addition of a snake to the blinding of Polyphemus.[64] But, however restricted the original intention may have been, frequently the actual impact must have been to refocus the myth in a more religious or moral direction. Thus, the tragic intensity of Ajax's suicide draws us away from any identification with Odysseus, whose behaviour had caused the incident, just as the sight of King Priam of Troy pleading for the body of his son, Hector, turns us away from empathy with the triumphant Achilles, where once the focus of the narrative had lain.[65] A greater sympathy and compassion is thus extracted from the viewer, whether or not this was the artist's primary motive, or indeed his motive at all. So, simply in virtue of how the visual arts function, further developments necessarily take place; precisely because the artist must focus on one incident rather than another as his reminder of the narrative as a whole, in effect a new narrative emerges. It is a point which, as a later chapter will demonstrate, applies as much to Christian as to Greek art.

However, the telling of the narrative version can itself also change substantially and indeed had to, if the myths were still to speak to a society which in due course had no major external threat to fear such as Persia or Sparta and which also now understood the

[63] Aphrodite arising from the foam of the sea is common in art from 460 BC, while no allusion is ever made to the reason given for the foam in the earlier narrative: the castration of the god Uranus. Carpenter, *Art and Myth*, 69. Botticelli's painting *The Birth of Venus* also develops the myth by giving it a strong Neo-Platonic context: E. H. Gombrich, *Symbolic Images* (Oxford: Phaedon, 3rd edn., 1975), 31–78, esp. 72–5.

[64] Illustrated in H. A. Shapiro, *Myth into Art* (London: Routledge, 1994), 53.

[65] For Ajax, ibid., 149–54, esp. figure 107; for Priam, ibid., 38–45, esp. figure 24. Shapiro also gives a number of other examples. We need also to guard against thinking that the artist is always dependent on some literary model; cf. Carpenter, *Art and Myth*, 11.

nature of the gods very differently. The difference which the Roman Empire made can be seen in the use to which the gods are put by the Roman poets, Vergil and Ovid, for both of whom Augustus and the protection afforded by the State bulk large.[66] Some commentators insist that for Vergil the existence of the gods is an irrelevance,[67] but this is to ignore the way in which he stands at the end of a long line of poetic tradition that had used the gods as a way of articulating religious experience. It has its own set of rules, like opera, which means that we cannot immediately infer the poet's own views, but with caution we can still speak of a Zeus or Jupiter 'considerably refined'.[68] Even Ovid, who speaks of poetry creating the gods, also insists on their ultimate invulnerability,[69] though his heart cannot really be said to be in the religion in the way it is in the story-telling.

The later poet, Statius (d. AD 96), with his extensive use of allegory, more truly represents the direction in which the classical tradition was to go, and indeed had already largely gone. The attempts of philosophers of his own day and later to allegorize Homer are commonly regarded with contempt, and indeed many such proposed readings can only strike us, like much of the medieval allegorizing of Scripture, as forced and artificial.[70] Yet it would be unfair to universalize this judgement, when so much of Stoicism and Neo-Platonism used such allegorization as a way of analysing their own sense of the divine. Though Plotinus never mentions Homer by name, significantly it is to the *Iliad* that he appeals to characterize his own deeply felt religious experience.

---

[66] Vergil is much the more subtle of the two. Augustus is named only twice or thrice in the *Aeneid*, whereas Ovid frequently resorts to flattery, and indeed ends his *Metamorphoses* with what can only strike the modern mind as a cringing eulogy of the imperial house: 15.746 ff.

[67] e.g. G. W. Williams, *Technique and Ideas in the Aeneid* (New Haven: Yale University Press, 1983), *passim*, but esp. 28, 213.

[68] A powerful defence of this view is given by D. C. Feeney, *The Gods in Epic* (Oxford: Clarendon Press, 1991), esp. 43–8, 152–59 (esp.153), 176–80.

[69] Ovid, *Ex Ponto*, 4.8.55: di quoque carminibus, si fas est dicere, fiunt; *Ars Amatoria* 1.637: expedit esse deos et, ut expedit, esse putemus. Contrast *Metamorphoses* 2.621–2: neque enim caelestia tingui ora licet lacrimis (for heavenly faces are not permitted to be moistened by tears).

[70] For some examples, Proclus's treatment of the *Iliad* discussed in R. Lamberton, *Homer the Theologian* (Berkeley: University of California Press, 1986), 199–221.

Coming to a perception of the divine in things, he maintains, is rather like when Achilles was grasped from behind by the goddess Athena, and so enabled to see her awesome glory.[71] Origen too makes a comparison between such readings and his own multivalent reading of Scripture.[72] Accordingly, just as we must exercise imagination in recognizing that this is how the Scriptures were experienced by Origen, so also we need to acknowledge that Homer was often now experienced in a similar fashion in the ancient world. As with Scripture too, there was a similar tension between whether a morally acceptable literal meaning had to be found, or whether literal and deeper meaning could be allowed to pull in different directions.[73] For later Neo-Platonism the blind seer Demodocus became Homer's self-portrait as the religious visionary at work,[74] while their image of Odysseus as pilgrim is one to which we shall return shortly.

The power of such transformations is well indicated by the extent of their incorporation into the new religion of Christianity. Though the gods were to take on some strange guises in the Middle Ages, phenomena as varied as the key role of Vergil in Dante or the Order of the Golden Fleece at the Burgundian court illustrate the continuing, wide ranging influence of classical myth.[75] A still larger role was to be achieved at the Renaissance. Nor can this be regarded as simply a thin veneer for something other than Christianity. Sometimes no doubt it was, but more commonly Christian and classical values were thoroughly integrated. Zwingli

[71] Homer, *Iliad* 1. 188–222, esp. 199–200; Plotinus, *Enneads* 6.5.7.

[72] Origen, *Contra Celsum* 1. 42. For an early example of an attempt to incorporate the appeal of Homer into the lives of the apostles, in *The Acts of Andrew*: D. R. MacDonald, *Christianizing Homer* (New York: Oxford University Press, 1994).

[73] Porphyry appears sometimes to have insisted on the moral acceptability of a literal reading before allegory should proceed: Lamberton, *Homer the Theologian*, 124. By contrast Proclus took the unacceptability of the literal as indicative of a deeper meaning: *In Rep.* 1. 193. 26—194. 11.

[74] Demodocus plays a large role in *Odyssey* 8. Added force to this religious dimension was given by the tradition of Homer being blind, like the famous seer, Tiresias. The author of the *Homeric Hymn to Apollo* identifies himself as blind: 3. 172.

[75] In tracing the continuing influence of classical myth through the Middle Ages, particularly useful is J. Seznec, *The Survival of the Pagan Gods* (Princeton, NJ: Princeton University Press, 1953).

even promised King Francis I that he would one day see both Adam and Hercules in heaven, while Erasmus declared that an allegorical reading of myth was preferable to much Scripture taken literally.[76] Much the same applies in art. Vergil's powerful evocation of Aeneas' consulting the Sibyl at Cumae, near Naples, we now know to be based on an actual site (discovered in 1932).[77] The acceptance of such pagan prophets came early in Christianity, partly because of Jewish interpolations in the *Sibylline Books*.[78] But the presence of sibyls alongside prophets on the ceiling of the Sistine Chapel witnesses to a much stronger claim that would have been shared alike by Michelangelo and his papal patrons:[79] that the classical world, no less than the biblical, witnesses to the presence of God.[80] Again, if we take another committed Christian artist, Rubens, we completely misread his mythological paintings unless we perceive them as Christian allegories.

In the fourteenth century the anonymous *Ovid moralisé* and Boccaccio's *Genealogia deorum* had led the way. At one level the lack of historical sensitivity reflected in such writings is to be regretted. For its recovery, though, classical studies was to pay a huge price. Precisely because their myths were now seen as reflecting only a world that is past, classical texts began to lose their power for the present and so any major perceived worth in their study. Much contemporary research now focuses on the history of that influence. In a perceptive study of one such particular case, the story of Daedalus and Icarus, the author traces the way in which over time it has been variously used to explore the legitimacy or otherwise of human aspirations. Significantly, he ends by speaking of our right to use the language of truth, as we judge the attempts of the myth by 'assuming new shapes and answering new

---

[76] Zwingli, *Christiani fidei brevis et clara expositio* of 1531; Erasmus, *Enchiridion militis Christiani* of 1518: 'Immo fortasse plusculo fructu legetur poetica cum allegoria, quam narratio sacrorum librorum, si consistas in cortice.'

[77] Vergil, *Aeneid* 6. 35 ff; H. W. Parke, *Sibyls and Sibylline Prophecy* (London: Routledge, 1988), 71–99, esp. 80.

[78] Ibid., 152–73.

[79] For the complex symbolism behind Michelangelo's seven prophets and five sibyls, E. Wind, 'Michelangelo's prophets and sibyls' in G. Holmes (ed.), *Art and Politics in Renaissance Italy* (Oxford: Oxford University Press, 1993), 263–300.

[80] A less well known but quite splendid example in wood of such use of the sibyls is to be found in the choir stalls in the Münster at Ulm, made by Syrlin the Elder *c.*1470.

needs' to reflect those questions.[81] Certainly, if classical literature is ever again to recover its pre-eminence, what would be needed is not only recognition of contexts and meanings that are past, but also new readings that can continue to speak to the present.[82] Therein surely also lies a lesson for Judaism and Christianity for their own relations to their specific traditions.

Some anticipatory examples

Let me conclude this discussion of the role of myth in the classical world with consideration of a few specific examples that will allow us to anticipate some of the issues which the next section will raise with regard to the three patriarchal figures, Abraham, Isaac, and Joseph. Though the differences must not be underestimated, significant points of comparison will emerge, as we shall see in due course. Here I shall treat each of the classical figures in their own right, but lurking behind their introduction is the thought that Abraham may usefully be compared with Odysseus (Ulysses in Latin), Isaac with Iphigenia, and Joseph, perhaps rather more surprisingly, with Helen and Ganymede.

Odysseus

The opening line of the *Odyssey* describes its hero as *polutropos*. It is likely that the phrase is deliberately ambiguous ('a man of many turns'), intended to conjure up not only the length and variety of Odysseus' many wanderings before his eventual return home but also his need to adopt many wiles or strategies to secure that return. Already in the first line of the poem we have the foundation for the two very different directions in which his story was later to develop: the image of the journey as spiritual quest ('home' in an enlarged sense) and meditation on whether the wiles employed to get there should be viewed as cleverness in a good or

---

[81] N. Rudd, 'Daedalus and Icarus' in C. Martindale, *Ovid Renewed* (Cambridge: Cambridge University Press, 1988), 21–53, esp. 35, 53.

[82] For examples of contemporary poets attempting this with Ovid, M. Hoffmann and J. Lasdun (eds.), *After Ovid: New Metamorphoses* (London: Faber and Faber, 1994).

bad sense. Abraham's journeys were of course likewise given a larger significance. Though less prominent, there are also later indications of doubts about the propriety of some of Abraham's actions, just as those of Odysseus were to be challenged, though not by Homer himself.

As questioning of the legitimacy of Odysseus' actions arose long before any use was made of his journey as an image for spiritual pilgrimage, let us first note developments in this regard. Given the exalted position assigned to Homer in Greek society, it is surprising to observe how extensively his positive characterization of Odysseus was already being undermined in the fifth century. Homer had treated Ajax as a foil to Odysseus, and his gruff words to Achilles in *Iliad* 9 are contrasted with those of the more diplomatic Odysseus. In *Iliad* 23 Ajax loses to Odysseus in a foot-race, not significant in itself, but prophetic of a more troubling defeat in the contest for the award of Achilles' armour. Here a speech was required (Odysseus' forte). Ajax takes the loss so badly that not only does he go mad and commit suicide but his ghost also refuses to speak to Odysseus, who appears to him in Hades (*Odyssey* 11) and addresses him with 'honeyed words'. No less than three times does Pindar refer to the dispute, implying on each occasion that Ajax's simple sincerity had been abused by the wily Odysseus.[83] With Euripides Odysseus fares no better. In *Hecuba* he is portrayed as a cynical, unscrupulous and chauvinistic politician, while in *Troades*, though he never appears personally on stage, his is seen as the malign influence responsible for the death of Astyanax, Hector's son.

But perhaps the most hostile portrayal of all comes from the elderly Sophocles in his late play *Philoctetes*. At an early stage Odysseus advises Neoptolemus that lying is justified for the public good, and continues in that vein throughout the play: 'We shall appear just once more. But now for the brief span of a day turn yourself over to me for shameless conduct, and then for the rest of time you will be called most pious of all mortal men.'[84] Forty years earlier in his *Ajax* Sophocles had offered a more sympathetic portrait of Odysseus, with Ajax presented as unnecessarily intransigent. Yet

---

[83] *Nemean* 7. 23–30; *Nemean* 8. 21–32; *Isthmian* 4.35 ff.

[84] *Philoctetes* 82–5 (my trans.) This play dates from 409 BC, when Sophocles was in his eighties. The date of *Ajax* is less certain.

even here the play opens with the goddess Athena hailing Odysseus: 'Son of Laertius, I have always seen you hunting for some means of snatching at your foes.'[85] The two speeches from Antisthenes, the Cynic, follower of Socrates, which end up favouring Odysseus, suggest that a lively debate about the nature of political morality was mediated through the story of Odysseus. No doubt those commentators are right who suggest that Athenian disillusionment with political intrigue played a large part in generating changed attitudes.[86]

Vergil continued the negative trend. Though the end of Hesiod's *Theogony* would have allowed the Romans to trace their origins to Odysseus himself,[87] instead Vergil opted for the defeated Trojans and thus there entered firmly into the European tradition the notion of the renamed Ulysses as devious, with the equation of 'Greek' with scheming and 'Trojan' with manly.[88] It was not till the Renaissance that any significant attempt was made to redress the balance, with Petrarch's translation of the *Odyssey* into Latin in the 1360s and the recovery of the influence of Plutarch's more positive attitude. Commentators disagree about how Shakespeare intends us to judge Ulysses in *Troilus and Cressida*. 'The policy of ... that same dog-fox, Ulysses, is not proved worth a blackberry,' declares Thersites, but on the other side needs to be set Thersites' generally low view of all the participants, while to Ulysses is given an impressive speech on the importance of order in society.[89] That speech, however, can too easily be pulled out of its context. A more likely judgement, therefore, is that Shakespeare intended to use Ulysses as a vehicle for opening up debate, rather than specifically committing himself either way. By contrast, seventeenth-century France adopted firm convictions. Though Racine in his play *Iphigénie en Aulide* remains hostile,

[85] *Ajax* 1–2 (my trans.)

[86] So W. B. Stanford, *The Ulysses Theme* (Oxford: Blackwell, 1954), 102–17, esp. 109. Less plausible is his attempt to impute personal motives, such as racial prejudice to Pindar (94), personal failure to Euripides (116), or simply dramatic purpose for the change of attitude in *Philoctetes* (110–11).

[87] *Theogony* 1011–13: Latinus as the son of Odysseus.

[88] *Aeneid* 2 is unrelentingly negative. Ironically, American use of 'Trojan' as a term for a condom means that Vergil's sense survives (admittedly, in a debased way) among millions who have never heard of either him or the Trojan war.

[89] For Thersites' comment, 5. 4; for the famous speech on 'degrees', 1.3.

Archbishop Fénelon in his *Aventures de Télémaque* of 1699 goes so far as to use Ulysses as his chief exemplar of how a prince ought to behave, a pattern which is repeated by Vico in Italy in the following century. At one level such vicissitudes could of course be read as no more than attempts to return to the Homeric portrait, but that would, I think, be a mistake. In effect, the story had become a handle for considering the complex issues of political morality. It allowed these to be discussed at a safe distance from the particularities of the present, and as such this constitutes one major factor that helps explain the continuing popularity of this man 'of many turns'.

But still more important was the other meaning of that phrase, the reference to Odysseus' many journeys, as he embarked on his long meanderings back from Troy. In the nineteenth century Schliemann's famous archaeological investigations at Troy were to give a considerable boost to belief in the essential historicity of the Homeric poems, which were confidently thought to reflect both the Mycenaean world and a decisive fall of Troy at the end of the thirteenth century BC. It was a confidence which was to last until at least the 1950s, and for some scholars much longer.[90] In an influential book the distinguished ancient historian, Moses Finley, ridicules the position, observing for instance the way in which all knowledge of chariot fighting has been lost, with the result that the poet can find no better use for the chariot than as means of transport to bring warriors to a suitable place for combat on foot![91] His solution is to suggest that both poems are essentially fictitious creations, from the Dark Age of the tenth or ninth century BC, with an occasional (often ill-understood) anachronism. While he seems right that there is nothing that requires an earlier date, and much to make it problematic (the most likely candidate, Troy VIIa, is 'a pitiful, poverty-stricken little place', compared to Schliemann's original suggestion of Troy II),[92] an orally developing poetry does allow the possibility of considerable changes over the centuries as the

---

[90] H. Lorimer, *Homer and the Monuments* (1950) gives a lengthy list of alleged Mycenaean parallels. A. J. B. Wace and F. H. Stubbings (eds.), *A Companion to Homer* (London: Macmillan, 1962), exhibits a similar confidence.

[91] M. I. Finley, *The World of Odysseus* (Harmondsworth: Penguin, 2nd edn., 1978), 45.

[92] Ibid., 164. Schliemann himself withdrew his identification with Troy II in 1890.

bards sought to make their stories more readily intelligible to their immediate audience. So a fragile historical core is not altogether impossible. The problem is worth noting since there has been, as we shall see, a similar decline in confidence in what had once seemed to be the proven historicity of the patriarchal narratives.

As with biblical studies, it was the eighteenth century that had initiated this renewed interest in the historicity of the Homeric narrative. One finds it reflected, for instance, in the notes to Alexander Pope's translation, where he is insistent that Odysseus should be judged by the standards of his own time, as also in the attempts of artists to respond to Winckelmann's censures that costume and manner should reflect those of the ancient world. Two classical scholars reviewing that past in 1974 comment on the 'fairness' of the more balanced portrait offered in the twentieth century by Joyce and Kazantzakis, a comment that turns out to be premised not only on their relation to Homer but also on an assumption of Homer's own basis in history.[93] Yet, as their own survey reveals, what has really given Odysseus his power, even in these two twentieth-century adaptations, is not really the journeys in themselves, but their mythic quality, and it is that trend which has continued even into the late twentieth century, as, for instance, in Derek Walcott's epic poem *Omeros* or Theo Angelopoulos' film *Ulysses' Gaze*.[94] Indeed, in Joyce's case the analogy is transformed into a single day's wanderings through the city of Dublin. Though Joyce attempts detailed parallels with Homer (Circe, for example, becomes a brothel keeper), these remain unknown to the principal actor, Leopold Bloom, whose own parallels are drawn from his own lineage as son of an Hungarian Jew. So in his own perception Bloom might be construed as a kind of Abraham figure, searching for Zion while lost by the waters of Babylon.[95] Abraham and

[93] W. B. Stanford and J. V. Luce, *The Quest for Ulysses* (Oxford: Phaidon, 1974), 220, 233.

[94] Though *Omeros* (London: Faber & Faber, 1990) does include literal wanderings through America and Europe (Bks. 4, 5), the spiritual return of Achilles to Africa in Book 3 underlines the deeper intention. Similarly, *Ulysses' Gaze* (1995) makes thirty-five years of absence away from home conclude with a search for deeper self-understanding in further wanderings through the Balkans.

[95] Bloom is a Jew by birth and a Roman Catholic by baptism, though non-practising. The extent of any analogy, though, is complicated by Bloom often getting comically wrong what little he has learnt of the two faiths.

Ulysses to some degree thus merge, with both engaged in a similar type of spiritual quest. Yet it is the quest for a secular Zion compared to Kanzantzakis' more mystic vision.[96] Indeed, the religious element predominates in most of what preceded Joyce, where parallels are to be found drawn not only with Abraham but even with Christ himself. Neo-Platonism helped set an example. Plotinus, for instance, provides us with a fine passage in which our personal spiritual quest is seen in terms of Odysseus' own search for his homeland, though Proclus did later try to qualify such an approach by insisting also upon the moral appropriateness of a literal reading.[97] Among the Church Fathers both Origen and Gregory of Nyssa seem to have been attracted by this type of reading.[98] Yet, though interpretation of Odysseus tied to the mast before the Sirens as a prefiguration of Christ comes early,[99] the best known medieval treatment is of quite a different kind.

For Dante Ulysses is the pre-eminent example of a journey wrongly pursued, of knowledge sought without limit, and so he stands condemned in Hell:

> No tenderness for my son, nor piety
> …
> Could conquer in me the restless itch to rove
> And rummage through the world exploring it,
> All human worth and wickedness to prove.[100]

In such terms does Ulysses describe his attempt to sail the uncharted waters of the Atlantic. Ironically, the man after whom America is named, Americo Vespucci, took Dante's images literally and attempted to correct him, as he himself sailed beyond that

[96] The religious import of Kanzantzakis' very long poem (his *Odyssey* is 33, 333 lines long) is hard to interpret. At one point God appears on a mountain as a lonely and rather frightened old tramp, but the religious character of the quest continues with both Orthodox and Buddhist overtones.

[97] Plotinus, *Enneads* 1.6.8; Proclus *In Rep.* 1.131. 5–14.

[98] e.g. Origen, *Contra Celsum* 3, 66; Gregory of Nyssa, *Letters* 8.

[99] H. Rahner, 'Odysseus am Mastbaum', in *Symbole der Kirche* (Salzburg: Müller, 1954), 239–71; idem, *Greek Myths and Christian Mystery* (London: Burns & Oates, 1963), 353–86.

[100] Dante, *Inferno* 26. 94–9. D. L. Sayers' translation in *Divine Comedy* I *Hell* (Harmondsworth: Penguin, 1949).

western limit. It makes fascinating reading to observe how such a revised Dantean Ulysses and Christopher Columbus' more Messianic interpretation compete, as the new world is explored.[101] A return to Dante's pessimism was to become a marked feature of nineteenth- and twentieth-century accounts, as absolute confidence in scientific advance declined, among which must be numbered Tennyson's *Ulysses* despite its famous self-description:

> And this grey spirit yearning in desire
> To follow knowledge like a sinking star,
> Beyond the utmost bound of human thought.[102]

Yet he is more optimistic than Newman in a poem from the previous year (1832), despite the latter's explicit comparison with Christ.[103] As such, Newman is in marked contrast to most other Christian treatments. For instance, Spenser uses a parallel with Ulysses for Guyon in Book 2 of his *Faerie Queene* (1590) to imply that victory in this life can be assured. Early in the following century Chapman is also positive about this 'wise and God-observing man' who 'turns through many and various ways towards the truth';[104] so too was the dramatist Calderón in Spain, who attempted the theme twice, though once with a strong element of penitence introduced.[105]

At one level it is possible to read such variations in the treatment of Ulysses' travels as no more than reflections of the specific cultural circumstances of the society in which they happen to be set: Dante amidst medieval suspicion of alchemy, Spenser at the centre of optimism about the new, reformed faith and English expansionism, modern uncertainties in Joyce and Kazantzakis over what this century has wrought. But that would be to tell only half

---

[101] Cf. P. Boitani, *The Shadow of Ulysses* (Oxford: Clarendon Press, 1994), 44–123, esp. 55 ff.

[102] Tennyson, *Ulysses* 30–2. Tennyson was only 24 at the time, but the poem clearly reflects his own determination to go on, despite his friend Hallam's death and uncertainty about what the future may bring.

[103] J. H. Newman, *Verses on Various Occasions* 37 'Isle of the Sirens'; note also R. S. Edgecombe's comments on the poem in *Two Poets of the Oxford Movement* (London: Associated University Presses, 1996), 208–9.

[104] Preface to Chapman, *Homer's Odyssey* (1616).

[105] The second play *Los encantos de la culpa*, written after he had become a priest, is a more allegorical version of the first, *El mayor encanto, amor*.

the tale. One aspect of Greek religion is often forgotten: that Greeks consulted the shrines of heroes no less than the oracles of the gods.[106] Stanford ends his survey of this long tradition by suggesting that, just as the worshipper once felt invigorated at the hero's shrine, so later in history 'a mutually energising power was exchanged between the author and the hero'.[107] That was a wise insight. For, however much social conditioning may have been involved, there is no reason to think that it had the final or exclusive say. Just as the journeys of Abraham had their good and bad aspects and so prompted further thought about life's pilgrimage, so those of Ulysses also elicited further reflection on the patterning of readers' lives. If in Dante's day they allowed the warning to be heard of 'enough and no more', so in our own even more pessimistic twentieth century the very image of those journeys refused pessimism the last word.[108] For even those most tempted to make that judgement today still end declaring the necessity of the spiritual journey, even if they are altogether uncertain where it might lead.[109]

Iphigenia

Of the three, Iphigenia is the parallel which may be dealt with most briefly at this stage. As will become apparent when we consider Isaac in the next chapter, there is a similar wrestling with the issue of sacrifice: who may demand it and why, and whether the principal focus should be on parent or child.

Though some have found the basis of the Iphigenia myth in rituals of sacrificing deer preparatory to marriage,[110] clearly the written version has broken free of any such possible constraints.

[106] One review makes this the main point of critique of a seminal work which we discussed earlier, G. S. Kirk's *Myth* and its attempt to divorce myth from religion: J. G. Griffiths, *Classical Review* (1972), 235–8.

[107] Stanford *The Ulysses Theme*, 246.

[108] Perhaps seen most clearly in the conclusion of Joyce's novel with its repeated use of 'yes', culminating in 'and yes I said yes I will Yes': *Ulysses* (Harmondsworth: Penguin, 1968), 704.

[109] This is the conclusion reached by Boitani in his survey of other twentieth-century applications such as those of Joseph Conrad and Primo Levi, and despite his own conviction that we live 'in a world where belief in God is no longer possible': *Shadow*, 149–88, esp. 165.

[110] Dowden, *Uses*, 107.

The fact that Homer gives her name in a rather different form, and fails even to mention the most famous story associated with her, has been taken as evidence of his dislike for that particular tale, but more probably it merely represents his concern that Agamemnon should not be presented in either too tragic or too sympathetic a light.[111] Aeschylus has no such hesitations, and so it is in his play *Agamemnon* that the myth first survives in its full gruesome form: the only way of appeasing the wrath of the goddess Artemis (who has becalmed the Greek fleet at Aulis before it can even set forth for Troy) is for its commander, Agamemnon, to sacrifice his own daughter. Later versions explain Artemis' wrath as due to Agamemnon having killed an animal sacred to her and perhaps also boasted in consequence of his superiority to the goddess,[112] whereas Aeschylus leaves us without any explicit explanation. The chorus speak of two eagles devouring a pregnant hare, but this is probably not an explanation, but rather a metaphor for what Agamemnon is about to do to his daughter. The result is that many commentators pronounce the play incoherent.[113]

The plot of Euripides' *Iphigenia at Aulis* is very different. Here Artemis intervenes to snatch the girl away, substituting in her place a deer, but not before, in what is clearly the heart of the play, she has moved from resistance to voluntary self-sacrifice.[114] It is clearly an issue that interested Euripides, as the theme of human sacrifice is taken up by him in a number of his other plays. In *Iphigenia in Tauris* Iphigenia is about to be forced by the natives of this remote place (situated in the Crimea) to sacrifice her brother when she recognizes him and they both flee, while in his *Hecuba* we find the dead Achilles demanding the sacrifice of the Trojan Polyxena at his tomb. In that latter play the virtue and nobility of Polyxena is contrasted with the violence and boorishness of the Greeks.

In later treatments it is Euripides' version which prevails. We find Iphigenia's offer treated as a symbol both of the triumph of

[111] 'Iphianassa' in *Iliad* 9. 144–5; T. Ganz, *Early Greek Myth* (Baltimore: Johns Hopkins University Press, 1993), 582.

[112] Though Euripides in *Iphigenia in Tauris* offers yet another explanation: that Agamemnon had made a vow to give to Artemis the most beautiful thing which that year would bring forth (15–25).

[113] Aeschylus, *Agamemnon* 104–21; M. Simpson (ed.) *Gods and Heroes of the Greeks: The Library of Apollodorus* (Amherst: University of Massachusetts Press, 1976), 283–5.   [114] *Iphigenia at Aulis* 1368 ff.

the common good over private affection, and of the integrity of self-sacrifice.[115] Both father and child are thus portrayed in a favourable light, even if the divine is in some versions left as arbitrary and unfeeling. Lucretius used the sacrifice to condemn religion: 'such was the enormity of evil that was urged upon humanity by religion.'[116] Yet seldom is the myth appropriated in this way elsewhere, not least because Agamemnon's initial arrogance could so easily be stressed, as also Artemis' care for the girl. In a Christian context Giambattista Tiepelo's painting of the scene in the Villa Valmarana in Vicenza illustrates the myth's potential. On entering the room one is confronted with a willing Iphigenia already on the altar, while her father's face is buried in his cloak, so overcome is he by grief. But Iphigenia is looking to heaven, and forces our gaze also to the ceiling, where at the furthest end the goddess is already appearing. Love, we are being told, must be willing to yield to duty, even if the sacrifice is not always required.[117]

Even if only mediated through Ovid, for much of Christian history the sacrifice of Iphigenia has been almost as well known as that of Isaac. Though it is hard to prove direct influence, undoubtedly, as we shall see in the next chapter, many similar considerations and reflections have been applied in both cases. For some that may be an occasion for regret, but I fail to see why God should not have used a similar story to help illuminate how the Scriptures can themselves best be appropriated.

Helen and Ganymede

With Joseph our anticipatory parallels are less direct, and to the uninitiated will no doubt appear somewhat surprising, since they refer less to the biblical text itself, and more to its subsequent use, where the incident with Potiphar's wife becomes the focus for

---

[115] Both points are stressed in Ovid's brief account: *Metamorphoses* 12. 25 ff.

[116] Lucretius, *De Rerum Natura* 1. 84–101 (my trans). Significantly, he makes the sacrifice happen, and so fully justifies his final line: *tantum religio potuit suadere malorum*. The use of a spondaic word within the first foot of the hexameter is rare and deliberately emphatic. G. K. Chesterton used the line to complain when he had to get out of bed for early Mass.

[117] For illustrations and discussion of the painting, M. Levey, *Giambattista Tiepelo* (New Haven: Yale University Press, 1986), 229–32.

sustained reflection on the nature of temptation, and marriage to Aseneth a spur to thinking about conversion. The nature of virtue and religious experience is thus effectively explored through sexual relations, and this is what we also find to some degree in the changes that are made to the stories of Helen and Ganymede. However, before turning to these, one word of caution seems appropriate. While it must be conceded that in general Greek attitudes to women were more negative than those to be found within the Bible and Christian tradition, it is important to observe that the generality of that truth need not apply in every specific instance, and that is what I think we find with Helen. Perhaps another example will help to make the point even more strongly, and that is the treatment of Pandora. Hesiod's very negative treatment of the first woman is well-known,[118] and it would be easy to make a rash jump from that early presentation to the fault of her later largely negative image in the Christian era as lying at the door of the Greeks. But this will not do. As a matter of fact she occurs very seldom in the classical tradition, and then mostly in a strongly positive light.[119] What made the difference was the attempt by some Church Fathers to draw a parallel with Eve. When these texts became available once more at the Renaissance along with Hesiod's, the sanctioning of the negative image became too powerful to resist.[120] So, when we think of the many negative artistic images of women that Pandora was used to convey, it is Christianity for once that must shoulder the greater blame, not Greece. Though the negative interpretations nearest to our own time seldom make an explicit reference to Eve, very many from earlier generations do.[121]

---

[118] Hesiod, *Works and Days* 57–101; *Theogony* 570–90.

[119] Pandora does not occur in Ovid or Vergil, while in the Greek tradition her use on the base of Pheidias' statue of Athene in the Parthenon must be positive (Spivey, *Greek Sculpture*, 168–9), as clearly also is Plotinus' play on her name to indicate the material world as the source of many blessings: *Enneads* 4.3.14.

[120] The parallel is found, for instance, in Gregory of Nazianzus, *Adversus mulieres se nimis ornantes* 115 ff.; Origen, *Contra Celsum* IV, 38. Neither Hesiod nor Origen's *Contra Celsum* were available in Latin until the late fifteenth century: D. and E. Panofsky, *Pandora's Box* (2nd edn., Princeton, NJ: Princeton University Press, 1962), 14.

[121] For more recent treatments of the theme from Rossetti, Klee and Beckmann, Panofsky, *Pandora's Box*, illus. 56–7, 59–60. As examples of the connection being made, one might note in the sixteenth century the title Jean

Goethe did not adopt that approach. Instead, in his three explorations of the Pandora myth, a positive, allegorical account is offered,[122] and this is how we also find him treating Helen. Whereas for Marlowe in his *Doctor Faustus* she is no more than the embodiment of sensual beauty ('the face that launched a thousand ships'), for Goethe in his version of the Faustus legend she has clearly become a symbol of all that is best in classical humanism.[123] The classical world did not itself go that far, but almost from the beginning of written presentations we find it debated how far she could herself be blamed for the Trojan war. Jew and Greek did of course have very different attitudes to sexuality, and so sexual temptation could never have quite the same meaning for the Greek as it did for the Jew, but the Helen myth does seem to have stimulated some parallel degree of reflection regarding the extent to which the woman might legitimately herself be blamed.

In Homer two tendencies are present: the first is to blame Helen, and indeed she sometimes blames herself; the second is to blame the gods.[124] But already with Hesiod we find the existence of an alternative version, according to which only a phantom went in her stead, while Helen herself travelled to Egypt.[125] This is the account the historian Herodotus received from Egyptian priests and which he accepts, arguing that the Trojans would never have fought a war to defend such a worthless seducer as Paris, who had robbed Menelaus of his wife.[126] Plato recounts how the poet Stesichorus recanted his earlier acceptance of the Homeric version that blamed Helen. A papyrus (only published in 1963) also now reveals that Stesichorus was equally critical of Hesiod's version, seeking for his own 'true account'.[127] What that was we do not know precisely, but the fact that Plato tells us Stesichorus was blinded for accepting Homer's version surely suggests that his revisions must have lain in either exonerating Helen or at the very

---

Clousin chose for his painting in the Louvre (*Eva Prima Pandora*), while in the eighteenth Sir James Barry makes similar connections in his notes to his painting 'Creation of Pandora': Panofsky, 61–2, 87–9.

[122] Ibid., 122–9.

[123] Marlowe, *Doctor Faustus*, 1328–34; Goethe, *Faustus* 2.1. 6487–6500.

[124] Both tendencies are present in *Iliad* 3.161–80, while at *Odyssey* 4. 259–64 she blames Aphrodite.   [125] Hesiod, fr. 358.

[126] Herodotus, *Histories* 2. 113–19.

[127] Plato, *Phaedrus* 243 a–b; Feeney, *Gods in Epic*, 14–15.

least making Paris equally culpable. The play which Euripides named after Helen is also sympathetic to her, though its deeper theme is the deceptiveness of surface reality in general: Helen is the innocent wife of Menelaus, though the world thinks her an adulteress.[128]

What is interesting about these developments is the way in which reflection through the myth enables a complete reassessment of the roles of the two principal actors. In early versions Helen had to bear the brunt of the blame, and that despite the fact that it was Aphrodite who has made her Paris' plaything, as the goddess' reward for his favourable judgement on her beauty in the famous, so-called Judgement of Paris. On that scenario Paris and Aphrodite both got off remarkably lightly, whereas later accounts rebel, and assert Paris's full responsibility, while also showing varying degrees of sympathy for Helen herself, as well as some willingness to accord her dignity and status. As we shall note in the next chapter, Joseph's relations with Potiphar's wife are similarly used as a handle upon which to reflect about questions of responsibility and blame in the face of temptation, with similarly no single answer being given.

Goethe's treatment of Helen as a symbol of goodness has already been noted. However, for a truer parallel to Joseph's relations with Aseneth and a use of sexuality as an image of conversion and spiritual quest from within the classical world, it is to the story of Ganymede that we must turn. Inevitably, the choice will strike most readers as somewhat odd, and it is true that one stream of tradition continued to offer an account quite incompatible with any such treatment. Yet even the early origins of the myth admit of more than one reading. The image of the young Ganymede being carried off to heaven by Zeus may have had its origins in Cretan adolescents being carried off by older men to be prepared for adulthood before being returned to the community.[129] If so, an element of education was already present, though it is also not inconceivable that the myth was appropriated for such practices at a later date. Certainly, Homer's version appears to lack any

---

[128] Cf. C. H. Whitman, *Euridipes and the Full Circle of Myth* (Cambridge, Mass.: Harvard University Press, 1974), 37–9.

[129] Dowden, *Uses*, 112–17; additional support would seem to be offered by Plato's accusation that the myth was invented by Cretans to justify their pederasty (*Laws* 1. 636D).

suggestion that homosexual seduction or lust lay at the heart of the story, for it is the gods as a whole who judge Ganymede too beautiful to remain on earth.[130] The *Homeric Hymn to Aphrodite* probably has the same meaning, though this time it is Zeus himself who makes the decision.[131] In the third century BC, however, Apollonius of Rhodes leaves us in no doubt about Zeus's homosexual intent; nor does Ovid, who appears to be the first to add that Zeus adapted the guise of an eagle in order to achieve the seduction.[132]

Yet against such a pattern of development needs to be set on the other side the allegorical reading of both Plato and Xenophon that the abduction represents the ascent of the pure soul to knowledge of the divine,[133] and it is in this sense (suitably modified by a doctrine of grace) that it survives as a major image within Christianity. In the poem *Ovid moralisé* there is made what proves to be the rather unappealing suggestion that the eagle symbolizes Christ and the lad John the Baptist. The difficulty with the image thus understood was that, apart from legitimating an appropriate difference in status between Christ and John, it would seem otherwise to misrepresent the relation between the two figures. Much more acceptable, therefore, was the proposal of the Florentine Platonist, Marsilio Ficino, that Ganymede be taken to represent the soul being drawn up towards God, and it is in this sense that it entered the work of Michelangelo: the soul ravished by ecstatic union with God. That Michelangelo's drawings on the subject reflect an erotic undercurrent to his relations with Tommaso de' Cavalieri is not in doubt, but this can be exaggerated, especially as Michelangelo's poetry of the time uses equally strong erotic imagery to describe his relation with God.[134] Certainly, many Renaissance paintings were less innocent,[135] but

---

[130] *Iliad* 20. 234–5.

[131] 202–17; cf. also T. Ganz, *Early Greek Myth*, 558.

[132] Apollonius, *Argonautica* 3. 115–17; Ovid, *Metamorphoses* 10. 152–61.

[133] Plato, *Phaedrus* 255; Xenophon, *Symposium* 8. 28–30.

[134] George Bull is more plausible than James Saslow, who despite conceding Michelangelo's celibacy ends up by insisting on most prominence for homosexual content. G. Bull, *Michelangelo: A Biography* (Harmondsworth: Penguin, 1995), 249–59; J. M. Saslow, *Ganymede in the Renaissance* (New Haven: Yale University Press, 1986), 17–62, esp. 39, 62.

[135] Here Saslow is more helpful, with his stress on Ganymede's bisexual appeal: *Ganymede*, 63 ff.

the power of the imagery also breaks through in Rubens, for whom, however, the experience of being caught up into the divine presence is without any of the violent associations it had for Michelangelo.[136] His contemporary Rembrandt, though, was to sound the death-knell of this way of reading the myth: in his parody Ganymede becomes an unattractive child, urinating in fright.[137]

In this last case I do not pretend that the way in which the Joseph story developed offers particularly close parallels. My point rather is that long before Freud sexuality was being read metaphorically, as indicative of deeper levels of lived experience, and the changing pattern of myth was being used to work towards such deeper understandings. Moral and religious insight were deepened, not by endlessly identical repetitions of the same story but by willingness to hear it in new ways. The same, I believe, applies to the patriarchal narratives. Their power lies in the new ways in which they were read, no less than in the form in which they had their origins. Tradition can of course develop in bad directions as well as good, but to canonize the past simply because it is past is the way to the death of a tradition, not its life.

---

[136] C. Scribner III, *Rubens* (New York: Harry Abrams, 1989), 60–1 for illustration and commentary.

[137] Saslow, *Ganymede*, 186 for illustration, though I find his allegorical reading implausible (187–9).

5
Victim into saint: Patriarchal retellings

IN the previous chapter we observed the numerous variations to which many of the classical world's most famous myths were subject. These I argued were a source of strength rather than weakness, a vehicle through which new religious and moral insights could emerge. Even so, it is tempting to suppose Christianity essentially different, both in virtue of being an historical religion (God became incarnate at a fixed point in history) and because it has a fixed canon in a written text. That presumed contrast, I shall be concerned here to deny. For, though Christianity would not be the same religion without certain key historical claims, it by no means follows from this that history has always been, or should be, its sole controlling factor. Neither history nor canon can be allowed to function as final arbiters, since more fundamental are questions of significance. What we need to consider is whether theologically or spiritually the new versions of a story or a new use to which it is put had something valuable to say in its new context, and so perhaps also to us today.

In my chapter on revelation I argued that a developing tradition characterizes the canon as such, and that it would be arbitrary sharply to differentiate biblical and post-biblical reflection of this kind, especially as exactly the same pattern of response is to be detected in the later period to changing questions and challenges as these arose. The most common way of referring to what is seen as acceptable post-biblical change is to talk of changes in interpretation rather than changes to the text itself, but to my mind as a description of what happens that is quite inadequate. For so radical can these changes be that it is only in the most trivial sense that the text remains the same: the words on the page do not alter. Its content, focus and themes are so restructured, however, that effectively a wholly new grid has been imposed, with what is most important often seen as hidden, as it were, in the interstices of the text. The parallel with the classical world thus becomes much closer than might initially have been supposed, and 'moving text' rather than static deposit the best way of characterizing the biblical inheritance, no less than the classical.

In this chapter I want to test that claim in respect of stories that were being narrated and altered over roughly the same period of time as classical myth, namely the patriarchal narratives. In Chapter 3 we saw how a living tradition is never something static, but rather continually developing in response to the various social circumstances with which it is faced. There I emphasized that this was in no sense to advocate cultural determinism, but it was to observe that a response is most likely when certain questions become pressing, and even then the nature of the response will be conditioned in part by the range of options already existing within the tradition. Inevitably, in a Bible that claims to preserve almost two thousand years of history from Abraham leaving Ur to Paul awaiting death at Rome[1] huge social changes occurred that necessitated new ways of appropriating the past. Though, as we shall see, some more recent work has challenged the age of the patriarchal traditions, much Old Testament research this century has endorsed such a notion of developing tradition and indeed this is made explicit in the German name for one form of biblical criticism as this is applied to the Old Testament: *Traditionsgeschichte* or *Uberlieferungsgeschichte*.[2]

Even so, for me there is something deeply unsatisfactory about most Old Testament scholarship when it moves beyond the tracing

---

[1] The most popular date for Abraham has been to place him somewhere in the Middle Bronze Age (2000–1500 BC). That, it is argued, would allow him to accord well both with biblical dating and with the archaeology of the period in respect of customs generally and specific Semitic migrations in that part of the world. Paul's martyrdom is normally dated *c.* AD 65. Even if oral traditions are denied, written developments are still likely to span a thousand years from the Court History embedded in the life of David (1010–970 BC) to the early or mid-second century AD.

[2] For a good account of the various ways in which the two terms have been used, D. A. Knight, *Rediscovering the Traditions of Israel* (Missoula, Mont.: Society of Biblical Literature, 1973); for some examples of 'tradition criticism' in practice, D. A. Knight (ed.), *Tradition and Theology in the Old Testament* (London: SPCK, 1977). Gerhard von Rad is perhaps the best known Old Testament scholar associated with such an approach. In his case its use is intimately linked with the application of Form Criticism.

of such history into questions of 'meaning' or, still more problematic, revelatory significance. For the tendency remains to 'freeze' one particular reading of the text as normative, whether it be original context, the presumed intentions of particular sources, the book's final canonical form, or its significance when viewed in the light of the New Testament. Nor do more recent, literary approaches necessarily avoid this problem.[3] Some of its advocates do remain sensitive to the past history of the text, but with others reference to historical context appears sometimes to be taken as a challenge to the integrity of the text, and then there is a real danger that all in the end we are left with is the prioritizing of the assumptions and prejudices of the present moment. What instead I am concerned to advocate here is that we take seriously each stage of the development as at least in principle capable of informing our present understanding.

In saying this I am concerned to advocate rather more than a simple willingness to listen to the plurality of the past. What I want to do is detach the reader from supposing that only certain forms of imposition upon an earlier text are acceptable, those that are canonical or which reflect our present day concerns. For, if by their most natural interpretation changes within the canon already exhibit a relative lack of restraint, why should we necessarily despise a similar pattern in later history? Would that not be to fossilize the message? It would be to assume that God's activity can be caught at one instant of time, as though tradition, whether human or divine, could be artificially pulled out of the specifics of its historical setting. Rather, what I suggest we have are numerous points in a development; some permanently enlightening, others not.

Admittedly, one could concede a plurality of such points within the Scriptures, and then deny any subsequent development. But, if so, two very serious objections need to be faced. First, if such conditioning is the mark of developments within Scripture, why should the normal pattern of the development of the tradition cease when every other form of historical change continues? Does

---

[3] The most influential has been the work of Robert Alter: *The Art of Biblical Narrative* (London: HarperCollins, 1981); *The World of Biblical Literature* (London: SPCK, 1992); *Genesis* (New York: Norton, 1996). Unlike many of his followers, Alter is not guilty of the fault of which I complain in the text.

it not make the Bible an arbitrary and inexplicable exception to the normal patterns of human thinking, which always work within a developing context? Or, putting the point in more explicitly theological terms, if God accepted such conditioning as part of his dialogue with humanity within the period of the canon, why should it ever have ceased? Secondly, since as a matter of fact we know that such developments did continue, what theological explanation are we to give of them, if for most of the history of the three monotheistic religions, for almost all their adherents, what has been believed and transmitted is not some photographed original instant, but a constantly developing and still running film? Does it not suggest that divine action continued in the same way as it had once operated within the canonical communities, with God taking seriously the new social contexts in which the communities of faith now found themselves? Of course each of the three religions have traditionally seen themselves as alternatives to one another, but even so it would be odd if they were to make the ways of providence even more difficult to comprehend by insisting that what has passed for revealed truth through most of their own history was no such thing.

Such a perspective confers one important added advantage: it entails the possibility of an alternative form of dialogue between the three main monotheistic religions. Instead of setting them in simple opposition to one another, account needs to be taken of how a developing tradition has shaped the story in each case. The result will be that what appears to be deep conflict will sometimes turn out not after all to be so. I shall try to illustrate the point in what follows. So, for instance, the fact that within Islam Ishmael is normally taken as the subject of Abraham's sacrifice rather than Isaac might seem irreconcilable, whereas my contention will be that the Muslim choice exhibits a similar rationale for change as is to be found within later Jewish and Christian forms of the story, though differently implemented. Again, Paul so fundamentally alters the original meaning of the Abraham story that greater respect for comparable degrees of change within Judaism and Islam is required, if Christians are not to find themselves committed to condemning their own tradition.

But my argument is unlikely to carry conviction without detailed consideration of specific examples. To these, therefore, I now turn. Despite the repeated scriptural formula linking Jacob with Abraham and Isaac,[4] I have decided to substitute Joseph in his place for consideration here. This is because, despite the profound use to which Jacob's wrestling at Peniel was put within the Christian tradition (Gen. 32: 22–32),[5] and even a possible parallel with Oedipus,[6] as a whole what happens is less interesting than with Joseph. Perhaps precisely because Jacob became the eponymous founder of Israel, apart from compliments Judaism is very reserved, while Islam almost wholly ignores him.[7] To describe, as in the title of the chapter, what happens in the developing tradition to these three patriarchs as the transformation of 'victim into saint' may seem singularly inapposite for a narrative so full of action, but its justification will, I hope, become clear once the reader has been made aware of those particular features of the narrative on which I wish to focus. The easiest to indicate briefly is Isaac as sacrificial victim. We begin, however, with Abraham. Apart from historical order this has one added advantage. The change in his case is often thought not to be radical. But, if we can establish otherwise, then it may perhaps make the reader more inclined to view favourably the still more extensive alterations that were applied in the case of Isaac and Joseph. In each of the three examples, we shall note the criteria that might be used to legitimate such changes. As we shall see, more often than not, what is

---

[4] In both Old and New Testaments, e.g. Exod. 3: 6; Matt. 22: 32.

[5] As an analysis of prayer, perhaps now best known through Charles Wesley's fine poem 'Wrestling Jacob': e.g. in D. Davie (ed.), *New Oxford Book of Christian Verse* (Oxford: Oxford University Press, 1981), 167–9. For a general survey of the history of interpretation, J. Rogerson, 'Wrestling with the angel: a study in historical and literary interpretation' in A. Loades and M. McLain (eds.), *Hermeneutics, the Bible and Literary Criticism* (London: Macmillan, 1992), 131–44.

[6] G. G. Nicol, 'Jacob as Oedipus: Old Testament narrative as mythology', in *Expository Times* 108 (1996), 43–4.

[7] The Qur'an has four references (2.132–3, 6.84; 19.49; 21.72), in each of which he is linked with one or more other patriarch and no story told of him. In Judaism there is a reluctance to identify the agent with whom he wrestled as God, and the major focus for prayer moves to Bethel; for some treatments, E. G. Clarke, 'Jacob's dream at Bethel as interpreted in the targums and the New Testament', in *Sciences Religieuses* 4 (1974–5), 366–77. The difficulty is well illustrated by the conversion of Jacob's assailant into Essau's guardian angel in *Midrash Rabbah* (77–8), as by the failure of even Elie Wiesel's imaginative powers to extract anything more from the tradition than self-wrestling: E. Wiesel, *Messengers of God* (New York: Summit, 1976), 103–35.

involved is much more than a simple trajectory. Instead, the developing tradition turns back upon itself, to effect a new text.

Journeying with Abraham

In the previous chapter we saw how the wanderings of Odysseus came to function as a metaphor for something rather different. Though the historical element never entirely recedes in Abraham's case, it is true of Judaism no less than of Christianity and Islam that Abraham also is given a similar, larger role. In the process the stress falls less on God's direction of his journey and much more on his particular responses, and in that sense Abraham becomes less the passive 'victim' of events beyond his comprehension, more the initiator through God's grace of what is to come. Though 'victim' may seem too strong a term for such a contrast, there is one person in the narrative as a whole to whom its application is entirely justified, the slave-girl Hagar. Modern feminist studies have rediscovered her voice. What is less well known is how Islam transformed her desert wanderings: no more a mere victim of persecution she has become a model to be imitated by all Muslims. It is with her treatment that I shall conclude this section.

Interfaith dialogue and biblical origins

In due course we shall consider how Abraham was treated in the history of each of the three main monotheistic religions, but before doing so I want first to consider the wider issue of methodology. Because all three see in the same text to varying degrees God's revelatory hand at work, it is tempting to suppose that there already exists a shared consensus upon which we can build. In one sense that is right, but it can all too easily be used to disguise from ourselves deeper conflicts, and these need to be faced. To illustrate the point I shall use a recent work by the distinguished German scholar, Karl-Josef Kuschel. In contrast to his own conclusions, it will be my contention that in its original significance the text's most natural trajectory is towards Judaism. How that can be reconciled with the use to which Abraham is put within the New Testament will be considered in due course, but in trying to understand the development of tradition it is surely important to take seriously the issue of how each tradition develops, however problematic that might appear to be to one's own faith. 'Historical original' and present, presumed meaning can diverge considerably, and it is important to trace that development; important also to consider whether it is a development that extends behind the text to an historical personage or not. That way, not only can the possibility of various loci of revelation in that history be duly acknowledged but also the distinctiveness of each religion's development of the story be given its proper place.

Kuschel examines the development of the various traditions in some detail, but, as already noted, it is Abraham in his original significance that he finds most promising as 'a symbol of hope for Jews, Christians and Muslims' (the subtitle of his book) rather than these later traditions, which he more often than not views negatively. This is all the more surprising, when one notes that his analysis is accompanied by full endorsement of the same key role for development through cultural context which we have been advocating: 'recollection of the stories of Abraham has always been part of the theology for a specific community of faith; it has been a creative theological reaction to new historical demands which the people of Israel was not spared in its tremendous history. Christianity and Islam were simply to continue to write creative Abraham theology on their own account.'[8] Yet, despite such comments, his judgement on subsequent developments is largely negative; where he finds his symbol of hope is in the tradition's original emphases, in its universalism (a blessing on all humanity), and its stress on faith, and not in its subsequent elaboration, except where confirmation is provided for these original insights. Thus, for example, he concludes by talking about 'the normativity of the original Abraham traditions in the book of Genesis', which in his view must pass judgement upon 'narrow-minded applications of Abraham by synagogue, church and Umma', among which are included also certain developments even within the canons of the three religions concerned.[9]

What is worrying about such a conclusion is not his general

[8] K.-J. Kuschel, *Abraham: A Symbol of Hope for Jews, Christians and Muslims* (London: SCM Press, 1995), 5.

[9] Ibid., 204–5. He finds John's Gospel particularly deficient in this respect, 110–29.

moral and religious sentiments, with which I more often than not agree (Kuschel's heart is clearly in the right place in terms of tolerance and compassion), but the sense with which one feels that he is, as it were, rigging the books to obtain his conclusion. So, for example, throughout he equates the key concepts of Judaism, Christianity, and Islam (*emuna*, *pistis*, and *islam*) as 'dedicated trust' without recognizing the subtle but important differences between them. Again, we are told that the Qur'an is 'not opposed' to recognizing the authority of Genesis since it 'recognises the authority of the Hebrew Bible as a source of revelation'.[10] This is misleading to say the least since for the Muslim where the latter dissents from the Qur'an this is seen as due to a corrupt text. Likewise, the fact that Islam overwhelmingly assumes Ishmael to have been the child intended for sacrifice is passed over in a brief paragraph that mentions first the minority Muslim tradition which accepts the other two religions' endorsement of Isaac as the child involved. This is hardly adequate for so central a feature of the Muslim tradition. Again, those aspects of Christianity that reject a continuing central role for Judaism are severely criticized as disloyal to the original tradition, as though the sole motive could be bigotry, rather than issues to be given serious consideration in their own right.[11] But most worrying of all is the fact that Kuschel leaves unexamined the question of why the original version should hold such authority, especially as he appears quite willing to concede the usual scholarly doubts about how much of the tradition is in any case historical.[12] For if the universalism he detects in the text is an interpretation of past history rather than integral to the history itself, it is far from clear why it should it hold a preeminent place rather than other versions of the same story. This is surely a question that requires an answer if the charge is to be avoided, that support for such universalism has come first. So it seems to me that we need to start again, and examine afresh both the earliest versions we possess and some of the key changes subsequently made. I shall begin with the text itself in its original context so far as this is recoverable, taking each of these two key issues of universalism and faith in turn.

'God's action proclaimed in the promises to Abraham is not

[10] Ibid., 204–5.   [11] Ibid., 110–29; 214–16.
[12] Ibid., 4.

limited to him and his posterity, but reaches its goal when it includes all the families of the earth'; so Westermann,[13] and numerous other biblical scholars. But can we be quite so confident of finding such an unqualified universalism in the text? In Chapter 17, for instance, Abraham is promised that God will make him 'the father of a multitude of nations' (v. 4–5). But note that this is interpreted literally in the following verse, by the promise that 'kings shall come forth from you'. In other words, 'father' is not a metaphor of blessing as it was to become in the later Jewish and Christian tradition (e.g. Hos 11: 1–4; Luke 12: 30); instead the verse surely alludes to the literal claims for descent made elsewhere in Genesis, for various neighbouring peoples such as Moab and Edom, and in view of the treatment assigned to them it must surely indicate an inferior blessing. Esau as ancestor of Edom, for instance, though blessed by God, is promised very much less than Jacob.[14] Again, if we take the twice repeated declaration that 'by you all the families of the earth shall bless themselves' (Gen. 12: 2 and 18: 17 RSV) from our contemporary perspective this sounds clearly universalist, but one immediate limitation to be noted is that the author's perspective would not have extended much, if at all, beyond the Middle East.

Indeed, whether one approaches the issue on the basis on the assumptions of source criticism or from the internal logic of the Genesis narrative itself, either way such a narrowing of perspective seems forced upon us as the correct interpretation. As we shall note shortly, source criticism is now widely under attack, but here I want the reader to note that, whatever methodology is employed, the same conclusions must follow. So I shall begin with source criticism. The twice repeated declaration of the previous paragraph has been assigned to the work of J, the Yahwist perhaps writing under David or Solomon, when the blessing would have come most obviously in the dubious form of imperial expansion. Chapter 15 is normally assigned to E, the Elohist writing perhaps in the eighth century in the northern kingdom at a time when David's Empire was no more. Nonetheless, perhaps recalling that empire, he promises to give to Abraham's descendants 'this land

---

[13] C. Westermann, *Genesis: A Commentary* (London: SPCK, 1985), II, 152.
[14] For Esau and Edom, Gen. 36: 9; for Moab's descent from Lot, Gen. 19: 30–8, esp. 37.

from the river of Egypt to the great river, the River Euphrates' (v.
18). Did E envisage a restoration and enlargement of David's
empire at some future period? And if this is his meaning, might
this not reinforce how we have suggested J should be read, with
empire seen as the precise way in which other peoples were
blessed, through being ruled by the Hebrews? P, the priestly writer
whose version was the first to be quoted in the previous paragraph
(Gen. 17), is also assigned the role of editing the text as a whole.
Writing as he was in post-exilic times, the question that raises itself
is how he might have understood J and E in a way that allowed
him to include their accounts without substantial modification.
Might the answer be that for him the blessing meant that the Jews
now dispersed throughout the Middle East would act as a leaven
in the lump, partly through the help and enlightenment they could
bring to those among whom they lived, and perhaps because if
God is to bless his people at all he must do so through blessing
those to whom they are now subject. One might compare
Jeremiah's injunction to the exiles for a similar sentiment: 'Seek
the welfare of the city where I have sent you into exile, and pray
to the Lord on its behalf, for in its welfare you will find your
welfare' (Jer. 29: 7 RSV).

As we shall observe shortly, source criticism is now less popular than it once was. Even so, very similar conclusions seem forced
upon us even if we confine our attentions to the internal logic of
the Genesis narrative as a whole. For the closest parallels elsewhere
in the Pentateuch that also speak of blessings and curses alike
envisage these more limited territorial ambitions. So, for instance,
the blessing accorded Jacob follows closely that accorded Abraham
but with this narrower perspective made explicit (Gen. 12: 3 and
27: 28–29).[15] One further point is worth making. Much is often
made of the fact that Abraham was not himself an Israelite,[16] and
that he had free and intimate relations with non-Jews. But one
needs to observe that such behaviour is in any case required by the
logic of the story, since those who will eventually be called Jews
are as yet confined to a single family, and even that is scattered in
its wanderings throughout the Middle East. This presumably also
helps explain why there is none of the hostility to the Canaanites

---

[15] A similar pattern also emerges in Num. 22: 6 and 24: 7.
[16] So, e.g. Kuschel, *Abraham*, 14.

that characterizes later history, since the single family must at this
stage still be presumed to be heavily dependent on its neighbours,
though even so Isaac is still told to marry from within his own
kindred (Gen. 24: 3). None of this is to argue against some degree
of openness to other peoples, but it is to suggest that one cannot
jump from the absence of narrow exclusivism to anything
remotely approaching modern notions of universal concern.

Similar qualifications are forced upon us if we turn to Kuschel's
other common theme, that of faith. Certainly questions of faith are
not absent from the Genesis account, but it is all too easy for the
Christian to impose Paul's interpretation as the natural reading,
which it is not; other, more plausible alternatives are available.
Already in Chapter 1 of Romans Paul had wrung a very different
meaning from a verse of Habakkuk, transforming the prophet's
declaration that the righteous shall live by their faithfulness (their
obedience) into his own, distinctive claim that it is through being
righteous (justified) by faith that we live (Hab. 2: 4; Rom. 1: 17
RSV).[17] Trustful attitude has taken the place of faithful, obedient
action, and this is the pattern which Paul repeats in Chapter 4,
verse 3 with his quotation and interpretation of Genesis 15: 6:
'Abraham believed the Lord, and the Lord reckoned it to him as
righteousness.' Here most modern translations continue to support
the Pauline interpretation of the text, but are they right?
Significantly, many Jewish commentators offer a very different
account. The verse is taken to refer to Abraham's faithful obedience and its reward by God, and so quite a different translation
emerges: 'He put his trust in Yahweh, who accounted it to his
merit,' and a number of Christian scholars also now follow this
interpretation.[18] In any case, Paul's account leaves it a puzzle why
Abraham's faith should be singled out for praise at precisely this
point in the narrative, when far greater tests are demanded of him
elsewhere. By contrast, the Jewish view makes the verse function

[17] For some of the issues, J. Ziesler, *Paul's Letter to the Romans* (London: SCM
Press, 1989), 71–2; J. A. Fitzmyer, *Romans* (New York: Anchor Bible,
Doubleday, 1992), 264–5. The question of how far Paul departs from the Hebrew
text is complicated by the existence of three variant readings in the Septuagint.

[18] A similar issue arises in respect of how the divine response to Phinehas'
conduct in Psalm 106. 31 is best interpreted. For a very helpful discussion of the
issues, R. W. L. Moberly, 'Abraham's righteousness (Genesis 15: 6)', in R. W. L.
Moberly, *From Eden to Golgotha* (Atlanta, Georgia: Scholars Press, 1992), 30–54.

as part of a continuing story of faithful obedience. The promise is repeatedly made (in Chapters 12, 15, 17, 18, and 22). That surely suggests, instead of the Pauline view, a pattern of increasing confirmation, a confirmation that culminates in Chapter 22 in Abraham's successful passing of the test of being summoned to sacrifice his son. Significantly, that passage ends by declaring: '*because* you have done this … I will indeed bless you' (Gen. 22: 16–17 RSV).[19] I submit, therefore that the Jewish interpretation is the more natural: that at the core of the narrative lies the question of obedient action, faithfulness, rather than Pauline faith.[20]

It is no perverse pleasure which has led me to stress the distance of the patriarchal narratives from the concerns of the New Testament. How they might once more be united we will consider in due course. But it is important that we should first be made aware of that distance, and for several reasons. To begin with, we need to respect the integrity of each of the stages through which the revelatory process has gone. If early stages speaks of human limitations, so too does our own context. Secondly, aware-ness of such distance will help us better appreciate how tradition works, or, putting it more theologically, how God engages the human imagination by building upon what we already understand of him. Thirdly, by seeing the complexity in the growth of our own developed tradition, it will make us more sympathetic to similar patterns of development in other religions. Finally, it will enable us better to appreciate why even where there is an histori-cal core there is pressure to generate a text that goes beyond any desire simply to transmit the tradition as received.

That last point will be well illustrated in the two subsequent chapters by what happens with Christology and the way in which

---

[19] For a similar view, R. W. L. Moberly, 'The earliest commentary on the Akedah', in ibid., 55–73. Some critics might wish to make something of the contrast between the unconditional character of the promises in Genesis and their provisionality in passages like Deuteronomy 28, but this seems to me to have more to do with differences in function than theology. A sermon addressed to future conduct is one thing; a narrative where the outcome of the promise is already known quite another.

[20] For a modern aesthetic example of a similar conclusion being drawn from the narrative, cf. the Hollywood epic, *The Bible: In the Beginning* (1966). There, though the script-writer was a Christian (Christopher Fry) the story of Abraham is made to culminate in the declaration: 'In all things we must obey him.'

even the life of Jesus was rewritten to bring out the significance that he was now believed to have. But the point applies no less to traditions connected with Abraham. Even though later writers had no doubt that Abraham was an historical figure, nonetheless their dissatisfaction with the story as it stood led to major alterations in the way it was told. In modern times apparent confirmation of historicity led to many seeing the hand of God in the events themselves, and so these as the primacy *loci* of divine revelation. More recently, such confidence has once more declined, and so we need to consider to what degree it matters, if at all, whether we can trace the story of Abraham to some event in the external world.

So long as the conclusions of source criticism appeared secure, an historical core seemed certain, even if much was thought to be later adaptation for fresh applications in new historical contexts. Archaeology was also used very effectively to reinforce such a view. The documentary hypothesis has, however, itself come under attack in recent years, particularly through the influential work of John Van Seters who eliminates E and places the writing of J and P entirely within the post-exilic periods.[21] This is reinforced by his attack on the attempts by W. F. Albright, G. E. Wright and others to find archaeological parallels from the second millennium BC.[22] For such changing perspectives and their dependence on the interrelation between text and archaeology there are interesting parallels with the decline in confidence in Homer's historicity of which we took note in the previous chapter. Both have occurred over (very roughly) the same period of time. A wide range of positions on the historicity of the Old Testament now exists. With external supporting evidence available for the general framework only from Ahab onwards, the existence of

[21] J. Van Seters, *Abraham in History and Tradition* (New Haven: Yale University Press, 1975); J. Van Seters, *Prologue to History: The Yahwist as Historian in Genesis* (Louisville, Kentucky: Westminster, 1992); T. D. Alexander, *Abraham in the Negev* (Carlisle: Paternoster Press, 1997). For an extended argument the other way, indicating good grounds for continued acceptance of the documentary hypothesis: E. Nicholson, *The Pentateuch in the Twentieth Century* (Oxford: Clarendon Press, 1998). The likelihood that some of the sources are pre-exilic (239–40), though, does not of itself establish the historicity of the patriarchs.
[22] e.g. W. F. Albright, 'Abram the Hebrew: a new archaeological interpretation', in *Bulletin of the American School of Oriental Research* 163 (1961), 36–54; G. E. Wright, *Biblical Archaeology* (London: Duckworth, 1962), esp. 40–52.

David and Solomon has even been called into question, far less Abraham.[23]

This is not the place to enter into the details of such disputes, but the case against Genesis seems to me less strongly proven than with Homer. Admittedly, Van Seters is able to point to numerous historical anachronisms, such as camels instead of donkeys, the wrong use of Hittite, or the assumption of a settlement at Beersheba when none existed before the Iron Age;[24] also many practices which one might have assumed to be ancient, such as the very special inheritance rights attaching to the first-born, he demonstrates continued into Babylonian times.[25] Our attention is likewise drawn to the fact that the two places from which Abraham migrates—Ur and Haran—were in fact prominent during the Neo-Babylonian period.[26] Although such points do tell decisively against any supposition of oral tradition faithfully transmitted unaltered, much can surely be explained in terms of the natural retelling of a story in terms more readily intelligible to a contemporary audience. Thus, for example, the original placing of the Hittites in Anatolia had no doubt passed from memory. Likewise, the Bible itself reveals that what in the narrative appears to be the name by which Abraham identified a particular place was in fact known to have had a more ancient name, as with Luz rather than Bethel or Laish rather than Dan.[27] None of this proves antiquity; it merely shows that even numerous anachronisms do not preclude an historical core, and the retellings argued for by source criticism. What, however, does make such a development inherently more likely is the way in which Van Seters' theory of a sixth-century invention completely fails to explain why the story is told in the way it is, in such marked contrast to the religion of the time. To invent a Jewish world in which Law had no significant place suggests an extraordinary indifference to Law among some Jews of the time that is hard to comprehend. After all, it is one thing to inherit stories of a different, distant world; quite another, to conjure them up as legitimate options in one's own day.

[23] The range of positions is well represented in L. L. Grabbe (ed.), *Can a 'History of Israel' be Written?* (Sheffield: Sheffield Academic Press, 1997). The size claimed for the empire under David and Solomon is where doubt most commonly begins.   [24] Van Seters, *Abraham*, 17, 45–6, 111.
[25] Ibid., 87–95.   [26] Ibid., 24.
[27] On Bethel, contrast Gen. 12: 8 and Gen. 28: 19; on Dan, Gen. 14: 14 and Judg. 18: 29.

But what weight should be given to questions of historicity in this particular case? One reason why the issue might be deemed important is because that is seen as the only way God could endorse one people's special commitment to the land of Israel. But there is no reason why this should not have come later, for instance with Moses or even later still. Even if all such stories of the chosen people originating from elsewhere were to prove entirely unhistorical, there are still plenty of parallels in imaginatively treated origins generating just as strong a commitment to a particular place, as for instance among the Aztecs whose origin myth also spoke of a divinely guided migration and of a change of name.[28] This is not to say that history never matters (the following chapter will insist upon its vital importance), but it does not follow from this that it always matters, and, as we now examine the developments within each of the three religions in turn, we shall observe each concerned with something more important, what might be described as a spiritual journey of vocation.[29]

Spiritual pilgrimage

Within Judaism   Though the various writers concerned never explicitly say so, since for them the meaning they discover is actually already present in the text, it seems clear that the motivation for such new readings lies at least in part in dissatisfaction with the apparent theological content of the Genesis narrative. For while it leaves us in no doubt about God's guidance and care for the future nation, the human contribution is seen as more deeply problematic. Though it plays its part, this is caused less by the desire that Abraham be a good and holy man, and much more by the feeling that there should be some clear impact upon Abraham of God's transforming presence.

[28]   As with 'Abram' to 'Abraham', from 'Azteca' in the place of origin to the new name, 'Mexica'. Some scholars draw the parallel with Genesis; e.g. M. D. Coe, *Mexico: From the Olmecs to the Aztecs* (London: Thames & Hudson, 1962), 158–9. Others suspect an underlying core of historicity; e.g. E. Baquedano, *Los Aztecas* (Mexico City: Panorama Editorial, 1992), 22–6.

[29]   For a similar tension between history and spiritual significance, note the repeated attempt to apply the story of Israel's early migrations to the history of the Anglo-Saxons: N. Howe, *Migration and Mythmaking in Anglo-Saxon England* (New Haven: Yale University Press, 1989).

Even within the biblical narrative one can detect signs that such worries were already present from an early stage. Thus if we assume source criticism and compare the two versions of Abraham passing off Sarah as his sister, Genesis 12: 10–17 (J) and 20: 1–18 (E), we find that the second version offers a much less morally ambiguous tale. No more does God punish someone unaware of Sarah's true status; again, Abraham is now only given presents after the deception has been disclosed; finally, in the second version Sarah turns out to be his half-sister (v. 12), and so, strictly speaking, no lie has been told. As one distinguished Old Testament scholar has put it, 'our Elohistic narrative gives much more consideration to the requirements of a reflective, indeed sensitive, and theologically refined readership'.[30] Indeed, the theory has even been advanced that it was precisely moral worries about the conduct of Abraham in Genesis 12 which generated the legal prohibition in Deuteronomy against remarrying a wife whom one had once discarded (Deut. 24: 1–4).[31] Whether so or not, it does look as though it is already within the canon that the search for a more spiritually uplifting narrative begins.

Modern readers of the narrative will vary greatly over how pressing they see the need for such a retelling. The sympathetic ear which finds no significant problems perhaps requires the jolt of discovering how very differently others hear the same story. One writer, for instance, describes the portrait of Abraham which emerges as of 'an unscrupulous entrepreneur, a get-rich-quick merchant' whose real interest over Sodom is not compassion but simply in preserving his kinsman, Lot.[32] Others describe him as 'a man with little to recommend him' who sacrifices one member of his family after another to his own interest.[33] Yet another asks us to read the story from the perspective of an Egyptian or Canaanite,

---

[30] G. von Rad, *Genesis* (London: SCM Press, 1972), 226; cf. 230.

[31] D. Daube and C. Carmichael, *The Return of the Divorcée* (Oxford: Yarnton Trust, 1993), esp. 15–28; for further examples of the same relation between law and patriarchal narrative, C. M. Carmichael, *Law and Narrative in the Bible* (Ithaca: Cornell University Press, 1985), esp. 150–5, 185–205.

[32] P. R. Davies, *Whose Bible Is It Anyway?* (Sheffield: Sheffield Academic Press, 1995), 95–113, esp. 101 and 109–10. He points out that Gen. 29: 19 implies that the real motive was concern for Lot.

[33] D. N. Fewell and D. M. Gunn, *Gender, Power and Promise* (Nashville: Abingdon Press, 1993), 39–55, esp. 39.

and observes how very unappealing is the result.[34] No doubt some of their claims are exaggerated, but it does help us to comprehend why the narrative was to be changed so substantially in later Jewish tradition. The journey in effect becomes one of conversion and commitment. Apart from two exceptions, Kuschel detects in what follows only increasing exclusivism.[35] But such an analysis is premised on two mistaken assumptions, that the motivation behind such rewriting was generally to exclude others rather than commit oneself more deeply, and that to expect others to convert to one's own point of view is necessarily a sign of intolerance.

Surprisingly, Joshua 24 is taken as already marking the beginning of the decline, inasmuch as it takes as its model for the renouncing of pagan gods the way in which Abraham rejects the gods of his father, Terah. For Kuschel 'nothing is left here of Abraham's readiness for peace which is shown in Genesis, or of the blessing for the world of the peoples'.[36] Admittedly, the chapter is part of a book which is ruthless in its extermination of the native, pagan population, but it would be a mistake to assume this an inevitable consequence of such undivided commitment. For if so, it would argue for indifference right across the entire spectrum of our beliefs.[37] In fact, the most common use of the incident is as a handle to discuss the question of conversion, and only secondarily, if at all, hostility to others. So, for instance, in the second century BC in *Jubilees* we find not only Abraham committed at an early age to a life of prayer but also doing everything in his power to win his father over from the worship of idols (*Jub.* 11:14–12:8).[38] Even in the second-century AD *Apocalypse of Abraham* where we have a very judgmental Abraham it is his growth into a 'friend of God' which seems most stressed.[39] For Josephus it is as an innovator in religion that

---

[34] D. J. Clines, 'The God of the Pentateuch', in *Epworth Review* 23 (1996), 55–64.

[35] Philo and Josephus are the exceptions; Kuschel, *Abraham*, 40–9.

[36] Ibid., 31.

[37] True tolerance presupposes competing, strong commitments, not indifference; D. Brown, 'Tolerance: virtue or vice?', in D. R. Bromham et al. (eds.), *Ethics in Reproductive Medicine* (London: Springer-Verlag, 1992), 201–10.

[38] J. H. Charlesworth (ed.), *The Old Testament Pseudepigrapha* (New York: Doubleday, 1985), II, 79–80.

[39] Abraham is judgemental in 1–8, but at 10.5 the strength of his commitment has made him God's friend; Charlesworth, *Pseudepigrapha*, I, 694.

Abraham has significance,[40] while Philo offers an extended allegorical treatment of the narrative, according to which Abraham is
conceived of as advancing beyond pantheist materialism through
the relative commitment characterized by Hagar towards the fullness of vision which Sarah symbolizes. Sandmel concludes his
examination of what Philo has done by declaring that it 'reflects a
marginal, aberrative version of Judaism,'[41] but his own detailed
analysis suggests a very different reading. Philo's Abraham is on a
spiritual journey (from the adolescence of Canaan to the commitment of the desert), but so too was he in the rabbis' account, with
his journey south turned into a journey towards the Temple and
the type of commitment that characterized.[42] The final objective
may differ radically, but not the placing of the spiritual journey
above any mere migration to a new land. The imagination engages
with a journey one is also able personally to make.

One form that such commitment took was in observance of the
Law. At its most basic what this allowed was an easier identification with Abraham on the part of the devout Jewish reader. The
process can already be seen to be at work in the way in which P
projects the importance of circumcision back into the patriarch's
story. Thus in Chapter 17, where Abraham's circumcision is
described, in the attempt to connect Abraham with what had
become the definitive mark of every male Jew, P indulges in what
might legitimately be described as 'overkill', with the word
'covenant' used no less than thirteen times, and lauded in terms
such as 'everlasting' and for 'generation upon generation' (e.g. v. 7).
It is surely into this context that we should fit Ben Sira's identification of Abraham as an observant follower of the Law, as also his
depiction in most of later Judaism. Thus Ecclesiasticus declares: 'he
kept the law of the Most High, and was taken into covenant with
him; he established the covenant in his flesh, and when he was
tested he was found faithful' (Sir. 44: 20 RSV). Explicable too in

---

[40] *Jewish Antiquities* I, iv, 77; I, vii, 154–5.
[41] S. Sandmel, 'Philo's place in Judaism: a study of conceptions of Abraham
in Jewish literature', *Hebrew Union College Annual* 26 (1955), 155–332, esp. 332.
[42] For Philo Gen. 12: 9 (*De Abrahamo* 88) meant a journey into the desert;
for *Genesis Rabbah* (39) a turn southwards towards the Temple. The alternative
accounts are greatly aided by the different readings in the Hebrew and in the
Septuagint.

this way is the rabbinic decision to treat him as the arch-disciple of the law, even anticipating the observance of Passover and functioning like a priest.[43]

Yet it would be a mistake to interpret such alterations exclusively in terms of a wish for closer identification, for they are clearly part of something wider, the desire to find in Abraham someone who has benefited, morally and spiritually, from being a friend of God. Philo interprets his change of name as itself indicative of moral change.[44] In the *Genesis Apocryphon* we find Abraham's accumulation of wealth carefully dissociated from deception,[45] while in a book which it may have influenced, *Jubilees*, quite a number of such potentially embarrassing incidents are either omitted or circumvented. Such considerations also appear to have affected the way in which the conduct of his wife was treated. Thus, even Josephus, normally fairly loyal to the biblical narrative, expands a single biblical verse to leave us in no doubt about the extreme character of Hagar's conduct and thus of the legitimacy of her first expulsion, while in respect of the second we are told that Sarah loved Ishmael no less than Isaac and that the motivation this time was her conviction that the difference in age between the two boys was too great for them to be brought up together.[46] Again, in the Targums we find the third-century AD *Neofiti* stressing Abraham's commitment to prayer,[47] whilst the very much later *Pseudo-Jonathan*, though conceding failure in Abraham, is equally insistent upon God's willingness generally to forgive.[48] Particularly fascinating is what happens in the second-century AD *Testament of Abraham*. Abraham is so perfect that he

[43] *Genesis Rabbah* 42 and 55.

[44] In *De Mutatione Nominum* 65–76 Philo argues that we have a move from Abram the astrologer to Abraham the lover of virtue and wisdom.

[45] For translation and commentary, G. Vermes, *Scripture and Tradition in Judaism* (Leiden: Brill, 1973), 96–126, esp. 100–2 and 114.

[46] *Jewish Antiquities* I, x.4.; xii.3. Unlike the first, the second passage could scarcely be justified as a natural expansion. Cf. Gen. 16: 4; 21: 9–10.

[47] e.g. his first thought on defeating the kings is a prayer that success in this life may not deprive him of a deeper relation with God in the next; M. McNamara (ed.), *Targum Neofiti I: Genesis* (Edinburgh: T & T Clark, 1992), 15.1 (94).

[48] M. Maher (ed.), *Targum Pseudo-Jonathan: Genesis* (Edinburgh: T & T Clark, 1992); for failure, 15.3 (60); for God's readiness to forgive, 18.20–2 and 19.24 (68 and 71). This Targum may be as late as the eleventh century.

needs to be taught compassion by God, and this is done through the archangel Michael giving him a dramatic world tour.[49]

Though I have tried to indicate some underlying common themes, even this brief survey demonstrates a wide variety of approaches, some more appealing than others. It was certainly no part of my intention to claim uniform progress in how Abraham is treated. The *Apocalypse of Abraham* and Pseudo-Philo are particularly gruesome. In the former Abraham calmly accepts the destruction of his father and his house by thunderbolt without any trace of compassion, while in the latter Abraham's deliverance from the fiery furnace is said to involve the loss of 83,500 lives.[50] Fortunately, however, other versions continued to be current, while even in these more gruesome tales we need to note the religious dimension. So, for example, for Pseudo-Philo idolatry seems to have been regarded as equivalent to being a Gentile,[51] and so Judaism is seen as a religion which must turn inwards if it is to maintain the strength of its commitment. That is the protective course to which religions so often turn when they believe that the values they embody are under threat. But there is an alternative. For, by contrast, in much rabbinical writing we find Abraham used as a model for evangelism. His hospitality, as he runs from his tent to greet passers-by, was taken as indicative of something much deeper, while the fact that he was not circumcized until he was ninety-nine years old was used to demonstrate that the door to conversion never closes.[52] In arguing thus the rabbis were in effect assuming the wider sense of blessing now associated with the verses we discussed earlier. What God gives must be shared if its true value is to be demonstrated.

Judaism over the course of its history thus wrestled with forging a more satisfactory and more relevant image of its founding patriarch, with some right turns and some wrong, and throughout with factual detail firmly subordinated to other more fundamental

---

[49] The key chapter for a change of heart is Chapter 14; Charlesworth, *Old Testament Pseudepigrapha* I, 890–1.

[50] *Apocalypse* 8.1–6 (Charlesworth, *Pseudepigrapha*, I, 693); Pseudo-Philo, *Antiquities* VI, 3–18. Scholars continue to debate whether the fiery furnace is a borrowing from Daniel or a pun on Ur as 'fire'.

[51] F. J. Murphy, *Pseudo-Philo: Rewriting the Bible* (New York: Oxford University Press, 1993), 252–4.

[52] *Genesis Rabbah* 48 and 46 (Gen. 17: 1 and 11).

concerns, but so too, as we shall see, did Christianity. So need either religion despise the other as it sought to put Abraham to fresh use? To that fresh use within my own community I now turn.

Within Christianity Earlier we argued that it would be wrong to claim for the original meaning of the story Paul's stress on either faith or universalism. Yet for the modern Christian both emphases are essential. Though Pauline exegesis is strained, one could of course observe that it obeys the rules of the day, and so in its own context it would not have been seen as quite so idiosyncratic. Pertinent too is the observation that, if God wished to speak to Paul in a way he could understand, then this is the approach even God would have needed to adopt. Even so, there is something unsatisfactory in exegesis which not only leaves much of the Old Testament deeply problematic but also seems to force Christianity into an antagonistic attitude towards Judaism. So I want to briefly examine these two issues once more, to see whether Paul's conclusions may be given a gentler nuance. What I shall argue is that Paul uses a christological criterion to impose a harsher interpretation on Jewish tradition than Christianity in fact requires. Nonetheless, noting the application has the advantage of highlighting a similar process at work within Scripture to what we earlier claimed sometimes legitimately happens beyond the canon, in later developments providing a critique and corrective of earlier canonical approaches.[53] Rather than always generating a linear development, tradition sometimes, as it were, turns back upon itself to provide a new reading.

Consider first the issue of universalism. Though attempts are sometimes made to defend Paul's appeal to the use of the singular 'seed' in the promise to Abraham, it would be widely acknowledged that this 'certainly strains the intended meaning of the biblical text', while I have already noted earlier the more limited range that is the likely meaning of the promise that 'in your seed all the nations of the earth will be blessed' (Gal. 3: 16, based on the LXX, Gen. 22: 18).[54] For Paul the seed is 'Christ', and it is clear that a

---

[53] Ch. 2 gave the example of new attitudes to the significance of Christ's childhood; Ch. 7 will consider changing attitudes to images and art.

[54] For a defence of Paul's interpretation, F. F. Bruce, *The Epistle to the Galatians* (Exeter: Paternoster, 1982), 171–3; for a contrary view, J. W. Aageson, *Written Also For Our Sake: Paul and the Art of Biblical Interpretation* (Louisville, Kentucky: Westminster, 1993), 73–88. The quotation is from Aageson, 73.

christological criterion is being used to generate the new sense he gives to the Old Testament passage, as he reflects upon the universal significance of Christ and so on what he thinks the passage must mean for his own day. Unfortunately, as part of that argument Paul feels bound to demote the status of the law and of circumcision in particular.[55] Whereas rabbinical thought had seen in the lateness of Abraham's circumcision an argument for a generous attitude towards evangelism, Paul's attempt to be generous to Gentiles leads him to deduce the insignificance of circumcision. Thereby, not only is a rite held dear by Jews of today called into question, but also the possibility precluded of contemporary Christians acknowledging any legitimacy to such a conviction.[56]

Yet an alternative trajectory in handling the story of Abraham, less hostile to Judaism, is to be found elsewhere in the New Testament, where we find Abraham used in a way much closer to the unqualified generosity of the rabbinical interpretation. Abraham's hospitality is the key theme. So in Jesus' teaching we discover Abraham hosting an eschatological banquet at which many will come from east and west and sit with him, and from the context it is clear that Gentiles are included.[57] Again the sick and despised are specifically identified as children of Abraham, as in the case of the crippled woman who is called a 'daughter of Abraham', or Zacchaeus the tax collector who is called a 'son of Abraham' (Luke 13: 10–17, esp. 16; Luke 19: 1–10, esp. 9). Though, as the following chapter indicates, we cannot deduce from this that Jesus had precisely the same attitudes to Gentiles as Paul, we can say that there is an openness in valuing those allegedly outside the community that already prepares the way. Significantly, however, the grounds for exclusion are very different. Whereas Paul is polemical in relation to Judaism, Jesus only excludes from the bosom of Abraham those who fail to value others, and it is for this reason that 'Dives' is excluded (Luke 16: 19–31).[58]

---

[55] Two of the principal themes of Galatians as a whole.

[56] As some Jewish Christians of today demonstrate, it is possible to hold both to faith in Christ and to the importance of circumcision as a mark of Jewish identity and responsibility.

[57] Matt. 8: 11, told in the context of Jesus healing the centurion's servant (8: 5–13). The point is probably the same in Luke, though he gives the saying a different context: Luke 13: 28–9.

[58] The Latin name for the 'rich man' is surely worth retaining for someone who otherwise remains nameless.

Nor does this stress on hospitality cease in the later history of Christianity. So popular has the Andrei Rublev's icon of the Trinity become that we tend to forget that not only did Abraham welcoming souls to his bosom in heaven become a major figure in liturgy and art,[59] even the passage on which Rublev based his icon was more commonly interpreted in the West as indicative of Abraham's generosity to the stranger.[60] One can quote examples as varied as fifth-century mosaics in Santa Maria Maggiore at Rome, a medieval sculpture at Salisbury, its inclusion as part of the seven Works of Mercy by Murillo for the Church of the Hospital de la Caridad in Seville or Rembrandt's *Abraham Serving the Three Angels*.[61] With Abraham also envisaged as encountering Christ in the mysterious figure of Melchizedek, the two grounds for universalism (christological and Abrahamic) in effect became one (Gen. 14: 18–20).[62] The generosity of Christ as Melchizedek anticipates Abraham's own. Of course it did not happen like this, but that does not mean that it is untrue. The rewritten narrative presents imaginatively the criteria on the basis of which the new conclusions were drawn.

In drawing such implications Christianity needs to acknowledge its debt to Jewish exegesis. So, for instance, Abraham interceding in the Lazarus parable has clear parallels in rabbinical discussion (Luke 16: 19–31; *Genesis Rabbah* 48), just as the use of Melchizedek's priesthood in Hebrews finds obvious antecedents in Jewish projections of the Temple cult back into the life of Abraham. Tradition identified him as Shem, king of Jerusalem, and the Jerusalem connection not only made the priestly continuity argument possible but also his treatment in the messianic context of Psalm 110.[63] So one clear advantage that would emerge

---

[59] For Abraham's role in the liturgy, B. Bolte, 'Abraham dans la liturgie', *Cahiers Sion* 5 (1951), 88–95, esp. 92–3; there are fine sculptural examples of Abraham welcoming souls at Moissac and Rheims.

[60] The three angels at Mamre, Gen. 18: 1–15; even in the East the theme of hospitality is also found, as in some of the Greek monasteries on Mount Athos.

[61] Illustrated in S. Partsch, *Rembrandt* (London: Weidenfeld & Nicholson, 1991), 129.

[62] Helped by the typology of Hebrews 7, by the fifteenth century so close had the identification become that a tabernacle containing the host was commonly called a melchizedek.

[63] I. Jacobs, *The Midrashic Process* (Cambridge: Cambridge University Press, 1995), 108–32.

in giving greater prominence to these other trajectories towards universalism in the story of Abraham is that not only are they not derogatory to the later history of Judaism they also resonate with similar tendencies within the Jewish tradition itself. They would thus appear to open up the possibility of a more fruitful dialogue.

If Paul's use of 'seed' in Galatians 3 to derive universalism is problematic, so also in his argument in the following chapter for rejecting Sinai and substituting faith in its place. Indeed, it is hard not to convict Paul of an exegesis that is strained even by midrashic standards, as well as one which seems inevitably, once more, to force Christianity into a contemptuous attitude towards the history of Judaism. In outline what we are told is that Sinai is part of the heritage of the slave Hagar whereas Sarah represents the promise which the new faith brings (4: 21–26). What is wrong with this is not allegory in itself,[64] nor even its specific form as typology (reading the Old Testament as an anticipation of the New), but the strange inversion which effectively destroys any claims to a real parallel. Exegetes suggest that this may be Paul responding to a more obvious version used to justify the superiority of Jewish Christians,[65] but even if so, it hardly gives any more plausibility to the exegesis. However, it does at least have the merit of warning Christians against too hasty a dismissal of similar radical exegesis in other religions. For by comparison the Muslim substitution of Ishmael for Isaac in the story of the sacrifice (discussed in the next section) would seem quite mild.

Both Luther and Calvin show some embarrassment over Paul's approach at this point. Luther informs us that 'allegories do not strongly persuade', while Calvin observes that 'this may seem absurd at first sight'.[66] Of the two Luther is closer to the apparent implications of Paul's argument in making the contrast with Judaism as such, whereas Calvin, perhaps following Augustine and

---

[64] Philo had already treated Hagar and Sarah in such a way; *De Abrahamo*, 68; *De Fuga et Inventione*, 128, 209 ff; *De Mutatione Nominum*, 255.

[65] C. K. Barrett, 'The allegory of Abraham, Sarah and Hagar in the argument of Galatians' in J. Friedrich et al. (eds.), *Rechtfertigung: Festschrift für Ernst Käsemann* (Tübingen: J. B. Mohr, 1976), 1–16.

[66] M. Luther, *Commentary on Saint Paul's Epistle to the Galatians*, tr. P. S. Watson (Cambridge: James Clarke, 1953), 415–40, esp. 417; Calvin, *Epistles of Paul the Apostle to the Galatians, etc.*, tr. T. H. L. Parker (Edinburgh: Saint Andrew Press, 1965), 83–91, esp. 86.

ultimately Tyconius, sees the tension as one within the Church
and ourselves, rather than with those outside, and so stresses the
positive role of law as 'schoolmaster' (Gal. 3: 24).[67] In considering
the relation between the patriarchal narratives and the subsequent
Mosaic dispensation, various positions are possible. Some argue
the superiority of one to the other, while it is also possible to offer
a more nuanced view, with different judgements made in respect
of different aspects.[68] I do not wish to go into the matter in detail
here. One point, however, does seem important to stress, and that
is the dependence of the appropriateness of faith upon there being
a God in whom one can safely place one's trust.

I have already argued that faithfulness or faithful obedience is
the more natural reading of the story in its original context, and so
in respect of possible trajectories it is Judaism that has the stronger
case. So in this case if we are to offer a more plausible argument
than Paul's, we will need to consider whether the direction of
revelation as a whole might cast Abraham's obedience in a new
light. From the perspective of God's action in Christ we might
argue that a God who so fully identifies with the human condition
is one to be trusted, and so trust rather than obedience in itself can
legitimately come to the fore. Judaism is also in a position to justify
a similar perspective, through observing that, once the moral character of God has been firmly established in its later history, it too
may re-read the narrative as primarily a reflection on the notion of
trusting in God's goodness. Ironically, though, for such an argument to hold one needs the very thing Paul rejects as of much
significance, namely the Law. For it is surely precisely the Law that
gives God a definitely moral character which the patriarchal narratives as yet lack, and no doubt that is one major reason why the
text continued to be rewritten.

Some may think this comment unfair on the original narrative,
but, as I indicated earlier, I am by no means alone in finding its
portrayal of God deeply problematic. As such it makes the notion

---

[67] For the relevant sections of Tyconius, K. Froelich (ed.), *Biblical
Interpretation in the Early Church* (Philadelphia: Fortress, 1984), 114–32.

[68] For a rare challenge to the common view that Mosaic religion represents
an advance, H. W. F. Saggs, *The Encounter with the Divine in Mesopotamia and Israel*
(London: Athlone, 1978), 36–8; for a more nuanced position, R. W. L. Moberly,
The Old Testament of the Old Testament (Minneapolis: Fortress, 1992), esp. 159–66.

of trust more difficult to defend. For, though the narrative as it
stands amply justifies an obedience based on the power of God, on
his ability to bring about the apparently impossible, it looks more
shaky when one considers such obedience from the perspective of
the divine character. God's apparent approval for the way in
which Abraham treats some of the other characters in the narrative makes one wonder whether he is after all to be trusted, while
on one occasion when Abraham does behave conspicuously well,
in pleading for the cities of Sodom and Gomorrah, the narrative
leaves us wondering whether Abraham himself might not be a
more suitable object of trust than God. One might contrast the
Genesis version with the very moving expansion offered by the
Targum Pseudo-Jonathan in which the infinite kindness of God is
repeatedly stressed.[69] In other words, the Genesis narrative leaves
us with a sense of arbitrariness in the divine activity which only the
later versions dispel.

That is a point of no small significance. For trust, unlike obedience, carries with it heavy moral overtones. It is not just a matter
of promise, or even of one's ability to fulfil it; it requires a judgement that the person making the promise truly has one's best
interests at heart. And can that really be said of the sort of shabby
conduct God seems sometimes to endorse in this narrative? Sadly,
even Paul follows suit in expelling Hagar once more in the wilder-
ness (Gal. 4: 30). Thus I would argue that it was only the later
development of the tradition with its stress on the moral aspect as
embodied in the Law which made possible the move to Paul's
stress on trust. So despite what Paul says, far from Sinai being irrel-
evant, it was indispensable to producing a reading in which faith
and obedience could be held in creative and fruitful tension.

In short, Paul's projection of faith back into the text only
succeeds if those later developments of the tradition in a more
moral direction are assumed. Paul's polemic against his Jewish
inheritance has for long concealed a more balanced Paul beneath
the surface of his text, to which increasingly due acknowledgement is being given. Even so, when we hear James's question,
'Was not Abraham our father justified by his works, when he had

---

[69] In *Targum Pseudo-Jonathan* (68–9) punishment is proposed on account of
the oppression of the poor, while prayer for forgiveness is deemed sufficient to
avert punishment. Contrast Gen. 18: 16 ff.

offered Isaac his son upon the altar' (2: 21), we should guard
against too easy a reconciliation between Paul and James, as
though it was only a matter of different starting points that lead to
different emphases.[70] James, we have argued, is nearer the original
meaning and this generates tensions that need to be faced. But
equally Paul's reading should not be taken in isolation; it also went
with a very specific view of the character of God, one that only
became possible with the Sinai tradition. For all its faults, later
Christian tradition in speaking of the 'law of Christ' at least tried
to preserve the two essential sides of the equation, faith and a
moral God. To make that acknowledgement would once more
permit less strained relations with Judaism.

In Islam   As in Judaism and Christianity, so also in Islam we find
the same desire for someone with whose spiritual journey one
could more easily identify. So it is not surprising that we find
Abraham treated in the Qur'an as the first Muslim, as can be seen
in Abraham's prayer that he and his sons act as those who have
submitted (*muslimin*) to God.[71] Subsequent tradition went even
further, for on his miraculous ride to Jerusalem it was supposed
that Muhammad met Abraham in heaven and thereby discovered
their remarkable physical resemblance to one another.[72] Like later
Judaism the Qur'an also recounts the story of Abraham's rejection
of his father's idols at some length, though without any of the
harshness which we found in some Jewish versions. Instead,
Abraham's gentle pleading and forgiving spirit are movingly
contrasted with his father's intemperance; 'loving earnestness' and
'gentleness' is how one Muslim commentator describes Abraham's
attitude throughout.[73] Indeed, within contemporary Islam
Abraham's attitude to his father is often used to emphasize the
importance of filial care and respect, even when parents are

---

[70] A. C. Thiselton, *The Two Horizons* (Exeter: Paternoster, 1980), 422–7.
Though his comments are helpful, they do not seem to me to tell the full story.
[71] The repeated emphasis of Sura 2.127–35.
[72] A. Guillaume, *The Life of Mohammed* (Oxford: Oxford University Press,
1955), 186. Muhammad's biographer, Ishaq, descibes how on meeting with
Abraham in the seventh heaven Muhammad declared: 'Never have I seen a man
more like myself.'
[73] A. Y. Ali in his verse commentary, *The Holy Qur'an* (Leicester: Islamic
Foundation, 1975), 775, commenting on Sura 19.41–50.

disobedient to God. To this we might also add that within the Qur'an Abraham is specifically used several times to argue against the exclusivity of Judaism and Christianity (e.g. Sura 3: 65–7; 2: 135). So, despite the polemic, some similar trajectories are to be observed.

However, at one point there is a distinctive innovation, and that is in the treatment of Hagar. Traditional Christian treatments had often spoken of God's identification with the lowly and even of her words to God as 'the first Magnificat',[74] but modern feminist theology has drawn our attention to the more ambiguous elements in the biblical narrative, where, it is suggested, the natural reading is that 'the deity identifies ... not with the suffering slave but with her oppressors'.[75] Paul's analogy in Galatians has also been attacked as intensifying the problem.[76] As an alternative it is sometimes suggested that Hagar should now be seen as a 'suffering servant' whose release from bondage not only anticipates the exodus from Egypt (she herself is a foreigner living among a strange people)[77] but also in some ways the search on the part of modern women for release from male violence, as in the powerful story of the oppressed Celie in Alice Walker's novel *The Colour Purple*.[78] Such proposals seek to correct an earlier hermeneutic that has often been used to justify slavery, as in the American practice of referring to black slaves as 'Aunt Hagar's children'.[79]

Given the contempt with which Muslim attitudes to women

[74] Such distortions could still yield powerful sermons, as in A. Goes, *Hagar am Brunnen* (Frankfurt am Main: Fischer Bücherei, 1958), 21–6. For 'das erste Magnifikat,' Gen. 16: 13.

[75] P. Trible, *Texts of Terror* (London: SCM Press, 1984), 9–35, esp. 22, commenting on Gen. 16: 6–9; K. P. Darr, *Far More Precious Than Jewels* (Louisville, Kentucky: Westminster, 1991), 132–63.

[76] e.g. E. A. Castelli, 'Allegories of Hagar', in E. V. McKnight and E. S. Malboon, *The New Literary Criticism and the New Testament* (Sheffield: Sheffield Academic Press, 1994), 228–50, esp. 241 ff.

[77] There is also a reversal, since Hagar is herself an Egyptian suffering at the hands of Hebrews.

[78] For a comparison, C. A. Kirk-Duggan, 'Gender, violence and transformation in *The Colour Purple*', in M. I. Wallace and T. H. Smith (eds.), *Curing Violence* (Sonoma, California: Polebridge Press, 1994), 266–86.

[79] For an attempt to retrieve her for Black Theology, C. J. Sanders, 'Black women in biblical perspective' in C. J. Sanders (ed.), *Living the Intersection: Womanism and Afrocentrism Theology* (Minneapolis: Fortress, 1995), 131–8.

are often regarded in the West, it is salutary to discover a very different approach firmly embedded at this point in Islam. Already in the Qur'an some key events had been moved to Arabia, among them Abraham and Ishmael jointly restoring the Ka'ba at Mecca (Sura 2: 125–8). Later tradition also located Hagar's flight in Mecca,[80] and so today all pilgrims on the Hajj are expected to celebrate the deliverance by God of Hagar and her son in actions which copy those of Hagar. Thus she is envisaged in her anxiety to quench her son's thirst running back and forth between two small hills, and all pilgrims are expected to repeat that pattern (known as *sa'y*); the name of the spring that emerged is also taken to reflect the generosity of Allah's response to her prayers,[81] since it is called Zamzam after her words '*zam! zam!*' (the Arabic words for 'Stop! Stop!'), so quickly did the water gush forth. Men in their spiritual pilgrimage learning from a woman of God's great care for them in their need thus lies at the very heart of Islamic practice.[82] The drama and generosity of the Islamic version contrasts with the rather flat and grudging character of the biblical tale.[83] It surely does no violence to the core of their own traditions for the Jew or the Christian to concede this. To put the matter in explicitly Christian terms, the love of God we find reflected in Christ towards the foreigner, the slave and women is better represented by the Islamic version than any treatment of Hagar that the Christian tradition has itself generated.

A single minority tradition within Judaism speaks of Abraham

---

[80] A reference is assumed to be hidden in the Qur'an at 14.37. For more details on later developments, R. Firestone, *Journeys in Holy Lands: The Evolution of the Abraham-Ishmael Legend in Islamic Exegesis* (Albany, NY: SUNY, 1990), 105–51; B. F. Stowasser, *Women in the Qur'an, Traditions, and Interpretation* (New York: Oxford University Press, 1994), 43–9.

[81] The fact that in the biblical narrative God is described as responding to the cries of the child rather than the mother is often taken as yet another case of patriarchy, but on the other side one should note that the reason for Hagar's tears is in fact her dying child; S. P. Jeansonne, *The Women of Genesis* (Minneapolis: Fortress Press, 1990), 50. Even so, patriarchy is very much in evidence elsewhere in the narrative: Gen. 21: 11, 18 and 20.

[82] So, e.g. M. M. Ali, *The Religion of Islam* (Columbus, Ohio: Islamic Institute, 6th edn., 1990), 399; S. A. Ashraf, *Islam* (Cheltenham: Stanley Thornes, 1991), 79–80.

[83] Gen. 21: 8–20, though, admittedly, less savage in many ways than the related passage in Chapter 16.

being punished for his treatment of Hagar by being summoned to sacrifice his son Isaac.[84] To consideration of that sacrifice we now turn.

The sacrifice of Isaac

Here I want to concentrate upon a single incident (Gen. 22: 1–19), Abraham's readiness to sacrifice of Isaac. Partly in order to make my task more manageable, though I shall mention Islam's treatment of Ishmael in passing, my main focus will be on Judaism and Christianity. Thereby no slight is intended to Islam, for it seems to me that its substitution of a different son is less significant than it is often made out to be, not least because, as we shall see, the other two religions also move the focus towards the son. We shall in any case return to its contribution in our consideration of our final example, Joseph. My discussion here proceeds by three stages. First, we shall consider the potential for conflict between current common interpretations of the passage and its original biblical context; then we shall examine some of the motivations behind developments within the two religions; finally some assessment will be attempted of the conclusions reached within these developing traditions.

Reading the text then and now

A major factor in the positive appeal of the biblical version of the story must surely lie in the way in which at one level almost every religious reader can empathize with Abraham, and make the story his or her own. For conflict between one's religious vocation and other more purely human concerns is a virtually universal experience, with, for instance, the Catholic priest forced to choose between his love for a woman and the celibate interpretation of priesthood, or a mother wanting on the one hand as a mother to affirm her daughter's business successes and on the other her religious sense that they have been bought at the price of integrity or concern for others. The very brevity of the story also helps with such an identification; there is only one passing allusion to the value Abraham puts on his son: 'your only son Isaac, whom you

---

[84] So E. Wiesel quoted in K. P. Darr, *Far More Precious*, 150–1.

love' (v. 2). Thus bereft of detail, it makes it much easier for us to substitute some alternative sacrifice which we are called to make. But if that explains why at one level the story 'works', there are also problematic features which were to lead to significantly different retellings over the subsequent centuries.

The most obvious is that God appears to command what is without clear reason or moral justification. Not only are no grounds given for the sacrifice, it is also morally highly suspect: the command is to kill another human being and a child at that. Modern readers often make the issue easier for themselves by focusing on the introductory verse ('After these things God *tested* Abraham'), as though 'testing' already hints at something that will not be carried through to execution.[85] But this ignores Abraham's willingness to carry out the deed; is he wrongly praised for thinking that God could demand such a sacrifice? But in any case, though its consequences are obviously less, an evil command does not become any less evil, simply because it is withdrawn. It is hard therefore not to sympathize with the biblical commentator James Crenshaw when he remarks that 'no acquisition of fresh insight seems sufficiently precious to justify the private hell initiated by these words: Take your son and offer him as a burnt offering.'[86] Lest the reader think such comments only the result of modern squeamishness, perhaps they should be reminded of the reaction of Katie, Luther's wife: 'I do not believe it. God would not have treated his son like that.'[87]

Another, rather different strategy for making the narrative more acceptable might be to concentrate on the way in which the story ends, with God declaring: 'now I know that you *fear* God, seeing you have not withheld your son, your only son, from me' (Gen. 22: 12 RSV). It might then be argued that what is being stressed is the awe in which God should be held, his ways and purposes being infinitely more mysterious and wonderful than the human mind can comprehend.[88] Yet, though that is undoubtedly true,

---

[85] So we are told that it was 'a demand which God did not intend to take seriously'; G. von Rad, *Genesis* (London: SCM Press, 1972), 239.

[86] J. Crenshaw (ed.), *Theodicy in the Old Testament* (SPCK, 1983), 8.

[87] Quoted in R. H. Bainton, *Here I Stand: A Life of Martin Luther* (New York: Mentor, 1950), 290.

[88] This seems better than finding merely repetition of the theme of obedience, as in C. Westermann, *Genesis 12–36* (London: SPCK, 1985), 361–2, for then the problem of incomprehension remains.

there is still a great difference between an awe that concedes the respect due to a being infinitely richer than our limited human minds can grasp and one that unqualifiedly flies in the face of our deepest moral sensibilities. The latter cannot fail to set awe and trust in opposition to one another, which is no doubt why the New Testament sought to defuse the tension by giving Abraham grounds for continued trust: Abraham 'considered that God was able to raise men even from the dead' (Heb. 11: 19 RSV). Jesus' Jewish contemporary, Philo, likewise insists that Abraham acts thus not merely because he 'knows that to God all things are possible', but also because any hint of fear for the future can confidently be excluded, since Abraham knows that the God with whom he is dealing is of his very nature one who 'has the power to do everything yet wills only what is the best'.[89]

My remarks thus far may, however, be dismissed by many as superficial. What I want, therefore, to do now before considering how the tradition developed is two things: first, note how even the most sophisticated of modern readings fails, when it ignores the tradition; then, secondly, place the text in its historical setting, so that we can see more clearly what the pressures were towards change.

Now: Kierkegaard's interpretation   Kierkegaard's treatment of the incident in *Fear and Trembling* undoubtedly represents the most famous attempt to bypass the difficulties we have already noted and thus any necessity for new ways of telling the story. Abraham is portrayed as the great knight of faith prepared to go unquestionably wherever God calls.[90] The explanation given is as follows: 'The story of Abraham contains … a teleological suspension of the ethical. As the single individual he comes higher than the universal … If this is not Abraham's situation, then Abraham is not even a tragic hero but a murderer.'[91] The key thus becomes that there could be a higher religious demand than the purely ethical.[92]

---

[89]   Philo, *De Abrahamo* 32, 46 (my trans.); cf. also 34.
[90]   *Fear and Trembling*, eds. H. V. Hong and E. E. H. Hong (Princeton, NJ: Princeton University Press, 1983), *passim*, but esp. 20–2 and 35–7.
[91]   Ibid., 66.
[92]   For a very careful exposition of Kierkegaard's text, cf. E. F. Mooney, *Knights of Faith and Resignation: Reading Kierkegaard's Fear and Trembling* (Albany: State University of New York Press, 1991).

Presented thus starkly, it is easy to regard Kierkegaard as at the opposite extreme to the ethical rationalism of Kant, who denied that Abraham would have been right to obey such a divine command,[93] and in one sense this is right; Kierkegaard's repeated references to 'paradox' and to 'the absurd' would have won little sympathy from Kant. Yet, surprisingly perhaps, they also share much in common. First, Kierkegaard's philosophy in general can be interpreted as a revolt against Hegel and return to Kant and his recognition of the limits to human reason;[94] indeed, Kierkegaard's treatment of Abraham can be viewed as a protest against Hegel's relativizing of the symbolic status of the sacrifice as merely transitional towards a reconciliation with reason.[95] Secondly and more particularly, his ethical assumptions follow those of Kant rather than Hegel with the former's stress on universalizability rather than Hegel's on social context (*Sittlichkeit*).[96] Finally, Kant does not deny that the command should be obeyed if we knew that it truly issued from God; what he denies is that we could ever be certain that this was indeed the source—'the most remote possibility' is how he describes it.[97] However, while further reflections along these lines would, I believe, make Kierkegaard more accessible to those who share Kant's concern for intelligibility and rationality, even so the objections to Kierkegaard's position remain in my view overwhelming.

To begin with, there is the way in which he compartmentalizes human thinking. As is well known, he distinguishes various 'stages' or levels of human existence: the 'aesthetic', the 'ethical', 'religiousness A', and 'religiousness B'.[98] For somebody such as Kant,

93 *Religion Within the Limits of Reason Alone* 4.2.4. Kant is more emphatic in *The Conflict of the Faculties.*

94 Cf. D. Brown, *Continental Philosophy and Modern Theology* (Oxford: Blackwell, 1987), 16–19. Kant is too often parodied as the unqualified rationalist.

95 Cf. M. C. Taylor, *Altarity* (Chicago: University of Chicago Press, 1987), 5–11 and 348–53.

96 Note the use of 'universal' in the earlier quotation from Kierkegaard. For several other points of parallel with Kant, cf. R. L. Perkins, 'For Sanity's Sake: Kant, Kierkegaard and Father Abraham', in R. L. Perkins (ed.), *Kierkegaard's Fear and Trembling: Critical Appraisals* (Alabama: University of Alabama Press, 1981), 43–61.

97 *Religion Within the Limits of Reason Alone* 4.2.4. (New York: Harper & Row, 1960), 175.

98 For an outline, cf. D. R. Law, *Kierkegaard as Negative Theologian* (Oxford: Clarendon Press, 1993), 124–61.

or his follower in this, Richard Hare,[99] only formal criteria are needed to identify a person's morality: the willingness to universalize (requiring the same action of anyone in the same circumstances) and overridingness (treating the value in question as more binding than any other consideration). Yet on the other side (and in Kierkegaard's favour) may be set the way in which we tend to see morality in content terms, as essentially concerned with benefit and harm, and the introduction of other criteria as thereby stepping outside of morality.[100] Illustrative of this would be Genet's justification of betrayal as 'indispensable for achieving beauty',[101] Nietzsche's use of purely aesthetic criteria to guide action or to assess suffering,[102] and probably also Gauguin's justification of his flight to Tahiti in pursuit of his art.[103] This is not to say that such appeals are always opposed to conventional morality. Indeed, it is possible to envisage situations where ordinary morality could be justified on the basis of such non-moral criteria.[104] Yet Kierkegaard is right to this extent, that normally when people make such aesthetic criteria their overriding concern, they have stepped outside the usual understanding of what constitutes moral discussion and its criteria.

Even so, considerably greater difficulties arise when religion is substituted for aesthetics in the contrast. This is partly because the overlap with morals, with issues of benefit and harm, is in the religious case so self-evident. When we love someone we want them to flourish, and in that respect there can be no difference between our love for one another and God's love for us. But even when we turn to consider our love for God, while it would be absurd to suppose that it is through such love that we enable God to flourish, the object of our love will still nonetheless be to ensure that his projects flourish, in particular his purposes for the world. So, in this more limited sense it could be claimed that even here our aim

[99] R. M. Hare, *Freedom and Reason* (Oxford: Oxford University Press, 1963), 157 ff, esp. 168 ff.

[100] For key, opposing views on how morality should be defined, G. Wallace and A. D. M. Walker (eds.), *The Definition of Morality* (London: Methuen, 1970).

[101] *The Thief's Journal* (Harmondsworth: Penguin, 1967), 202.

[102] e.g. *Zur Genealogie der Moral* 1. 4; 2.17; *Jenseits von Gut und Böse*, 9, 270.

[103] *Noa, Noa*, trans. J. Griffin, (Oxford: Bruno Cassirer, 1961).

[104] Well argued by J. L. Stocks, *Morality and Purpose* (London: Routledge & Kegan Paul, 1969).

is that we should benefit someone, namely God. Much of worship in fact fits naturally into conventional moral categories, such as acknowledging another's worth, gratitude and so forth. Even if some aspects cannot be accommodated within such a moral frame- work, Kierkegaard's difficulties would still not be at an end. For if we are forced to say that God is the source of two distinct demands (the moral and the religious) that can conflict, then we seem to end up with a God divided against himself.

Kierkegaard is aware of such difficulties. That is no doubt why he insists that what happens in this instance is 'a teleological suspension of the ethical',[105] not a general pattern of overriding- ness. That also seems to be why he thinks the situation particularly traumatic, by contrast with the case of Agamemnon summoned to sacrifice his daughter Iphigenia, where he detects only conflict with natural inclination (love of daughter) suppressed in favour of a higher duty (the fleet sailing to rectify moral wrong). Yet as a comparative analysis it is surely badly deficient, since love for Iphigenia can equally be seen as morally binding, and so as offer- ing as traumatic a conflict within morality as anything Kierkegaard can present in respect of Abraham.[106]

Indeed, one might argue that in some ways it is the Agamemnon story that offers the more profound and more tragic dilemma. For, as we saw in the last chapter, Agamemnon is often given a reason why the sacrifice of his daughter should be demanded: because he has offended the goddess, Artemis. By contrast, when grounds are sought for why God might be justified in carrying the biblical test through to its conclusion, all we can fall back on is God's absolute right over our lives as their source and origin. It is a justification with a long history, but as Aquinas' support makes clear,[107] where comparison is drawn with God's apparent endorsement within Scripture of theft and adultery (cf. Exod. 12: 35; Hos. 1: 2 ff.), on this scenario all we are left with is a conflict between God's property rights and human love, hardly the most edifying of comparisons.

[105] For a helpful clarification of what is meant by the phrase, cf. A. Hannay, *Kierkegaard* (London: Routledge & Kegan Paul, 1982), 73–84.
[106] P. Quinn, 'Agamemnon and Abraham: The Tragic Dilemma of Kierkegaard's Knight of Faith', *Journal of Literature and Theology*, 4.2 (1990), 181–93.   [107] *Summa Theologiae*, 1a2ae. 94.5.

Kierkegaard's solution then is untenable for these two reasons. First, his sharp distinction between the religious and the ethical cannot be sustained; secondly, once reduced to a tragic conflict between two ethical norms, the divine norm then emerges as an unacceptable reduction of humanity to property. What makes matters worse is that once we return the passage to its likely original context, Abraham's own likely legitimization also turns out to be a form of this property argument.

Then: its value in its historical context So far as the original meaning of the story is concerned, of one thing we can be quite certain, that its point cannot lie in the rejection of human sacrifice. For the story is robbed of its dramatic power unless Abraham's virtue lies precisely in his willingness to carry through the deed at God's behest. Indeed, the agony becomes all the more real if the cultural context made this not altogether unlikely as a divine command. Jon Levenson in his recent book argues exactly this point,[108] observing that similarly elsewhere in Scripture Jephthah is not condemned for sacrificing his daughter, while King Mesha's sacrifice of his oldest son seems to be treated as though it met with positive acceptance on the part of God (Judg. 11: 29–40; 2 Kings 3: 26–27). Again, the injunction in Exodus that 'the first-born of your sons you shall give to me' is accompanied by no warning that it should not be interpreted as literally as the rest of its context (Exod. 22: 29 RSV). From evidence such as this Levenson concludes that prophetic denunciations were campaigning against something rather more than occasional backsliding (e.g. Jer. 7: 31; Ezek. 20: 25–31).

How plausible these claims are, I leave to others to judge, but it does seem that to make sense of the tale we need to assume that child sacrifice was not totally ruled out of court. It would also help with its plausibility if the story-teller is assuming the absolute rights of a father over his children, for then none of the obvious moral difficulties that arise in the modern context would have inhibited appreciation of the story. By the time of the great medieval kabbalistic work, the *Zohar*, we find the story completely rewritten, so perplexed was the author by the question: 'Who has ever

---

[108] J. Levenson, *The Death and Resurrection of the Beloved Son* (New Haven: Yale University Press, 1993), 3–52.

seen a compassionate father turn cruel?'[109] But in the ancient
world generally the view was that children were simply part of the
property of their father and thus without any independent rights,
and there are a number of biblical passages which seem to imply a
similar perspective.[110] So, though Abraham loved Isaac, there
would still be no need for Isaac's interests to be independently
considered apart from his own. The Old Testament exhibits some
tensions between corporate and more personal understandings of
responsibility and human worth,[111] but, as Chapter 2 argued, it
was only gradually and long after the closure of the canon that the
full implications for the evaluation of children have been drawn.
    That being so, it would be unfair to judge the story in purely
modern terms. One needs instead to enter imaginatively into a
world where children were viewed very differently and where the
dilemma would have been seen quite otherwise from the way in
which it is viewed today. Certainly, Abraham loved Isaac, but in
the final analysis the child had no rights: the power of life and
death lay with him as father. In one very obvious sense Aquinas is
much nearer to that thought world than we are, with his suggestion that God's command also reflected the issue of property
rights. A thousand years earlier Philo attempted a similar defence.
For Aquinas God has the right to abrogate laws of murder, theft
and adultery because everything that is belongs to him as its
Creator. Philo in similar vein argues that God may take back his
gifts at any time. On the positive side such a perspective draws
attention to the fact that we owe everything to God, and no doubt
even today some sense can be made of the story in these terms. But
there is a very high price to be paid, in the way in which it undermines the generosity of God. Gifts that are conditional and may be
withdrawn seem only in some attenuated sense 'gifts'.[112] It was
perhaps to avoid any hint that questions of ownership were the

---

[109] *Zohar*, trans. D. C. Matt (London: SPCK, 1983), 74.

[110] In Roman law fathers had the right to put their children to death, and this
also seems to be assumed in a number of Old Testament stories: Gen. 38: 24–5;
42: 37; Judg. 11: 34–40.

[111] Contrast Exod. 20: 5 and Jos. 7 with Jer. 31: 29 and Ezek. 18: 2.

[112] A somewhat different way of presenting the dilemma would be as follows.
Once the creation involved in human fatherhood is seen as conferring only
limited rights, in due course the same question must arise in respect of the greater
creator and father, God.

issue on either side that alternative explanations for both the command and for the response were soon being sought. It is to these that I now turn.

Motivation and a developing tradition

Here I want to draw attention to two rather different types of strategy which were employed in the attempt to integrate the story more effectively within a developing understanding of the nature of revelation and the kind of God it revealed. The first illustrates the extent to which various implausible avenues were explored, only to be rejected in due course; the second, the foundation for upgrading the incident such that it comes to be seen as definitive of the divine–human relationship. I consider first the search for a more intelligible command; then, that for a more fitting response.

A more intelligible command   Perhaps the easiest way of avoiding any suggestion of arbitrariness or lack of generosity in God was to deny that the command was after all his. It is a strategy which we find employed in a number of authors, as in the second-century BC with the Book of *Jubilees* (treated as canonical at Qumran), where Mastema or Satan is blamed for initiating the deed.[113] In the author's view it was quite unnecessary, but vindicated by the additional status it gives to Mount Zion, where the deed is now located (a process of identification which has already begun within Scripture at 2 Chron. 3: 1). Origen's *De Principiis* exhibits a similar pattern, though now the role of Satan has become more unqualifiedly evil. Origen, however, was clearly undecided about the best explanation to offer, since in his *Homilies* this element is omitted, and replaced by the likely resurrection of Isaac were he to die on the altar.[114] Yet more variants are to be found in later Judaism. One version in the *Babylonian Talmud* models its account on what happened to Job; it was God's way of proving to Satan Abraham's righteousness and thereby legitimating his reward of him.[115] Another is closer to Origen's, and finds a powerful ally in

---

[113] *Jubilees* 17.15–18.19; Charlesworth, *Pseudepigrapha*, II. 90–1.
[114] *De Principiis* 3. 2.1; *Homilies*, on Genesis 22.
[115] *Sanhedrin* 89b.

Elie Wiesel: 'Satan personifies the doubt Abraham *had* to have in order to remain human.'[116]

A rather different version of this tactic of directing responsibility away from God is to blame Abraham himself, instead of Satan. This is what happens in the Midrash *Bereshit Rabba* as also in the medieval *Zohar* where the testing becomes a punishment for Abraham's neglect of the poor.[117] Here we have one of the ironies of development. Abraham's story had begun by lacking strong moral content; by the time of *Jubilees* he has become a paragon of virtue; but so many versions emerged with him as a moral prig that once more the story was rewritten, to teach him humility, whether as in this version or in the second-century AD *Testament of Abraham* where, as we saw earlier, some powerful experiences are invented to teach him compassion for human frailty.

Very different, and more common, though, is the tactic of lessening the severity of the test. The modern reader's assumption that it was *only* a test in effect takes this form, but it has a long history, particularly where Abraham is conceived as knowing that God could raise Isaac from the dead. As we have seen, both Hebrews and Origen adopt this version. There is not a hint of any such belief throughout Genesis; so we can be certain that no such thought had crossed the narrator's mind, but it does of course solve the problem of the cruel father. Even Kierkegaard resorts to a not dissimilar strategy: Abraham 'did not have faith that he would be blessed in a future life but that he would be blessed here in the world. God could give him a new Isaac, could restore to life the one sacrificed.'[118] But at most this might be true to the sentiments of the original narrator in the sense that a substitute child could be envisaged, not that Isaac himself could be brought back to life.[119]

Unfortunately, these are rather ad hoc strategies; they are better at indicating a problem, than at producing a viable solution. Indeed, the introduction of Satan might be read as simply a dramatic way of labelling the problem! More honest, therefore, might be judged another passage of the Babylonian Talmud which

[116] Elie Wiesel, *Messengers of God* (New York: Summit Books, 1976), 86, author's own italics. [117] *Zohar* 70, 224.
[118] Kierkegaard, *Fear and Trembling*, 36.
[119] There is the no parallel for the latter, whereas the miraculous birth of Isaac itself provides a precedent for the former.

rejects altogether any didactic worth to the story.[120] Appeal to resurrection is also not much better, especially in its this-world version. For if Isaac is to be resurrected shortly thereafter, though there is of course the terrible pain of the pyre, from the perspective of the person whose faith is in question—Abraham's—the act seems only a momentary interlude before his calm is restored. In other words, all these answers share a common fault: they fail to tackle the problem of the person whose greater potential tragedy the story conceals—Isaac.

A more fitting response   Though in turning to consideration of the response it may seem as though we are neglecting the unresolved issue of the arbitrariness of the divine command, what we shall in fact discover is that the two are closely related: that a different conception of the response allows a fresh view of the command. What is worrying about Abraham's conduct can be well illustrated by contrasting this story of father and son with another from Hinduism, in which Nachiketas, the son, protests to his father that the only adequate sacrifice is self-sacrifice and promptly offers himself.[121] It is the way in which the infant seems dispensable within the 'greater' purposes of God and Abraham that makes one so recoil from the biblical version of the narrative. The real sufferer is left without a voice, and without any chance to find meaning in his own death.

That is no doubt why in both later Jewish and Christian versions the central focus moves towards the contribution of Isaac himself and as a necessary corollary someone of more mature years.[122] Within the Jewish context scholars disagree in their explanations as to why this happened. Because Isaac's offering is often seen as atoning, making, for instance, the exodus deliverance possible, there has been much debate over whether here Judaism shows indebtedness to Christianity or vice versa. For some the

---

[120] Ta'anit 4a; cf. also M. Roshwald's comments on 'The Meaning of Faith', *Modern Theology* 7 (1991), 381–401, esp. 395–6.

[121] *Upanishads* 'Katha' 1–3 (Harmondsworth: Penguin, 1965), 55–61.

[122] Despite the 'lad' of v. 5 occasionally commentators on the biblical text also attempt this move, with Isaac a young adult who displays a 'faith that co-operates'; V. R. Hamilton, *Genesis 18–50* (Grand Rapids, Michigan: Eerdmans, 1995), 100, 110.

changed perspective comes in response to Christian claims for the significance of Christ's death, while for others it is Christianity that incorporates an already changed Jewish perspective.[123] The problem with the latter argument is the uncertain dating of so many of the relevant texts and the fairly minor role which the parallel with Isaac plays within the New Testament; the difficulty with the former that indisputably such changes have already begun before the advent of Christianity, while, though there are signs of what could be Christian influence, they are much less marked than might otherwise have been supposed.[124] Certainly, the right to claim the heritage of Isaac was something over which the two religions fought,[125] but the best interpretation of the available evidence suggests two parallel developments, occasionally enriching one another rather than one dominating the other.[126]

Authors do not usually give the reasons for the changes— primarily of course because they do not see them as changes—but even as early as *Jubilees*, long before Christianity, the author seems concerned to indicate that Isaac was a responsible individual, with his implied age at the time being that of a fourteen-year-old.[127] Again, early in the first century AD in 4 Maccabees we find Isaac used as a model for the Maccabean martyrs: 'Courage, brother, said one ... And another recalling the past, said, "Remember whence you came and at the hand of what a father Isaac gave himself to be sacrificed for piety's sake" ' (13: 10–12).[128] Other first

[123] For the former, P. R. Davies and B. D. Chilton, 'The Aqedah: a revised tradition history', *Catholic Biblical Quarterly* 40 (1978), 514–46; for the latter, Vermes, *Scripture and Tradition*, 193–227. For an assessment of the debate, C. T. R. Hayward, 'The present state of research into the Targumic account of the sacrifice of Isaac', *Journal of Jewish Studies* 32 (1981), 127–50.

[124] For an example in the relatively minor role played by Isaac's 'blood', C. T. R. Hayward, 'The sacrifice of Isaac and Jewish polemic against Christianity', *Catholic Biblical Quarterly* 52 (1990), 292–306.

[125] For an example, R. L. Wilken, 'Melito, the Jewish community at Sardis, and the sacrifice of Isaac', *Theological Studies* 37 (1976), 53–69.

[126] S. Spiegel, *The Last Trial* (New York: Behrman, 1979), 77–120, esp. 103–4, 116–18; A. F. Segal, *The Other Judaisms of Late Antiquity* (Atlanta, Georgia: Scholars Press, 1987), 109–30, esp. 129.

[127] E. Nestle, 'Wie alt war Isaak bei der Opferung?', *Zeitschrift für die alttestamentliche Wissenschaft* 26 (1906), 281–2. His argument is based on 17: 15–16.

[128] Charlesworth, *Pseudepigrapha*, II.558. It has been suggested that the reason why the parallel passage in the earlier 2 Maccabees makes no such appeal is because a similar spirituality was first attempted through the three young men in

century writers take a similar line. Pseudo-Philo portrays Isaac as gladly giving his assent,[129] while Josephus not only repeats this pattern, but identifies Isaac as an adult of twenty-five years of age.[130] The midrash *Genesis Rabbah* at one point opts for a similar age—twenty-six—but elsewhere for what was to become the standard Jewish pattern, an Isaac aged thirty-seven.[131]

The age was not arbitrarily chosen. The argument was that since Sarah's death follows immediately this must have been in response to news of the terrible events recorded in the previous chapter. Since she died at one hundred and twenty-seven and bore Isaac at ninety, this means that Isaac must have been thirty-seven at the time. Though this may have been what prompted the change, the motives are unlikely to have been entirely exegetical. The medieval *Zohar*, for instance, takes Isaac's age as indicative of his personal responsibility, while the Hebrew particle *et* is used to argue that Isaac was tested no less than Abraham.[132] Perhaps a couple of centuries earlier in the Aramaic paraphrase of Genesis in *Targum Pseudo-Jonathan* a different tactic is employed: Isaac is seen as himself initiating the testing. Ishmael boasts that because he had not been circumcised until he was thirteen, it was his own decision to identify with God, unlike Isaac who had the rites imposed upon him at eight days old. Isaac's response is interesting: 'Behold, today I am thirty-seven years old, and if the Holy One, blessed be he, were to ask all my members, I would not refuse.' Abraham and Isaac then go together to the place of sacrifice 'with a perfect heart', and Isaac, though not Abraham, is then vouchsafed a vision of the angels in heaven observing their complete unanimity of action.[133]

Many of these details are shared with the very much earlier *Targum Neofiti*, but not Pseudo-Jonathan's decision to make Isaac

the fiery furnace of Daniel 3; C. Thoma, 'Observations on the concept and the early forms of Akedah spirituality', in A. Finkel and L. Fizzell (eds.), *Standing before God: Studies on Prayer in Scripture and Tradition* (New York: Ktav, 1981), 213–22.

[129] *Biblical Antiquities* 40.2–3. A similar treatment is accorded Jephthah's daughter; for a detailed analysis, C. Baker, 'Pseudo-Philo and the transformation of Jephthah's daughter', in M. Bal (ed.), *Anti-Covenant: Counter-Reading Women's Lives in the Hebrew Bible* (Sheffield: Almond, 1989), 195–209.

[130] *Jewish Antiquities* 1. 232; 1. 227.

[131] For the former, *Genesis Rabbah* 58.5.

[132] *Zohar*, 73. For commentary on this surprising use of the accusative particle, 214.   [133] *Targum Pseudo-Jonathan* 77–81, esp. 78, 79.

go off immediately afterwards to 'the schoolhouse of Shem the Great'. The author's desire (which is given exegetical justification) is clearly to make Isaac correspond still more closely to the practice of the orthodox Jew. A similar desire for such identification also explains what happens within Islam. Though Muhammad *may* have conceived of Isaac as the sacrifice,[134] high praise is heaped upon his brother Ishmael because 'he was strictly true to what he had promised', and it is this verse which is normally used to interpret the longer passage which describes the sacrifice, though neither son is mentioned by name, except Isaac at the very end.[135] There is, however, a certain naturalness in assuming that Ishmael is intended since the immediately preceding verse had spoken of a reward and most Muslim commentators assume that the 'good news' is the birth of Abraham's second son, Isaac. In *Jubilees* the descendants of Ishmael are identified as Arabs, an assumption which may already be present within the biblical canon.[136] If so, we have yet another example of the search for personal identification with those whose example one's religious life seeks to emulate. Certainly in popular Muslim piety today the various actions of the *hajj* or pilgrimage at Mecca are made to correspond closely to the actions of Abraham, Hagar and Ishmael in what are interpreted as deeds of voluntary self-sacrifice in relation to God and one's fellow human beings. Moreover, whether or not one is in Mecca, each year there is offered the sacrifice of a sheep or some other suitable animal on *Id al-Adha* (the feast of sacrifice) in annual commemoration of this act of the two patriarchs, and it is celebrated as a major feast day in the Muslim calendar.

[134] Only with Ibn Ishaq (d. 767) does Ishmael become the dominant contender. In explaining why he came to hold almost exclusive sway, commentators point to the increasing ritual importance of Mecca and the rise of Arab identity; S. Bashear, 'Abraham's sacrifice of his son and related issues', *Der Islam* 67 (1990), 243–77, esp. 264 ff.; R. Firestone, 'Abraham's son as the intended sacrifice: issues in Qur'anic exegesis', *Journal of Semitic Studies* 34 (1989), 95–131, esp. 129 ff. A Jewish counter-reaction was perhaps inevitable; for an early example, M. Ohana, 'La polémique judéo-islamique et l'image d'Ismael dans Targum Pseudo-Jonathan et dans Pirke de Rabbi Eliezer', *Augustinianum* 15 (1975), 367–87.

[135] Sura 19. 54–5; and footnote 2506, *The Holy Qur'an*, 779; for the sacrifice itself, Sura 37.100–13.

[136] *Jubilees* 20.11–13. For within the canon, A. Jeffrey in *Interpreter's Dictionary of the Bible* (New York: Abingdon, 1962), Vol. 1, 182.

Thus Islam no less than Judaism and Christianity moves the focus to the act of the son. A range of motives has been noted, among them moral concerns, the characterization of God and desire for suitable models to imitate. Not yet noted, however, is the extent to which the new form of the story came not only to define the nature of the religion as such but also offered a version which could draw the apparently conflicting traditions closer together.

Self-sacrifice as religious norm

I noted earlier that the issue of which son offered himself in sacrifice is an issue of very secondary importance, even if the answer is recoverable historically. For the real importance of the story lies elsewhere, and so there would seem no reason in principle why Jew, Christian and Muslim alike should not mutually endorse these two rather different but related expressions of their common desire to aspire towards a more self-sacrificial form of life. All that stands in the way are legends of historical descent, neither of which is likely to be true when measured against the complexities of Middle-Eastern history. More promising, therefore, is further exploration of how the story has come to symbolize the very nature of religious commitment. I shall illustrate this from Judaism and Christianity in turn. At the same time it will be important to note what criteria might be employed to justify such moves.

Akedah as universal norm   Within Judaism Isaac was to become the norm for life understood as self-sacrificial dedication to God, and, significantly, the incident ceased to be known as Abraham's testing but instead acquired its new title as 'the binding' of Isaac, the *Akedah*.[137] As we have observed, the Maccabean martyrs were envisaged as appealing to the example of Isaac, and that was a pattern that was to repeat itself through much subsequent Jewish suffering. This is no doubt why in some expositions it was even assumed that Isaac had actually been sacrificed, an inference not entirely without textual support, since only

---

[137] The first occurrence of the term is in Mekilta de-Rabbi Ishmael; so Spiegel, *The Last Trial*, xix–xx.

Abraham is mentioned as returning.[138] However, for most the intention was enough. 'Here is a story that contains a Jewish identity in its totality ... Every major theme, every passion and obsession that makes Judaism the adventure that it is, can be traced back to it.' So writes Elie Wiesel.[139] The major importance that the binding has for later Judaism, in such marked contrast to the absence of any reference anywhere in the Hebrew Bible, can in part be explained by the tragedies of Jewish history: sacrifice was an inescapable category. But this is by no means the whole story.

It was also taken as the clue to understanding Israel's worship, which could now be read as a symbolic, substitutionary offering of ourselves, and indeed, it was even seen as necessary to legitimate the killing that is involved in the consumption of any animal food.[140] It is sometimes argued that allusions to Jerusalem are already lurking in the biblical text,[141] but whether so or not, by the time of Chronicles this is made explicit, and it becomes the established pattern for all later literature. Indeed, *Jubilees* with its elaborate dating makes it the pattern for Passover, while one of the Targums links the two, together with the beginning and the end of the world, into what it calls 'the four nights' of world history.[142] The intention seems to be to declare that the liberation of Israel at the end of time will be achieved by a combination of divine care, as witnessed in the Passover, and human self-offering, as demonstrated by Isaac.

In contemporary Judaism the *Akedah* is celebrated at the New Year feast, Rosh Ha-Shanah, rather than at Passover, where some think its liturgical celebration may have had its origin. Additional prominence, though, has been acquired through its association with the Holocaust. In Hebrew a more neutral term is used (*Shoah*—destruction). It seems likely that 'holocaust' has become the favoured term in English largely because of its extensive usage

---

[138] Cf. Levenson, *Death and Resurrection*, 192–6; for the mention of only Abraham, Gen. 22: 19.   [139] Wiesel, *Messengers*, 69.

[140] For the former, *Leviticus Rabbah* 2.11 on Lev. 1: 5 and 11; for the latter, *Genesis Rabbah* 56. 3.

[141] For some of the arguments, cf. Levenson, *Death and Resurrection* 114–23; cf. also Gen. 22: 2; 2 Chron. 3: 1; *Jubilees* 18. 13.

[142] *Jubilees* 17.15–16;Targum of Exodus 12: 41–2; quoted in P. Grelot, *What are the Targums?* (Collegeville, Minnesota: The Liturgical Press, 1992), 40–2.

in the writings of Elie Wiesel.[143] His own use has been termed a
'sacred parody' because the religious significance of the term still
remains in doubt, whereas for other Jewish writers it continues to
have the appropriate resonance. Yet others resort to alternative
analogies such as those of Cain and Abel.[144] In trying to account
for this ambivalent attitude among so many modern Jewish writers, one notes the marked contrast to the enthusiasm with which
the image of the *Akedah* was employed in dealing with Christian
butchery at the time of the Crusades. During this period the story
was sometimes even further modified to include Isaac's actual
death and subsequent resurrection.[145] To attribute the difference
solely to the number of deaths in the Holocaust seems inadequate
as an explanation since the pogroms of the Middle Ages were also
experienced with great severity. More likely as an explanation is
the difficulty the modern world in general has in appropriating the
notion of sacrifice.[146]

We find it hard to accept the apparently mysterious connection
between one person's death and another's life, but is that not in part
due to a failure of imagination? Isaac's sacrifice lived in the imagination of the medieval martyrs, and so informed their deaths,
whereas for the modern mind it often remains no more than a story
about the distant past. Though various forms of connection were
proposed, the irony is that to those earlier generations the offer of
self-sacrifice was sufficient in itself to establish a relationship. It

---

[143] So Z. Garber and B. Zuckerman, 'Why do we call the holocaust "the
holocaust?" ', *Modern Judaism* 9 (1989), 197–211.

[144] For Wiesel contrasted with the 'literal recall' of Eliezer Berkovits, I.
Wollaston, 'Traditions of remembrance: post-holocaust interpretations of Genesis
22' in J. Davies et al. (eds.), *Words Remembered, Texts Renewed* (Sheffield: Sheffield
Academic Press, 1995), 41–51; for a not dissimilar contrast between A. B.
Yehoshua and Moshe Shamir and others, E. A. Coffin, 'The binding of Isaac in
modern Israeli literature' in M. P. O'Connor and D. N. Freedman (eds.),
Backgrounds for the Bible (Winona Lake, Indiana: Eisenbrauns, 1987), 293–308; for
Dan Pagis' substitution of Cain and Abel, S. D. Ezrahi, 'Shattering memories',
The New Republic 204 (1991), 36–9.

[145] Spiegel, *The Last Trial*, 17–27 and 129 ff. The long poem of Rabbi
Ephraim ben Jacob of Bonn includes the modification, 143–52, esp. 148–9.

[146] The inadequacies of all existing theories are rightly highlighted by B.
Chilton in 'The hungry knife: towards a sense of sacrifice', in M. D. Carroll et
al. (eds.), *The Bible in Human Society* (Sheffield: Sheffield Academic Press, 1996),
122–38.

could then live in the mind as a commitment that brought Isaac and recipient together in a shared bond of fellowship. If we then ask what generated that new understanding, attention has already been drawn to some of the prompts in exegetical and moral reflection, but that is to tell only half the story. Given the original stress in the incident on obedience, it would be hard to justify what happened as a natural trajectory from the way in which the tale was first told. Instead, what we appear to have is something rather like what happened with Paul in respect of his treatment of Abraham, a later focus of the tradition turning back upon its roots to offer a new perspective on them. In this case reflection on worship grounded in sacrifice seems to have produced the requisite result, when combined with certain attitudes towards suffering. Concepts of atonement clearly played a key role, and this is no less true of Christianity.

Isaac as type of Christ   In reaching that point, as with Judaism, stress upon the voluntary aspect of the sacrifice and its intimate connection with worship also helped shape the Christian tradition's understanding of how the story should be read, as too did the desire to make of the story a present, imagined reality. This was achieved through finding in the story of Isaac an anticipation or type of the sacrificial death of Christ. The degree to which the connection is already made in the New Testament is a matter of some dispute. Paul's talk of a God 'who did not spare his own Son' might be an allusion, but if so it is surprising that he does not take advantage of the opportunity to give added force to the comparison through any use of the Septuagint description of Isaac as the 'beloved' son. Similarly, even where this phrase is used—in the baptismal narrative, one observes that Luke took it as a reference to Psalm 2 and not Genesis 22.[147] So the development of the comparison may be much more strongly post-biblical than is often assumed.[148]

---

[147] The Septuagint of Gen. 22 has 'beloved' three times at v. 2, 12 and 16. The western text of Luke 3.22 adds 'today I have begotten you' to Mark's presumed quotation at 1: 11 of Ps. 2: 7.

[148] But for a contrary view in respect of the Epistle to the Hebrews, J. Swetnam, *Jesus and Isaac* (Rome: Biblical Institute, 1981). He reads Heb. 2: 5–18 in the light of Jewish understandings of the *Akedah*: 130–77.

However that may be, as it proceeded apace, it clearly went with stress upon the voluntary character of Isaac's act, helped in part, no doubt, by Christ's own age at the crucifixion. So, for instance, Clement of Rome informs us that because 'Isaac knew with confidence what was about to happen, it was with gladness that he was lead forth as a sacrificial victim,' while Irenaeus urges us to 'take up our cross as Isaac took up his bundle of sticks'.[149] Tertullian exhibits a similar pattern: 'Isaac ... when delivered up by his father for a sacrifice, himself carried the wood for himself, and did at that early date set forth the death of Christ who, when surrendered as a victim by his Father, carried the wood of his own passion.'[150] One notes that, though in Genesis Abraham places the burden of the wood upon his son (22: 6), Tertullian's Latin (*sibi ipse*) implies personal responsibility, an impression inevitably intensified by the intended parallel with Christ. More generally among the Fathers, two other patterns are also to be observed: one in which, because Isaac is not himself sacrificed, the ram in the thicket is taken as the principal type for Christ, and the other where the ram is treated as a symbol of Christ's humanity (which did die) and Isaac of his divinity (which did not). Examples of the former we find in Justin, Melito and Tertullian, and of the latter in Origen and Theodoret.[151] This alternative, more indirect analogy was aided by the fact that in both Latin and Greek the word for horns can also mean the extremities of a piece of wood, such as a cross. In Christian history as a whole, however, identification with Isaac was to remain the dominant image. Indeed, sometimes so intense was the desire to make Isaac's sacrifice voluntary that it can almost come to stand inadvertently in contrast to Christ's. Ambrose can even inform us: 'Isaac did not hesitate when he followed his father with his unequal steps; he did not weep when bound, nor did he ask for delay when presented on the altar.'[152] Likewise, in medieval plays on the theme 'it is Isaac who is the

---

[149] Clement, *First Letter to Corinthians* 31 (my trans.); Irenaeus, *Adversus Haereses* 4.10 (my trans.).

[150] *Adversus Marcionem* 3.18, trans. E. Evans (Oxford: Clarendon Press, 1972), 225; cf. also Melito *De Pascha*, 59.

[151] J. Daniélou, 'La typologie d'Isaac dans le christianisme primitif', *Biblica* 28 (1947), 363–93, esp. 370–76.

[152] Ambrose, *De Virginitate* 2. 9 (my trans.). No doubt, Ambrose is showing here the influence of Stoicism.

hero', so much so that he is even shown giving thought for his mother as he prepares for death.[153] In Renaissance drama a rather different tack is employed: with some obvious borrowings from the story of Iphigenia, in George Buchanan's *Jephthes* Jephthah's daughter becomes a type for Christ in her sacrificial self-giving.[154] Iconographically there are similar developments. In the catacomb of Calixtus Abraham and Isaac are portrayed, jointly giving thanks for their deliverance, while in the catacomb on the Via Latina the artist takes the moment at which we find the action halted, with both listening to an unseen God.[155] The latter depiction has a pagan altar, and it remains pagan in structure until superseded at Chartres and elsewhere by one obviously Christian in form. By the eighteenth century the altar is less common. In its place Tiepolo gives to Isaac the priestly vestments of martyrdom. In that painting (in the Metropolitan in New York) Isaac is clearly a young man, and though bound and blindfolded, the blindfold is gently held and there is no suggestion of a struggle.[156] William Blake is more traditional in retaining the altar, but innovative in assigning to Isaac the discovery of the ram; to Isaac thus belongs the new age.[157] Occasionally artists did try to return to the old focus. In 1401 in the competition for the bronze doors for the Baptistry at Florence Brunelleschi offered a relief in which Isaac looks in agony as his father draws the knife, but, significantly, such a conception was rejected in favour of Ghiberti's alternative proposal: here Isaac looks with total confidence at the angel whom Abraham has yet to see.[158] That, then, is overwhelmingly how the

---

[153] Thus paralleling the crucifixion. R. Woolf, *Art and Doctrine: Essays on Medieval Literature* (London: Hambledon Press, 1986), 49–75, esp. 59 ff.

[154] In token of the debt, the girl is named 'Iphis'. For a comparison between Buchanan's play and Beza's *Abraham sacrificiant*: D. K. Shuger, *The Renaissance Bible* (Berkeley: University of California, 1994), 128–66.

[155] For illustration of the latter, A. Ferrua, *The Unknown Catacomb* (New Lanark, Geddes & Grosset, 1991), 91; for discussion of early developments, I. S. Van Woerden, 'The iconography of the sacrifice of Abraham' in *Vigiliae Christianae* 15 (1961), 214–55.

[156] R. Mühlberger, *The Bible in Art: The Old Testament* (New York: Portland House, 1991), 48–9.

[157] Painted in 1799; for illustration and commentary, R. Lister, *The Paintings of William Blake* (Cambridge: Cambridge University Press, 1986), No. 21.

[158] For illustrations and commentary, F. Hartt, *History of Italian Renaissance Art* (New York: Abrams, 4th edn., 1994), 167–9.

tradition came to read the narrative. Even apparent exceptions may not be so. Though on a famous carving at Souillac Abraham appears to grasp Isaac savagely by the hair and Isaac recoil in fear, closer inspection reveals otherwise, as the poet R. S. Thomas has noted:

> And the son's face is calm;
> There is trust there.[159]

Perhaps the best example of the degree to which the imagination had rewritten the story is provided by the ninth-century Kildalton cross from the island of Islay in the Western Hebrides. There on one arm Cain cudgels his brother with a club while on the other Isaac, calmly facing his father, offers himself on the altar: the first vicious murder contrasted with the first perfect self-sacrifice.

In effect, the story has been redefined in the light of Christ's crucifixion. The helpless victim has become the saint who anticipates Christ's own sacrifice. This is made quite explicit in the Coptic church where Isaac is assigned a specific saint's day, and the second-century AD *Testament of Isaac* used to celebrate that day. It speaks of Isaac as purified silver, the perfume of whose sacrifice penetrates the veil of heaven, with us enjoined to follow his example, particularly in sacrificial giving to the poor.[160]

Conclusion What is fascinating about this history is that two independent, developing traditions have nonetheless coalesced round a similar retelling of the familiar tale, with Judaism and Christianity alike finding in Isaac's self-sacrificial offering the 'real' text. This is not to deny considerable differences of detail in respect of atonement theology, but it is to note the opportunities thereby created for fruitful dialogue, and indeed the possibility of mutual enrichment through attention to underlying atonement theologies in the other's faith. Where, for instance, Christianity is prepared to speak of the appropriateness of atonement rather than

[159] R. S. Thomas, 'Souillac: le sacrifice d'Abraham', in *Collected Poems 1945–90* (London: Dent, 1993), 147; for a discussion of some of his other uses, S. Volk-Birke, 'World history from BC to AD: R. S. Thomas' *Counterpoint*', *Literature and Theology* 9 (1995), 199–226.

[160] In Charlesworth, *Pseudepigrapha* I, 905–11, esp. 911 (ch. 8). September 3rd is his saint's day.

its necessity, the closeness to the Jewish position would seem particularly clear.[161] This is, however, not the place to begin such dialogue.

It is, though, the place to acknowledge how much is lost if either or both religions seek to recover a primary place for the passage in something like its original significance. One indication of the consequences is provided in what sometimes happened as a result of the new interest in more literal readings that was generated among Protestant and Catholic alike during the sixteenth century and thereafter. In his commentary on Genesis Calvin had insisted upon a literal reading, and this has led some to detect in Rembrandt's depiction of the scene a revolt against earlier presentations.[162] To some degree this seems true, in that the Bible is followed more closely, with Abraham clearly the central figure. Even so, Isaac remains a youth rather than a child, and, as comparison with a pupil's imitation shows, at least in his most famous version gentleness and acceptance are still the primary motifs.[163] So a better example perhaps comes from the Catholic world, in the artist whose style so influenced that of Rembrandt, namely Caravaggio. For it is his version more than any other which shows us what is so profoundly wrong with the biblical version: Abraham is shown pinning down his victim, a squirming and screaming son.[164] None of this is to deny that on occasion preachers succeed marvellously in using the narrative as it stands to advocate readiness to sacrifice to God all we hold most dear, and sometimes even through consciously drawing attention to all the agonies that

---

[161] On the Jewish view Isaac is prepared, rather than required, to offer himself. For the distinction in Christian theology: D. Brown, ' "Necessary" and "fitting" reasons in Christian theology', in W. J. Abraham and S. W. Holtzer (eds.), *The Rationality of Religious Belief* (Oxford: Clarendon Press, 1987), 211–30.

[162] D. R. Smith, 'Towards a Protestant aesthetics: Rembrandt's 1655 *Sacrifice of Isaac*', *Art History* 8 (1985), 290–302. The debate on the nature of Protestant aesthetics is continued by D. T. Jenkins and Donald Davie in *Journal of Literature and Theology* 2 (1988), 153–73.

[163] The etching of 1655 is more sharply focused on Abraham's agonies than is the Leningrad painting of 1635. For the comparison with a pupil's version, S. Partsch, *Rembrandt* (London: Weidenfeld and Nicholson, 1991), 108–111.

[164] For illustration and commentary, A. Moir, *Caravaggio* (London: Thames & Hudson, 1989), 94–5.

Abraham must have undergone.[165] Even so, it is one thing to offer
oneself; quite another to offer someone else. It would be a tragedy
if our modern retreat from tradition also meant a return to what is
in the end not only the more troubling but also the less evocative
image.[166]

What may make some Christians hesitate is the doubt already
noted as to whether such a retelling had already been explicitly
endorsed by the New Testament itself. For me that cannot be the
final arbitrator. The fact that Christ went voluntarily to the cross
in itself demands that reinterpretation. Perhaps what inhibited
early endorsement was the conservative character of New
Testament imagery. It tends to speak of God 'giving' or 'sending'
or 'not sparing' his own Son (e.g. John 3: 16–17; Rom. 8: 32),
rather than of the Son himself making the decision. Thereby the
way was open to a similar subordination of purpose to that which
we find in the Abraham story. It was a line of thought which later
Christianity was to close doctrinally through its formulation of the
doctrine of the Trinity and the equality of the three persons. The
next chapter will argue that this imposition was justified, though
almost certainly not the original meaning. Similarly here, we may
contend that tradition in the power of the Spirit gave the passage
a very different, though legitimate, meaning. The Church's reflection on the significance of Christ had enabled new insights to be
appropriated that go well beyond any literal or natural reading of
the existing text.

But it is a Spirit at work not only within the Christian tradition. Judaism and Islam (and Hinduism in the story of
Nachiketas) were also able to move in this direction, of a life

[165] For a more academic example, cf. von Rad's treatment where a very
Lutheran reading is offered, with Abraham, like Christ, thrown into a world of
'Godforsakenness'; *Genesis*, 237–45, esp. 244. For an aesthetic, the way in which
Abraham is driven almost mad, wandering through the ruins of Sodom, before
he finally yields, in the film *The Bible: In the Beginning* (1966).

[166] A good example of the problem is the recent decision of York Minster in
restoring the sculptures on its Great West Door to abandon the traditional typology, and in consequence place a bound and naked Isaac already cowering on the
pyre (Rory Young, 1997–8). By way of contrast, note the parallel fifteenth-
century roof boss in Norwich Cathedral, in which Isaac is portrayed unbound
and in prayer: illustrated in M. Rose and J. Hedgecoe, *Stories in Stone* (London:
Herbert Press, 1997), 52.

voluntarily given for others, without benefit of Christology. That does not make Christology dispensable. Each tradition has its own integrity, and a distinctive story that needs hearing in how it arrived at what we might call an 'atonement' perception; so in any dialogue that distinctiveness needs to be taken with the maximum seriousness. Even so, recognition of these alternative routes does hint that the application of Christology may not always be an advantage. Sometimes it can be an inhibitor in the task of imaginatively appropriating past texts, and this is well illustrated by my final example in this chapter, the story of Joseph.

The temptations of Joseph

One factor which makes Joseph's treatment in tradition so particularly interesting is the warning it contains of the dangers that can sometimes lurk in too facile or superficial a christocentric approach. For, while the Jewish tradition made very effective use of him as a medium for moral reflection, Christianity came to an insignificant halt. In a number of the Fathers—Tertullian, Ambrose, Cyril of Alexandria, and Chrysostom—Joseph, like Isaac, is seen as prefiguring Christ: sold as he was, like Jesus, by those whom he trusted.[167] But precisely because of that comparison with Jesus, excluded was any serious consideration of moral growth and how that might occur.[168] Perhaps because of this even when the story is taken on its own terms, as in Chrysostom, we are offered none of the profound reflections that were to characterize the Jewish and Muslim traditions. Instead, young men are simply urged to copy the chastity of Joseph before Potiphar's wife.[169]

To my mind, as it stands the biblical version can hardly be said to offer any profound moral illumination, however dynamic and exciting it is as a narrative. In Chapter 37 we are introduced to a

---

[167] Tertullian, *Adversus Marcionem* 3.18; Cyril of Alexandria, *Glaphyra in Genesim*, 6 (*PG* 69. 283 ff.).

[168] Well illustrated by Ambrose, *De Joseph Patriarcha* (*PL* 14. 641). Because of the parallel, his forgiveness of others is seen as immediate (1.3), and all inclination to sexual sin absent (5. 22–24).   [169] e.g. *Homiliae in Genesim* 62. 4.

favoured child whose undiplomatic truthfulness results in his misery;[170] in Chapter 39 we find him resisting a temptation where all the blame is put on Potiphar's wife, and little explanation given to account for his successful resistance;[171] finally Chapters 41 and following record his material success and reconciliation with his family but only after some rather cruel teasing of them on his part. Admittedly, some have found in the story of the relation between Joseph and his brothers 'people ... refined by suffering' into a profound capacity to forgive,[172] but caution is necessary in drawing such a lesson. Not only does the narrative show little interest in psychological motivations,[173] if the final chapter of Genesis is taken as part of the same narrative, even at the time of Jacob's death the brothers clearly still do not believe that Joseph had forgiven them.[174]

Careful scrutiny of the text suggests that it is the character of Judah, one of Joseph's brothers, rather than that of Joseph himself, which is most transformed over the course of the narrative,[175] and indeed it is with Judah's family that the long-term destiny of God's

[170] A low estimate of the treatment of his brothers has often been voiced; e.g. Wiesel, *Messengers* 156, 160. Wiesel suggest ostentatious luxury as the reason why his brothers do not recognize him.

[171] Gen. 39: 8–9 puts all the emphasis on his standing with his master, and only mentions sinning against God briefly at the end. Some find in this a reflection of the Wisdom literature's appeal to the practical consequences of adultery: V. P. Hamilton, *The Book of Genesis: Chapters 18–50* (Grand Rapids, Mich.: Eerdmans, 1995), 463.

[172] G, von Rad, *Old Testament Theology* (Edinburgh: Oliver & Boyd, 1962), I, 173; and Genesis commentary, *passim*. For a particularly well argued version of this view, R. M. Schwartz, 'Joseph's bones and the resurrection of the text: remembering in the Bible', in Schwartz (ed.), *The Book and the Text: The Bible and Literary Theory* (Oxford: Blackwell, 1990), 40–59.

[173] Stressed by C. Westermann, *Joseph* (Edinburgh: T & T Clark, 1996), 6–7, 28–9. The acquisition and loss of garments take the place of psychological reflections.

[174] All we have to go on at 45: 15 is that 'his brothers talked with him'. Genesis 50: 15–21 then discloses continuing, residual suspicions. This makes it difficult to take the development of conscience as one of the narrative's main themes, the view of T. L. Hettema, *Reading for Good* (Kampen: Kok Pharos, 1996), esp. 229–34. More plausible is Hettema's recognition of the difficulties in appropriating the narrative for today: 264–9.

[175] Through his relations with Tamar (38, esp. v. 26) and in his offer to serve as a slave in Benjamin's place (44, esp. vv. 33–4).

people would lie.[176] Yet, in its immediate context it looks as though the incident of Judah's intercourse with Tamar had a quite different function, to underline the contrast with Joseph's chastity in the subsequent chapter. That being so, it is perhaps not unexpected that, so far from the narrator consciously contributing positive moral weight to David's ancestor, he provoked a felt need in the author of the book of Ruth for an alternative version of the past.[177] Sordid relations with a presumed prostitute are countered by the moving story of Boaz and Ruth, likewise ancestor and foreigner. With that attack on David's line and the already noted ambiguities in Joseph's conduct, it is all the more surprising that Joseph was to become the Jewish tradition's pre-eminent example of a *Tzaddik* or righteous one. Instead of twice being victimized, once by his brothers and once by Potiphar's wife, he is portrayed as the saint in training. Yet that is what happened, and a not dissimilar pattern emerges within Islam.

Jewish and Muslim developments

The ascription of sanctity came early, but one has to wait rather longer for deep psychological insight. Depending on the date of the book of Esther, as early as the fourth or third century BC Joseph is already being used as illustrative of the need to resist temptation, while in the second century BC Ben Sira declares that 'no one else ever born has been like Joseph'.[178] Among the latter's

---

[176] Not only is Judah the ancestor of King David, David is taunted by Shimei of 'the house of Joseph,' (2 Sam. 19: 20). A complicated relationship culminates in David on his death-bed finally ordering Shimei's execution: 2 Sam. 16: 5–14; 19: 16–24; 1 Kings 2: 8–9. For some fascinating reflections on the implications of the story, G. Josipovici, *The Book of God* (New Haven: Yale University Press, 1988), 75–89.

[177] For a more detailed argument that this was the intention, K. Nielson, *Ruth* (London: SCM Press, 1997), 12–17. The parallel assumes that both the women involved were foreigners, Tamar a Canaanite, Ruth a Moabite, but it is possible that Genesis implies no such thing. For Tamar is not specifically identified as a Canaanite, whereas a few verses earlier another woman is: contrast Gen. 38: 6 and 38: 2.

[178] For Ben Sira, Ecclus. 49: 15 (JB). Mordecai's rejection of idolatry is deliberately expressed through verbal echoes of the Genesis passage: so J. D. Levenson, *Esther* (London: SCM Press, 1997), 68. For other parallels with the Joseph story, ibid., 21; S. B. Berg, *Book of Esther* (Missoula, Mont.: Scholars Press, 1979), 123–42.

contemporaries the author of *Jubilees* makes only one significant addition, in helping to justify such a judgement: Joseph resists temptation through remembering that the death penalty attaches to adultery. For the writer of the *Testament of the Twelve Patriarchs*, on the other hand, it has become an endurance test, lasting no less than seven years, with 'patience and prayer' Joseph's resources against temptation. Unfortunately, neither narrative offers much expansion of what they have in mind, and so our understanding of how temptation might be resisted is not really significantly advanced.[179]

Even so, a precedent had been set, in terms of how Joseph's story was to be used. That is no doubt why it came to function as a launching pad for a large body of thought both on how sanctity might be created in an individual and in particular on the role that temptation might play in this process. Moral growth might be expected as part of such a story, and that is no doubt why several writers reserve their harshest criticisms for Joseph's initial behaviour towards his brothers, while at the same time searching for extenuating reasons to explain his later conduct towards his family as a whole. Philo is one example of this. In his treatise *On Dreams* Joseph's brothers are actually praised for resisting his dreams, while in his work *On Joseph* his father reprimands him. It is against such a backdrop that Philo portrays Joseph's growth into the ideal statesman, learning self-restraint, as he does, through his relations with Potiphar's wife, and a proper analysis of motives through his testing (not teasing) of his brothers once they are in Egypt.[180] At the other extreme is the *Targum Pseudo-Jonathan* which uses the story of Joseph to warn of the danger of decline from virtue. In its version of Chapter 37 the brothers are seen wholly to blame, with Joseph a model of innocent virtue that is confirmed in the testing of Chapter 39. However in Chapter 40 he is condemned for trusting in men rather than God when he speaks to the chief cupbearer, and asks for his support. Further indication of that decline is then seen in his treatment of his family, so much so in fact that

---

[179] *Jubilees* 39. 6 (Charlesworth, *Pseudepigrapha* I.129); *Testament of Joseph* 2–16 (Charlesworth II. 819–23); for a helpful analysis of the latter, W. H. Hollander, *Joseph as an Ethical Model in the Testament of the Twelve Patriarchs* (Leiden: Brill, 1981).

[180] *De Somniis* II, 14. 3; *De Iosepho* 2. 9; 9. 40 ff.; 39. 232 ff.

in Chapter 46 his life is shortened as a punishment, though by Chapter 50 (the final chapter) we are informed that he has at last learnt humility.[181]

However, following the biblical precedent, inevitably the strongest focus is placed on the temptation by Potiphar's wife. Here the role of internalized command, precedent (in his father's example) and context (was Joseph wise to be there in the first place?) are all fully explored. So, for instance, on the last point (context), a number of Midrash explicitly blame Joseph, one even observing that Joseph could not possibly have lost a garment so firmly attached to his body as the *beged* was, unless he had unravelled it of his own accord.[182] Thomas Mann in his massive novel *Joseph and His Brothers*, though displaying wide knowledge of the range of factors to which appeal had been made, also significantly focuses on the temptations of overconfident virtue.[183] Yet, though reflection continued to revolve round that specific temptation, in effect it had become the impetus for considering the issue of temptation in general. This is well illustrated by how the matter is treated in the medieval *Zohar*, where Joseph has become the pattern of all successful resistance to temptation. One needs to acknowledge its seductive power, the 'beautiful clothes', while at the same time appreciating that the only effective response is something equally powerful and deeply entrenched, God's law and 'compassion for the world'.[184]

A similar development occurs in Islam. The Qur'an devotes a

[181] For clear instances of the perceived decline, *Targum Pseudo-Jonathan* (Aramaic Bible edition, 134, 151, with contrast, 165). More generally, M. Niehoff, 'The figure of Joseph in the Targums', *Journal of Jewish Studies* 39 (1988), 234–50.

[182] *Midrash Tanhuma*: Vayyeshev 9. The great commentator Rashi reports that the reference to Joseph going into the house 'to do his work' at Gen. 39: 11 was often interpreted to imply Joseph's intention to yield to the woman; N. Leibovitz, *Studies in Bereshit* (Jerusalem: Nehama, 1974), 415. Some have seen in the biblical text itself a hint of such intention through punning on a similar word meaning unfaithfulness (*bagad*); V. P. Hamilton, *Genesis 18–50*, 465.

[183] It was his desire to be 'a virtuoso of virtue' that led to 'his second descent into the grave'; T. Mann, *Joseph and his Brothers* (Harmondsworth: Penguin, 1978), 748–57, esp. 757, 751.

[184] *Zohar*, 84–90, esp. 87, 89. In similar vein in the sixth-century *Mekilta de Rabbi Ishmael* attempts to link each of the Ten Commandments to Joseph's style of life.

whole chapter to the story of Joseph, and in it the temptation plays a major and expanded role. Muslim commentators see it as part of Joseph's training, and draws attention to the way in which he shows no signs of pride in his strength of resolve, but attributes to God alone his ability to resist.[185] Attention is also drawn to the unqualified character of his forgiveness of his brothers, and that Muhammad himself used this as a model for his relations with the Quraysh who had conspired against him.[186] The exhaustive commentary of Mawdudi is at great pain to stress the moral lessons that can be drawn from the version in the Qur'an in contrast to the biblical account which he finds confused and at time corrupting.[187] It is interesting, though, to note that he himself retreats from the most natural reading of the text when it speaks of Joseph's restraint working in due course a conversion in the heart of the woman herself.[188] No new speaker is indicated. Nonetheless, most commentators want to assign the relevant verses to Joseph. Some modern Muslim writers, though, do defend the earlier minority tradition, and so are willing to see in the words that are then attributed to the woman an 'awakened spiritual consciousness ... that Joseph ... was true in every sense', and so awareness in her at the last of 'the true meaning of spiritual love'.[189]

Certainly, it was that alternative early interpretation which led to some importance being attached to the woman being given a name. So, though within Islam Potiphar is identified only by his court title Aziz, in subsequent Islamic tradition his wife is normally called Zulaikha. That developing tradition also attempted to lessen the culpability of her lust, not only through stressing Joseph's beauty but also the fact that as an Egyptian court official Aziz would have been a eunuch.[190] So though in some Islamic versions

[185] S. A. A. Mawdudi, *Towards Understanding the Qur'an* (Leicester: Islamic Foundation, 1993), IV, 143–215, esp. 163–4, 168.

[186] Ibid., 144–5, 209.

[187] He claims the biblical account implies Joseph's guilt: 165–6. For an example of an inconsistency correctly detected: 158–9.

[188] Qur'an 12. 52–3; Mawdudi, 182–3; cf. 160.

[189] A. Y. Ali, *Holy Quran*, 570, 571. Mawdudi concedes Muslim scholars of the past have supported this interpretation: e.g. Ibn Taymiyyah (d. 1328).

[190] The Hebrew *saris* in Gen. 39: 1, though often translated simply as 'court official', is usually taken to mean a 'eunuch'. So, the potential for stressing extenuating circumstances was already present in the earliest form of the story.

the woman is indeed spoken of in derogatory terms, that is by no means the dominant presentation over time, and indeed, as we have already noted, in the Qur'an Joseph himself is presented as only successfully resisting because of divine assistance: 'and (with passion) did she desire him, and he would have desired her, but that he saw the evidence of his Lord.'[191] Again, as with the Jewish tradition the nature of both temptation and relationship are explored well beyond the scope of the purely sexual. This is particularly true of Sufi poetry and mysticism, such as the great fifteenth-century Persian poem *Yusuf and Zukaikha* by Jami; in it, Zulaikha's pursuit of Joseph is taken as an allegory of the soul's pursuit of heavenly love with many temptations on the way before success is achieved at the last, with their hearts united in love of God. That poem was written when the poet was in his seventies, as indeed apparently was its great predecessor of the same name, written by Firdawsi about 1010. The profound effect of developments of the incident within Islamic culture is well illustrated by the fact that, despite the Muslim ban on religious representational art, Joseph was to acquire more representations than any other figure from the Qur'an.[192]

One of the most remarkable additions in the Qur'an version is the way in which Zulaikha seeks to defend her reputation after the incident with the shirt. She invites all the ladies of the court to a banquet and when they are busy with their knives (cutting a citrus or some other fruit), Joseph is summoned. So overwhelmed are they by his beauty that they cut their hands (Sura 12: 31). Before we smile too patronizingly it is as well to recall that related notions also find a place in Jewish and Christian exegesis. Though in most modern translations Jacob's blessing of Joseph is taken to mean that 'Joseph is a fruitful bough by a spring: his branches run over a wall' (Gen. 49: 22 RSV), the Hebrew word *banot* (here translated 'branches') literally means 'daughters' or 'girls', and so this led to

---

[191] *Holy Qur'an*, Sura 12. 24 (558). Though usually interpreted as a reference to God, it is sometimes taken to mean Jacob, which would bring the account nearer to that in *Jubilees*.

[192] Not of course directly in mosques or sacred texts, but most commonly through illustrations of such poems as are mentioned in the text. For an example, with the other women looking on from above, Plate X in T. W. Arnold, *The Old and New Testament in Muslim Religious Art* (London: British Academy, 1932); cf. also 25–7, 46.

Jerome's version in the Vulgate: 'A growing son, Joseph, a growing son and handsome in appearance; the girls ran about upon the
wall', which he justified in terms of them being overwhelmed and
excited by his beauty.[193] James Kugel takes us on a trail as fascinating as any detective novel to discover the antecedents of the
story in careful Jewish questioning and exegesis of the biblical text.
This is not the place to pursue the matter in detail. One illustration of the method will suffice. After Joseph flees from Potiphar's
wife, she is portrayed as calling to the members of the household
and saying to them: 'See, he has brought among us a Hebrew to
insult us.' Yet three verses earlier we had been told that the reason
for the incident was that everyone has gone away. It was argued,
therefore, that allusion was being made to a separate incident, one
in which not only are other women present but also Joseph
himself.[194] Thereby not only was an additional dramatic incident
invented, but also, more importantly, the possibility of greater
sympathy for Zulaikha's plight. The extraordinary power of physical beauty for good or ill was highlighted, especially in those later
versions where Zulaikha and Joseph are eventually reconciled.[195]
Here readers should recall the previous chapter, and the way in
which Helen was also portrayed in a new light in later versions of
her myth, as fresh insights were sought into the relative blame
attaching to situations of sexual temptation.[196] Parallel too is the

---

[193] Vulgate of Gen 49: 42 (my trans.). Cf. Jerome, *Hebrew Questions on Genesis*
49: 22–6.

[194] Gen. 39.11–14; J. L. Kugel, *In Potiphar's House* (Cambridge,
Massachussetts: Harvard University Press, 2nd edn., 1994), 28–65, esp. 40–51.
The use of 'See' was taken to imply Joseph's actual presence.

[195] The poetic texts of Rumi and Jami would be cases in point. The starting
point for such reflection may be the Hebrew Bible itself, since Joseph's beauty is
described in exactly the same terms as that of Rachel, which led to Jacob's love
for her: Gen. 39: 6; 29: 17–18. In *The Thousand and One Nights* we find women
described 'as beautiful as Jusuf in form'.

[196] In response to attempts by Stowasser, Bouhdiba and others to note the more
positive evaluation of women implied in some versions of the story, others have
declared that in them all 'Zulaykha is crafted by heterosexual male desire and imagination,' so that 'even in Jami's version, the most generous one in its construction
of Zulaykha, she loses agency in the end': G. K. Merguerian and A. Najmabadi,
'Zulaykha and Yusuf: whose "best story"?', *International Journal of Middle Eastern
Studies* 29 (1997), 485–508, esp. 500, 501. But such comments strike me as unfair,
especially as it is premised on the assumption that any presentation of woman as an
object of male desire is necessarily less than fully respectful of women.

way in which in the Ganymede myth sexual desire becomes a metaphor for spiritual transformation. For, if reflective exegesis was one spur to development, another was the invention of a wholly new story, such as we find in the late first-century AD Jewish work *Joseph and Aseneth*. Scripture tells of the marriage of Joseph to an Egyptian of that name, and nothing more, whereas in this story we learn how the virgin Aseneth is likewise tempted by Joseph's beauty, but this time Joseph (who is also declared a virgin) becomes the instrument of her moral growth, with the story culminating in her intercession on behalf of those who have done her wrong. Commentators have observed how she is the real hero of the tale, functioning not only as the model of the perfect proselyte conversion but 'like a walled mother-city' for all who seek forgiveness.[197] The work was to enter the Bible of the Armenian Church in due course, and thanks to Vincent of Beauvais it became popular in the West from the thirteenth century onwards.[198] So Christianity was not entirely unaffected by such developments.

Assessment

It seems to me unfair to describe such inventions as entirely arbitrary; rather, they arose precisely because of detailed meditation and reflection upon the text. If so, it cannot be improper to raise the question whether revelation was not being mediated afresh through such contemplation; that the life of the text lay not solely in the past, but also in its current reshaping in the community's life. To suggest this with respect to the incident of the knives which gives the initial impression of being no more than an amusing invention may seem quite absurd, but, as I have tried to indicate, in fact it is part of a process of the deepening of the community's consciousness on the whole question of temptation. In the biblical narrative, temptation is not really the point; no

---

[197] Gen. 41: 45 (there pointed as Asenath); *Joseph and Aseneth* 16.16; for Aseneth as central focus, R. D. Chesnutt, *From Death to Life: Conversion in Joseph and Aseneth* (Sheffield: Sheffield Academic Press, 1995), esp. 268–9; for her visionary, non-sexist role, E. McE. Humphrey, *The Ladies and the Cities* (Sheffield: Sheffield Academic Press, 1995), 13–55, 150–76, esp. 168 ff.

[198] Vincent of Beauvais, *Speculum historiale* I. 118–24. The influence, though, is literary rather than visual.

description is offered of the wife, and the function of the tale is really as part of the larger narrative, to explain why Joseph ends up in prison.[199] By *Jubilees* temptation has become the focus, but unfortunately in a rather priggish, self-righteous kind of way. By constantly recalling the commandment against adultery, Joseph has no difficulty in resisting Potiphar's wife not merely 'day after day' as in the biblical version but for a whole year (Gen. 39: 10; *Jub.* 39: 5–8). That power of resistance no doubt helps explain why by the beginning of the Christian era Joseph had become a figure of wisdom,[200] but along with such exaltation of Joseph's powers of resistance goes a rival, more subtle and more religiously engaging account.

We have already noted some signs of sympathy with the temptress as herself subject to temptation. We also find moves towards greater realism in the presentation of Joseph's side of the temptation. His too becomes a real battle with an evil desire, and by the time of the Babylonian Talmud his example lies not in being a paragon of virtue beyond temptation but as one who narrowly succeeds in avoiding a fall, or even, very occasionally, actually falls.[201] Careful, detailed consideration is likewise given to what might achieve successful resistance. Though the answers are on the surface quite varied, what they all have in common is the importance of remembrance, whether it be of God's omnipresence, of specific injunctions or habits of the past or the vision of the hurt countenance of someone who has taught one a better way. Serious engagement with the complexities of the ordinary human experience of temptation and possible means towards their resolution were now at the heart of the religious understanding, instead of at its periphery, and with that we can see a significant

---

[199] It has even been suggested that demonstration of his loyalty to his master is the real point in narrating the incident; so Westermann, *Joseph* 25–7. Against is the contrast from the previous chapter with Judah's yielding to Tamar: Gen. 38.

[200] With Joseph, and not Benjamin, described as the son of Jacob's old age in Gen. 37.3, the puzzle was resolved by 'old age' being taken to mean 'wisdom'; hence 'son of wisdom' in, e. g. *Targum Onkelos*. Von Rad took the view that the Genesis text was itself already intending to offer Joseph as a model of wisdom; for a critique of this view, S. Weeks, *Early Israelite Wisdom* (Oxford: Clarendon Press, 1994), ch. 6.

[201] As in *Aggadot ha-Talmud*: 'the two of them went naked into bed'; quoted in Kugel, 120 n. 4.

advance on what appear to be the primary concerns of the biblical
text. What a developing tradition had in effect allowed was a lively
debate about the nature of virtue, what contributes to its growth
and in particular its relation to temptation. Judaism and Islam by
having in effect an open text gave permission for that lively debate,
and the result is that Joseph remains a major figure for both religions. By contrast, for most contemporary Christians Joseph has
sunk into relative oblivion. Coverdale's one-line transformation
may be taken as symptomatic of how little was achieved.[202] Of
course, it by no means follows that all that emerged in Judaism or
Islam was good. Much of it was little more than folklore, but even
here caution is necessary. The power attributed to Joseph to overcome the effect of 'the evil eye' had been acquired, it would be
argued, by his own victory over envy and the roving eye.[203]

Though the Epistle to the Hebrews declares that Christ was
tempted as we are, the Christology of certainty and infused
knowledge that has dominated the history of Christianity
prevented any comparable insights being mediated through the
story of Christ's temptations. Nor could the story of Joseph offer
any help, once he was aligned as antetype to Christ. Instead, he
quickly became a self-congratulatory model for bishops.[204] The
Christian tradition had thus to look elsewhere. In effect, it rewrote
another biblical narrative, the life of Mary Magdalene, to tell its
own story of sin and growth towards holiness,[205] but that does not
mean that it should ignore the trajectory which we have examined
here. Consideration of the kind of life-style God wanted from
humanity was in effect mediated through such figures, and the
three religions can learn much from each other as they discover

---

[202] In the Book of Common Prayer's version of Ps. 105: 18, where his
mistranslation, 'the iron entered into his soul' invites a deeper level of reflection
than merely having an iron collar put round his neck, as modern translations
propose.

[203] S. Goldman, *The Wiles of Women/The Wiles of Men* (New York: SUNY,
1995), 132–43 esp. 142.

[204] Ambrose sometimes represents this tendency, but for an artistic example,
note the scenes from the life of Joseph on the throne of Archbishop Maximianus
(d. 554) at Ravenna: M. Schapiro, *Late Antique, Early Christian and Medieval Art*
(London: Chatto and Windus, 1980), 34–48.

[205] Discussed in chapter I of my *Discipleship and Imagination*.

what issues were seen as significant and requiring further imaginative exploration.

To some Christians, though, all such efforts will seem unnecessary, precisely because they assume that such reflection must be mediated through the life of Christ or not at all. Why matters are not that simple will be our subject for study in the final part of this volume.

PART THREE
Christ: Change and imagination

IN the second Part of this book I argued that, appearances
notwithstanding, the biblical stories of the patriarchs can be seen
to exhibit many of the features of the formative narratives of the
classical world. The changing content of the latter was used as a
handle for continuing reflection on religious and moral issues, but
the same was no less true for the lives of Abraham, Isaac and
Joseph. Despite the appearance of a fixed text, it was a developing
tradition that had both generated the canonical version and also
insisted that reflection should continue. So far from being embarrassed by this 'moving text', I argued that it contains trajectories of
which we can approve, as well as even, on occasion, appropriate
critiques of the dominant biblical way of viewing some particular
matter. I also suggested that seeing the three major monotheistic
religions developing within their own traditions allowed for a
healthier respect both for the process and for the current position
within each, while even the classical world need not be seen as
entirely set apart from God's revelatory action in the world. Once
function within their respective developing frames has been fully
explored, surface conflict is sometimes discovered after all not to
run deep. It is time now, though, for us to focus on Christianity
alone. Yet even here, as we shall see, questions regarding other
faiths cannot be entirely disregarded. Chapter 7, for instance, will
note the way in which medieval Christianity projected on to Islam
its own anxieties about idolatry.

For many, perhaps the majority, of Christians, so long as the
analysis I am proposing is confined to the Old Testament, there
might be thought to be little at stake. In the final Part of this book,
therefore, it is appropriate that we turn to the very heart of
Christianity, to the story of Jesus and what significance the Church
has drawn from it. Obviously, this is a vast subject. So only a small
range of issues can be considered here. In Chapter 6, 'Divine

Accommodation', I shall argue that the incarnation itself exhibits the same sort of pattern as we have already noted elsewhere: divine revelation accommodating itself to particular social contexts and further developments occurring in consequence. Jesus, to make the maximum impact on his own day and people, had in certain key respects to be, as it were, a child of his own time. Their issues had to be his. Nonetheless, Jesus can be viewed as opening up trajectories, in relation to which the way in which his own person and teaching were eventually understood can be seen as an entirely natural, if not inevitable, development.

Chapter 7, 'Art as Revelation', will then carry that argument one stage further, by observing two ways in which later Christianity was still further modified by the doctrine of Christ's divinity as it had gradually emerged through the New Testament and beyond. More abstract doctrinal themes might have been considered, but integral to the argument of this book has been the contention that the imaginative element in Christian belief has been wrongly demoted. A brief Conclusion will then attempt to drawn the threads together, by asking where we stand today. I shall use some examples from modern film and art to indicate what I would regard as the most acute challenges now facing Christology. Such reflections will also help me to identify where the deficiencies in my present argument lie, and thus why I think a further book necessary on the theme of tradition and imagination, this time focused on the issue of discipleship.

6

Divine accommodation

FOR most of Christian history the notion of a developing tradition underlying the New Testament witness to Christ has gone unnoticed. It is only with the growth of biblical criticism that such a recognition has been forced upon us. The result is that talk of a divorce between 'the Jesus of history' and 'the Christ of faith' has become commonplace. Some have welcomed the new pristine Jesus as normative, especially when portrayed as stripped of all dogma; others have insisted that all that matters is the Christ of faith; yet others have attempted to bridge the gap. My own inclination is to flow with that last stream, not least because development is the pattern of revelation which we have detected elsewhere. That does not entail that the same pattern must apply in the case of Christ also (God could have chosen to act differently in this case), but, if this indeed proves so, the justification for seeing all revelation as of this kind will have been immeasurably strengthened. Even at the point of his greatest involvement with humanity, God submitted perception of himself to the vagaries of a developing tradition; so why not elsewhere also?

But can we discover anything about the historical Jesus? Pessimistic comments about the failure of previous quests abound, and are now often used to argue for focusing predominantly or even exclusively on the text as we now have it.[1] But there are two objections to such an inference. The first is that Christianity is at its heart an historical religion, and so it matters hugely what sort of incarnation it was. How we conceive the human Jesus to have lived will also fundamentally affect how in general we understand God's relation with the world and ourselves. Secondly, as Chapter I argued, the danger in relying exclusively on more literary

---

[1] e.g. R. Morgan with J. Barton, *Biblical Interpretation* (Oxford: Oxford University Press, 1988), 121–4.

approaches is that the Church will fail to acknowledge development within Scripture, and so the necessity for continuing development beyond. Of course the Enlightenment hope of ever providing a single answer to the quest must now be seen as unrealizable. Scholarly reflection is caught in the particularities of the moment no less than was Jesus himself. But it is possible to reflect on the current consensus and assess its implications. Some may find my analysis too 'liberal', with too 'fallible' a Jesus. The tide may even already be turning in quite another direction.[2] The advantage of what follows, though, is that it faces squarely the principal difficulties involved in conceding a very high degree of accommodation to the human condition in the incarnation.

In trying to comprehend why such an accommodation might be appropriate, there appear to be at least two essential elements which need be considered, and each of these we shall examine in some detail in this chapter. The first is whether there could be a real entering into the human condition without some abandonment of the usual accompaniments of divinity, and what implications this might have for how Jesus came eventually to be perceived as divine. The second type of issue concerns his teaching. It is tempting to try and make Jesus' words always immediately bear universal significance, but if he were to achieve maximum relevance to the people of his own immediate time and place, might this not mean that what he said had to be reinterpreted within a growing tradition, as fresh applications were sought for new situations, and perhaps even to a considerable degree? In considering such questions one of my principal concerns will be to highlight the key role played by the imagination in such developments. Though the relation between truth and imagination is a complex one, they certainly must not be prised apart.

---

[2] By any standard N. T. Wright's projected five-volumed *Christian Origins and the Question of God* (London: SPCK, 1992 ff.) is an impressive achievement. Its conclusions, though, are so distinctive that it would have diverted me too far from my main task to consider its arguments here. If widely accepted, they would push New Testament scholarship in a more conservative direction than that pursued in my text. There are of course others pushing in the opposite direction, as in the agnosticism of the Jesus Seminar: R. W. Funk and R. W. Hoover (eds.), *The Five Gospels* (New York: Macmillan, 1993).

From human being to divine Son

The growth of incarnational doctrine within Scripture is a topic
which I tackled at length, more than a decade ago, as part of a
book on the Trinity.[3] Inevitably the passage of time has brought
with it the desire to have expressed some things differently. Talk
of the 'separate identity' of the three persons of the Trinity misled
some critics to suppose that my intention was to advocate a
stronger degree of distinctness between the three persons than was
in fact the case, and this needed correcting in subsequent writing.[4]
Similarly, use of the term 'intervention' to describe God's action
in the world was unfortunate, since it could so easily be taken to
imply that God was absent except where he was intervening. That
too I attempted to correct in later articles by substituting the term
'interaction' and insisting that most divine action in the world had
no need to be brought under the rubric of 'miracle'.[5] It is also the
case that I was too dogmatic in advocating only one possible line
of development. New Testament studies are always to some
degree in a state of flux, and, though inevitably I currently think
some scenarios more plausible than others, there are in fact quite
a number, any of which would be consistent with the general
pattern of argument which I seek to elaborate below.

Even with all these qualifications, however, I still wish to stand
by the general thrust of that earlier book. Where the difference
comes in what follows is rather where precisely the spotlight falls.
Here I shall ignore entirely the conceptual question of how Jesus

[3] D. Brown, *The Divine Trinity* (London: Duckworth, 1985; La Salle,
Illinois: Open Court, 1995), esp. 101–58 and 219–71.

[4] D. Brown, 'Wittgenstein against the Wittgensteinians', *Modern Theology* 2
(1986), 257–76; idem., 'Trinitarian Personhood and Individuality', in R. J.
Feenstra and C. Plantinga (eds.), *Trinity, Incarnation and Atonement* (Indiana:
University of Notre Dame Press, 1989), 48–78. Some theologians are reluctant to
acknowledge the capacity of other minds to develop and change: cf. the criticisms
of me by J. P. Mackey, 'Are there Christian alternatives to trinitarian thinking?',
in J. M. Byrne, *The Christian Understanding of God Today* (Dublin: Columba,
1993), 66–75, esp. 70.

[5] D. Brown, 'God and Symbolic Action', in B. Hebblethwaite and E.
Henderson (eds.), *Divine Action* (Edinburgh: T. & T. Clark, 1990), 103–22, esp.
104–10; idem., 'Butler and Deism', in C. Cunliffe (ed.), *Joseph Butler's Moral and
Religious Thought* (Oxford: Clarendon Press, 1992), 7–28, esp. 24–6.

could be at once divine and human. The only element of my previous discussion of which the reader should be made aware is my earlier insistence (which would be widely shared) that it is impossible for someone who is truly human sanely to believe himself divine. This is because being human implies a range of predicates which are necessarily not true of the divine, as for example being tempted, having limited knowledge, thinking sequentially, and so forth. Accordingly, however it was achieved, if God wanted to identify completely with the human condition, he had to accept such characteristic human limitations, at least in so far as they came to expression in the humanity of Jesus. So, rather than Jesus making any explicit claim to divinity, what Jesus said and did could have at most implied as much.

To my mind it is one of the great glories of the incarnation that God chose to identify so completely with the human condition that he was willing even to incorporate into himself all the limitations inherent in our mortal nature. Such identification did not fall short of total. But it is one thing to assert this claim, quite another to make it a reasonable belief. In part that is a matter of conceptual considerations, of how the relation between, and union of, divine and human in one person might best be presented.[6] In that earlier work I suggested that it might bear some remote analogy to the relation between our own unconscious or subconscious selves and full consciousness: as Freud and Jung have made us all, at times too painfully, aware, there is much going on beneath our explicit consciousness that nonetheless fundamentally influences and shapes our identity. Jesus' deepest consciousness might thus have been suffused with the divine in a way that ours is not. Whether a good analogy or not, of necessity our focus here must be rather different. It is a matter of asking ourselves whether there was anything in the complex of events associated with Jesus which might legitimate our ascribing divinity to him. What I will suggest is that what God in effect did in the incarnation was commit himself to a developing tradition. Not only did he expose himself to the vagaries of being human, he also submitted himself to the

---

[6] For my discussion of the conceptual problems, *The Divine Trinity*, esp. 245–71; for a more detailed discussion where many of the conclusions are of a similar kind, T. V. Morris, *The Logic of God Incarnate* (Ithaca: Cornell University Press, 1986).

uncertainties of human comprehension in abandoning himself to humanity's most characteristic way of thinking:[7] gradual perception through creative retelling of the story of his identification with us in Jesus. Even the incarnation could only be made known as part of a developing tradition.

It would be tedious to repeat the arguments and examples of a decade earlier. Though historical grounds for believing in the divinity of Christ are still given, my primary intention now lies elsewhere. What I want to concentrate upon is the various ways in which the imagination could help or hinder Christians then and now in appropriation of the significance of Christ. I proceed by two stages. My discussion opens by examining why appeal to the life of Jesus is inadequate of itself to justify belief in his divinity. This is used as a platform to initiate consideration of why it is that truths that go beyond the merely historical are required to play such a key role in the Gospel narratives. Then, secondly, having given my own grounds for belief in Christ's divinity, I use one key element to illustrate how the logic of imaginative story-telling has the capacity fundamentally to distort, as well as illumine, our understanding, unless we are always careful to identify what type of question it is that we wish to address to the narrative. Imagination is thus by no means always a sure guide to truth. Nonetheless, without it the Gospel narratives would be enormously impoverished.

Imagination and the historical Jesus

We begin then by considering why appeal to the words and actions of Jesus is inadequate to the task. Despite occasional arguments to the contrary,[8] there is almost nothing in earlier Jewish tradition to suggest that the contemporaries of Jesus might have found it easy to make any sense of a claim on his part to be God.

[7] Most characteristic, if not today, at least so far as the great sweep of human history is concerned.

[8] e.g. M. Barker, The Great Angel: A Study of Israel's Second God (London: SPCK, 1992), where El and Yahweh are sharply distinguished and Memra and Melchizedek viewed as later equivalents for this second god. More plausible anticipations, such as Wisdom treated as an hypostasis, are considered below. More recently, she has applied similar arguments to Jesus himself: M. Barker, The Risen Lord (Edinburgh: T & T Clark, 1996).

Nor can classical heroes or deified emperors count since the limitations in power or moral perfection that these notions imply find no analogy in the Jewish treatment of God. Yet attempts continue to be made to justify belief in Christ's divinity on the basis of his life alone. This seems to me in large part motivated by a misplaced deference to Scripture: misplaced, because, as I hope to demonstrate, it wrongly confines truth to the narrowly historical.

As no one person dominates the field, to some degree it is arbitrary whom we take as representative of this type of approach.[9] Among the most impressive of recent examples is the work of the American scholar Ben Witherington. *The Christology of Jesus* well indicates by its title his central focus on what Jesus himself thought about his own role. Relying exclusively on evidence from the Synoptic Gospels and taking successively the relationships, deeds and words of Jesus, he argues that even from these Gospels alone we may conclude that Jesus saw himself as Wisdom incarnate, possibly pre-existent but certainly destined to 'assume a position of divine power and authority as God's right-hand man'.[10] Though each passage that is analysed is handled with care, two major reservations about his approach as a whole cannot be avoided. As both are popular misconceptions and by no means rare among professional scholars, both failings are worth noting. The first is the wide use of what might be described as persuasive definition. Though a footnote expresses a preference in terminology for 'transcendent' over 'divine consciousness',[11] it is the word 'divine' which more commonly occurs. Thus frequent mention is made of Jesus' 'divine authority', 'divine mission', 'divine role', and so forth,[12] but no attempt made to analyse whether what is asserted only God himself could do. So, for instance, 'a divine mission of reclaiming

[9] The second volume of N. T. Wright's major project might have been another possibility. But it would seem unfair to treat the intricacies of its arguments with the brevity required here. Suffice it to note, though, that, despite his subscription to the third quest for the historical Jesus, I find his description of Jesus' conception of his role hard to draw as a natural reading from the synoptic narratives. Jesus, he suggests, 'saw himself in the role of the strange quasi-messianic figure who would share the very throne of Israel's one God': *Jesus and the Victory of God* (Minneapolis: Fortress Press, 1996), 648.

[10] B. Witherington, *The Christology of Jesus* (Minneapolis: Fortress Press, 1990), esp. 51, 227, 233, 261.   [11] Ibid., 25 n. 95.

[12] Ibid., e.g. 136, 143. The quotation is from 136.

Israel for God' surely means no more than something initiated and supported by God, not something only a divine being could perform. Secondly, there is a tendency to suppose that it is sufficient to defend the authenticity of particular verses that seem to imply a high Christology, without any recourse to the wider conceptual issue of why, if such a reading is correct, it has failed to make much impact elsewhere. So, for example, the words of the Father at Jesus' baptism that speak of Jesus' unique sonship are defended as coming from Jesus' own experience (Mark 1: 11),[13] but, if so, why did they have so little impact on what Jesus had to say in public? The only obvious exception is the so-called Johannine thunderbolt (Matt. 11: 27), but that very description indicates its exceptional character, and thus what has made even some conservative scholars try to identify a primitive form of the saying that might more naturally accord with the more reticent language Jesus uses of himself elsewhere.[14]

Non-biblical scholars often misinterpret such moves. Though no doubt sometimes motivated by lack of belief in incarnational doctrine, that is seldom the key issue. Jesus could easily have had the visions recorded of him in respect of his baptism and temptation, and indeed given the assumptions of the time this is in theory not at all unlikely. Even so, caution is necessary. Not only does the heavenly voice at his baptism fail to permeate Jesus' teaching, the evangelists present its message as meant for our benefit rather than that of Jesus. So in Mark's narrative no one, not even Jesus, is allowed subsequently to show any awareness of the earlier incident,[15] while in Matthew that the focus is on the reader is made even more explicit by his alteration of the heavenly words from 'you are ...' to 'this is my beloved son'.[16] John goes one stage

---

[13] Witherington, *Christology*, 148–55.

[14] It has been suggested that the original form of the saying may only have intended to indicate that Jesus' relationship with God is as intimate as that of any father and son: 'just as only a father (really) knows his son, so only a son (really) knows his father'. So J. Jeremias, *New Testament Theology: The Proclamation of Jesus* (London: SCM Press, 1971), 59.

[15] The stress on the reader is found in E. Haenchen, *Der Weg Jesu* (Berlin: Topelmann, 1966), 61.

[16] Contrast Mark 1: 11 and Matt. 3: 17. That Matthew intended John the Baptist as the addressee of the latter seems unlikely since the narrative fails to give him any appropriate response.

Christ: change and imagination

further, with the baptismal vision now an experience of John
rather than Jesus (John 1: 32–34), while the flight into the wilder-
ness receives no mention. Is it not likely therefore that the two
incidents are there for a different reason than purely factual record?
In all probability the baptism of Jesus by John did mark the inauguration of his ministry, and from that point on he had a firm
conviction of the very special role to which he was called, in part
perhaps based upon some visionary or mystical experience he had
at the time.[17] But it is a large leap to go on from this to assert that
it took precisely the character that the Gospels describe, where the
unique sonship characteristic of the Church's later proclamation
has become the primary focus. John's Gospel well illustrates the
growth of such an adaptation, where not only is Jesus declared Son
but also Lamb of God (John 1: 35–36), a phrase that is unintelligible in its immediate context and only becomes so in the light of
his later death. Equally, though Jesus may well have had visions of
the devil, the kind of temptations to which he becomes subject
speak of a range of possibilities that only make sense in the light of
whom Christians now know him to be. For could the opportunity of ruling the entire world (Matt. 4: 8–9) really have been seen
as a realistic option for the human consciousness of someone with
as yet only a mere handful of unarmed and powerless followers?

It is thus only if we scale down considerably the character of
both incidents that they begin to have some semblance of historical plausibility. Yet, that said, we ought not to jump from this
admission to the conclusion that the stories are therefore untrue.
By that I do not intend to allude to the core of historical truth
which I have already identified, nor the further elements of
historicity of which biblical scholars commonly take cognisance,
such as the presence in the baptismal narrative of an early incipient Christology that identified that point as Jesus' adoption
through the Spirit. Rather, what I have in mind is our need to
come to terms with a notion of truth much larger than the purely
historical. Not only can truth be more powerful in its effect when
mediated through the imagination, imaginative rewriting can
convey aspects of truth which might otherwise be neglected in a

---

[17] This is the view adopted by C. Rowland, *The Open Heaven* (New York:
Crossroads, 1982), 358–60; cf. J. Marcus, 'Jesus' baptismal vision', *New Testament
Studies* 41 (1995), 512–21.

purely factual account. This is especially so in respect of questions of significance or meaning. Jesus in the vividness of his parables and in the dramatic character of his actions initiated a trend which continued as later tradition rewrote his life to bring out his full significance, as the community of faith now saw it. The parables invite us to imagine ourselves one of the participants in the drama (for example, the prodigal son). His actions functioned no differently. His miracles, for instance, as we shall see, might appropriately be described as enacted parables. It was therefore little wonder that the later Church continued that pattern of imaginative reflection.

Whether it drew the right conclusions we shall consider in due course, but that the imagination exercises considerable power is well illustrated by observing that John also alludes to Jesus being subject to temptations similar to those mentioned by the synoptics,[18] but precisely because they are recorded in the form of bare fact they pass most readers by and so we fail to accord them any significance. By contrast, the accounts in Matthew and Luke immediately engage our imagination, and so the reader is forced immediately to face the contrasts in the very different character of the kingdom that Christ will bring. Facts can, of course, of themselves sometimes attract our interest, but, as I tried to stress in Chapter 1, whether they do so or not is often immeasurably aided by the way in which they are presented to us. They need that extra spur in order to be appropriated. It is through appealing to our imagination that they are enabled to become 'truths for us', as it were. Though the conventions of our own day are hugely different, modern writers no less than ancient must resort to rhetoric and literary 'licence' if they are to win over their readers to their own particular perspective. Not that the imagination's additions always make for success; the riot of imagery in the book of Revelation is one major reason why for so many Christians today it remains a closed book.

Equally, however, we need to be on our guard against supposing that the historical fact and imaginative truth can always easily

---

[18] John parallels the three temptations by putting them into the mouths first of 'the people', then members of Jesus' audience and finally his own brothers: 6: 15; 6: 30–2; 7: 1–5. So R. E. Brown, *The Gospel According To John* (Garden City, NY: Anchor Bible, Doubleday, 1966), 308.

be separated out and distinguished. So, for instance, the status of Jesus' miracles is often presented in terms of an either-or: either historical or symbolic. But of course there is no reason why they should not have been both, and not only in John where their 'sign' character is made explicit. The fact that the same word is commonly used for 'heal' and 'save' would have quickly alerted the original Greek readers to the fact that something rather more was in play,[19] as would the juxtaposition of incidents illustrative of physical and spiritual blindness and so forth (e.g. Mark 8: 13–26).[20] Nowadays, Jesus' miracles are most commonly read as demonstrations of his divine power, but this ignores the frequency of belief in similar miracles not only in the subsequent Christian tradition but also in the ancient world, particularly at the shrines of the pagan healing god, Asclepius.[21] This is not to say that Jesus' miracles would not have been regarded as out of the ordinary, but it is to claim that in the ancient world both witnesses and readers would have been more interested in what was being said by them rather than by the mere fact of their occurrence. This is in no sense an attempt to undermine their historicity. Indeed, in terms of attestation the most securely rooted is also one of the most spectacular: the feeding of the five thousand.[22] But it is to suggest that we distort their role in the narrative if we place our primary emphasis on mere historicity. No doubt divine power is part of what is at stake, but their main narrative function is symbolic, to enable readers imaginatively to grasp that a new order of reality in which all are cared for is dawning. Nor have we any reason to

[19] The Authorised Version nicely captures the wider sense of the verb when it translates Matt. 9: 21 as: 'if I may but touch his garment, I shall be whole.' In Luke 7: 50 *sozomai* is used of purely spiritual healing. For a development of this point, D. Brown, *The Word To Set You Free* (London: SPCK, 1995), 123–7.

[20] So M. D. Hooker, *Gospel according to St Mark* (London: A & C Black, 1991), 197, 252.

[21] E. J. Edelstein and L. Edelstein, *Asclepius: A Collection and Interpretation of the Testimonies* (2 vols. Baltimore: Johns Hopkins, 1945); Cf. also R. L. Fox, *Pagans and Christians* (Harmondsworth: Penguin, 1986), 102–67, esp. 117–18.

[22] It is the only one attested by all four gospels, and indeed old enough to have developed two independent forms (Mark 6: 32–45; 8: 1–10) unless one or other was invented by Mark for symbolic purposes, either to indicate the relevance of the miracle for both Jew and Gentile or else to underline the continuing incomprehension of the disciples. M. D. Hooker takes the latter view: *St Mark*, 187–9.

think that Jesus himself viewed them any differently. That is to make a difficult, though not necessarily illegitimate, inference to what lies behind the narratives we possess, for if Jesus thought of himself as inaugurating a new order then healing miracles might well have been seen as symbolic for him also as part of this wider dimension.

Such an intricate intertwining of historical and imaginative truth obviously provides no automatic guarantee of the presence of the former in each specific case. We have already noted how the baptismal and temptation narratives are likely to contain an element of retrospective exaggeration. The same might also hold with some miracles. Take the case of the turning of water into wine at Cana (John 2: 1–11; esp. vv. 1, 4 and 6). Despite the attempt of some scholars to defend the appropriateness of 'Dionysiac' imagery in a Palestinian context,[23] the incongruity of the miracle at a literal level remains. Not only is the deed trivial in comparison with Jesus' other responses to human need, there is also an absurd over-provision, amounting to some 120 gallons in modern terms! On the other hand, symbolically there are numerous hints towards some other deeper meaning; to name but a few, 'on the third day', 'my hour … not yet come', the use of stone water jars normally used in Jewish rites of purification, and the indication that there were six of them, one short of the customary complete or perfect number, all suggesting that a new order is here. Nothing compels the abandonment of a literal reading, but what can with confidence be asserted is that anyone who makes that meaning primary would have lost the main point of the story, in the marvellous over-abundance of the good and rich life that Christ has come to bring.

Commentators who advocate a purely symbolic interpretation sometimes insist that John must have inherited the story as historical, as though the only way of defending John's truthfulness is by insisting that he himself was not responsible for the invention.[24] But is this not to apply the conventions of the twentieth century

[23] M. Hengel, 'The Dionysiac Messiah', in idem., *Studies in Early Christology* (Edinburgh: T & T Clark, 1995), 293–331; for a different view, C. K. Barrett, *Gospel According To St John* (London; SPCK, 2nd edn., 1978), 188–9.
[24] e.g. S. Smalley, *John—Evangelist and Interpreter* (Exeter: Paternoster, 1983 edn.), 174–8.

to the first? If we accept the integrity of the author, presumably on such a scenario John presupposed that Cana was precisely the sort of thing Christ could literally have done and in some sense metaphorically still does: bringing out of mere water the wine of new life. For him it was thus imaginatively true, as well as being also a useful narrative device right at the beginning of his Gospel, for drawing out the contrast with the form of Judaism (as represented by the purificatory jars) with which he saw the Gospel taking issue.[25] To concede the existence of such a type of inference and resultant invention does of course leave us uncertain of how widely the practice might have extended, but that is not as acute a problem as it might initially appear, since for the inference to be drawn in the first place there must have been some miracles assumed to be factually true.

Considerations of imaginative significance, however, are likely to have had an impact not only on the way in which particular incidents are told and in the generation of some new stories, but also on the very shape and structure of the narrative as a whole. How extensive these changes can be we have already observed in Chapter 2 when examining the infancy narratives. The beginnings of Christ's life are told in a way that presumes its end throughout. Yet we must not draw from this the conclusion that it is an issue that only affects writing of the distant past. The problems can be observed in both personal and historical narratives of our own day. Something that seems apparently minor at the time may in retrospect come to be regarded as decisive in determining one's future marriage or job or even one's conversion to Christianity. As Sartre observed: 'Who shall decide whether that mystic crisis in my fifteenth year "was" a pure accident of puberty, or, on the contrary, the first sign of a future conversion. I myself, according to whether I shall decide—at twenty years of age, at thirty years, to be converted.'[26] Likewise, on the more public plain, the assassin's bullet at Sarajevo in 1914 was at one point seen as launching 'a war to end all wars', only later to be reinterpreted as but a prelude to a still more extensive world war, while the recent agonies of that city

---

[25] A stronger contrast with Judaism as such might be the intention, but in view of the depth of engagement with Jewish ideas in this gospel it seems safer to suppose that the link with Judaism has not yet quite been severed.

[26] J.-P. Sartre, *Being and Nothingness* (London: Methuen, 1969), 498.

and the break-up of the former Yugoslavia offer the possibility of yet another reassessment. Each will require a very different structure to the historian's narrative, with the relative significance of Serbian nationalism each time assessed quite differently. Admittedly, in the modern world we think it improper for the professional historian also to use imaginative rewriting as an element in such a restructuring of the narrative,[27] but that it can help with understanding even in our own context is well illustrated by the success of the historical novel. So, for instance, Salmon Rushdie's novel *Midnight's Children* is more effective than many a more mundane historical analysis in comprehending the factors that led to the partition of India in 1947. But if fiction even in our day can sometimes achieve the greater success, why not sometimes also the mixture of fact and fiction that characterized so much historical narrative in the ancient world, and in particular the Gospels themselves? It is to the consideration of what such rewriting implied that we next turn.

Competing logics: ontology and imagination

Though some philosophers such as Plato and Kierkegaard have attempted to integrate philosophy and the imagination, it still remains a common assumption that the two modes of thought are necessarily opposed. In the case of the New Testament, it is maintained that the attempt to go beyond its imagery into the ontological categories of the creeds was not only a mistake but stultifying of the life of the gospel. I want to present a rather different picture here: to indicate how strong the pressure was from various New Testament trajectories towards the incarnational content of the creeds,[28] while noting that, so far from the imagination always

---

[27] For an exception to such rules, cf. S. Schama, *Dead Certainties* (London: Granta, 1991), particularly his 'Afterword.' and 'Note on Sources': 319–33. He describes his historical writing as 'a work of the imagination' and admits to creating 'fictitious dialogues … worked up from my own understanding of the sources as to how such a scene might have taken place' (327).

[28] Almost nothing in history is inevitable, and in this case there were of course other groups such as Jewish and Gnostic Christians who were to advocate a different route. Even so, I would contend that the trajectory investigated in the text was the most natural, with Jewish Christians inhibited by conservatism and Gnostic Christians by lack of imaginative constraint.

being liberating, it too can sometimes stultify. To my mind, therefore, rather than playing imagination and ontology off against one
another, they should be seen as generating similar challenges and
similar problems. To a much greater degree than any of the other
evangelists, it is John who is commonly regarded as having thrown
back into the life of Jesus the perception of him which the later
Church came to hold. One way of posing our first question about
the logic of ontology is therefore to ask whether we have any
reason to follow him. For that to be the case, there must be
enough about Jesus' life that makes it natural, if not inevitable, for
the later Church to ascribe divinity to him, and secondly the post-
resurrection ascription must itself be seen to be securely based.
Both requirements on my view can be met.

On the first point it is important to observe that for this to be
so it is not at all necessary that biblical scholars come up with only
one particular way of reading the New Testament evidence.
Witherington, as we saw, focused on Jesus' use of Wisdom
language; for an earlier generation it was the Son of Man;[29] for a
still earlier generation, Son of God.[30] Each of these claims is
contentious. Bultmann, for instance, argued that Jesus expected
vindication from a Son of Man distinct from himself,[31] and on his
side is the fact that, though frequently the phrase is found as a
periphrasis for 'I', nowhere does Jesus unambiguously identify the
exalted Son of Man with himself.[32] Even so, what can be said is
that, however deeply we probe beneath the surface to the original

---

[29] As in C. F. D. Moule, *The Origin of Christology* (Cambridge: Cambridge
University Press, 1977), though, as subsequent, private correspondence made
clear, in *The Divine Trinity* (105–9) I exaggerated the degree to which he wanted
to rely on such a claim.

[30] The most common appeal before the rise of biblical criticism, which
observed that the Old Testament uses the term in a non-metaphysical way, as in
the relation between God and the king: 2 Sam. 7.14 ff. This impression is reinforced by the way in which Luke appears not to think much at stake when he
substitutes for the centurion's confession in Mark that this was the Son of God:
'Certainly this was a righteous man' (AV): Luke 23: 47; cf. Mark 15: 39.

[31] R. Bultmann, *The History of the Synoptic Tradition* (Oxford: Blackwell,
1963), 152. He is followed by G. Bornkamm, *Jesus of Nazareth* (London: Hodder
and Stoughton, 1973 edn.), 175–8.

[32] The three key passages in Mark could all be read otherwise: 8: 38; 13: 26;
14: 62. Similar passages from Q in Matthew also fail to make an explicit identification: 13: 41; 19: 28.

Jesus, what emerges is still a very exalted (though not divine) sense of his mission. A scholar such as E. P. Sanders, who sees his task as purely an historical one, has no hesitation in concluding not only that we can know a great deal about the historical Jesus[33] but also that, even though it may be contested whether any of the various titles are Jesus' own, he still thought of himself as having a unique role as God's instrument in inaugurating a new age. Even the calling of the Twelve indicates as much, with Jesus envisaging them as presiding judges under him (Matt. 19: 28), as does his entry into Jerusalem with its implicit claim to a kingdom of sorts, since Jesus rides on an ass to fulfil a regal prophecy of Zechariah (9: 9: 'Rejoice greatly, O daughter of Zion! ... Lo, your king comes to you ... humble and riding on an ass' RSV). As Sanders remarks: 'Jesus was clearly above the disciples; a person who is above the judges of Israel is very high indeed. ... My own favourite term for his conception of himself is "viceroy". God was king, but Jesus represented him and would represent him in the coming kingdom.'[34]

Nor, it seems to me, is an early commitment to Christ's divinity on the part of his followers any less securely based.[35] Here I must repeat briefly my argument of a decade ago. New Testament scholars have rightly drawn attention to the very large extent to which early Christology was functional rather than ontological: that is, it spoke of Christ functioning in place of God rather than being himself God. So, for instance, Philippians 2: 6–11 may mean something very different from what it has traditionally been taken to mean. Rather than claiming for Christ pre-existent divine status, it asserts that like Adam he reflected the divine image ('the form of God') but unlike Adam he did not overreach himself by

---

[33] 'We know a lot about Jesus'; E. P. Sanders, *The Historical Figure of Jesus* (Harmondsworth: Penguin, 1993), xiv. For a similar positive estimate based on recent archaeological discoveries, J. H. Charlesworth, *Jesus within Judaism* (London: SPCK, 1989).

[34] Sanders, *Historical Figure*, 238–48, esp. 248.

[35] Because of my earlier discussion in *The Divine Trinity* of what is meant by divinity in the context of the incarnation (101–58, 245–71), I have left the notion here relatively undefined, but at the very least it must entail at some stage for Christ the exercise of divine power in his own right, and not merely through delegation.

trying to grasp at equality with God.[36] Yet in response we may note that functional language can entail ontological implications, and such extensive powers are accorded Christ (nothing less than ruler of the universe in God's place in 1 Cor. 15: 24–28) that we may legitimately conclude that he is implicitly acknowledged as divine throughout Scripture, even if it is only with John's Gospel that this is made completely explicit.

This is, unfortunately, a point which is still not widely acknowledged. The most impressive book on Christology of recent years is perhaps Karl-Josef Kuschel's *Born Before all Time?* It is a laudable attempt to integrate systematic reflection and the work of New Testament scholars. Many of his complaints against the failure of systematic theologians to engage sufficiently with the results of biblical research hit their target very effectively.[37] Equally, he shows a commendable care to interpret the christo-logical passages of Scripture in context, which rightly generates the conclusion that not only is the content mostly functional rather than ontological but also that their focus is overwhelmingly towards Christ's future rather than his past. In his view Paul 'still does not represent an incarnational theology' and it is only with the non-Pauline Colossians and John that we get the notion of Christ's pre-existence, though even here the main stress remains on the future: 'What is important is not protology and a sphere of speculation and mythology, but soteriology as a dynamic move-ment of God in favour of liberation on earth.'[38] As an analysis of where the stress in the New Testament lies, there is little with which I would wish to take issue.

However, it by no means follows from this admission that we are required to accept Kuschel's conclusion that the Church

---

[36] J. D. G. Dunn, *Christology in the Making* (London: SCM Press, 1980), 114–21. This book contains numerous other examples, explored at length. In the particular case of Phil. 2, though, 'most scholars' apparently still follow the tradi-tional ontological interpretation; so R. E. Brown, *An Introduction to New Testament Christology* (London: Geoffrey Chapman, 1994), 135.

[37] K.-J. Kuschel, *Born Before All Time?* (London: SCM Press, 1992). Detailed consideration is given to almost all the major systematic theologians of the twen-tieth century, including Harnack, Barth, Bultmann, Pannenberg, Rahner, Jüngel, Motmann, Kasper, Küng, and Schillebeeckx: 35–175; 397–482. Barth is particu-larly criticised for 'simply seeking biblical confirmation after the event' (173).

[38] Ibid., 307, 383.

should therefore abandon pre-existence and the claims that follow from it and return to a more primitive Christology. There are two fundamental flaws in his argument. The first and less important of the two stems from a key underlying motive for his analysis which he reveals in his final section—the desire for some kind of reconciliation with Judaism.[39] He seems to assume that the less the difference, the greater the tolerance, but, it seems to me, religious dialogue is more likely to be fruitful if differences are acknowledged rather than denied, and their role in their respective traditions fully and properly explored. Mutual respect surely comes from understanding, not from the levelling of differences.[40] Then, secondly and more importantly, Kuschel in the end commits precisely the mistake of which he complains in so many of the theologians he discusses: a failure to integrate adequately systematic theology and New Testament studies.[41] For on several occasions he reiterates the normative, controlling character of Scripture,[42] yet at the same time notes the way it has been influenced by sociological factors. But, if this is so, then are not we who are placed in a different social setting allowed the possibility of drawing different conclusions from the text's surface meaning? To make the point clearer, Kuschel argues that pre-existence is asserted because of a decline in confidence in human ability to bring about change in the world; so, for instance, the argument of Colossians is set in the context of the earthquake which took place at Colossae in AD 61.[43] Whether this is a plausible explanation or not need not concern us here. What is important to note is that whether that was the instigating factor or not does not affect the truth of the epistle's underlying claim. That must be judged on other grounds. Likewise, the absence of pre-existence claims cannot be the final criterion. Not only may their absence have had

---

[39] Ibid., 505, 513 ff.

[40] For a more detailed consideration of the contrast, D. Brown, 'Tolerance: virtue or vice?', in D. R. Bromham et al., *Ethics in Reproductive Medicine* (London: Springer-Verlag, 1992), 201–9.

[41] 'A deep hiatus between the biblical evidence and classical dogmatics' (Kuschel, *Born Before All Time?*, 399).

[42] Ibid., e.g. 426, 487. One section is even headed: 'dogmatics as consistent exegesis' (489 ff.).

[43] Ibid., 327–40; for other examples of pre-existence as a theology of crisis, 181–207, esp. 199, 205.

motivating factors unconnected with questions of truth,[44] but also statements with quite different emphases could carry implications of which their authors were either unaware or only subliminally so. So, for instance, we are surely entitled to ask how a community that has no longer such a exclusive and pressing focus on the future as the early Church seems to have had would now express the same conviction of Christ's importance. A Christ who is Lord of the future quickly becomes Lord of the past as well, as the advance of time absorbs that future, and so makes urgent the question of the status of those now dead, who had expected a different, imminent destiny. In addition, any claim to control the future already contains an implicit claim to control the past, for the obvious reason that what the future brings is in part a function of the past. So even with Kuschel's unusual slant to functional Christology, my point about ontological implications still applies.

As for what induced the early Church to ascribe such extensive powers to Christ, in part the answer must lie in Jesus' own expectations. Even if he had thought of the Son of Man as a distinct heavenly figure who would help inaugurate his new role, the earliest experience of the risen Christ was such as to convince the early Church that the two figures were identical.[45] So the earliest Christology we find is of a Christ exalted to God's right hand like the Son of Man, and it is in particular to Psalm 110 that repeated appeal is made (e.g. Acts 2: 33; 5: 31; 7: 55–56; Rom. 8: 34; Eph. 1: 20 ff.; Col. 3: 1). Talk of Christ's exaltation, however, extends beyond the use of this psalm. Not only do we find such language in what looks like a pre-Pauline credal formula at the beginning of Romans (1: 3–4), but it recurs many times elsewhere either with alternative imagery or with 'right hand' subtly modified to include a closer identity with God's throne.[46] Though parallels to language

---

[44] Kuschel himself concedes as much in respect of Mark: ibid., 314.

[45] M. Hengel inclines, if somewhat hesitantly, to this view in his exhaustive study, 'Sit at my right hand', in M. Hengel, 'Dionysiac Messiah', 119–225, esp. 173–4. Cf. 108–9.

[46] For alternative imagery, Phil. 2: 5–11, though Hengel surely goes too far in suggesting that 'the name which is above every name' refers to the divine tetragramm (155–6); for occupying the same throne as Father, Rev. 3: 21. Still later, the primary focus of Ps. 110 moves elsewhere, to Christ's pre-existence and priesthood in vv. 3–4, as in Justin Martyr (*Dialogue* 19. 4; 33. 1; 45. 4; 76. 7; 83. 4; 96. 1; 113. 5; 118. 1).

of ascent can be found in Jewish literature, and also treatment of various figures as exalted such as Enoch or one of the angels (Metatron and Michael/Melchizedek), there is nothing that quite parallels the range of claims made for Christ.[47] Indeed, though non-canonical Christianity continued to experiment with an angel Christology, we find this already firmly abandoned as inadequate in Hebrews,[48] and in the book of Revelation the worship of Jesus set firmly alongside that of God.[49]

Some contemporary New Testament scholars continue to use 'imagination' in a derogatory sense. One even suggests that belief in the incarnation was no more than a wild elaboration from one way of speaking of the continuing significance of a martyr's death.[50] But imagination too can have its controls, and in this case they appear substantial, in the experiences that generated such an early felt need to use the language of exaltation. Indeed, the linguistic restraint is impressive, particularly as this is reflected in the way in which any ontological commitment is allowed only to follow, not precede, images drawn from experience. Thus, though the experiential language alludes to a highly exalted figure, it is in the main left to us to draw any conclusion in respect of divinity. Yet that sometimes lies not far beneath the surface. The immediate

[47] In Qumran fragment 11Q Melchizedek Michael/Melchizedek seems to be treated in a similar way to the future Son of Man of the Gospels (Hengel, 'Dionysiac Messiah', 111–12). In Jewish apocalyptic literature, perhaps under pressure of an increasing sense of divine distance, reference is common to the exaltation of the outstandingly righteous to existence among the angels; for a helpful discussion, M. Himmelfarb, *Ascent to Heaven in Jewish and Christian Apocalypses* (New York: Oxford University Press, 1993). The exalted are seldom made superior to the angels, though a conspicuous exception is to be found in *The Similitudes of Enoch*: Himmelfarb, 59–61, for other exceptions, 49, 57.

[48] Contrast *Shepherd of Hermas* (e.g. Visions 5, 2; Mandates 5. 1.7) and Heb. 1: 3–4 and 13–14. Even so, the author of the *Shepherd* occasionally also seems to want to draw the contrast: e. g. Similitudes 9, 12.7–8: cf. J. Daniélou, *The Theology of Jewish Christianity* (Philadelphia: Westminster Press, 1964), 122.

[49] For an excellent discussion of the range of positions currently held on the worship of angels in Judaism and early Christianity and its possible relevance or otherwise to the theology of the Book of Revelation, L. T. Stuckenbruck, *Angel Veneration and Christology* (Tübingen: Mohr/Siebeck, 1994). He warns against too ready a tendency to generalize, and not enough attention to specific context, as, for example, with the argument of the Epistle to the Hebrews: 119–39.

[50] B. L. Mack, *A Myth of Innocence* (Philadelphia: Fortress Press, 1988), 102–13; for the derogatory use of 'imagination', esp. 353–76, esp. 376.

response in Matthew from the disciples is worship (28: 16–20),[51] while both Jewish and Christian scholars have recently analysed Paul's allusions to his experience in terms of a *merkabah* mysticism that equates the object of the experience with God.[52] Again, one needs some account of why imagery from Psalm 110 appears so prominently in the Church's early mission, and one possible explanation might lie in that being the content of some at least of the resurrection appearances listed by Paul (1 Cor. 15: 5–8). An allusion to the first which he lists—that to Peter—may be buried in a verse in Luke that sounds suspiciously like a credal formula, while it is significant that what is often taken to be an early hymn assumes exaltation rather than an earthly resurrection to be the conclusion of Jesus' ministry (Luke 24: 34; Phil. 2: 5–10, esp. 9–10: the latter moves straight from death to exaltation). Hints of the existence of other exaltation experiences, now lost, have been detected behind the Transfiguration and Pentecost narratives, as well as in occasional verses elsewhere.[53]

These last comments are, of course, pure speculation. It has, however, a certain necessity since the difficulties inherent in the existing resurrection accounts are still seldom dealt with adequately

---

[51] The trinitarian language calls into question the precise historicity of the expressions used, but not necessarily the experience itself, nor the fact of having been a commission.

[52] In *Paul the Convert* (New Haven: Yale University Press, 1990), 34–71, A. F. Segal maintains that not only does the publication of the Angelic Liturgy from Qumran establish such mysticism as already in existence in New Testament times (40), but also Paul's own experience is best seen in such a context (esp. 56–8). Frances Young has argued that such language from Paul is best seen in sacramental terms: 'From analysis to overlay: a sacramental approach to christology', in D. Brown and A. Loades (eds.), *Christ: The Sacramental Word* (London: SPCK, 1996), 40–56. However, precisely because of the greater readiness generally of mystics to use divine language, caution is necessary in interpreting Paul. In my view even with this evidence we would still need the type of argument from function to ontology which has characterized the main body of the text.

[53] For the possibility of the Transfiguration as a transferred resurrection appearance, A. M. Ramsey, *The Glory of God and the Transfiguration of Christ* (London: Longmans, Green & Co., 1949). C. F. Evans' objection that it does not resemble the other resurrection appearances seems misplaced, since the point would be that it would be more like earlier exaltation appearances: C. F. Evans, *Saint Luke* (London: SCM Press, 1990), 413–14. Pentecost as such an experience is suggested by Hengel, 'Dionysiac Messiah', 214. A similar suggestion has also been made in respect of John 1: 51.

by modern systematic theologians. This is a point rightly made by Peter Carnley in his exhaustive study. Against the objectivist approach of Pannenberg the complaint is made that, like Westcott in an earlier age, he assumes too easy a reconciliation of the conflicting narratives, with a consequent failure to appreciate the degree to which even they are already being written at a 'middle distance' from the events to which they refer.[54] They are too distinctive of each evangelist's personal approach to guarantee easily a solid historical core. Unlike Pannenberg, Barth and Bultmann tried to circumvent the problem of historicity by insisting that the significance of the narratives lies beyond the normal canons of historical investigation, but this receives, if anything, even more devastating criticism.[55] In particular, attention is drawn to the implausibility of their claim that Paul was either not interested in evidence (Barth) or occasionally slipped (Bultmann), as also in the oddity of them both advocating that faith take risks but yet themselves trying to avoid all historical risk.[56] Finally, of Schillebeeckx it is observed that, though he claims to take the question of evidence seriously, in the end his position is one of equivocation. For he argues that the earliest form that faith took after the death of Jesus was conviction of experience of the power of his forgiveness and certainty of his future parousia, but, even if this were so, the question of the grounds for such belief would still arise, since they only make sense on the assumption that Jesus remains alive.[57] All these points seem to me powerful objections against the most influential approaches adopted this century.

Carnley's own solution, however, I do not find persuasive. This is to appeal to the ubiquitous references to experiences of the Spirit of Jesus in the New Testament to justify the conviction of the disciples that Jesus was still alive and our own conviction by analogy with similar experiences within today's Church.[58]

---

[54] P. Carnley, *The Structure of Resurrection Belief* (Oxford: Clarendon Press, 1987), 29–95. Difficulties are identified in narratives of both the empty tomb (44–62) and appearances (62–72), which leads him, at the end of his book, to speak of them being written from a 'middle distance' (367).

[55] Ibid., 96–147.

[56] For the issue of 1 Cor. 15: 3–8 as an attempt to offer proof, 108–11, 137–40; for the oddity of approach to risk, 133–6.

[57] Ibid., 199–222, esp. 206.

[58] Ibid., 223–368, esp. 249–59 and 267 ff.

Though stemming from the entirely laudable desire to identify factors in the early Church's experience which could justify both their faith and ours, his approach seems to me unnecessarily pessimistic, in appealing to such vague experiences. To me it would seem more satisfactory to admit that we are being invited to identify with a tradition, not all elements of which are now fully recoverable. But we still know the most important thing, the very early implicit acceptance of Christ's divinity. However deeply we burrow, it is still there in our earliest accessible post-resurrection Church.

The language of exaltation is so common in the New Testament that it requires no detailed examination here. Repeated use is made of the opening verse of Psalm 110,[59] while at least one early credal formula that uses the language of resurrection seems really to have exaltation in mind.[60] Indeed, so frequent are such imagery and assumptions that, whatever the historical value of Luke's account of Stephen's death in Acts 7, his vision of Jesus standing at the right hand of God 'is in all likelihood an accurate reflection of the sort of visionary experiences that were formative of earliest Christian belief and devotion.'[61] Yet a puzzle remains, and this may be used to illustrate how imagination can sometimes mislead and stultify. Though so much of the early material, so far as this is recoverable, seems thus to have focused on exaltation, this is no longer the emphasis with which we are most familiar from the best known of the resurrection stories, where the stress is on the continuity of Christ's humanity. This is particularly so in Luke, but is true even of John where one might have expected otherwise,[62] especially given the repeated references to ascension throughout his narrative. Thomas's ejaculation, 'My Lord and my God' (John 20: 28) is appropriate as a response to John's Gospel as a whole but strangely overdone if only the immediate context is

---

[59] For a detailed investigation of the texts, D. M. Hay, *Glory at the Right Hand* (Nashville: Abingdon Press, 1973).

[60] As in Rom. 1: 3–4, which speaks of Christ as 'designated Son of God in power ... by his resurrection from the dead' (RSV).

[61] L. W. Hurtado, *One God, One Lord* (Philadelphia: Fortress Press, 1988), 93–124, esp. 118.

[62] Contrast the mention of 'worship' in both Matthew's appearances (28: 9 and 17) and the stress on the humanity in Luke and John: Luke 24: 30 and 39–43 and John 20–21.

assumed, where the physicality of the resurrection is being stressed. My suspicion is that the resurrection appearances took a variety of different forms, some exalted, some more human, but that by the time the Gospels came to be written it was the more human that there was the most need to record, in order to establish the continuity of the now exalted Lord with the once earthly Christ.[63]

It is all too easy for us to suppose that the imaginative logic of narrative is the only possible construction of events, as though discovery of the empty tomb must come first, then human-like appearances, with only exaltation and ascension at the end to remove Christ from the scene. But such a natural progression seems challenged by Mark who, despite recording the empty tomb, seems to place the first appearances not there but in Galilee (Mark 16: 7),[64] while, despite his failure to record any such event, John's repeated allusions to the ascension imply that he attaches an importance to it that his narrative, like Luke's, fails to disclose (John 1: 51; 3: 13; 6: 62; 20: 17). So it is not impossible that imaginative considerations—the need for a developing narrative—have produced the present culmination in an ascension, rather than that the existing narratives represent the actual balance of resurrection appearances. If so, it would provide an excellent illustration of how the requirements of the imagination can distort the historical record in quite subtle as well as more obvious ways. Putting it crudely, the requirements of a good story pulled in precisely the opposite direction from the order in which events may have occurred. The irony is that because the logic of story falls first on empty tomb and very earthly resurrection appearances those are the poles round which most contemporary discussion revolves, whereas were we to take the weight of the New Testament witness as a whole it is exaltation and ascension that is most deeply embedded. Because the ascension is treated literally as a sort of full stop at the end of the story, it has lost the imaginative power it once had, as the primary vehicle for conveying Christ's ultimate significance.

[63] In John clearly in response to gnostic pressures, but perhaps also in Luke too.

[64] As the earliest tradition, this effectively undermines any claim that the appearances at the tomb were first, as indeed does Luke's suggestion that all the appearances took place in the city itself. In Luke's case apologetic considerations seen to have proved decisive, in allowing his narrative to move from provincial Galilee to Jerusalem and then on (in Acts) to the imperial capital, Rome.

But doctrinal ontology, it may be replied, fares no better: it stifles creativity in the way in which we are allowed to think of Jesus. That this has often been the case, I would not deny. Nonetheless, its strengths as well as its weaknesses need to be acknowledged, and I want to end the first half of this chapter by illustrating both from what happens within the New Testament itself. All four evangelists were faced one way or another with the same problem: that Christ's significance was now seen very differently from the way it had been perceived during his lifetime. Though only John makes the claims to full divinity explicit (and even then he remains subordinationist in his theology),[65] all four rewrite the narrative to varying degrees so that new significance can be grasped by the reader. New Testament scholars continue to disagree about the extent of such activity. Has, for instance, the use of Jonah to illuminate Jesus' forthcoming death and resurrection evolved out of something much less precise?[66] The questions flood in. What, however, cannot be disputed is that this happens, and that they do so with varying degrees of success. To take but one problematic instance, Matthew deliberately modifies Mark to avoid any suggestion that there were certain things Jesus could not do.[67] Yet, so far from enhancing Christ's status, it robs us of any notion (as in Mark) of Jesus waiting on human response.

Indeed, more often than not the alterations in the Synoptics simply generate further tensions, as with the addition of the infancy narratives where their post-resurrection confidence is hard to integrate with the obvious signs of growth in perception that characterize the narrative that follows. That is why John's much more radical solution can seem much more attractive. Though still taking care to build upon historical incidents, and indeed in consequence

---

[65] Most obviously at 14: 28: 'The Father is greater than I.'

[66] Contrast Matt. 12: 39–40 with its allusion to Christ's resurrection and Luke 11: 29–32 with its very different suggestion that the point of comparison is the effect of their preaching.

[67] Most obviously in Matt. 13: 58 (contrast Mark 6: 5), but there are several other examples, such as the omission of Jesus' question about who touched him in the crowd, or his rejection of the suggestion that a healing by Jesus might happen gradually, though Mark probably introduces such gradualism to illustrate how difficult it is to dislodge spiritual blindness: contrast Matt. 9: 22 and Mark 5: 30–1 and note the omission of Mark 8: 22–6, despite parallels for Mark 8: 14–21 and 27–30 in Matt. 16: 5–20.

even at times offering a more accurate record than the Synoptics,[68] he plays free with how the actors respond to those incidents, with Jesus fully aware of his divinity throughout. The result is that we get, as we have seen, the historically impossible confession of John the Baptist at Jesus' baptism, the implausible miracle at Cana, and numerous speeches that build on phrases and parables from the Synoptics that flesh out how the Church now sees Jesus. For some the result is a docetic Christ who has lost all real contact with his humanity,[69] but for most readers it works remarkably well, with some of the best loved touches of Jesus' humanity (his relations with the beloved disciple and Mary Magdalene)[70] coming from this Gospel. Even so there are tensions which sometimes come to the surface, where it is really only by the reader relying surreptitiously on the Synoptics that the situation is saved.[71]

Raymond Brown has claimed that the historical Jesus would have endorsed John's judgement on himself.[72] That is a claim which I do not find plausible. It is only the exalted Jesus who would, like the Church, have understood the full significance of who he was. The incarnation was a real kenosis that necessitated gradual development in the understanding of who Jesus was, and so the necessary exercise of the imagination as the story was retold in the light of that new understanding. History matters, but only when set in the context of the fullest perception of truth. John immeasurably advanced that process, but even he needed correction not only

[68] This is true of his account of Jesus' trial, though this could be due more to greater astuteness in understanding what might have happened than to better sources or any greater concern for historical accuracy; so Sanders, *Historical Figure*, 67 and 72.

[69] E. Käsemann, *The Testament of Jesus* (Philadephia: Fortress Press, 1968); for a reply, M. M. Thompson, *The Humanity of Jesus in the Fourth Gospel* (Philadelphia: Fortress Press, 1988).

[70] Though these are not necessarily in themselves historical. That the portrayal of the beloved disciple at the very least contains an idealized element is widely acknowledged: e.g. R. E. Brown, *Gospel According to John* (New York: Doubleday, 1966), xciv–xcv.

[71] For the discussion of one example, D. Brown, 'The healing of a corpse', *Expository Times* 12 (1996), 373–4.

[72] 'I have no difficulty with the thesis that if Jesus … could have read John, he would have found that Gospel a suitable expression of his identity'; R. E. Brown, 'Did Jesus know he was God?', *Biblical Theology Bulletin* 15 (1985), 74–9, esp. 77–8.

from the Synoptics but also by the later Church.[73] When the Council of Nicaea condemned Arius in 325, it also by implication condemned even John's Christology as inadequate in some respects. All elements of subordinationism were now removed. In effect, the Church asked: if Christ enjoys all the powers of God,[74] why not unqualifiedly so?

Christian theologians often write as though the Bible should be given the first and last word. Certainly as revelation it needs to be given the first word, but if even the Gospels themselves are an evolving tradition in which not only does Matthew correct Mark and John, Matthew all but corrects even the perceptions of Jesus himself, why should that evolving tradition have ceased? Indeed, we know that it did not. At the beginning of the second century Ignatius uses 'God' unqualifiedly of Jesus' earthly life,[75] while the copyists of the New Testament manuscripts did not hesitate to alter the text where it failed to correspond with sufficient clarity to later perceptions. According to one recent study this was not in any sense attempted systematically but rather wherever particular scribes thought that the text lay exposed to an heretical misreading, such as adoptionism, docetism, or gnosticism.[76] In some cases, so confused did the situation become that the orthodox even accused heretics of altering texts that had in fact been originally tampered with by their co-religionists.[77]

In considering this phenomenon it is important that we give full weight to both the positive and negative contributions that doctrine and imagination could make. Sometimes much would be lost were we deprived of the original version of what the text said. For instance, despite the attempt of many a later scribe to eliminate such a reference, it is still possible to discover in Matthew's high Christology a willingness to admit some ignorance in the

[73] On the need for correction by the synoptics, see Brown himself in R. E. Brown, *An Introduction to New Testament Christology* (London: Geoffrey Chapman, 1994), 121–4, esp. 122 and 33 n. 37.

[74] As in both early and late New Testament passages: 1 Cor. 15: 24–8; Matt. 28: 18.

[75] e.g. *Ephesians* 18. 2 and 19. 3.

[76] B. D. Ehrman, *The Orthodox Corruption of Scripture* (New York: Oxford University Press, 1993); for intentions, 98 and 274–80.

[77] As in Tertullian's complaint that the plural had been wrongly substituted for the singular in John 1: 13; Ehrman, *Orthodox Corruption*, 26–7, 59.

Son.[78] Such an awareness on our part helps in understanding both Jesus' life and the growth of belief about him. But in other cases the situation is quite otherwise. For example, the anti-docetic verses added to Luke that speak of Jesus dropping blood in Gethsemane not only make more powerful appeal to our imaginations in terms of the struggles which prayer involves than Luke's insipid original, they can also, precisely on those grounds, lay a greater claim to truth (Luke 22: 43–44).[79] One could, of course, appeal for support to Scripture elsewhere, in that the addition brings Lucan theology closer to the Marcan version of what happened (Mark 14: 32–36). But even without that parallel one might argue that the verses offer a more realistic account of what Jesus' prayerful struggle must have involved. Thereby one would be appealing to a much wider criterion of what the Church believes itself to have derived from Scripture, and not always deductively. In a similar way I would argue that the addition of 'Son of God' to the opening verse of Mark's Gospel enables that Gospel's message to be more effectively read today than if the title were only allowed to emerge later in his narrative and then with a possibly adoptionist sense, whether or not that was Mark's original intention.[80]

Whether we change the meaning[81] or, as with those scribes, change the written text, what we have is once more what Part Two described as 'a moving text', one which of necessity changes as new perceptions arise. Reflecting on the fluidity of the early manuscript tradition, one recent writer declares that 'the quest for a single authoritative text is itself a distortion of the tradition'.[82]

---

[78] The bulk of manuscripts omit the ignorance of the Son in Matt. 24: 36; Ehrman, *Orthodox Corruption*, 91–2.

[79] Ibid., 187–94. For the appropriateness of the description to prayer, D. Brown, *The Word*, 151–5.

[80] For arguments that the phrase is not original to Mark 1: 1, Ehrman, *Orthodox Corruption*, 72–5. Without it, Jesus' adoption at his baptism becomes a plausible reading.

[81] To most modern Christians the phrase 'Son of God' automatically connotes Christ's divinity; in its original sense it spoke only of a special intimacy: e.g. C. Rowland, *Christian Origins* (London: SPCK, 1985), 178–9.

[82] D. C. Parker, *The Living Text of the Gospels* (Cambridge: Cambridge University Press, 1997), 202. He takes as his benchmark the 'remarkably free text' of the Codex Bezae which could be as early as the second century.

That in my view is an exaggeration,[83] but it does emphasize how implausible it is for anyone automatically to be dismissive of textual variants and other such developments. Each new perception needs to be weighed, but it is my contention that if growth in incarnational doctrine is so weighed, it will not be found wanting. Its faults lay not in what was accrued (divinity) but in what was sometimes thereby diminished (Christ's humanity). But, it may be objected, it is one thing to concede such developments in respect of Jesus' consciousness where kenosis was essential to his full humanity, quite another to make the claim in respect of any aspect of his teaching. That subject will be the next topic of our investigation.

From Jewish charismatic to universal teacher

In this section I wish to consider some claims commonly made about the difference between the teaching of Jesus and that of the Church which came after him. Some contentions are of course quite incompatible with his goodness, far less his divinity. These are often the ones to hit the newspaper headlines. What, however, I have in mind here are the more modest and more widely canvassed claims of a kind that, though not impugning Jesus' integrity, do open up a wide gap between what he taught and the mind of the later Church, some of which might be thought to call into question whether there is a continuing tradition after all. Though in all three cases which I am about to consider it seems to me quite likely that there was such a divorce, the reader should note that I am less interested in which particular cases are true than in the principles upon which continuity might still be defended. The section will end with a brief discussion of the implications for Jesus' perfection, but I begin with my illustrative cases: the view that unlike the later Church he continued in obedience to the Law; the supposition that Jesus thought that a new, apocalyptic age would dawn which in fact never came; and the related issue of whether he died in despair.

---

[83] In our desire to take the variants seriously, we must not exaggerate the extent of divergence.

Law: obedience and abolition

Though there is no shortage of distinguished advocates of the view that the positions of Jesus and Paul on the Law were virtually identical,[84] there are powerful, countervailing arguments, the principal of which is that without some major difference it becomes virtually impossible to explain why the question of obedience to the Law figured so prominently as a contentious issue in early Christianity. For, had Jesus abrogated the force of the Law, that would surely have put all such argument at an end. Yet, to take a particularly striking example, Luke tells us in Acts that Peter required a special revelation before he would accept the view that all foods were clean (Acts 10, esp. 9–16). Bultmann used the criterion of dissimilarity from the surrounding culture to argue that Jesus' pronouncement on the matter as reported in Mark must be original (Mark 7: 15),[85] but here at least we seem pulled in a different direction by the need to make sense of what happened later, in respect not only of Peter's vision but also the more certainly historical confrontation between Peter and Paul as recorded in Galatians (Gal. 2: 11 ff.). The Matthean version of the saying therefore looks more likely to be closer to what Jesus may actually have said. Both Mark's phrasing and editorial comment leave us in no doubt of the absolute conclusion we are to draw, whereas not only does Matthew omit the editorial comment, but also small grammatical changes allow the accent to fall instead on the contrast: it is not so much the externals that matter as the internals.[86] The stress in Jesus' teaching would thus have been on the greater importance of internal dispositions, and that was then expanded by the early Church from an original relativization of food rules to their actual abolition.

Were that the sole case of change in Jesus' teaching on the Law,

---

[84] e.g. E. Käsemann, *Essays on New Testament Themes* (London: SCM Press, 1964), 37–8.

[85] R. Bultmann, *History of the Synoptic Tradition* (Oxford: Blackwell, 1963), 105; N. Perrin, *Rediscovering the Teaching of Jesus* (London: SCM Press, 1967), 150.

[86] Matt. 15: 11: 'Not what goes into the mouth defiles a man, but what comes out of the mouth' (RSV). Contrast Mark. 7: 15: 'There is nothing outside a man which by going into him can defile him' and v. 19: 'Thus he declared all foods clean.' For a very helpful discussion of the contrast, J. D. G. Dunn, *Jesus, Paul and the Law* (London: SPCK, 1990), 37–60.

the matter might not be of any great moment, but increasingly New Testament scholars are coming to the recognition that nowhere need Jesus be seen as advocating the abolition of the Law, and indeed it makes better sense of the evidence to suggest that he did not. Particularly prominent in this approach has been the work of E. P. Sanders. He has argued that Jesus' confrontation with the Pharisees over legal issues is manufactured by the early Church and is in fact a reflection of later disputes. What the Gospels offer us is a parody of what the Pharisees taught. So, for instance, he ridicules the idea that the Pharisees could ever have sent out scouts to spy on Jesus and his disciples plucking ears of corn on the sabbath,[87] as also the notion that they could ever have believed that the great majority of their fellow Jews were sinners simply in virtue of not adhering to the high standards that they themselves demanded.[88] What shocked Jesus' contemporaries was not Jesus' valuing of the ordinary people of the land but his acceptance of those who were sinners by any standard, and his suggesting that they were already valued and accepted by God even before they repented. Though many think Sanders' rehabilitation of the Pharisees overdone, there appears widespread agreement that in general the strong corrective he offers is long overdue.

If this is so, the various passages that appear to be attacking the Law as such would then need to be rethought. Only once does Sanders himself find Jesus abrogating the Law (and only then in deference to the demands of the coming kingdom) in his declaration, 'let the dead bury their dead' (Matt. 8: 21–22),[89] though even here some have advocated an alternative, less radical interpretation.[90] Similarly on the question of sabbath observance, Jesus' concern would not have been to reject the practice as such but rather, as with the food laws, to draw attention to priorities. The dramatic antitheses in the Sermon of the Mount would then fit

---

[87] E. P. Sanders, *Jesus and Judaism* (London: SCM Press, 1985), 264–7; *Historical Figure*, 214.

[88] Sanders, *Jesus and Judaism*, 174–211. Among those advocating the wider sense of the term 'sinner' is J. Jeremias, *New Testament Theology I* (London: SCM Press, 1971), esp. 112.

[89] Sanders, *Jesus and Judaism*, 252–5.

[90] That it addresses excuses for procrastination, rather than an actual violation of the fifth commandment; so G. Vermes, *The Religion of Jesus the Jew* (London: SCM Press, 1993), 26–9.

into a similar pattern. However, in attempting to identify the motives behind such reordering, Sanders is less helpful. He informs us that 'Jesus did not oppose the Mosaic code, but he did find it to be inadequate' and yet concludes that Jesus was 'no reformer'.[91] Presumably, in part it depends what one means by reform. Certainly, the Jewish scholar Geza Vermes is prepared to declare that 'the most outstanding feature in Jesus' attitude is an all-pervading concern with the ultimate purpose of the Law', while the Christian Graham Stanton talks of love as the interpretative 'lens' that now makes radical demands.[92] It is a matter of Jesus helping us to identify the moral core or heart of the Law. Some of his intensified demands find parallels at Qumran as on the questions of divorce or oaths,[93] but there are also important contrasts. At Qumran love of neighbour and hatred of enemy were effectively conjoined,[94] while in his invitation to the messianic banquet Jesus specifically includes those banned by the desert community: 'the maimed, the lame and the blind' (Luke 14: 12–14).[95] The positive expression of the golden rule that forms the climax of Matthew's version of the Sermon also seems without parallel in Judaism.[96] So, while the search for the heart of the Law and its moral intensification find parallels elsewhere, Jesus' teaching remains unmatched among surviving Jewish literature of the period in its strength and focus.

Such an account of his teaching has two obvious advantages. The first is that it explains why Jesus would have had immediate appeal within the specifically Jewish context of Palestine. He would not be seen as attacking Judaism as such, but as summoning his co-religionists to a deeper appreciation of their inheritance. We thus no longer have the historically implausible scenario of Jesus calling his fellow Jews to abandon their identity and all that seemed to define them as having a special role in the providence

[91] Sanders, *Jesus and Judaism*, 260, 269.

[92] Vermes, *Religion of Jesus*, 44–5; G. Stanton, *A Gospel for a New People* (Edinburgh: T & T Clark, 1992), 285–306, esp. 304–6.

[93] On divorce, Matt. 5: 31–32, 19: 3–9 and Damascus Document: CD 4. 21 (though even here the issue of divorce is only implicit, polygamy being the main issue); on oaths, Matt. 5: 33–37 and Josephus on Essenes, *Jewish War*, 2.135.

[94] Qumran Community Rule: 1 QS 1.9–10. Contrast Matt. 5. 43–8.

[95] Contrast Qumran Rule of the Congregation: 1 Q Sa 2.5 ff.

[96] So Vermes, *Religion of Jesus*, 38–41; Matt. 7: 12.

of God. But, secondly, this also helps in making explicable the different picture that emerges once the Gentile mission began after Jesus' death. The trajectory of the relative importance of various parts of the Law that Jesus had laid down now called into question the legitimacy of imposing on Gentiles those parts of Law that merely defined Jews as Jews. It is thus possible to argue that even if the jettisoning of parts of the Law by the early Christian community was by no means inevitable, it had after all a certain naturalness. This is not to assert that Jesus saw this implication. Rather, we must concede that the status of Gentiles scarcely entered his horizons, as the difficulty the evangelists had in finding suitable precedents well illustrates, where we are offered little more than two miracles at a distance.[97] But it is to claim that he set the Church's reflection in the direction that made such a change possible. Paul is commonly given the credit for this. Though not denying the importance of his contribution, it does seem to me that more attention needs to be paid to the role played by the Church as a whole, not least by Matthew.

Admittedly, some have seen in Matthew's Gospel a conservative Jewish reaction against drawing the legitimate conclusions of just such a trajectory.[98] Some parts of Matthew do admit of just such an interpretation: 'not an iota, not a dot, will pass from the law until all is accomplished' (Matt. 5: 17 RSV). Yet, just as Matthew stretches the meaning of Old Testament verses to insist upon their fulfilment, might not the same phenomenon be happening in this case? The jot and tittle are fulfilled in Jesus' more demanding understanding of the Law: 'unless your righteousness exceeds ... you will never enter the kingdom of heaven' (Matt. 5: 20).[99] This is not to say that Matthew never regresses. From his use

---

[97] The Syro-Phoenician woman's daughter in Mark 7: 24–30; the centurion's servant in Matt. 8: 5–13. This is even conceded by Jeremias, *Jesus' Promise to the Nations* (London: SCM Press, 1958), 29.

[98] G. D. Kilpatrick, W. D. Davies, and the earlier G. Bornkamm all saw this Gospel as focused upon internal disputes within Judaism: for a summary of their views, Stanton, *A Gospel*, 118–24.

[99] Jot and tittle are the AV form of v. 17. Like its less conspicuous parallel in Luke (16: 16–17), as it stands verse 17 seems to imply a dispensational view, with the law in due course superseded, whereas verse 20 allows us a Jesus once more concerned with priorities, for whom even the least commandment could have its legitimate place, provided it evoked the right moral disposition.

of 'little ones' elsewhere in his Gospel, scholars have deduced that the well-known passage that speaks of our feeding, clothing and visiting Christ in disguise was originally intended in its present context as a rather narrow reassurance to persecuted disciples (the nations will be judged in accordance with how they have treated them),[100] whereas for Jesus the meaning may well have been a radical demand upon the disciples[101]—and even if not, that is how the matter has been presented for most of Christian history. So my point is not that Matthew always gets it right, but that, despite his apparent inconsistencies, he deserves more credit as a theologian than he is normally given.[102]

Paul may in fact be much more confused than Matthew. Certainly, in his search for an adequate justification for going beyond Jesus' explicit teaching he resorts to a bewildering variety of arguments against the Law.[103] In response to Sanders it has been argued that while he is right to discount the traditional view that for Paul the main point of contention is justification by faith, his central concern nonetheless was a significant innovation upon questions of the Law: that it should no longer be seen as the embodiment of nationalist privilege.[104] But against this it must be observed that, if this is indeed Paul's view, he fails to state it with much clarity. Law is only grudgingly given credit (e.g. Rom. 7: 4–25; Gal. 2: 19–25), and the more natural interpretation is surely that Paul is desperately floundering in his attempt to find suitable arguments to undermine its central role, rather than that he has a coherent theology about its significance. So even those most well disposed to Paul find themselves remarking on the oddity of his

---

[100] Matt. 25: 31–46. cf. 10: 42, 18. 6; Stanton, *A Gospel*, 207–31.

[101] So, for instance, D. R. Catchpole, 'The poor on earth and the Son of Man in heaven: a reappraisal of Mt. 25.31–46', *Bulletin of John Rylands Library Manchester* 61 (1979), 335–97.

[102] For a similar, very positive estimate of Matthew by a modern ethicist, T. W. Ogletree, *The Use of the Bible in Christian Ethics* (Philadelphia: Fortress Press, 1983), esp. 104–16.

[103] Heikki Räisänen presents a powerful case for the view that 'Paul's thought on the law is full of difficulties and inconsistencies' and that, in so far as he was 'an original and imaginative thinker,' he is best understood as working by 'intuition' rather than by careful, reasoned argument: *Paul and the Law* (Tübingen: Mohr/Siebeck, 1983), esp. 264–9. For the implications of this for inter-faith dialogue, see further my discussion of Paul's treatment of Abraham in Chapter 5.

[104] Dunn, *Jesus, Paul and the Law*, esp. 183 ff.

arguments,[105] while among the general community of biblical scholars even more hostile comments are not uncommon, with his position described as a mass of 'self-contradiction' and 'oceans ... away from the religion of Jesus the Jew'.[106] This is not to deny the importance of Paul's contribution, only to insist that the limitations of his approach need to be acknowledged.

That Paul was extraordinarily perceptive on a large range of issues surely does not entail that he must have been equally insightful in everything. So far as I can see, Paul failed to get much beyond his understanding of Law as deeply problematic, whereas Matthew at least perceived how continuity could be argued, and this he did quite brilliantly. Indeed, even where in all probability Matthew narrowed Jesus' teaching, as in Chapter 25, he did so in a way that, as we have seen, at least allowed its subsequent enlargement. Any ordinary believer now hearing this text takes it in the wider sense, however narrowly it may once have been intended. To look at Paul alone might easily mislead one into supposing that he invented a wholly new Christian position on the subject, whereas Matthew demonstrates that there was no radical discontinuity but a continuing, developing tradition. Indeed, it was a trajectory that continued beyond the canon, as elements in his own writing were themselves subject to reinterpretation.

Imminent eschatology and imaginative density

On the question of what Jesus expected in the immediate future, Sanders' suggestion that he advocated what he dubs a 'restoration eschatology', with stress on a new Temple to inaugurate a new age,[107] has won much less wide favour than has his account of Jesus' attitude to the Law. In part this is because, if true, it makes extremely puzzling the great mass of Jesus' teaching since, apart from those few sayings upon which Sanders so heavily relies,[108]

---

[105] As sometimes Dunn himself: 'an arbitrary hermeneutical procedure' (202); 'open to sharp criticism' (247).

[106] E. P. Sanders, *Paul, the Law and the Jewish People* (Philadelphia: Fortress Press, 1983), 147, cf. 123; Vermes, *Religion of Jesus*, 212.

[107] Sanders, *Jesus and Judaism*, 61–119.

[108] Most obviously, Mark 13: 1–2, 14: 57–8. Vermes describes Sanders' view of the importance of the Temple as 'vastly overestimated' (*Religion of Jesus*, 185 n. 1).

Jesus is portrayed as no more concerned with the Temple than any other observant Jew. Moreover, Jesus' action in overturning the tables of the money-changers in the outer court of the Temple hardly seems an obvious way of symbolizing the Temple's impending destruction, as Sanders claims. The symbolism of breaking something within the Temple precincts would surely be more natural.[109] So, while there seems little doubt that Jesus did expect a new order to dawn shortly,[110] what precise form that was supposed to take must remain uncertain.

Numerous attempts have been made to extricate Jesus from any such assertion of an imminent eschatology.[111] A common strategy has been to suggest that this was an imposition of the nascent Church, while the attempt has even been made to lay the blame at the foot of John the Baptist.[112] Much ink, though, has been wasted unnecessarily on the question of present versus future eschatology. There is no reason why both should not have been present in Jesus' mind. Caird offers a promising compromise: for Jesus God's final vindication still remains in the future, but the battle and victory over Satan is already breaking through in his own life.[113] It is also important to stress that to anticipate some dramatic divine intervention in the world is not necessarily to presuppose the world's imminent demise. As much recent scholarship has underlined, apocalyptic cannot automatically be equated with the world's end. Nor should we suppose any single vision of what the future will bring.[114]

---

[109] Especially had the act been performed in the inner court nearer the building itself rather than in the more distant Court of the Gentiles.

[110] As, e.g. in Matt. 10: 23 and Mark 14: 62, or the imminence assumed throughout Mark 13.

[111] For a promising attempt to argue that all that is meant is the beginning of an end-time, C. E. B. Cranfield, 'Thoughts on New Testament eschatology', *Scottish Journal of Theology* 35 (1982), 497–512. But for me it seems wiser to take the most obvious meaning from passages such as Matt. 10: 23 or 1 Cor. 7: 29.

[112] e.g. W. Schenk, 'Gefangenschaft und Tod des Täufers', *New Testament Studies* 29 (1983), 455 ff.

[113] G. B. Caird, *The Language and Imagery of the Bible* (London: Duckworth, 1980), 12.

[114] For a magisterial study, C. Rowland, *The Open Heaven* (London: SPCK, 1982). Though in the main body of the text I have made no distinction between the concerns of apocalyptic and eschatology, Rowland rightly observes (e.g. 445) that apocalyptic's visionary focus carried the potential for undermining interest in a historically realized eschatology.

So, for instance, in his lifetime Jesus appears to have modified significantly the eschatology of John the Baptist. Judgement was not now the heart of God's message, nor necessarily a subordinate place for the Gentiles.[115] Instead, even though he continues to find a special place for his people and their traditions, his message is one of universal divine love and grace.[116] Even so, care must be taken to avoid substituting too comfortable an image. The threat of hell still remains an element, however deeply we probe.[117] Again, many a modern writer assumes too easily that eschatology and apocalyptic are the language of the downtrodden and an identification with them. As one recent, important study has underlined, apocalyptic notions are just as likely to arise among the upper echelons of society as among the marginalized, and indeed the post-exilic priesthood is quite likely to have been the source in the Jewish context.[118] This is in no way to challenge the view that Jesus identified with the underdog (we have already seen as much in his attitude to 'sinners'), but it is to call into question whether that is the most helpful category for understanding why eschatological and apocalyptic language came to function so decisively in his thought.

Instead, I suggest that we focus upon what we might call the notion of imaginative density (or intensity) and its implications. Even in a secular context followers are most inspired by the leader whose vision is such that a different world seems just around the

[115] Though John laid great stress on Christ coming with the fire of judgement (Matt. 3: 11–12), Jesus in his response to him (Matt. 11: 4 ff.) omits the negative verses which immediately follow his Old Testament allusions: J. Fitzmyer, *Gospel According to Luke 1–9* (New York: Doubleday, 1981), 667. Again, in his use of the traditional expectation of the Gentiles sharing in the messianic banquet Jesus excludes the subservient role for them which dominates Old Testament thinking. Contrast Luke 13: 28–30 and summary of earlier attitudes in Sanders, *Jesus and Judaism*, 214.

[116] Note how God's providential care in letting the sun shine on the just and unjust is linked by Jesus with his demand for love of enemies: Matt. 5: 43–8.

[117] Though Matthew's use six times of 'weeping and gnashing of teeth' occurs only once elsewhere (Luke 13: 28) and his 'outer darkness' not all, Mark does once have similar language (9: 43–8).

[118] S. L. Cook, *Prophecy and Apocalypticism* (Minneapolis: Fortress Press, 1995), 19–84. The Free Spirit Brethren, the followers of Savonarola and the Irvingites, for instance, all included the wealthy and privileged among their members (35–9).

corner. The alternative reality is allowed to 'come alive' for them in the here and now. Nor is it any different in the religious case, except to this extent: instead of the leader doing all the work, it is a matter of God's drawing so close that everything about him and his purposes is felt as near at hand. It is often forgotten that the issue of Jesus' apocalyptic consciousness is not just a matter of his teaching, but also, no less, of the kinds of experience to which he was subject. It is commonplace to find the baptism and temptation treated as purely internal experiences, the dramatization of which is then seen as due solely to the presentational skills of the evangelists. No doubt this is in large part so, but the preservation of the image of a dove for which the evangelists seem unable to offer any clear meaning hints that this aspect may well go back to Jesus himself, and, if so, it may well imply an original vision of Jesus that spoke to him of the beginning of a new order.[119] Again, the evangelists' accounts of Jesus' temptations and Jesus' own repeated allusions elsewhere to his battle with Satan may well also have had their origins in visionary experiences.[120] These are features of Jesus' consciousness with which the modern mind finds it peculiarly difficult to engage. Contemporary Christians find it hard to admit that Jesus could himself have seen a Satan, in the existence of whom they themselves may not believe.

But such difficulties need to be faced. In particular, it should be noted that such features are part and parcel of the same imaginative density that also envisaged aspects that readily admit of contemporary endorsement, such as the messianic banquet, to which all the marginalized are invited. The difficulty of 'decoding'

---

[119] Though there is one non-biblical parallel for treating the Spirit as like a dove at creation (Rowland, *Open Heaven*, 358–63), the evangelists fail to make such a connection, and the easiest, original allusion to comprehend is therefore the dove that begins a new order after the disaster of the Flood (Gen. 8: 8–12). This is not to deny the appropriateness of its later usurpation for trinitarian imagery.

[120] Though the temptation narratives have no doubt been elaborated, a growing body of opinion is now prepared to see Jesus as subject to apocalyptic visions, of which the fall of Satan from heaven (Luke 11: 18) might be another example; M. J. Borg, *Jesus: A New Vision* (San Francisco: Harper & Row, 1987), 33–4, 43. Even Mark speaks of Jesus being tested by Satan, and this may well indicate the same specific type of temptation of vocation as is claimed by Matthew and Luke; J. B. Gibson, *The Temptations of Jesus in Early Christianity* (Sheffield: Sheffield Academic Press, 1995), 58–60.

Satan is surely no more a difficulty than 'the stars ... falling from heaven' (Mark 13: 25 RSV, part of the apocalyptic chapter). The images are a lived reality appropriate for that time, however differently we might express the same ideas. The density is such that the future becomes present, and there, here. That the transformation of place, no less than that of time, is also a feature of such ways of thinking can be illustrated widely from the New Testament. To give but two examples, Matthew can assert of Christ both that he is at God's right hand and that he is in the believers' midst, while Paul can use language of exaltation and of meeting 'the Lord in the air' at the same time as he insists upon mutual indwelling (Matt. 18: 20; 1 Thess. 4: 17 RSV).

It was little wonder then that such apparent inconsistencies opened up the possibility of two very different trajectories. Some, such as Mark and the early Paul, continued to use the language of imminence, while in others, particularly Luke, we find it firmly abandoned, and in its place a long history envisaged for the Church.[121] It could also generate very different attitudes to the State, as in the contrast between Paul's attitude in Romans (13: 1–7) and the uncompromising hostility adopted by the author of the book of Revelation. At one level, there is no choice. The 'bizarre' riot of images offered us by the latter is clearly much nearer the apocalyptic mindset.[122] Yet there is also a tragic price, in the lack of charity shown in envisaging millions condemned to a terrible death. Nor is that price by any means unique. Quite often in the history of the Church apocalyptic ideas have gone with a harsh judgementalism, and not just towards those outside the community. The rule of love has sometimes been experienced as a severe and troubling discipline. Faults, though, can equally be detected on the other side, in a loss of enthusiasm and an easy conformity to the world. That suggests to me that we in fact need both trajectories, each there with the possibility of correcting the other.

Perhaps the point I am struggling towards can be made clearer if

---

[121] For the early Paul, e. g. 1 Thess. 4: 15; 1 Cor. 7: 29. Luke not only removes the sense of imminence, but also sometimes makes future expectation present reality, as in Jesus' words before the Sanhedrin: contrast Mark 14: 62 and Luke 22: 69.

[122] Rowland readily admits 'the bizarre nature of the symbolism' found in apocalyptic, *Open Heaven*, (447).

I take a specific instance, the question of pacifism. Though I have myself adopted this strategy in the past,[123] it now seems to me too easy a reconciliation of Jesus' pacifism and the Church's later policy of just war to say that Jesus only addressed the conduct of the individual under threat, whereas the later Church was forced to face the State's corporate responsibilities, where third-party interests are necessarily involved: it is one thing to sacrifice one's own interests, quite another those of someone else. It is not that this line of argument is wrong, but that it ignores the possibility of evoking a very different order of reality. That this is sometimes capable of realization is well illustrated by the lives of Mahatma Gandhi and Martin Luther King. Yet the apocalyptic pacifism of 'I have a dream' also has its dangers. Lack of engagement on the part of Christians with the powers that be can mean that something much worse is the result, with even the basic principles of justice flouted.[124] The Geneva Convention and other such attempts to bring an element of humanity into warfare came not through the example of pacifism but, in part at least, from the long tradition of Christian reflection on just war theory. That is surely immeasurably better than two unreconciled absolutes facing one another: pacifism and unlimited warfare. In similar fashion, it is good to hear from the sidelines an idealist critique of government social policies, but it is important also that others be prepared to offer more pragmatic criticisms in terms of what is currently deemed to be economically feasible. The two forms of Christian witness thus need one another, in much the same way as we have seen that in the antitheses of the Sermon on the Mount Jesus did not abrogate the more basic requirements of the Law but at the same time constantly challenged his audience to recognition of a higher way.

The cry of dereliction

Related to the issue we have just discussed is the manner of Jesus' death. If the imaginative density of his eschatological vision was

---

[123] D. Brown, *Choices: Ethics and the Christian* (Oxford: Blackwell, 1983), 133–9.

[124] Willingness to face such issues is what one misses in even subtle, modern defences of pacifism; e.g. S. Hauerwas, *The Peaceable Kingdom* (London: SCM Press, 1983), 72–95 and 135–51; J. H. Yoder, *The Politics of Jesus* (Grand Rapids: Eerdmans, 2nd edn. 1994).

such that more distant future and immediate present were fused in the manner suggested, then it becomes quite likely that his death would have been experienced as the frustration of all his hopes. The society directly ruled by God never came, and the result was what many have described as a life that ended in despair. As one distinguished Jewish scholar has described the cry of dereliction, it speaks of 'the broken heart of a man of faith' in 'the terrible moment when he saw that God had abandoned him'.[125]

The traditional Christian response has been to deny that this could conceivably have been so. In the history of the exegesis of Mark 15: 34, the two most popular alternative explanations for the verse have been sought either in Jesus' representational role or in the distinction between his divine and human natures.[126] But to have Jesus reflecting on himself as bearer of the sins of the world is hard to draw from the evidence of the Gospels on their own, while the more limited consciousness we found reason earlier to attribute to Jesus would argue for a more firmly context-based reflection in the disappointment of his hopes. Yet both Luke and John do portray a Christ who is more confident on the cross than the one we find in Mark.[127] The fact Mark chooses to quote Jesus' words in Aramaic argues for the authenticity of the cry,[128] but one should not dismiss too hastily the possibility of some historical justification for Luke and John also, however unlikely the actual words may have been.[129] For it could be argued that all they are doing is bringing out the full implications of Jesus' use of the

---

[125] Vermes, op. cit., 207, on Mark 15: 34.

[126] As an example of representation on behalf of sinful humanity, Augustine, *Exposition of the Psalms* 37. 6, where he is supported by the Septuagint's and Vulgate's mistranslation of 'groaning' in Ps. 22: 2 as 'my sins'; on the basis of the two natures, Aquinas, *Summa Theologiae* 3. 46. 12. For detailed treatment of the use of the verse, G. Rossé, *The Cry of Jesus on the Cross* (New York: Paulist Press, 1987).

[127] 'Father, into thy hands I commit my spirit' (Luke 23: 46 RSV); 'it is accomplished' (John 19: 30).

[128] Matthew alone follows Mark, though even he modifies the Aramaic *Eloi* to the Hebrew *Eli*, presumably to make more plausible the crowd's misunderstanding of the cry as a reference to the prophet Elijah: Matt. 27: 46.

[129] John's final word with its use of the Greek perfect is too closely bound up with his theology of the cross as victory to inspire confidence, while Luke's likewise reflects his wider editorial policy of suggesting a consistent, ordained path: Luke 24: 46; John 19: 30.

opening verse of Psalm 22 in his cry. Though we do not know what exegesis of the psalm was being followed in Jesus' own lifetime, the normal pattern did become prophetic of a suffering Israel and her eventual happy restoration.[130] The psalm ends on a confident note, and so it could be argued that in appealing to his Father in this way what Jesus is implicitly doing is presupposing that God will similarly bring his own agony to a more confident end. One might add that whatever Mark thought he was doing in recording the cry of dereliction he could not have thought that it was a cry of absolute despair, since the very point of his writing a Gospel must be that he has some good news to offer that takes us beyond despair.

Yet this seems too easy a resolution. It may have happened thus, but the truth is that we do not know where Jesus' reflections had reached at the point of death. In addition, we must reckon with the fact that such hope as Mark offers appears not to lie so much in the death itself as in promised resurrection appearances in Galilee (16: 6–8, the last authentic words of the Gospel). So an alternative way of reading the additions in Luke and John is to suppose that they are imposing on the death itself a truth that in fact finds its resolution somewhere beyond Jesus' death. Luke finds this working itself out in the gift of the Spirit in the history of the Church, while John projects his message back into the already existing life of the believer: resurrection happens as soon as the Christian message is appropriated. Both thus fundamentally alter the nature of Jesus' eschatology, and it is these new conceptions which help provide legitimization for the way in which they choose to present Christ's death.

What we find, I suggest, is tradition once more adapting to new circumstances, yet in a way that remains, despite surface appearances, in essential continuity with Jesus' own hopes and aspirations. Initially, this may seem a rather astonishing claim to make, so often is it voiced as a criticism that what Jesus proclaimed was the imminence of the kingdom whereas what in fact arrived was

---

[130] Ironically, to counter such a reading, Bucer assigned the two halves of the psalm to different periods of David's life, though insisting on reference to a single incident in the case of Christ himself: R. G. Hobbs, 'Martin Bucer on Psalm 22', in O. Fatio and P. Fraenkel (eds.), *Histoire de l'exégèse au XVIe siècle* (Geneva: Librairie Droz, 1978), 144–63.

the Church. In the literal sense of his words, Jesus of course got it badly wrong. Yet there surely remains a deeper sense (at least for the Christian) in which he got it right. For what the kingdom was about in Jesus' mind was a new sense of God's presence on earth, and that is precisely what arrived according to Christian conviction. Luke spoke of its gradual realization in the history of the Church and John of its immediate appropriation in the life of the individual believer, but neither doubted its fulfilment. So in putting on the lips of the crucified Christ related claims, though they may well have been telling a literal falsehood, that does not undermine the greater, imaginative truth. Jesus' imagination had worked along one set of tracks; its fulfilment came along quite another, but the two were nonetheless closely related. Whatever Jesus may have thought at his last gasp, his resurrection offered unequivocal evidence that his hopes had been fulfilled: God was now indeed closer to his people than ever before.

In assessing such freedom with the 'text' of Christ's own life, two factors in particular need to be borne in mind. The first is that, however Jesus thought of his death, its significance was quite transformed by later events. So, had we only Mark's account, some degree of distortion would have been the inevitable result, and this would necessarily have precluded full imaginative engagement on the part of the believer at that stage of the narrative. John's great cry of triumph at the end remains integral to how Christians should respond to Christ's death: so far from death bringing defeat, it too can open up the way to new life. A common modern response to such a line of argument would be to say that it is Mark's words that are the most profound, since they speak of God fully entering into the worst kind of experience that human beings could endure. It is at this point that my second factor becomes relevant, that modern preoccupations involve no less a rewriting of the text.

I shall argue this point at greater length in Chapter 7, where reasons for the change in emphasis will be explored. Here, suffice it to note that in writing still struggling towards recognition of the full divinity of Christ, it is rather implausible to suggest that this was already seen as one of the main purposes of Christ's suffering. Earlier Christian reflection had viewed talk of Christ's descent into hell as concerned with his liberation of those devout souls who antedated his coming (based particularly on 1 Pet. 3: 18–20 and

Matt. 27: 52–53). Though there are some anticipations, to identify 'descent' with the despairing cry is essentially a modern conception.[131] The idea has often been powerfully and movingly expressed, but we must take care not to exaggerate. Many human beings have suffered much worse,[132] while the fact that Jesus still acknowledges the existence of God in his cry demonstrates that there were still further depths to which he did not go. But that is a small qualification, compared with the reality of what in retrospect can now be claimed. Even though Jesus was unaware of it at the time, this was God himself entering into the dreadful horror of what human beings most fear.

But I must end with the qualification. Those inclined to mock Luke's righteous martyr and John's triumphant victor as the products of a facile escapism which cannot deal with the agony of the cry need to be reminded that modern impositions have no less difficulties, though of a different kind. A suffering that was without hope and short lived has little to offer many a contemporary enduring torture or hunger over a decade or more. An adequate imaginative presentation of Christ's significance is thus no easy task. That is why not only the New Testament rewrote his death but also, as we shall see, so did later tradition as it sought to apply later hermeneutical frameworks to the challenges of its own day.

A perfect life

It remains now to face one last issue, whether to tell the story of Jesus in this way is inevitably to call into question any claim to his perfection. Does it not speak of a thoroughly limited human being, far less divinity incarnate? I fail to see why. A recurring theme of this book has been that to be human entails being part of

---

[131] Though 'despair' is not an expression which Calvin would have liked, for him 'descent into hell' does include Jesus experiencing a sense of total alienation from God: *Institutes of the Christian Religion* (Philadelphia: Westminster Press, 1960), I, 512–20, esp. 516–17 (2.16. 8–12). Balthasar has argued for a deeper alienation in death itself: *Mysterium Pascale* (Edinburgh: T & T Clark, 1990), 148–88, esp. 168 ff.

[132] 'Years of torture producing a wasted body that is finally just dumped in an anonymous grave' was the example I quoted in an earlier essay: D. Brown, 'The problem of pain' in R. Morgan (ed.), *The Religion of the Incarnation* (Bristol: Bristol Classical Press, 1989), 46–59, esp. 54 ff.

one social context rather than another, and that, though this does not determine what one thinks, it heavily conditions and shapes all one's thought. Why then should a divine incarnation have been any different? Indeed, to be truly such, must not Jesus have been subject to the normal assumptions of first-century Palestinian thought? This is normally readily conceded in terms of a three-decker universe, or Mosaic and Davidic authorship of the Pentateuch and Psalms; but can such an admission not be carried much further?

It is in no way my contention that Jesus had to accept the Law or the necessity of an apocalyptic framework, but I do wish to assert not only that neither perspective was incompatible with a kenotic understanding of incarnation, but also, more importantly, that their acceptance allowed the closest possible identification with the way human thinking in general works, not by necessity but by close conditioning. So in the case of the Law it enabled Jesus to speak more powerfully to the people of his own race and day, while at the same time opening up the possibility of the application of a new, liberating Law of the heart to all humanity. Similarly on apocalyptic, such ideas, though by no means universal in first century Palestine, were quite common. They were, however, dominant in the context within which Jesus grew up, for almost certainly it was over against the ideas of John the Baptist that his sense of mission was forged, and as we have already noted, this led him to make significant modifications to John's position, in being both more open and less judgemental. We have already noted the unusual character of Jesus' baptismal experience and what for some seems his bizarre confrontation with a personal devil. At that point one level of possible explanation was offered, but we still need to probe more deeply. Why was it that even God the Son should have had experiences which do not necessarily directly correspond with reality, in the sense of there being one supreme personal devil or a dove that indicates a new order rather than the third person of the Trinity?

In response, it may be said that what we need to note is the alternative. In popular presentations of Christianity one is often offered only three options—Jesus as mad, bad or God. But this is surely precisely the nature of the problem. In effect, these are the only alternatives offered by John's Gospel, but the result is that Jesus' humanity is called into question. Had only John's Gospel survived, we might well have doubted whether there ever had been a full and complete incarnation. It is only by reading that Gospel as descriptive of something other than Jesus' humanity (either his divinity or our relation with that divinity) that we are really able to come to terms with its message. It was thus essential that Jesus should speak of things other than himself so long as he remained in this world. Paradoxically, God had to reveal himself by being other than God, just as Jesus had to speak of a kingdom of which he was not the king, for it to become plain that it was indeed his kingdom that was being revealed. John at least saw this, and that is why he portrays Jesus not as he was but as he is now known to be, with even Christ's eucharistic blood holding a promise beyond the wildest imaginative leap of the historical Jesus. For John it promises participation in the eternity of his divine life, whereas for the historical Jesus any notion of his disciples drinking his blood could only have brought disgust or 'nausea'.[133]

For some, such a portrayal will seem quite incompatible with any postulated human perfection for Jesus, because moral and spiritual truths are held to be universal and not dependent on the contingencies of history. But why should we hold to such a view? In Chapter 1, while challenging modern relativism, I also spoke against the absolutism of the Enlightenment. For better or worse all human thought is placed in specific contexts, and surely, if this is so, Jesus can have been no exception. Indeed, the main argument of this book has been that certain truths can only come naturally to consciousness as a result of specific historical pressures. We can be absolutely certain that Jesus' idealism would have taken a very different form had he been born in a different century or place. Imaginative density is what gave his mission its particular force and power, but that this took a definite particular form in visions of the devil and a dove, or rural images of sheep and hillside banquets should not delude us into thinking that more general conclusions are prohibited, though these too will require modification as later generations discover the pressures of distortion to which our own age has also inevitably been subject.

---

[133] The reaction proposed by Vermes because of the Jewish 'profoundly rooted blood taboo' (16). The version in Paul and Luke—'the new covenant in my blood' (Luke 22: 21; 1 Cor. 11: 25) is therefore more likely to be correct than 'my blood in the covenant' (Mark 14: 24; Matt. 26: 28). For some reflections on its further development in John 6: D. Brown, *The Word*, 146–50.

'Perfection' is in any case a misnomer, since what incarnation
requires is something rather different: sinlessness. Here moral
absolutes are not in play, but rather the absence of anything which
would inhibit Jesus' relation with the divine, and so make impossible the assertion of Christ as both divine and human. The
tensions are already evident in the contradictions to which the
author of the First Letter of John finds himself exposed.[134] But as
many a biblical scholar has remarked,[135] it is impossible to prove a
negative ('never sinned') and so our judgement of such a claim
must in the final analysis be theological, and not purely historical.
What that entails can perhaps best be indicated by highlighting the
similar understandings of sinlessness adopted by the nineteenth-
century theologian Schleiermacher and the twentieth-century
biblical scholar, John Knox, though they drew very different
conclusions. For both sinlessness is taken to involve an unclouded
consciousness for which any serious engagement with temptation
must therefore be an impossibility.[136] That is precisely what I
would be concerned to deny. For Jesus engagement with sin was
so real that it took visual form, despair so deep that he probably
believed he died a failure. Yet nowhere do the Gospels record him
ever doubting God's love and goodness, nowhere ever repenting
of a sin. Sinlessness is not about the absence of clouds, but about
what always remains at the forefront of one's vision. Yet even so
it seems to me not altogether inconceivable that this vision of Jesus
might have included some sense of his own sinfulness. That at any
rate would make more readily intelligible his desire to be baptized

[134] Sinfulness within the community is asserted at 1.8 ff. only to be denied as
impossible if a relation with God is to be maintained in 3. 4 ff. 'The apparent
contradiction is probably not to be eliminated', remarks C. H. Dodd, *The
Johannine Epistles* (London: Hodder & Stoughton, 1946), 78–81, esp. 80.
[135] E.g. J. A. T. Robinson, 'Need Jesus have been perfect?', in S. W. Sykes
and J. P. Clayton (eds.), *Christ, Faith and History* (Cambridge: Cambridge
University Press, 1972), 39–52, esp. 44.
[136] Schleiermacher, *Christian Faith* (Edinburgh: T & T Clark, 1928), 413–16;
J. Knox, *The Humanity and Divinity of Christ* (Cambridge: Cambridge University
Press, 1967), 68 ff; cf. 47. Where they differ is that while Schleiermacher insists
upon that unclouded consciousness and so makes temptation problematic, Knox
declares that for Jesus to have had a real humanity this must have involved temp-
tations that themselves partook of sin. For an extended discussion of both, J. P.
Sheehy, 'The sinlessness of Christ as a problem in modern systematic theology'
(D.Phil thesis, Oxford, 1989), 140–206.

by John. The act would have been motivated by his sense of sharing in the corporate responsibility of his people for their failure to live up to God's demands upon them. But that would hardly make Jesus himself a sinner, though it would once more exhibit the extent to which his experience was identified with our own.

Thus I conclude this chapter by observing that the approach advocated to tradition in this book finds ample confirmation not only in how the life and teaching of Jesus was treated by the New Testament Church, but also, more importantly, in how he himself lived and thought. The incarnation was a lived narrative of accommodation to the human condition, within which imagination played an indispensable part. But the contribution of the imagination to understanding the significance of Christ by no means ended with the closure of the New Testament canon. With the doctrine of the incarnation now secure, later tradition demanded some fundamental correctives to the general thrust of Scripture. It is to consideration of these that I turn next.

7

Art as revelation

So used are theologians to engaging with the written word that it is
all too easy for them to forget that for most of Christian history,
with the great mass of the population illiterate, most Christians'
primary experience of their faith will have been visual and, though
probably to a lesser degree, aural. The drama of the liturgy, hymns
and sermons, re-enactments of the biblical stories in mystery plays,
and the visual imagery present throughout the church building
would have been what inspired and directed their faith. Against such
a backdrop it would seem odd to discount all mediation of revelation through the eye.[1] The previous chapter has in any case already
noted what a key role the visual played in Jesus' own experience. It
would be wrong, though, to think of later visual experience as
merely the mediation of what previous generations already knew.
As we have already observed, just as the written text acquired new
meanings, so too did the visual. Two innovations in particular were
of enormous importance for the future of Christianity: new attitudes
to creativity and to God's identification with humanity. Though
both derive from the doctrine of the incarnation, neither, in my
view, can be wholly explained by appeal to Scripture. Instead, their
history and significance are best explored through the history of pre-
Reformation art. First, however, a brief word about the relation
between innovation and tradition in art.

Innovation and tradition in art

Beryl Smalley opens her well-known book, *The Study of the Bible
in the Middle Ages* with the remark that 'the Bible was the most

---

[1] Even modern stress on revelation as narrative can remain essentially cere-
bral. It is refreshing, therefore, when its essential content is identified as 'the gift
of an image' as in J. F. Haught, *Mystery and Promise: A Theology of Revelation*
(Collegeville, Minnesota: Liturgical Press, 1993), esp. 21–8.

studied book in the middle ages',[2] and, lest the reader is inclined
to dismiss it all as the wrong kind of study, one may note that
Smalley herself launched her career with a study of someone for
whom the literal sense was central, namely Andrew of St. Victor.[3]
So in what follows the conclusion should not be drawn that I wish
in any way to discount the importance of the Bible for pre-
Reformation Christianity. Yet it remains true that access to the
written word remained the privilege of the few, and so, though
sermons in the vernacular no doubt played their part, it was the
visual which had the decisive role. A heavy responsibility therefore
fell on artists and those who commissioned them. Generalizations
about the role of the artist become more and more difficult from
the Renaissance onwards, as secular commissions gained an
increasing role and a great plurality of approaches developed. The
danger, though, is that, as our sights turn further back in history,
we are drawn into artificial contrasts, believing innovation to be
the essential characteristic of the later period and an unchanging
tradition the mark of earlier times. Both presentations are carica-
tures. Except for very recent developments, such as conceptual art,
we will find that, whatever age we take, artists, like expositors of
the word, operated within a tradition of interpretation, yet one
that was no less 'a moving text': a gradually changing content,
whose images had the latent power radically to reshape the nature
of the faith they were expounding.

We need to disabuse ourselves of a number of misconceptions.
Since at least the Romantic movement and perhaps earlier, our
conception of the artist has been of the isolated genius, the very
reverse of someone working within a tradition. Changing attitudes
are well illustrated by the history of the term 'masterpiece'.
Originally it meant a piece of work which demonstrated that one
had successfully learnt the skills and traditions of one's trade, and
it was not till the fifteenth century that it was used as an independent term of praise. Even then it was only slowly extended to
painting, whereas by the nineteenth century it had become such a

[2] B. Smalley, *The Study of the Bible in the Middle Ages* (Notre Dame, Ind.:
University of Notre Dame Press, 1964), xi.

[3] 'Beryl Smalley and the place of the Bible in medieval studies', in K. Walsh
and D. Wood (eds.), *The Bible in the Medieval World* (Oxford: Blackwell, 1985),
1–16, esp. 8 ff.

feat of solitary endeavour as more likely to produce despair than realization.[4] One restraint on such an image of artists has been their own continued identification with various schools, such as the Fauvist or Blaue Reiter at the beginning of this century. Even so, such movements are more often than not interpreted as episodic, original bursts of vigour rather than as new elements within a continuous creative tradition. Each school is then seen as owing little to its predecessors. The result is that even with earlier periods such as Romanesque, Gothic, and Renaissance are quite commonly taken as indicative of decisive breaks, rather than, as I shall argue, important innovations amid essential continuities.

In response it may be objected that such continuities as exist are essentially artificial, generated as they are by a shared content in the Christian faith. In actual fact, as we shall see, the continuities run deeper than this, in artistic form and conventions also. More immediately, however, there is a need to challenge the notion of an unchanging content to the Christian faith. In what follows I shall argue that the Christian artistic tradition drew its strength from its ability to innovate—its capacity to transmit the biblical story in ways which at times could speak more powerfully to contemporaries than the original deposit. To some the claim will seem controversial or even false, not because of my stress on innovation, but because of where I place its source. The tendency remains to attribute such innovation not to the artists themselves, but to the clergy and other patrons who commissioned the works. Yet, while in some cases such as Abbot Suger the patron did pay close attention to detail,[5] we have no reason to think this generally so. In fact one recent study (written jointly by an intellectual and an art historian) has concluded that the degree of architectural freedom in the Middle Ages precisely parallels the degree of scholastic freedom: that, in the eleventh century while academic scholasticism was still being forged, decisions were similarly being

---

[4] W. Cahn, *Masterpieces: Chapters on the History of an Idea* (Princeton, NJ: Princeton University Press, 1979), esp. 5, 45–6, 66, 131–4.

[5] Cf. his own description in E. Panofsky (ed.), *Abbot Suger on the Abbey Church of St. Denis and its Art Treasures* (Princeton, NJ: Princeton University Press, 1979).

made as the building progressed; by the early twelfth century, however, problems were being solved sequentially as in the logic of Abelard; while the later twelfth century witnessed variation within a set framework, much like the controlling pattern exercised by the growth of set texts such as Peter Lombard's *Sentences*.[6]

Nor have we any reason to doubt that a comparable degree of freedom existed for more representational arts. The fact that most, though by no means all, artists of an earlier age were anonymous should not be taken to imply complete subservience to the wishes of their patrons; rather, it tells us something about their social status, as artisans, a quite different thing. In the course of what follows I shall return to this issue a number of times.[7] That religious writers and changing patterns of piety had their effect, no one could deny, but that influence runs in more than one direction is well indicated by the way in which many a saint's religious experience was decisively shaped by pictorial representations. Think of Francis converted before the crucifix in San Damiano or allusions to the effect of art on her visions in the life of St Catherine of Siena. Indeed, it appears quite likely that it was artistic inspiration that moved the stigmata in a more christological direction.[8]

The growth of the two insights upon which I intend to focus cannot be narrowly confined to one particular period. Nor were such developments linear or inevitable. Yet the decisive contribution does in one case come from the earlier medieval period, the other from the later. So, to simplify matters, our story is pursued historically, and suitably modified, as further qualifications suggest themselves.

[6] So C. M. Radding and W. W. Clark, *Medieval Architecture, Medieval Learning: Builders and Masters in the Age of Romanesque and Gothic* (New Haven: Yale University Press, 1992).

[7] Note in particular the section on *factors for change* in the second half of the chapter. For a similar interactionist view, B. Cassidy, 'Introduction: iconography, texts and audience' in idem (ed.), *Iconography at the Crossroads* (Princeton, NJ: Princeton University Press, 1993), 3–16.

[8] The dominant element in Francis' vision was of a seraph. For artistic developments, M. Meiss, *Painting in Florence and Siena after the Black Death* (Princeton, NJ: Princeton University Press, 1951), 105–31, esp. 116 ff.

Roman to Romanesque: Incarnation as creativity's endorsement

Though the argument from the incarnation that justifies Christianity's endorsement of artistic creativity was, as we shall see, made explicit only in the Eastern iconoclastic controversy, it was in many ways Western Christendom which took the greater advantage of its implications. For the conclusion was drawn that God, in sketching or defining himself through the human, had in effect endorsed all that was best in human creativity, and the result was what might almost be described as a riot in range of reference and borrowing. This is particularly evident in Romanesque art, but is already evident even in the Roman period. That is where I shall begin. Thereafter I turn to iconoclasm and Byzantine attitudes, before concluding the section with the contrast between Romanesque exuberance and biblical restraints. Why I want to speak of continuing revelation will become clear in due course. The issue hangs on how biblical attitudes should be interpreted.

Empire and innovation

We begin, though, with current scholarly dispute about what account should be given of the position of the Church in the immediate post-biblical period. So far, no Christian artefacts that can be dated earlier than 200 have come to light, while a number of early writers appear to combine a relentless critique of pagan imagery with strong advocacy of an aniconic God. Recently, however, it has been argued that this was more of a tactical device, and that, since Christian imagery is still early, we should assume that 'for the first two centuries of its history, the new religion exhibited a high degree of assimilation to Greco-Roman culture'.[9] Certainly, the position is more complicated than has often been claimed. The key passages can be read in a way that betokens a

[9] P. C. Finney, *The Invisible God* (New York: Oxford University Press, 1994), 293. I find implausible, though, his contention that written critiques were 'a purely apologetic device' intended 'to serve up an idealised portrayal of the new religionists' (58). For, given the general tenor of ancient thought, would it not have been a more effective strategy to endorse the value of art while denying it realistic content?

much more limited objective.[10] But, even if this were to be conclusively established in every case, we must wait until the Cappodocians before we have any unequivocal evidence of endorsement.[11] So, while it would be dangerous to infer uniform, intellectual resistance lasting longer than what happens in practice, it would be in my view equally unwise to assume a community united from the start in positive appreciation of the role of art. Even if we discount the influence of the Bible, not only did more negative attitudes give a powerful handle with which to attack paganism, the reserve shown by early Christianity in the types of art it favoured from the third century onwards suggests a more gradual appropriation of its religious value. There is a preference for symbols over direct representation of Christ,[12] while even when the latter begins to occur, it is his miracles which take precedence over what are seen as the more sacred elements of the story, including the crucifixion.[13]

In formulating their ideas, thinkers like the Apologists, Clement, and Origen leave us in no doubt about the great debt they owe to pagan thinking. The same is no less true of the origins of Christian art. The way in which art works innovatively but within a tradition is well illustrated by how Christian art was affected by its first cultural context. It used to be thought that the form taken by early representations should be traced to a desire to imbue Christ and the Christian religion with the awe attaching to the emperor in the late Roman empire, and this for example explains why he is made to face us.[14] However, more careful, recent analysis has convincingly (in my view) refuted this interpretation. It looks now as though what we have is the adaptation

[10] As was argued by M. C. Murray in her ground-breaking discussion 'Art and the early church', *Journal of Theological Studies* 28 (1977), 304–45. Tertullian, for example, is found to be confused (308–9), while Clement, despite his limitations to symbolism, is viewed as encouraging others rather than placing limits (322–3). Inevitably, some of her counter-interpretations seem more plausible than others.

[11] e.g. Gregory of Nyssa, *De deitate Filii et Spiritus Santi* (*PG.*, 46. 572); Gregory Nazianzen, *Oratio* 35, 3–4 (*PG.*, 36. 260–1).

[12] Some are discussed below. Even the Good Shepherd is symbol rather than representation, as the sheep over his back indicates.

[13] R. Milburn, *Early Christian Art and Architecture* (Aldershot: Scolon, 1988), esp. 243, 303.

[14] e.g. A. Grabar, *Christian Iconography, A Study of its Origins* (Princeton, NJ: Princeton University Press, 1968).

of pagan religious art to convey the intrinsic superiority of the new religion. Thus so far from Christ's entry into Jerusalem sharing most with an imperial triumph, we have him dressed as a philosopher and riding side-saddle on an ass; thereby at one and the same time reminding us of Dionysus but surpassing him in his claims to subvert the old order.[15] The wand, so far from indicating the staff of authority, is used to underline Christianity's claim to miraculous powers; Christ is shown in the garb of Asclepius, but without any reserve in his power to heal, unlike the Roman tradition which never portrayed their god of healing at work.[16] Again, though the size of portraits of Christ and the amount of gold used were traditional devices for indicating divinity, the usual trappings of imperial majesty—such as the royal diadem or the official imperial seat, the *sella curulis*—are absent. Finally, his androgynous character, varying from dark beard to effeminate long hair and even incipient breasts, indicates the claim that Christ includes within himself all that is most divine in Apollo or Dionysus as much as in Jupiter.[17]

Christians often respond to such facts with embarrassment, but there are at least two considerations which ought to weigh on the other side. The first is that comparable things were happening in theology itself, as Christianity sought to re-express itself in the thought-forms of pagan culture. Extensive use was made not only of pagan philosophy (particularly Platonic and Stoic) but also of pagan myth. Indeed, one of the fascinating features of the period is that, whereas the modern argument tends to be that if there are pagan parallels (for example for the Virgin Birth) it cannot be true, the ancient argument was that such myths proved the conceivability of God acting in this way. Such comparable behaviour among the theologians does not of course establish its rightness among the artists, but it may suggest what we have already noticed happened subsequently with respect to architecture, that the cultural climate made possible the two parallel lines of development rather than one

---

[15] T. F. Matthews, *The Clash of the Gods: a Reinterpretation of Early Christian Art* (Princeton, NJ: Princeton University Press, 1993), 23–53, esp. 45

[16] Ibid., 54–91, esp. 69–72.

[17] Ibid., 115–41, esp. 101–4 and 126–7. For a related example, the 'seated poetess', now reinterpreted as Christ teaching his followers, Milburn, *Early Christian Art*, 80, ill. 47.

necessarily determining the other. Certainly, when historians try to demonstrate the existence of 'a concentrated effort' to impose a particular theology upon artists, the attempt can sometimes go badly wrong.[18]

The second consideration is that these innovations did actually succeed in helping to ensure the triumph of Christianity and more controversially, I would add, advance its claims to the truth.

> The imagery that was formed for the new God drew upon a variety of potent sources—the gods, the philosophers, the magicians of antiquity ... Rising to the challenge, painters, sculptors, and mosaic workers invented without inhibition. The narratives of the Gospel they rewrote with freedom to forge images of memorable impact. By representing as many facets of his person as possible they tried to encompass somehow the totality of the unimaginable mystery. Their success spelt the death of the sacred imagery of classical antiquity.[19]

Such a conclusion seems to me to be largely true: it was by demonstrating that Christianity possessed all that was best in paganism, but also so much more, that it ensured its own triumph. But it is not quite true that artists 'invented without inhibition'. None of their images were incompatible with the Christian faith, and so there were controls, but they were not controls based on an unchangeable, sacred text. They thought that they could sometimes clarify or improve upon the message conveyed by biblical narrative, and sometimes they undoubtedly did. Some controversial, but illuminating borrowings from paganism may be used to illustrate the point.

Because according to ancient physiology breast milk was transmuted blood, from the second century onwards with Clement of Alexandria, the notion of Christ feeding us like a mother gained currency, and in the Middle Ages even occasionally generates pictures of Christ offering his nipple to the believer rather than blood from his wounded side.[20] Such imagery clearly has its parallels and

---

[18] As does Matthews, *Clash of the Gods*, 52–3, where one relief is used to argue a general case, generating in the process two theological misconceptions: Logos as created principle and the Entry to Jerusalem as an assertion of divinity.
[19] So Matthews ends his book, ibid., 180.
[20] Cf. C. W. Bynum, *Holy Feast and Holy Fast: The Religious Significance of Food to Medieval Women* (Berkeley: University of California Press, 1987), 269–72 and illus. 25 and 27.

antecedents in the way in which early Christian art was prepared
to identify Christ with the sexual ambiguity of Dionysus as we
noted above. Thereby his ability to be a saviour as much to
women as to men was clearly indicated, in a way that would have
been more difficult within the biblical narrative. It had its dangers
in its capacity to be read, not as an assertion of Christ's soterio-
logical inclusiveness, but as a denial that the incarnation included
the specifics of sexuality, which is perhaps why some Renaissance
painters deliberately go to the other extreme in emphasizing
Christ's male genital organs.[21]

Two other examples will suffice, the transformation of King
David into Orpheus and Jonah into Endymion. In the former case
this is a development to be noted within Judaism, for after the final
destruction of the Temple Old Testament hostility to imagery
increasingly relaxed, at least in some quarters. Thus the third-
century synagogue at Dura Europos (discovered in 1932) discloses
a wealth of imagery, including the figure of David as Orpheus, a
pattern that is found repeated at sixth-century Gaza.[22] Though
there are a few chronological and midrashic deviations from the
Old Testament, significantly this is the only borrowing from
paganism.[23] What motivated its inclusion was undoubtedly the
way in which it could reinforce other elements, particularly in the
Ezekiel cycle (based on chapter 37), which stressed the Jewish
hope for resurrection of the dead, despite the paucity of scriptural
reference. Not only had Orpheus's music tamed the wild beasts,
he had returned alive from Hades. With Christianity that message
could be made even more explicit, and Christ and David are fused,
for instance in the Catacomb of St Peter and Marcellinus at Rome,
though Christ retains Orpheus's cap and lyre rather than David's

[21] Cf. L. Steinberg, *The Sexuality of Christ in Renaissance Art and in Modern
Oblivion* (New York: Pantheon, 1983). Both book and issue are discussed in
Chapter 2.
[22] G. Sed-Rajna, *Ancient Jewish Art* (New Jersey: Chartwell, 1985), 63–88,
esp. 68–9; J. Stern, 'Orpheus in the synagogue of Dura-Europos', *Journal of the
Warburg and Courtauld Institutes*, 21, (1958), 1–7.
[23] Sed-Rajna, *Ancient Jewish Art*, 73, 83. Significantly, though, even within
Palestine itself synagogue floors and sarcophagi from the fourth and fifth centuries
have been found which mix Jewish and pagan motifs, particularly through placing the sun god Helios at the centre of a zodiac design: for illustrated examples,
S. Kochav, *Israel: Splendours of the Holy Land* (London: Thames and Hudson,
1995), 218–19 (Hamath Tiberias), 226–7 (Beth She'arim), 260–1 (Beth Alpha).

harp.[24] It is interesting to note that the lyre was the only pagan symbol that Clement of Alexandria listed among those acceptable for the Christian.[25] Was it because musical harmony is such a powerful symbol of the integration of what had been divided? Certainly, later Christian thought was to carry the analogy further. Partly through reading Psalm 57 christologically (with its reference to a harp in v. 8), the notion arose of the cross as itself a musical instrument which restores harmony, and it is this conception which survives in George Herbert's poem, 'Easter':

> His stretched sinews taught all strings, what key
> Is best to celebrate this most high day.[26]

Orpheus had come a long way, but was not Christianity the richer for such a musical image?

The modelling of Jonah on Endymion,[27] was not one destined, like Orpheus, to survive, but in its day it too must have had a very powerful impact. In classical mythology Endymion was granted a sleep of eternal youth thanks to the goddess of the night, Selene or Artemis. In Scripture the raising of the gourd over Jonah is intended to demonstrate God's concern for him (Jonah 4: 6–11), but it was only through combination with the Endymion legend that the concern is clearly declared to be eternal. Gourds are after all soon a thing of the past. Ironically, despite the New Testament (Matt. 12: 39–41), it took until the twelfth century before we find Jonah and the whale used to represent the theme of the resurrection.[28] But of course on that version it lacks the personal reference which the Endymion variant so clearly offers, and so it is not surprising to discover the latter on funeral monuments.

Iconoclasm and Byzantine reserve

It is astonishing to think that all developments in Christian art might well have come to a premature end in the eighth or ninth

---

[24] Illustrated in J. Hall, *History of Ideas and Images in Italian Art* (London: John Murray, 1983), 66.   [25] *Paedagogia* 3, 11.

[26] G. Herbert, *Complete English Poems* (Harmondsworth: Penguin, 1991), 37.

[27] Illustrated in Matthews, *Clash of the Gods*, 32.

[28] So Hall, *History of Ideas*, 70.

century, had one side achieved its goal in the so-called iconoclastic controversy (*c.* 730–843). For, though the debate was centred in the Byzantine empire, almost certainly its ramifications would have extended to Western Christendom, had the iconodules (supporters of icons) lost.[29] As so often in the history of Christianity, we have only a very imperfect knowledge of the motivations behind the losing side, in the main having to rely on select quotations by their opponents, even in the case of the emperor-theologian, Constantine V.[30] Direct Muslim influence is now discredited, but some continue to see political motives as primary, in the attempt by emperor and bishops to wrest control from monastic and popular piety.[31] Such factors should not be discounted, but, apart from the claim that only the eucharist could be a true icon of Christ,[32] it is innovation which seems most stressed, and which in turn is most countered. Much was made of St Luke's painting the Virgin and also of the emergence of the *acheiropoietos*, the holy face held to derive from the time of Christ himself and 'not made by human hands'. In fact both probably date only from the sixth century, but it was a useful fiction to insist that word and art arose at the same time.

The number of bishops prepared to take the iconoclastic side suggests quite a complicated debate, with a gradual growth in the importance attached to icons culminating in a crisis regarding their significance that was perhaps triggered by political complications. The fact that specific appeals to biblical texts were made by iconodules almost certainly implies corresponding arguments on the other side,[33] as does the search for suitable patristic quotations. Here the iconoclasts were on shakier ground in their use of some later Fathers, but, as already noted, rightly or wrongly strong

---

[29] Though Frankish political rivalries complicated the reception of decisions, we are still in the period of ecumenical councils.

[30] Fragments were preserved in Nicephorus' *Antirrhetici adversus Iconomachos*. Theodore the Studite provides some poems from the reign of Leo III, while we also have the decree from the heretical council of Hiereia in 754.

[31] e.g. G. Matthew, *Byzantine Aesthetics* (London: John Murray, 1963), 101–2. It is seen as 'a complex reaction' to a 'crisis generated by the Muslim advance', in J. Herrin, *The Formation of Christendom* (London: Fontana, 1989), 343.

[32] Because alone completely identical or *homoousios* with Christ.

[33] The Council of Nicaea in 787 appealed to Exod. 25: 17–22; Num. 7: 89; Ezek. 10: 16–20; Heb. 9: 1–5.

condemnations of imagery can easily be drawn from earlier writers such as the Apologists, Tertullian, Clement, and Origen.[34] In the end, though, the key argument turned on whether the exalted Christ could legitimately be 'circumscribed' (*perigraptos*) or not, given the fact that by definition the divine was not confined or restrained (*aperigraptos*) in any way.

The fact that both the leading iconodules appealed to the doctrine of the incarnation was to be of enormous significance for the later history of Christian art. John of Damascus argued that a 'likeness' of God only became possible with the incarnation, a likeness which was then maintained for all eternity because of the two natures (divine and human) in the one person. God had, as it were, violated his own commandment by himself giving his own image.[35] Theodore the Studite made very similar points. Of particular significance for future iconography was the way in which he appealed to the Transfiguration: here Christ's divinity was made manifest, but an image had remained.[36] Jaroslav Pelikan sums up well the significance of the successful resolution of the dispute: 'The ancient priority of hearing in biblical thought ... had now been forced to yield to the priority of seeing, as a consequence of the incarnation. ... As Word, he was still there to be heard and obeyed; but as Light, he was now there to be seen as well—and therefore to be visualised.'[37] Thanks to a controversy over art, Christianity had at last realized the full revolutionary implications of the New Testament, something of which the New Testament itself, in this respect at least, shows no awareness, and thus of the need, if not the necessity, to go beyond the strictures of the Old upon all imagery.

The irony, though, is that despite this dispute and clarification having taken place in the East, it is now often Eastern Christendom which is most resistant to carrying through the full implications of the incarnation for art. Thus it is not infrequent to

---

[34] For Clement, e.g. *Stromateis* VI, 16, 18 and *Exhortation to the Heathen*, IV, 57–62. For Origen, e.g. *Contra Celsum* VI. 66.

[35] *Orations on the Holy Icons*, esp. I, 15; II, 5; III, 8; III, 26.

[36] *Refutations* III, 1. 53. Of particular importance was the claim that the unity of Christ's person entailed his definition, without thereby implying that divinity was itself defined.

[37] J. Pelikan, *Imago Dei: The Byzantine Apologia for Icons* (Princeton, NJ: Princeton University Press, 1990), 99.

find among Eastern Christians objections to Western religious art
that it has sold the pass to secularism in paintings like Grünewald's
Isenheim altarpiece: the humanity has become so dominant that it
is possible only to speak of a divine absence.[38] But the question
could be posed in reverse: does Orthodoxy so stress the divinity
that the humanity is undermined? One particular problem has
been Orthodoxy's assumption that it is now in possession of very
definite canons for religious art,[39] and with that tends to go the
assumption that these canons have never changed.[40] As one art
historian remarks, 'despite the changes on every side, the
Byzantines maintained a fiction of continuity'.[41] But, just as its
liturgy has undergone a considerable number of developments,[42]
so too has the tradition of icon painting both thematically and on
this question of the presentation of the more human side of the
story of salvation.

Thus the eleventh and twelfth centuries do mark a considerable
softening of presentation, with a more motherly Mary and the first
appearance of Christ as the Man of Sorrows. In the late
Comnenian period we even find a frail, timid Virgin Mary and an
emotional Christ yielding to anger.[43] Changes in religious practice
may have facilitated these new emphases.[44] Further change under
Western influence is often equivocally condemned. While much
was of poor quality, it is interesting to find the early El Greco now
viewed as already a product of such a meeting of East and West,
with one of his predecessors in Crete even seen as a potential rival

---

[38] The view, for instance, of M. Quenot, *The Icon: Window on the Kingdom*
(London: Mowbray, 1992), 72–83, esp. 80.

[39] e.g. Quenot, Ibid., 66–72.

[40] Particularly marked are the repeated condemnations of innovation in L.
Ouspensky, *Theology of the Icon* (New York: St Vladimer's, Crestwood, 1992).
e.g. I, 144, 167; II, 323.

[41] J. Lowden, *Early Christian and Byzantine Art* (London: Phaidon, 1997),
187.

[42] Cf. H. Wybrew, *The Orthodox Liturgy* (London: SPCK, 1989).

[43] So K. Weitzmann, 'The icons of Constantinople', in K. Weitzmann et al.,
Icons (London: Studio Editions, 1987), 19, 64, 52, 64.

[44] H. Belting, *Bild und Kult: Eine Geschichte des Bildes vor dem Zeitalter der
Kunst* (Munich: C. H. Beck'sche Verlagsbuchhandlung (Oscar Beck), 1990), ch.
13; R. Cormack, *Painting the Soul* (London: Reaktion Books, 1997), 157 ff.
Changes in liturgy and in the internal form of the building (in the screen and in
the increasing introduction of icon stands) are both noted.

to Duccio in that creative mix.[45] While the acceptance of some influence for the good from Western art is still rare, it is not unknown even among the hierarchy.[46] However, with so much work still to be done on the history of the icon, it will be simpler if we confine ourselves here to what happened in the West, to illustrate the way in which through the developing tradition new perceptions were able to emerge out of the open character of the artistic text.

Romanesque exuberance and biblical restraint

Though art historians would now commonly acknowledge the way in which the Renaissance grew out of 'Gothic',[47] originally 'Gothic' was a term of disapprobation, coined by Vasari in the sixteenth century to denote the barbarism of the Goths from which Europe had only recently extricated itself. Discontinuity was thus stressed. It took until the nineteenth century before Romanesque was separately identified (in 1818).[48] Here too the term was pejorative, for, though at least continuity was acknow-ledged ('of the Roman'), the intention was still originally abusive, to suggest inferior copying. Nowadays for most people the origin of both terms is lost in the mists of history. Even so, the tendency remains to see the artists of those generations caught in the dead weight of tradition and deprived of significant opportunities for creative innovation that later generations were to enjoy. But, as Romanesque well illustrates, nothing could be further from the truth.

That there was borrowing from the Roman past no one would deny, either generally, as with the barrel vault, or more specifi-cally, as in the way in which the triple arch arrangement of the

[45] Cormack *Painting*, 167 ff. Angelos Akotantos (d. 1457) is compared to Duccio: 78, 182 ff.

[46] e.g. the lack of innovation in modern Greek icons is lamented by Metropolitan Athanasios Papas in 'Kontinuität und Erneuerung in der Ikonenmalerei', *L'icone dans la théologie et l'art* (Chambésy, Geneva: Éditions du Centre Orthodoxe, 1990), 265–74.

[47] With discontinuities of course also acknowledged: E. Panofsky, *Renaissance and Renascences* (New York: Harper & Row, 1969), 1–41, esp. 36 ff.

[48] For a fuller history and references, M. F. Hearn, *Romanesque Sculpture* (Oxford: Phaidon, 1981), 168 n. 28.

triforium of Autun Cathedral reflects the pattern of the Roman city's gates.[49] But nowadays a wider range of influence is generally acknowledged. One recent major investigation of the origins of the style,[50] for example, includes Byzantium, Armenia and both Muslim and Christian art in Syria. A heavy debt to the Middle East may seem implausible, until it is recalled how much movement of people in fact took place in early medieval Europe, not only through the monasteries and pilgrimage but also through conquest (e.g. Arabs in Spain, Normans in Sicily) and through trade (small-scale work in ivory could later be transposed to large-scale sculpture). John of Salisbury, for instance, made journeys across the Alps no less than ten times.[51] The result is that even in the Dark Ages and in distant Scotland there could emerge the eighth-century Ruthwell Cross whose themes and patterns are heavily indebted to Eastern models.[52]

Such range of borrowing suggests anything but narrowness of perspective, and indeed a number of commentators draw attention to the Romanesque's sheer aesthetic delight in creativity compared to the more didactic assumptions which prevailed under Gothic.[53] It was an attitude which could legitimate the incorporation of a Saracen saddle into a silver cross at Conques,[54] include a cameo of Augustus in the Lothar cross, and even give the head of the Empress Livia to Christ (Herimann cross) as well as copy on one of the doors of the cathedral at Le Puy in Kufic script the phrase 'All power to Allah'.[55] Only gradually, particularly with the Crusades, did more negative attitudes prevail.[56] All of this surely

---

[49] So A. Petzold, *Romanesque Art* (London: Weidenfeld & Nicolson, 1995), 143.

[50] V. I. Atroshenko and J. Collins, *The Origins of the Romanesque* (London: Lund Humphries, 1985).

[51] One of the examples given by G. Zarnecki in making the same point in *Romanesque* (Huntingdon, Cambs.: Herbert Press, 1989), 11–13.

[52] So Atroshenko and Collins, *Origins*, 130; supported by M. Schapiro, 'The religious meaning of the Ruthwell Cross', *Arts Bulletin* 26, (1944), 229–45; for more detailed recent analysis, B. Cassidy (ed.), *The Ruthwell Cross* (Princeton, NJ: Princeton University Press, 1992).

[53] e.g. M. Schapiro, 'On the aesthetic attitude in Romanesque art', *Selected Papers I: Romanesque Art* (London: Thames & Hudson, 1993), 1–27.

[54] Ibid., 17.   [55] Petzold, *Romanesque Art*, 141–2, 146.

[56] Contrast, for instance, the substantial Jewish town houses which survive from this earlier period at Norwich and Lincoln.

suggests a delight and joy in human creativity that is immeasurably wider than what was ever conceived or permitted by biblical revelation.

The most obvious evidence for such delight is in the building explosion itself, which took place following the collapse of expectations of an immediate end of the world at the turn of the first millennium.[57] Christians tend to forget how negative the Bible in fact is about building. The first building, Babel, is a symbol of human pride and arrogance (Gen. 11: 1–9). Even the building of God's own house, the Temple, is only conceded with reluctance (1 Chron. 28: 2–3), and is soon rescinded with the prophets' threats of its destruction, while the New Testament repeatedly underlines its view that we have here 'no continuing city' (Heb. 13: 14; cf. Matt. 6: 19; Luke 17: 28–29). If in response is set the continuing focus of Old Testament hopes on the city of Jerusalem and the way in which the book of Revelation takes up that theme with its longing for the new Jerusalem, one needs to note that what is stressed thereby is surely the importance of community and not any inherent value in architecture or any other form of artistic creativity. Indeed, the images of the city offered in the last book of the Bible defy the visual imagination.[58] Of course the Romanesque builders did not see themselves as rejecting the biblical view. Instead they found a mediating theology, according to which the building itself was seen as a model of the heavenly Jerusalem, like the biblical witness pointing beyond itself. But in effect their activity did open up for Christianity a new way of perceiving the world, still transient but also capable of being enjoyed in and for itself. Within such a context the pleasure that Reginald of Durham experiences in describing in detail the rich textiles which surrounded Cuthbert's body should occasion us no surprise.[59]

In some cases the borrowings may even have been subliminal. In a major study of the use of the classical orders in architecture from antiquity to the Renaissance John Onians has argued persuasively

[57] How influential these fears were is still hotly debated: B. McGinn, *Antichrist* (San Francisco: Harper, 1994), 97, 310.

[58] This issue is discussed in Chapter 3 of *Discipleship and Imagination*.

[59] Reginald of Durham, *Libellus de admirandis beati Cuthberti virtutibus*, ed. J. Raine (Surtees Society Publ., 1835), ch. 42, 87 ff.

for their symbolic use, even if more often than not, like our bodily gestures, they received (and needed) no explicit explanation in order to be understood.[60] In the Greek world, once Doric and Ionic came to be used in combination, Doric was in the main used for the outside of buildings, Ionic for the interior, and the Romans continued this practice of using the more intricate and complex to draw the worshipper into a building. In the Christian dispensation this practice appears to have been continued, with a progressive hierarchy of importance (with some exceptions) indicated by an ascending scale of Doric, Ionic, Corinthian, and Composite. It was a pattern which preceded from the outside in, culminating in wherever the high altar stood. Even apparent exceptions are given plausible alternative explanations by Onians.[61] Once again one notes the lack of embarrassment in such classical borrowings, however subliminally the symbolism may have been appropriated.

Although Onians is able to make occasional use of texts, such as the ninth-century writings of Rabanus Maurus, overwhelmingly it is to the plans of church buildings that he must appeal. A similar lack of written evidence prevents any incontestable answer as to why so many strange forms are sculptured on Romanesque churches. It was, famously, this feature to which St Bernard took such exception: 'To what purpose are those unclean apes, those fierce lions, those monstrous centaurs, those half men, those striped tigers, those fighting knights, those hunters winding their horns?'[62] Yet the previous sentence demonstrates that they were not without their power on Bernard also. For though asking 'what profit is there in these ridiculous monsters' he adds 'in that marvellous and deformed beauty, in that beautiful deformity?' His Latin even heightens the sense of paradox, showing that Bernard was not unaware of the strength of his own admission: *mira quaedam deformis formositas ac formosa deformitas.* Most commentators follow Bernard in assuming a purely aesthetic purpose. But, while that no

---

[60] J. Onians, *Bearers of Meaning* (Cambridge: Cambridge University Press, 1988), 5.

[61] For Pisa and Speyer, 102; 108–11; for another apparent counter-example from an earlier period, St Maria Maggiore, 67–8.

[62] From his *Apologia* (to William of St. Thierry) in *A Documentary History of Art*, ed. E. G. Holt (Princeton, NJ: Princeton University Press, 1947), 21.

doubt played its part, from looking at the representations themselves there is good reason to conclude that rather more was at stake.

Denis Grivot in his series of books on the magnificent Romanesque cathedral at Autun has been particularly effective in highlighting what this might be. In his *Bestiare d'Autun* he identifies a number of reasons: there is desire to declare all the world open to Christ, including the fabled creatures of distant parts; there is need to acknowledge the power of evil in all its forms and, more importantly, its subjection to Christ; finally, there is the desire to use every form of animal decoration, including that hallowed by the pre-Christian world.[63] In a few cases there is biblical precedent through the Vulgate. For instance, the men of Gammad, who in Ezekiel fight on behalf of Tyre from its towers, emerge as pygmies in Jerome's version, while one of the psalms has 'basilisk' (combination of bird and reptile) in place of the more mundane modern 'snake' (Ezek. 27: 11; Ps. 91: 13). The story of pygmies' battles against cranes is at least as old as Homer, and may indeed even have some basis in fact in the behaviour of the African Akka peoples.[64] Many of the more fabulous monsters, however, seem to derive ultimately from India, in particular from the travel lore of Ctesias, Greek physician to the Persian court, in the fourth century BC. Long after Honorius of Autun related such tales in the twelfth century they were still being accepted as fact in Western Europe. We do not here have gratuitous invention. At the same time their use is clearly also intended symbolically. Thus at Autun we find, for instance, the sculpture of a griffin (combination of eagle and lion) apparently triumphantly stepping on a man, unaware that a sword is already piercing his belly, a basilisk being defeated by a special shield through which he could not see, and even a naked man so confidently wielding a sword against a gigantic bird that we are left in no doubt who will win.[65] In the following century such defeat of the monsters is more commonly directly related to Christ, with their bodies trampled beneath the Saviour's feet. But

[63] D. Grivot, *Bestiare d'Autun* (Lyons: Ange Michel, 1973).
[64] Homer, *Iliad*, 3.1–7. Nineteenth century explorers discovered that the dwarfs of central Africa did in fact hunt cranes.
[65] D. Grivot, *Twelfth Century Sculpture in the Cathedral of Autun* (Colmar: SAEP, no date), 17–18, 61–3.

even so the message is surely still the same, given the context in which such sculptures are placed: that with Christ and his Church on one's side one has nothing more to fear.

There was of course another, more negative side which cannot be denied, the depiction of such monsters exacting terrible punishment upon sinners. But even here we must guard against confusing Romanesque with later medieval and more neurotic attitudes to death and judgement. A wide variety of factors needs to be noted, some of which touch closely upon our central theme of incarnation as the endorsement of artistic creativity. However, this is not to deny that part of the aim was to evoke terror at wrongdoing. Autun makes that clear in one of its Latin inscriptions: *terreat hic terror quos terreus alligat error*—'let this horror cower those bound by earthly wrong' (though even here there is beauty in the alliteration and punning). But there are at least three other factors to be borne in mind. The first (and least important) relates to the role of humour or satire. In a recent discussion of the way lust and its punishment were treated at this time, the authors make much of the role misogyny played.[66] But it seems to me that they are on stronger ground when they concede the often comic or absurd character of the figures displaying so publicly their private parts.[67] The spectator is forced to ask: Who wants to act the fool like that? Secondly, there is the way in which such depictions of punishment would answer to the viewer's sense of a fitting retribution. Significantly, despite God's promise to save the murderer Cain, later Jewish legend had him executed by Lamech and this finds its reflection in many a Romanesque Cathedral, including Autun and Modena.[68] Finally and most importantly, such judgement always remains set within the promise of salvation. It is no accident that the judgement theme is placed in the tympanum above the west door as one enters a church and so passes within the ark of salvation. It is here that Gislebertus, the great sculptor of Autun, chose to sign his name, and despite the seriousness of his theme he loses none of the liveliness, warmth and compassion which he shows

[66] A. Weir and J. Jerman, *Images of Lust* (London: Batsford, 1986), e.g. 22, 64.
[67] Ibid., 23 ff.
[68] J. L. Kugel, *In Potiphar's House* (Cambridge, Mass.: Harvard University Press, 1990), 159–72; Grivot, 39–40; B. Young, *The Villein's Bible: Stories in Romanesque Carving* (London: Barrie & Jenkins, 1990), 27.

elsewhere. So for instance the Archangel Michael is shown cheating in our favour on the scales, while three young children dance with joy about an angel.[69] The significance of that last factor is too often underestimated. Perhaps my point can be underlined most effectively by drawing a parallel with what I said about the nativity in Chapter 2 and the artistic transformations to which it was subject. For Matthew the wise men are astrologers, the pagan counterpart of the longings expressed in Old Testament prophecy. In the artistic tradition, however, they are transformed into three kings,[70] and as such (each representing a third of the known world) are found leading all humanity to Christ, as at St Apollinare Nuovo at Ravenna, and indeed even rushing to do so as on the facade of Verona Cathedral. The shepherds can then effectively represent poor people, while the addition of the animals[71] ensures that the wider creation too has become part of this scene of universal adoration. Instead of Gentile and pagan, the focus has moved; king and pauper, human and animal, all now find their fulfilment in Christ. All creation has been brought together in a single focused image.

That is, I believe, what happens also in Romanesque's treatment of the theme of judgement. Apart from its opening and closing chapters, for most Christians the Revelation of St John the Divine fails to work imaginatively, and the result is that the book is left mostly unread. In part the problem seems to lie in the author's own attitude to imagery, since a riot of Old Testament metaphor is offered without regard to its visual impact. In other words, what we have is essentially a literary rather than an imaginative creation. The book's failure on the visual level is well illustrated by the finest attempt to recreate it visually, in the late fourteenth-century Angers tapestry. Though beautifully worked, it lacks conviction and thus also impact. Dürer's fifteen woodcuts on the same theme seem to me even less successful, as is indicated by his need to add texts. Little wonder then that Romanesque sculptors resorted to composite images. It is fascinating to observe how far this in fact went. Though Christ in judgement is the

[69] Grivot, 4–5.   [70] Based on Isa. 60: 1–6; Ps. 72: 10–11.
[71] Based on Isa. 1: 3 and, though corrected in Jerome's Vulgate, the Septuagint version of Habakkuk 3: 2: 'in the midst of two creatures shalt thou be known.'

normal pattern, one also finds ascension and second coming merged (as at Charlieu and Moissac) and Christ's final significance even conveyed by means of Pentecost (as at Vézelay).[72] The aim was presumably to offer a theophany of Christ's presence and significance rather than place the imagery at a specific point in time.[73] In this the tympana succeed marvellously well. Of course like Revelation they take judgement seriously and so as with that book there are plenty of gruesome punishments portrayed, but these are never allowed to overwhelm in the way in which the consecutive character of a narrative treatment so easily can. Indeed, occasionally the punishments disappear altogether from the tympana as with Moissac's unqualified hymn of praise or Vézelay's refusal to limit those who stream towards Christ for salvation; included are pygmies, *cynocephali* (men with dog's heads) and Scythians with huge ears. Judgement placed at a specific point in history thus seems less important than lordship. Nothing is outside the Lord's domain. All creation, however odd, is his, as is all human creativity, whether explicitly Christian or not.

Now that the Reformation arguments about the destruction of images in churches are for most of us firmly in the past it is very easy to lose sight of how uncompromising the biblical attitude in fact is. Jerome's version of the second commandment could scarcely be more explicit: *Non facies tibi sculptile.*[74] Even treating it as only a part of the first commandment (as the medieval church and Luther did) might lessen the embarrassment, but the uncompromising character of the condemnation is still there for all to read: the sculpting of images is condemned unequivocally. As we shall see in the next section, this generated much anxiety in the later Middle Ages, long before the outbreak of the Reformation and among those for whom its specific type of reform would have held little appeal. For the truth, in my view, is that, if we rely on the general thrust of Scripture alone, the iconoclasts were right. The result has been a history of very gradual acceptance of the legitimacy of artistic images, with the Church only moving gradually from symbols to

---

[72] M. F. Hearn, *Romanesque Sculpture*, 135–7, 170–4. The interpretation of Vézelay is contested; for the rival interpretations and bibliography, ibid., 172.

[73] The view argued for by Hearn, *Romanesque Sculpture*, 169–91.

[74] Vulgate: Exod. 20: 4. Deut. 4: 15–31 is a passage of constantly reiterated hostility to images.

specific scenes and finally to the most sacred elements in the story, and all in the context of periodic counterattacks, which, as we shall see in our final chapter, have continued into our own day.

In the iconoclastic controversy, much was made of the various biblical passages in which reference is made to the role of the cherubim in the Temple or in visions of God. To these might be added God's appearance in fire, cloud and so forth, but, as Calvin remarked in his own iconoclastic attack, these need to be read in context, as declaring the incomprehensibility and invisibility of God, and thus his exclusion from representation. That is why symbols are used, and why the cherubim conceal the mercy seat with their wings.[75] Though we cannot now know for certain what was intended by the borrowing of the imagery of cherubim, the purpose may have been not only to mark the presence of divinity as in the surrounding paganism, but also the otherness of God: the very unnaturalism of the figures might suggest as much.[76] Certainly, in such passages it is hard to find any hint of joy in artistic creativity, or even in descriptions of the construction of the Temple, where what gives pride is not its artfulness, but rather its scale and the costliness of its materials (1 Kings 6). Among the tasks with which I was entrusted during the decade when I was a member of the Doctrine Commission of the Church of England was the writing of a chapter endorsing artistic creativity. Deference to the biblical presumptions of the other members required that I began with Scripture as a foundation, and I remember well how extraordinarily difficult it proved adequately so to found our position.[77]

One can of course contextualize biblical opposition, by noting the way in which in the Old Testament we have a people struggling to resist the allurements of larger nations and their religions, while in the New pre-occupation with the inauguration of the

[75] Calvin, *Institutes of the Christian Religion* (Philadelphia: Westminster Press, 1960), I, xi, 4 (I, 102–3). For the growth in Calvin's hostility, D. Augsburger, 'Calvin et le second commadement', in O. Fatio and P. Fraenkel (eds.), *Histoire de l'exégèse au XVIe siècle* (Geneva: Librairie Droz, 1978), 84–94.
[76] Usually, a winged lion or bull with a human face and wings, but other combinations occur.
[77] The result was 'The Spirit and creativity', in C. of E. Doctrine Commission Report, *We Believe in the Holy Spirit* (London: Church House Publishing, 1991), 147–69. Perhaps the most favoured passage is Exod. 35: 30 ff.

new age left no time to acknowledge the existing virtues of a passing civilization. But even with that said, we are left with little
upon which to build. The history of Judaism is surely in itself a
witness to the difficulty. For, despite the outstanding gifts of the
Jewish people in literature and music, it is not until modern times
that we find Judaism rivalling Christianity or even Islam in the
field of art.[78] Even then, the relationship of the artists to their
Jewish roots is seldom straightforward. Camille Pissarro avoided
religious themes, while R. B. Kitaj reflects as an agnostic on the
agonies of Jewish history.[79] Several American abstract expression-
ists were Jews, but significantly what their art stressed was the
possibility of at most hinting at the divine, not in any sense its
participation in the canvass. Chagall might seem the obvious
exception, but even here it is his own highly personalized and
inclusive creed that made the explicitly religious dimension in his
art possible.[80] More typical, therefore, are the dilemmas so powerfully exposed by Chaim Potok in his two moving novels about a
Hasidic Jew's calling to be an artist.[81]

The New Testament in itself provides no qualification of such
attitudes. We need therefore, in my view, to admit candidly that it
was only from the Church's later history that a critique could be
thrown back upon scriptural assumptions through a refocused
understanding of the full implications of the incarnation. It took the
very different social context of a now confident Church to trans-
form the Bible's suspicion of imagery as necessarily corrupting into
the aid to faith that it can undoubtedly be, and with it to bring a
still more powerful sense of the universality of the gospel message,
in both giving and receiving. None of this is to deny the numerous passages in the Bible that take divine creativity as their theme,
but it is to claim that for a proper assessment of human creativity

---

[78] This is not to deny the existence of some fine medieval manuscript illustrations: D. Godstein, *Hebrew Manuscript Painting* (London: British Library, 1985);
B. Narkiss, *The Golden Haggadah* (London: British Library, 1997).

[79] For Kitaj's relation to Judaism, M. Livingstone, *Kitaj* (London: Phaidon,
2nd edn., 1992), 7–46, esp. 29.

[80] The contrast between his Orthodox upbringing and own personal creed
are well brought out in his early biography of 1922: *My Life* (New York: Da
Capo, 1994) e.g. 115.

[81] *My Name is Asher Lev* (1988); *The Gift of Asher Lev* (1990). Both are available in Penguin (1992).

we must go beyond Scripture. The letter of Scripture misleads; so does its general thrust. Only by contemplating God's sketch or portrayal of himself in the incarnation, as did later Christianity both explicitly and implicitly, can we arrive at the truth. Continuing revelation has now taken us well beyond the canon of Scripture.

Gothic Art: incarnation as identification

In turning now to the history of Gothic, I shall begin and end by noting the degree of continuity or otherwise with Romanesque on the question of human creativity. As we shall see, the period opens with its strong endorsement, whereas by its end we note various anxieties which anticipate the Reformation. Yet, if in its attitude to other cultures Gothic in some ways narrowed Romanesque's largeness of vision, it could also claim to have carried further forward comprehension of the full implications of the doctrine of the incarnation in other ways. These in particular concern God's identification with us in Christ, and the related issue of our identification with him. My discussion proceeds by three stages. We look first at the extent of the developments in Gothic that took place up to the time of the Reformation, then at some of the factors that led to such changes. Finally, we consider how far they can be justified biblically, before concluding with some reflections on the price that was paid even in the Middle Ages for too close an observance of biblical injunctions.

From Saint-Denis to Grünewald

We begin then with a continuity. The origins of Gothic are commonly dated to the work of the Abbot Suger (d. 1151) at St-Denis, near Paris. What is less well known is his turbulent relation with St Bernard, whose hostility to the exuberance of Romanesque carvings we have already noted. Suger's innovations met with no less fierce a condemnation until Bernard's silence was bought by Suger's securing Bernard's uninhibited access to the French King.[82] Though the exotic creatures went, the extravagance and lack of

---

[82] So E. Panofsky, 'Abbot Suger of St. Denis', in *Meaning in the Visual Arts* (Harmondsworth: Penguin, 1970), 139–80, esp. 149–55.

simplicity remained. Yet there was at least a simplicity of architectural form, and this has led some to suggest that Bernard was influential after all, especially when taken in combination with the Platonic ideas of the school of Chartres, itself soon to have a cathedral exhibiting a similar pattern of innovation.[83]

St-Denis was of course dedicated to a saint who at that time was thought to be at once contemporary of Paul, and author of various Platonic writings.[84] Yet, however influential these may have been, Suger's own defence of his restoration and rebuilding of his monastery leaves us in no doubt that his primary inspiration is sacramental and incarnational. There is repeated emphasis on the ability of the material to point beyond itself, 'transferring that which is material to that which is immaterial'. So for instance when confronted with a richly adorned altar he declares: 'I can be transported from this inferior to that higher world in an anagogical manner.'[85] However, the Platonic overtones quickly merge into a strongly sacramental attitude, and thereby a strong connection with the incarnation is already established. Particularly pertinent to our present discussion is the way in which in pursuing such an argument Suger does not hesitate implicitly to expand (and even correct) Scripture. Commenting on the twelve central columns as symbolic of the twelve apostles and the others in the side aisles as representative of the prophets, he appeals to Ephesians 2: 19–22, but adds two glosses in the midst of the quotation: 'built upon the foundation of the apostles and the prophets, Jesus Christ himself being the cornerstone which joins one wall to the other; in whom all the building—whether spiritual or material—groweth into one holy temple in the Lord'.[86] If Panofsky is right,[87] the first addition ('joins one wall to another') alludes to Christ's two natures, and so would be a way of reinforcing the sacramental, incarnational point we have already noted, with the human or earthly as a medium towards the divine. But it has no justification

---

[83] O. von Simson, *The Gothic Cathedral* (Princeton, NJ: Princeton University Press, 3rd edn., 1988), esp. 21–58.

[84] Dionysius the Areopagite (*c.* 500) was identified with the person of the same name who heard Paul in Athens: Acts 17: 34.

[85] *De Administratione* 33; *Abbot Suger on the Abbey Treasures of St. Denis*, ed. and trans. E. Panofsky (Princeton, NJ: Princeton University Press, 2nd edn.), 63–5.   [86] *De Consecratione* 5; Panofsky, *Abbot Suger*, 105.

[87] Ibid., his commentary, 241–2.

in the original text; still less has the second gloss ('whether spiritual or material') which in fact subverts the original, where a purely metaphorical meaning for 'building' is clearly intended. Because Suger thus departs quite substantially from the intention of the author of the letter to the Ephesians, a natural reaction would be to dismiss immediately such a 'misuse' of Scripture. But it is also possible to view the matter differently: as the drawing out of ideas not fully appreciated at the time at which the biblical canon was formulated. In the previous section that was what I suggested happened in the Romanesque period, but here we have a rare example of the justification for such a procedure being made as explicit in the West as we found was the case in Eastern Christendom. Suger does more than gloss the text he uses; he fundamentally alters its meaning. Nowhere does Paul or any of his early followers endorse the creation of beautiful buildings. Indeed, almost certainly they would have regarded any such intention as at best an irrelevance, and at worst a blasphemy. Yet Suger, like John of Damascus and Theodore the Studite, saw that the incarnation made a quite different demand. Even so, such a view was to create terrible tensions in the Gothic world. For, as we shall see, the condemnatory force of Scripture was such that—absurdly—Jews and Muslims were made to take the blame for wrongful image-making, whereas in fact disobedience to the second commandment was—rightly—the Church's own. A Church no longer struggling to establish Christ's precise significance (almost no one now doubted his divinity) nor any more looking for the new age just over the horizon (the millennium was well past) could afford to reflect at leisure and draw different conclusions. Indeed, it is arguable that it was the Gothic age that gave greater significance to incarnation than any other.

Not that Gothic was by any means a uniform development across Europe. If we measure change by distinctive architectural elements, for instance, Germany was a full century later with Cologne Cathedral (begun in 1248), while Spain was only slightly earlier in following the French example with Burgos and Toledo.[88] Italy was even later: its most conspicuous exemplar was not to appear until work was begun on Milan cathedral in 1387. Till late in the day the superior building competence of the Italian

---

[88] Begun, respectively, in 1222 and 1226.

masons made them question whether they had anything to learn from foreigners.[89] It is hard to generalize, but of one thing we may be certain: that everywhere, however gradually, Gothic brought an increased emphasis on Christ's humanity. In a moment we shall have to consider the reasons for such a stress, but first we may simply note the phenomenon itself.

As one writer puts it,

> the Christian concept of the worth of the individual soul ... only achieved its first full expression eleven hundred years after the death of Christ, in the column statues of St-Denis and Chartres. The statues, seen by thousands of pilgrims at these important shrines ... gave new intensity to the doctrine of the incarnation through the radiance of the spirit proclaimed by the stone from which they were carved.[90]

Thus expressed we have of course a point that applies more widely than the treatment of Christ himself. Humanity (in the evaluative sense of the term), characterization, and sentiment are gradually applied right across the range of figures being represented. Insufficient survives from St-Denis to provide an illustration, but the various phases of the Chartres programme, the experts tell us, 'steadily increase in degree of humanisation'.[91] Somewhat paradoxically, even angels are eventually made to participate in this trend, as in the wonderful smile on the face of the thirteenth century angel of the annunciation at Rheims.[92]

Though this change, as we shall see, was motivated in part by a general change in attitude to what it is to be human, the key role played by a changing approach to the incarnation should not be underestimated. Our humanity becomes more personal because this is what has happened to Christ's. The contrast with what has gone before is well illustrated by the difference between the Romanesque Christ in judgement at Autun and how the same theme was now portrayed at Chartres. The former towers so

---

[89] So A. Martindale, *Gothic Art* (London: Thames & Hudson, 1967), 36–40, 145–6, 256.

[90] W. Anderson, *The Rise of the Gothic* (London: Hutchinson, 1985), 85.

[91] A. Katzenellenbogen, *The Sculptural Programs of Chartres Cathedral* (New York: Norton Library, 1964), 91.

[92] Illustration 109 in Anderson, *Rise*, 135; cf. ill. 92 in F. Deuchler, *Gothic* (London: Herbert Press, 1989).

hugely over all the other figures that awe before his divinity remains one's primary reaction, whereas at Chartres there is a soft-ness to his features (particularly his eyes) which suggests someone who has truly entered into our own condition.[93] It is an approach which one finds still more marked in depictions of Christ's birth and death, as their iconography developed. To Emile Mâle, whose multi-volumed work on the history of this period still dominates its interpretation, the thirteenth century represents its culmina-tion.[94] For him it has a mystery and serenity which later Gothic replaces by sentimentality and morbidity.[95] But it is also possible to view these developments more positively as a continuing powerful appropriation of the full meaning of the incarnation.

Let me return once more to the theme of how Christ's birth was portrayed, though this time giving some different examples from those noted in Chapter 2. Prior to *c.* 1300 the annunciation had an extremely simple format of two figures standing, as on the doorway of the Chapter House of Westminster Abbey,[96] whereas later presentations, partly under the influence of Pseudo-Bonaventure's *Meditations on the Life of Christ*,[97] make Gabriel and the Virgin kneel to each other in turn, the angel before the bearer of God incarnate and the Virgin as she hears his solemn words. Such a development made easier the viewer's active identification with Mary's thoughtful acceptance of her role, as in Giotto's moving portrayal, where both appear to kneel,[98] or Simone Martini's troubled Virgin, overwhelmed by the task which she has been assigned.[99] It was also thanks to Pseudo-Bonaventure that the

---

[93] Ill. 67 in Anderson, *Rise*, 92.

[94] E. Mâle, *L'art religieux du XIIIe siècle en France* (1898) and *L'art religieux de la fin du moyen âge en France* (1908). Available in English in two volumes as *Religious Art in France* (Princeton, NJ: Princeton University Press, 1984–6).

[95] This perspective emerges particularly clearly in his own summary of his ideas in *Religious Art from the Twelfth to the Eighteenth Century* (Princeton, NJ: Princeton University Press, 1982).

[96] Figs. 270, 271 in A. Gardner, *English Medieval Sculpture* (Cambridge: Cambridge University Press, 1951).

[97] Pseudo-Bonaventure, *Meditations on the Life of Christ*, eds. I. Ragusa and R. B. Green (Princeton, NJ: Princeton University Press, 1961), 14–21, esp. 14. Gabriel kneels first, then Mary.

[98] A. M. Spiazzi, *The Scrovegni Chapel in Padua* (Milan: Electra, 1993), 24–5.

[99] Ill. 152 in A. Martindale, *Gothic Art*, 205–6; C. Jannella, *Simone Martini* (Florence: Scala, 1989), 67–70.

depiction of Mary reading took on an increased importance. Originally intended merely to allude to Isaiah's prophecy (Isa. 7: 14) it now became the symbol of a woman at prayer (and thereby also implicitly of the entitlement of women to education).[100] Indeed, one of the surprises of any detailed investigation of modes of representation is the great extent to which the annunciation was used as a vehicle for exploring appropriate responses to the gospel.[101]

The birth itself also took on a more human character. Mâle waxes lyrical over the common thirteenth-century representation, as at Laon, where Mary lies in what looks like a church with the infant on its altar: 'In the presence of such a mystery, human feelings are silenced, even maternal love … Such a grand and theological conception is indeed far from the picturesque "crèches" which appeared in the fifteenth century and marked the end of great religious art.'[102] But, however powerfully it speaks of Christ's future sacrificial and eucharistic role, it fails to allow easily for our own identification with Christ, and so stands in marked contrast to the Holy Family scenes that were to emerge later and for which Mâle so often expresses scant respect. Around 1300 we already find Joseph lovingly holding the child, while 1400 sees the Holy Family as a model for the human family.[103] Mary and the child are also made to interact, sometimes in playful ways, as in the numerous variations on the child toying with his mother's veil.[104]

A similar pattern emerges for the end of Christ's life. The West slowly extricated itself from the traditional Byzantine way of displaying the crucifixion as a triumph rather than shared suffering. So instead of an empty cross, or one with a lamb or a human figure reigning in glory, we get Christ's sufferings shown in more and

[100] The theme was occasionally even expanded into lessons in music: M. Vloberg, *La Vierge et L'Enfant dans l'art francais* (Paris: Arthaud, 1954), 206–12.

[101] Stressed in P. Ladoué, 'La scène de l'annonciation vue par les peintres', *Gazette des beaux arts* 6 (1952), 351–70. Even Joseph makes an occasional appearance, as in work by the Master of Flémalle: 365.

[102] *Religious Art in France: The Thirteenth Century* (Princeton, NJ: Princeton University Press, 1984), 191–2, fig. 130.

[103] H. van Os, *The Art of Devotion* (London: Merrol Holberton, 1995), 76–7, 91–2, figs. 23 and 27. Joseph, however, did not assume major significance until the Counter-Reformation.

[104] F. Deuchler, *Gothic*, 82 and the thirteen illustrations listed there.

more explicit detail, not only in the crucifixion itself but also in a number of other focused images, particularly the Pietà of Mary cradling her dead son, and that of the Man of Sorrows. Ironically, the latter seems initially to have been based on Byzantine models, but in the West this soon went far beyond the simple inclination of the head of *c.* 1300 to indicate suffering, just as the *arma Christi* (the symbols of the Passion), which before 1300 had been seen exclusively as emblems of victory, were now turned into summonses towards empathy and compassion.[105]

It was a process which was to reach its culmination in 1515 in the Isenheim Altarpiece of the painter we now know as Matthias Grünewald. Reference has already been made to Quenot's negative judgement. One major reason for such negative verdicts is that the undoubtedly gruesome character of the work is so often pulled out of context. It is treated as a work of art, rather than as also an object with a specific purpose and working within a specific tradition. Here Andrée Hayum does well to remind us that it was originally intended for a hospital of the Antonite order, which cared for those suffering from a particularly ravaging illness that produced gangrene, boils, blackened skin and muscular spasms, caused by poisoned rye (ergot) and known then as St Antony's fire.[106] What is particularly original about Hayum's book is the considerable degree to which she finds the artist adapting his skills to say something to the patients in their condition. For instance, St Antony's temptations on one side of the panels become a means of addressing the patients' temptation to lose faith in the face of their great ordeal, made more personal by the fact that the demon on eye level is clearly suffering from a condition like their own, while the lamentation over the dead Christ on the predella splits in such a way that even Christ himself can be seen as a potential amputee.[107] There is not the space here to pursue her case further. Suffice it to observe that she succeeds in carrying much further the argument of the famous nineteenth-century French critic, J. K. Huysmans, who observed:

[105] van Os, 104–5; J. T. Rhodes, 'Ways of Seeing: Christ in Everything', in D. Brown and A. Loades (eds.), *The Sense of the Sacramental* (London: SPCK, 1995), 137–55.
[106] A. Hayum, *The Isenheim Altarpiece: God's Medicine and the Painter's Vision* (Princeton, NJ: Princeton University Press, 1989), 20–2.
[107] Ibid., 29–33.

That awful Christ who hung dying over the altar of the Isenheim hospital would seem to have been made in the image of the ergotics who prayed to him; they must surely have found consolation in the thought that this God they invoked had suffered the same repulsive torments as themselves, and had become flesh in a form as repulsive as their own; they must have felt less forsaken, less contemptible.[108]

Factors for change

Isenheim can thus be read in a very different way from Quenot's, as the culmination of incarnational discovery rather than its perversion. But to what does such a discovery of the full implications of the incarnation owe its origins, and to what extent do these allow the visual text to go beyond the biblical? The two questions are of course not unconnected, in that one set of cultural circumstances may make much easier a perception that is difficult in another, and this would seem to be true in this instance. The terrible ravages of the Black Death can hardly have been the decisive factor, coming as they did in the mid-fourteenth century. The first moves towards a suffering Christ clearly antedate the plague, and in any case would not explain the more joyful aspects of the humanization of Christ, such as in nativity or childhood scenes. In considering instances of the latter, such as Tewkesbury's Virgin teaching her child to walk, or Simone Martini's petulant twelve-year-old objecting to his mother's interrogation, Andrew Martindale suggests a correlation with a more observant, more empirical age.[109] Adolf Katzenellenbogen takes a similar line. In trying to explain what happened at Chartres in the twelfth century he draws attention to the contrast between the teaching of Hugh of St Victor (d. 1141) on the relation between soul and body and that of the local Chartrean philosopher, William of Conches (d. 1154): for the former the body is simply an appendage of the soul, whereas for the latter the soul truly animates and works from within.[110] It is a thesis which has been argued at length by Erwin Panofsky in his essay *Gothic Architecture and Scholasticism*, where he

---

[108] Quoted in E. Ruhmer, *Grünewald* (London: Phaidon, 1958), 25.

[109] A. Martindale, 'The child in the picture; a medieval perspective', in D. Wood (ed.), *The Church and Childhood* (Oxford: Blackwell, 1994), 197–232. esp. 228, 231–2 and frontispiece and plate 13.

[110] *Sculptural Programs*, 43–4 and notes, 123.

postulates more than mere parallel developments: 'It is not very probable that the builders of Gothic structures read Gilbert de la Porrée or Thomas Aquinas in the original. But they were exposed to the scholastic point of view in innumerable other ways,' ways that membership of the same church made possible, most obviously through the sermon.[111] Also, no doubt relevant is the growth of individualism that came with a changing social order, consequent on the growth of towns, and producing a new mercantile class and intellectual élite based first on cathedral schools and then on universities.[112]

In an influential essay it has been argued that initially at least the effect of the Black Death was to slow down such artistic trends. Instead, there was a return to a more majestic Christ, with stress on themes such as judgement, guilt and penance.[113] Though much challenged, the thesis has a plausible ring, inasmuch as the initial response of the time does seem to have been to interpret this plague that perhaps wiped out as much as a third of the population of Europe as an act of divine judgement. Certainly, the inevitable result was building delays and simplification of projects because of the shortage of labour.[114] But in the long term the effect was probably quite otherwise. That very shortage of labour meant greater openings for individual action, and so allowed the reintroduction of the desire for a personal and intimate Saviour.

Such social factors cannot of themselves, though, tell the whole story. Emile Mâle displays in his major study what seems to me a regrettable intellectualism. He declares that the 'artists of the Middle Ages ... were docile interpreters of a great body of thought ... They were rarely permitted to invent; the Church gave over to their fancy only purely decorative work,'[115] and in support of this contention he demonstrates how often the sculptural programmes have their parallels in Vincent of Beauvais's great encyclopedia, *Speculum Maius*. But the truth is that, but for the

---

[111] E. Panofsky, *Gothic Architecture and Scholasticism* (Cleveland: Meridian, 1957), 23.
[112] Cf. C. Morris, *The Discovery of the Individual 1050–1200* (London: SPCK, 1972), esp. ch. 3. [113] M. Meiss, *Painting in Florence*, esp. 70–93.
[114] The principal consequence in England according to P. Lindley, 'The Black Death and English art', in M. Ormrod and P. Lindley (eds.), *The Black Death in England* (Stamford: Paul Watkins, 1996), 125–46.
[115] Mâle, *Religious Art in France*, I, 400.

exceptional case such as Abbot Suger, we simply do not know
how tight a control was exercised. No doubt in some other
instances the controls were just as tight, and sometimes the
programme so intellectual as to necessitate a clerical inspiration.[116]
But at least two factors should be set on the other side. Often
greatest pride and interest was taken in movable artefacts (jewelled
ornaments, rich brocade and so forth) of which we fail to take due
account because the depredations of time and greed have removed
them from view. It was probably such artefacts (which of course
the clergy regularly used) which most attracted their attention, and
this may explain why someone like Gervase of Canterbury fails
even to mention in his account of the cathedral's rebuilding after
fire 'what was perhaps the most ambitious glazing programme
undertaken in Europe up to that date'.[117] Secondly, even where
there was control in some detail, the style would still depend more
on artistic considerations, and it is here, in characterization and
presentation rather than in formal content, that the real changes
were taking place. Small changes in expression or stance could
produce huge changes in the viewer's reaction, as in the loosening
of Christ's limbs over the course of the fourteenth century which
transformed the so-called Mercy-Seat Trinities from purely doctrinal expressions to ones which required an emotional reaction.[118]
Not that all such developments were necessarily enlightening; one
uncomprehending artist, for instance, misread the iconography of
Joseph being referred to heaven for an explanation of Mary's pregnancy and, thinking to heighten the effect, instead left him blinded
by a heavenly light![119] The way in which clerics sometimes
complained of artistic representations also suggest a different view,
since what need would there be to complain, if they had had total
control over the design? So too do the elaborate preparations,
prayerful as well as artistic, we know sculptors sometimes went
through before they undertook their task.[120]

What is particularly encouraging in more recent writing on the

---

[116]   As Mâle himself observes of the imagery for the Seven Liberal Arts, ibid.,
397.
[117]   T. S. Heslop, 'The visual arts and crafts', in B. Ford (ed.), *Medieval Britain*,
(Cambridge: Cambridge University Press, 1988), 173–8, esp. 173.
[118]   van Os, *The Art of Devotion*, 124–5.   [119]   Ibid., 74–5 and 11.
[120]   M. Camille, *The Gothic Idol* (Cambridge: Cambridge University Press,
1989), 211–13.

history of art is, as with Hayum on Isenheim, the way in which it takes much more seriously the artefact's functional role, something which could only be decided on site, as it were, and which demanded a much more serious interchange between artist and client than simply the latter dictating a programme. John Shearman has done this for the Renaissance by demonstrating the various ways in which the artist sought to engage the spectator. The picture, as it were, is 'transitive'; it deliberately invades our space. So, for instance, we are intended to be conscious of standing in the presence of a Pope, with Raphael's *Pope Julius II* (that is why he is seated), of the figures of Titian's *Pesaro Madonna* turning towards us from the side altar as we enter the main body of the church, or of Christ's body in Pontormo's *Entombment* being carried towards us out of the painting and into the burial vault of the church.[121] Shearman several times mentions the continuing influence of Pseudo-Bonaventure,[122] and this is also a text which bulks large in the very similar approach of the recent book from the current Director of the Rijksmuseum in Amsterdam, Henk van Os, *The Art of Devotion*. Though exclusively concerned with small artefacts for private devotion, there is no reason to think that his 'functional' approach[123] does not apply on the larger scale as well, with patrons determining the general nature of the commission and such things as the inclusion of their favourite saint, but the artist always concerned to develop existing artistic tradition in such a way as ensured a truly engaged spectator.

To understand the shared religious character of that engagement we need to travel back well beyond the late thirteenth-century writings of Pseudo-Bonaventure, to St Bernard (d. 1153). For it was he who set the Church upon the path of detailed meditation upon, and identification with events in Christ's life, a pattern that in many ways reached its culmination with the *Spiritual Exercises* of St Ignatius Loyola. Therein of course lies a splendid irony in that, as already noted, Bernard was severely critical of much of the art of his day and indeed at the level of explicit advocacy was responsible for the simple, unadorned churches of the earlier history of Cistercianism. But the passion of his engagement with Christ as

---

[121] J. Shearman, *Only Connect: Art and the Spectator in the Italian Renaissance* (Princeton, NJ: Princeton University Press, 1992), 90–3, 99, 127.

[122] Ibid., e.g. 33, 89.   [123] van Os, *The Art of Devotion*, 8.

reflected in his sermons on the Song of Songs legitimated an emotional identity with Christ's humanity that later spiritual writers were to exploit to the full, and which in turn helped generate a different range of incarnational expression within art. So, for instance, in a sermon on the power of Jesus' name (a veneration not fully developed till St Bernardino of Siena in the fifteenth century), he writes:

I place before myself a man ... who was also himself God almighty, who heals me by his example and strengthens me by his aid. ... So it is that I gather examples from the man and help from his divine power. The former act, as it were, as herbal plants, the latter as the means by which I give them bite, and I make a compound, the like of which no physician could make.[124]

It was a message that was reinforced by his friend and biographer, William of St. Thierry: 'The image of our Lord's humanity—his birth, passion and resurrection—is proposed for prayer and meditation, so that the weak soul, which does not know how to think save of bodies and bodily things might have something to which it might attach itself, to which it might cling in its own way with its own gaze of devotion'.[125]

But such a trend might well have fizzled out, had it not been for the social factors mentioned above and the additional impetus given by the new movement of the friars in the following century. The extent to which Francis was responsible for the inauguration of the crib has already been discussed in Chapter 2. His own lively version and the dramatic performances that it brought in its wake as a way of communicating the faith are believed to have had effects on art both great (increased focus on birth and crucifixion) and small (donkeys on wheels and bodies rising directly from the ground as from stage trap-doors). One recent study of the way in which the Passion was presented in thirteenth-century Italy argues that selective borrowing from Byzantine models resulted under Franciscan influence in major changes in how the narrative was understood. If some developments were unfortunate, on the whole what emerged was a Christ less firmly in control, and so one

---

[124] Bernard of Clairvaux, *Sermones super Cantica Canticorum* 15. 6 (my trans.).
[125] *Epistola ad fratres de Monte Dei*, 174 (my trans.).

with whom one could more fully empathize.[126] Francis' stress on the value of the particular and on observation likewise helped generate new attitudes that were to feed themselves into art. It has been argued that it is no accident that Giotto (d. 1337) was patronized by the Franciscans and contemporary with the nominalist stress on the particular that we find in the philosophy of the Franciscan William of Ockham.[127] Changing attitudes are well illustrated by the condemnation by Caesarius of Arles (d. 542) of the use of any images in monastic cells as contrasted with their enthusiastic endorsement almost a millennium later by the Dominican Henry Suso (d. 1366), who describes himself regularly practising his devotions by looking at images—*nach bildreicher Weise*.[128]

In that same century due account must also be taken of the key role women saints played in fostering such visual devotion, among them Birgitta of Sweden (d. 1377), Catharine of Siena (d. 1380) and Mother Julian of Norwich (d. 1413). Yet as we noted in respect of Catherine at the beginning of this chapter, we must be on our guard against the still dominant assumption that influence only went one way.[129] It is an insidious temptation on the part of the Christian to suppose that God only speaks to the Church through the most devout. Matters are in fact immeasurably more complex. Of course, people like Birgitta, Francis, and Bernard played key roles, but even they were affected by the cultural context in which they lived, however much they also changed it. Equally so were the artists. Sometimes they would consciously innovate, sometimes with little appreciation of what they were doing, but, either way, the ultimate effect on Christian self-understanding could be

---

[126] A, Derbes, *Picturing the Passion in Late Medieval Italy* (Cambridge: Cambridge University Press, 1996). In effect, a *Christus triumphans* gradually yields to a *Christus patiens*. The negative side is the exclusion of Pilate's role in preference to an exclusive focus on Jewish responsibility for the trial: 72–93.

[127] H. B. Gutman, 'The Rebirth of the Fine Arts and Franciscan Thought', *Franciscan Studies* 5 (1945), 215–34; 6 (1946), 3–29.

[128] Caesarius, *Regula Virginum*, 45: *Sources Chrétiennes*, (Paris: Les Éditions de Cerf, 1988) I, 230; *Das Leben des seligen Heinrich Seuse*, 35: K. Bihlmeyer (ed.), *Heinrich Seuse Deutsche Schriften* (Frankfurt: Minerva, 1961), 103.

[129] For an Eastern example of the argument: H. Maguire, *Art and Eloquence in Byzantium* (Princeton, NJ: Princeton University Press, 1981). What the author says is persuasive; it is what he omits that is worrying.

profound. Neither artistic nor religious engagement should be taken to imply passive acceptance. Rather, they gain their power precisely in their capacity to be transformed in the process of engagement.[130]

Biblical reserve: potential and penalty

With that background in the various formative influences in generating the new focus, we may now attempt some estimate of the extent to which these artistic developments may be described as genuinely innovative, in carrying the Christian revelation beyond its original biblical deposit. To clarify matters we need to note at least three senses of 'identification' that require consideration. We may identify with Christ by imitating him. We may identify through identifying with those who in turn identified with him, as for instance Mary rejoicing in the child to whom she has given birth or weeping over her dead son. Finally, God can identify with us in Christ. So, for instance, we may speak of God identifying with our suffering on the cross. Initially, we may think of all three as powerfully present in Scripture, since all three find their reflection in current Christian practice. But, when we probe more deeply, a different picture emerges. Certainly, the beginnings of the first form of identification is there, but the second only minimally and the third perhaps not at all.

Almost certainly Jesus did not speak of imitating himself but rather of imitating God.[131] So it is perhaps not altogether surprising that our earliest Christian writings—from Paul—show such a total lack of interest in the details of Christ's life. Had we to rely solely on Paul, we would know how important crucifixion and resurrection were theologically, and that we were expected to imitate Christ's humility, but we could hardly follow Jesus imaginatively on the way to Golgotha, and even with the resurrection, where Paul gives a little more detail, it is still not much more than a list.[132]

---

[130] For an example, in the way in which even Christ's body functioned as a contested concept in the life of Margery Kempe and others: S. Beckwith, *Christ's Body* (London: Routledge, 1993).

[131] For an excellent discussion, G. Vermes, *The Religion of Jesus the Jew* (London: SCM Press, 1993), 200–6.

[132] For humility, Phil. 2: 4–8; for resurrection, 1 Cor. 15: 4–8.

Indeed, when it comes to specifics, Paul is more likely to appeal to his own example than that of Jesus.[133] On first sight, the Gospels may seem to present a very different picture. But here too we need to ask about focus. In the Synoptics at least one verse that speaks of imitation is put retrospectively into the mouth of Jesus (Mark 8: 24),[134] but the focus is overwhelmingly upon obedience to God rather than imitation of Christ. Likewise, there is almost no room for identification in our second sense, since the disciples almost invariably, especially in Mark, function as an example not to be followed. John is different. At the Last Supper Christ explicitly enjoins imitation, while elsewhere the evangelist seems concerned to open up the possibility of identification through the actions of others in the drama, pre-eminently of course the beloved disciple. Yet that is only one author in New Testament. What at least it suggests, though, is the notion of a trajectory: an approach still weak in the New Testament, but growing and culminating in the Gothic period. In short, although neither element is present in Jesus' own teaching and nowhere strongly emphasized in the New Testament, the beginnings of *imitatio Christi* are already there in Paul, while positive identification through others in the drama is just developing by the end of the canonical period in John.

In understanding why there is little of such developments in the New Testament, we shall find part of our answer in a feature of its witness which we have already noted extensively in the previous chapter, namely that perception of the full significance of Christ was still growing in the biblical period and so, just as nowhere did it acknowledge a divinity for Christ of unqualified equality with the Father, it was also still struggling with the problem of the effective appropriation of his actions by the individual believer. There is also a deeper cultural factor of which we ought to take cognizance: the way in which the Bible shares the thought-world

[133] As, for instance, on the question of celibacy: 1 Cor. 7: 7. But the same is no less true when he is talking generally: 'Brethren, join in imitating me …' (Phil. 3: 17 RSV).

[134] Even those who think the reference to taking up the cross goes back to Jesus himself assume a general reference to martyrdom, rather than specific imitation, though this idea may be introduced in Luke's additional verse: C. E. B. Cranfield, *The Gospel according to St Mark* (Cambridge: Cambridge University Press, 1959), 282; cf. Luke 9: 23 and 27.

of the first millennium—that each of us has our own appropriate role in the scheme of things and that Christ's role was thus inevitably fundamentally different from ours. Whether as inaugurator of the new kingdom or as the one who makes atonement for our sins, his was a role which we could not be expected to emulate; our task was instead to follow and act in the way distinctive of followers rather than that of their unique leader. It was a thought-world with which the later Christus Victor and satisfaction theories of the atonement would naturally accord,[135] and these were to receive no serious challenge until the time of Abelard, who himself died at the dawn of the Gothic age (1142). It is thus not that there is nothing in the Bible to justify such moves, but that we deceive ourselves if we suppose we can establish it as a central biblical concern. The developments I have described happened because a particular nexus of social and individual factors, particularly in the Gothic period, made possible the perception of their importance, and we ought to give credit where credit is due.

When we turn to the third form of identification, however, the debt is even clearer. In its response to human suffering, the predominant response in contemporary theology is to appeal to God's identification with us as fellow sufferer on the cross. But not only does Scripture nowhere make such a move, the notion in any form is virtually absent. So familiar is the contemporary Church with reading the New Testament in this way that such a claim may well seem counter-intuitive. The reader, however, is asked to recall a similar issue in Chapter 2, where we found the original focus of the infancy narratives to lie elsewhere than in the new concerns that it was given in the Middle Ages and which continue into our own day. For Matthew and Luke the point was not to express God's total identification with our humanity in its infancy nor even to help us identify with Mary's love for her son, but partly to anticipate the significance of the cross, and partly to counter adoptionism and put in its place the idea that God's plan was prevenient throughout Christ's life.

Similarly, then, care is needed in analysing what significance the evangelists give to the close of Jesus' life. Though in no way

[135] F. W. Dillistone, *The Christian Understanding of the Atonement* (Nelwyn: Nisbet, 1968), chs. 3 and 5.

denying the fact of his suffering, it is in its atoning quality that they find its relevance, not in any sense of God thus identifying with us when we also suffer, of which there is not even a hint. On the contrary, as we saw in the previous chapter, Luke and John both show some embarrassment in how to treat the extremities of Jesus' suffering, and this is reflected in their omission of the cry of dereliction. Though those words are retained by Mark and Matthew, apart from historicity the enhancement of their atonement theology seems the most likely motive.[136] In fact, only one New Testament writing might be argued to anticipate later directions, but even in this case the issue is far from clear.

Certainly there are a couple of verses in the Epistle to the Hebrews that seem to come close to what we have in mind. On one occasion the author declares of Christ: 'since he has himself been through temptation, he is able to help others who are tempted' (Heb. 2: 18 JB);[137] on another: 'we have not a high priest who is unable to sympathise with our weaknesses, but one who in every respect has been tempted as we are, yet without sinning' (Heb. 4: 15 RSV). Out of context, the two verses might easily be taken as pointing decisively to the notion of divine identification with us in our humanity, but a number of qualifications need to be registered. First, the focus is on help in temptation rather than suffering, and this reflects the theme of the letter as whole: that Jesus has won for us direct access to God through his atoning sacrifice. Secondly, where Jesus' suffering on the cross is mentioned, it is in its quality as the completion of a perfect self-offering. The author's talk of Jesus made perfect through suffering thus has its focus not in the significance of suffering as such, but in how it contributed to Jesus' present exalted status.[138] As one commentator puts it, 'because of this perfect and completed sacrifice, he now

---

[136] Mark would therefore have intended 15: 34 to be interpreted in the light of the burden implied by 10: 45 (paralleled in Matthew at 20: 28, but not in Luke).

[137] The literal meaning of the Greek is best captured by the AV: 'for in that he himself hath suffered being tempted ...' Many modern translations make suffering and temptation two separate ideas in the protasis, but this not only distorts the Greek it also fails to give due weight to the fact that the apodosis refers to temptation alone.

[138] Where the stress lies in 2: 10: 'For it was fitting that he ... should make the pioneer of their salvation perfect through suffering' (RSV).

exercises his priesthood in heaven as the perfected Son'.[139] Finally, though Hebrews has a high Christology, one should note that it is Jesus' humanity that is held to be crucial and it is this which wins him his exalted state, rather than some prior divine status or intention. Christ is our 'pioneer' or 'leader', and so the theology might most naturally be viewed as anticipatory of the Christus Victor theology which came to dominate the first thousand years of Christianity.

If these qualifications are correct, then there would be insufficient justification for speaking even of the beginnings of a possible trajectory. Instead, resort would need to be made to a strategy similar to that which I employed in respect of Romanesque's distinctive contribution, incarnation as creativity's endorsement: a retrospective correction of the biblical witness. That the revelation of God's identification with human experience had to wait until the Gothic period may seem implausible. But it was only once the Church had securely established Christ's divinity that it could then afford itself the luxury of reflecting on the impact of that humanity upon his divinity. Even then some external stimulus was required, and that was what was provided in the Gothic period by its new empiricism and greater reflection on human experience in general. The notion of God becoming man had of course long since acquired the status of a commonplace within the tradition, but the way in which it was quickly heavily qualified (not to say, at times, wholly neutralized) in a monophysite direction for long delayed drawing what we can now see as the obvious conclusion. Among the church fathers the negative influence of Cyril of Alexandria is perhaps the most obvious, but even by the time of the Reformation the Church had still not decisively extricated itself from this difficulty.[140]

However, lest from the argument of this chapter the reader infer that I suppose that development always take a positive, welcome course, let me end my discussion of the Gothic period by drawing attention to the significant retreat it underwent on the

---

[139] H. W. Montefiore, *The Epistle to the Hebrews* (London: A & C Black, 1964), 61. Being perfected like a martyr is how he expands the sense.

[140] Though the claim seems to me exaggerated, some have not hesitated to call both Luther and Calvin 'almost monophysite'; e.g. G. L. Prestige, *Fathers and Heretics* (London: SPCK, 1940), 196.

theology of creativity, as compared to its Romanesque inheritance. The naturalism of Gothic and its concern with light make it so much more readily accessible to most of us than Romanesque that it is all too easy to judge the latter to be primitive by comparison.[141] But the possibility of an alternative view is well illustrated by the way in which so many modern artists such as Moore or Picasso have found at least part of their inspiration in Romanesque, Picasso even hanging a reproduction of a work of the San Clemente Master in his home.[142] By way of extenuation it is sometimes argued that Gothic was just as broad in its sympathies, with for example the adaptation of the pagan wheel of fortune to the rose window with God at its centre,[143] or the ready use of a pre-Christian symbol such as the Green Man.[144] But Michael Camille's survey in *The Gothic Idol* of attitudes opposed to its own suggests a different view. What makes the development particularly apposite for discussion here is the way it demonstrates how heavy a price may have to be paid, either by the Church or by outsiders, if clarity is not brought to the question of the extent to which the community of faith may legitimately go beyond the injunctions of Scripture.

What emerges is a society deeply insecure over its own creation of images, and as a result projecting upon others what can then be viewed as the forbidden versions of such creations. The profusion of images may initially suggest anything but uncertainty over their creation, but we need to recall that the Middle Ages never produced a sustained defence of their existence, and the Vulgate, as we have noted, could scarcely have been more explicit in its condemnation. Fortunately for us it ignored the injunction not to make sculptures for itself, but without any overarching theory for such rejection. The price paid was, unfortunately, the scapegoating of other groups as the real idol-makers. Among them were the Cathars (who in fact refused even to venerate the cross in case this be taken for idol worship), homosexuals, the Templars and perhaps most significantly of all, Muslims and Jews.[145] Muslims

---

[141] For the influence of Pseudo-Denys on Suger's approach to light, E. Panofsky, *Meaning in the Visual Arts*, 158–65.

[142] A. Petzold, *Romanesque Art*, 161–3.

[143] P. Cowen, *Rose Windows* (London: Thames & Hudson, 1979), esp. 86–90.

[144] W. Anderson, *Rise*, 105–24.

[145] Camille, *Gothic Idol*, 12–13, 90–6, 129–94, 271–81.

were actually provided with an alternative heretical Trinity, of Muhammad, Tergavant, and Apollo, while pagan deities generally came to be known as *mawmets*.[146] To Jews fell the misfortune of being branded as devils who attempted to misuse the true images for their own false purposes. The yellow badge and numerous other restrictions introduced at the Fourth Lateran Council in 1215 witness to a society deeply insecure about itself. Not that this was all to do with insecurity about images; economics clearly also played a part.[147] Nor is it to deny that there were also some who were more open, for example Marco Polo, who was willing to concede a degree of truth to other religions.[148] But it is to observe that the increased search for identification with Christ's humanity also sadly went with a diminution of respect for the humanity of many others. The one cannot invalidate the other, but it should make us recoil from any too facile a notion of the Christian tradition as uniformly a positive development.

[146] Camille, *Gothic Idol*, 135, 142.
[147] I. K. Little, *Religious Poverty and the Profit Economy in Medieval Europe* (London: Paul Elek, 1978), 42–57, esp. 55.
[148] Camille, *Gothic Idol*, 151.

CONCLUSION
Post/modernism and engagement

IN the previous chapters I have argued that changes in our conception of how the Bible came to be written and in the nature of its
impact in subsequent centuries require a different conception of
the relation between revelation and tradition than that which has
held sway throughout the history of Christianity. So far from
thinking of the Bible as the already fully painted canvas and the
traditions of the later Church as offering at most some optional
extra colouring, we need to think of a continuous dynamic of
tradition operating both within the Bible and beyond. That
'beyond' will then sometimes be found to merit status as revelation no less clear than what preceded it. Indeed, sometimes the
best interpretation of the situation will be that a corrective has
been provided to what was probably the dominant biblical view.

Such a perspective seems to me to have three major advantages.
The first is that it can release those of us who are Christians from
constantly trying to find in Scripture justifications for positions that
are more naturally read as later self-understandings. To give two
examples from earlier chapters, there ceases to be a need to look
for biblical passages that could in themselves legitimate either talk
of the complete equality of Christ with God the Father, or the use
of art in church. Equally, to take another two instances not previously considered, instead of the implausibility of urging that Jesus
was not opposed to divorce or Paul to homosexuality, it suggests
that discussion of such contemporary issues should be focused
upon the question of whether there are any principles thrown up
by the history of the tradition that might generate a critique of the
conclusions normally drawn from the clear biblical commitments.
Such reflection might not produce any different result, but it
would at least give a more realistic character to the shape of the
argument. Secondly, the Bible ceases to have an impossible burden
placed upon it, as somehow transcendent to all history. Though

for Christians God will still be seen as acting decisively in Christ, the pattern of divine accommodation exhibited in that life will be found to have its reflection both in the earlier history of the faith community and subsequently. Because biblical history thereby ceases to be a unique exception to the normal pattern of divine action, the perspective will require the Church to take its own history with the proper seriousness I believe it deserves. By that, though, I do not mean to endorse the views of either Orthodoxy or Rome. The former continues to speak of an unchanging tradition, while the latter in its official teaching presupposes continuous progress in understanding. To give an example from the previous chapter, the way in which image worship was so quickly projected upon Jew and Muslim surely indicates a more troubled history. Even where the Church gets the general principles for change right, their application can still go horribly wrong. Finally, the proposed model allows Christians to take seriously God's revelation operating in religions other than Christianity and indeed even more widely, through the impact of changing social conditions acting as a spur to the Church to think anew. It is, however, the possibility of a better understanding of other religions that I want most to stress here. To see God operating through a tradition means that it becomes no longer legitimate to pull isolated elements out from different religious traditions and throw them into automatic opposition to one other. Instead, context needs to be taken seriously, and that means that surface conflict will not always prove to be deeply embedded.

To leave matters there, though, would be to ignore my most important claim, and that is that the imagination is absolutely integral to the flourishing of any religion, Christianity included. The reader will recall that I began this book by considering the debate between modernism and postmodernism, and I insisted that the Church should situate itself between both. The Enlightenment was right to raise questions of historicity and objectivity, but postmodernism is also correct in noting the conditionedness of all thought and therefore the necessity for recognition of the role of community and tradition. Contemporary theologians often write as though of the two postmodernism were the one that is more naturally conducive to religious belief. In Chapter 1 I challenged that contention by observing how much Enlightenment thinking was also religiously motivated, however hostile it may have been to orthodox Christianity. Neither in fact seems to me particularly congenial to the religious desire for engagement. No doubt that is obvious in modernism's concern with objectivity, but it is no less true of postmodernism. There is a fascination with how a text functions rather than with what difference it might make to a person's life. Yet a religion like Christianity will succeed or fail not simply through the application of postmodernist concerns with internal coherence or the wider modernist desire to integrate reality as whole. It needs also an imaginative structure that can speak meaningfully to the life of contemporary believers, placed as they are at once both inside and outside their respective religious traditions. That requires a different conception of truth which is not quite captured by either position. I want therefore to end by highlighting where I detect continuing issues that need to be faced, not adequately covered by my discussion thus far but deeply rooted in the imaginative dilemmas thrown up by contemporary culture. It is these issues that I shall seek to address in my companion volume, *Discipleship and Imagination*.

Changes in visual impact: universal and particular

Much of this book has been concerned to stress the role of the imagination in the development of Christianity. Jesus himself, I suggested, experienced visions, while for most of the history of Christianity the eyes are likely to have been the primary vehicle through which religious truth was communicated. Even the retreat from images among Protestants had a less marked effect than is sometimes thought, not least because the emotional appeal of sermons was often through the listeners being urged to contemplate some particular image, such as the good shepherd, the suffering Christ or even the pains of hell.[1] The conveying of ideas, whether this be in the form of doctrine or injunctions on how to live, only gradually assumed the primary place it now has in the churches. What has caused this change is hard to say. A growing

---

[1] It is often forgotten how common religious imagery continued to remain in the home, from copies of Dürer woodcuts to Holman Hunt's hugely popular *The Light of the World* of 1856. In 1859 John Cassell's *Illustrated Family Bible* was selling 300,000 copies a week at a penny an issue: O. Chadwick, *The Victorian Church* (London: SCM Press, 2nd edn., 1972), Vol. 2, 56.

emphasis on the value of information in the culture as a whole may have played its part. So too has suspicion of appeal to the emotions, often so integral to the impact of visual images.

But one element in that decline I believe lies in the crisis within the visual arts themselves that had been going on ever since the invention of the camera. That posed in an acute form the question of what function was served by the artistic image. If representation could now be achieved more effectively by the camera, artists had to find their *raison d'être* elsewhere. In an impressive study of art and architecture in the twentieth century Mark Taylor has argued that the only proper conclusion to be drawn for theology from that history is a postmodernist one, that art in our own day is at its most significant when it hints at the transcendent other without ever promising to deliver. The reader would be right to detect the influence of Derrida, though in Taylor's case there is a stronger sense of something beyond the canvas, as when he declares of one artist's 'disfigured canvas' that 'it trembles with the approach of an Other it cannot figure'.[2] Significantly, though, he begins his book with modernist attempts to find the universal through abstract art, and rightly stresses the religious dimension in the aims of many of the artists involved.[3] If I read his argument correctly, he sees their work as magnificent failures, an excess of ambition that led almost inevitably either to totalitarian claims or else to despair in pure negativity.[4] In my view much more could be said on the other side.

That wider issue I shall not pursue here. What is interesting from the perspective of the issues raised in this book is the way in which that religious search for the universal has also been much more widely reflected in the uses to which Christian symbolism has been put in art of the twentieth century. One might almost say that, whereas in previous generations the particularity of Jesus' story was used to hint at wider, if not universal, applications, the process has now been reversed. The key artistic images begin with

---

[2] M. C. Taylor, *Disfiguring: Art, Architecture, Religion* (Chicago: University of Chicago Press, 1992), 305. He is speaking of a work by Anselm Kiefer. Others who in his view represent a similar trend include: Michelangelo Pistoletto, Michael Hiezer, and the architect Peter Eisenman.

[3] Not only at the beginning with Kandinsky, Mondrian, and Malevitch, but also in later American abstract expressionism, as well as in much minimalist architecture.   [4] Ibid., e.g. 94–5, 113, 132–3, 142.

the universal, and it is then left to the individual Christian whether or not applications are drawn for the life of Christ and thus for its relevance to the believer. An obvious example would be Henry Moore's sculptures of Mother and Child. The source of his inspiration was 'primitive' sculpture,[5] but its adoption in churches suggests that, though it begins as a universal, it can act as a cue to thinking of the relation between Mary and the infant Jesus, which in turn can reflect back upon the experience of the mother–child relationship in the percipient's own experience. Perhaps more surprisingly, the crucifixion is also found functioning in a similar way. In place of the particularity of one specific first century event, it has been usurped as an image of suffering in general. One can see such an appropriation at work already in the early Picasso,[6] but such an approach is particularly obvious in the case of Francis Bacon. The intention is to indicate the awfulness of suffering, and indeed its quality as irredeemable.[7] Though this indicates that the Church has no final control over its images, the same point applies no less for the artist. The advantage of such usage is that, even in a period of decline in explicit religious belief, the use of what was once explicit religious imagery can still throw up questions of meaning and significance.[8] The disadvantage, though, is that such imagery no longer immediately feeds into Christian belief and practice as a way of deepening the believer's engagement with the story. This is often true even of work done by practising Christians. For instance, Norman Adams' overpowering series of paintings on the theme of the Stations of the Cross so reduces the figurative detail that one's first thought must, I think, be the relation between

[5] P. James (ed.), *Henry Moore on Sculpture* (New York: Da Capo, 1992), 157–77, esp. 161–5.

[6] Picasso painted the crucifixion a number of times. Not all exhibit the universalizing tendency, but it is already noticeable in 1897. It is, however, the 1930s works that anticipate *Guernica* where particularity seems most left behind: G. Régnier (ed.), *The Body on the Cross* (Montreal: Museum of Fine Arts, 1993), ill. 6, 17–29; 74–83.

[7] 'Without any redemption': ibid., 141. Contrast Graham Sutherland: 'I was drawn to the crucifixion because … it is the most tragic of themes and yet it contains the promise of salvation:' ibid., 121.

[8] So Bacon can be read as a 'sacramental' invitation to 'purgation': W. Yates, 'Francis Bacon: the iconography of crucifixion', in J. L. Adams and R. P. Warren (eds.), *The Grotesque in Art and Literature* (Grand Rapids, Michigan: Eerdmans, 1997), 143–91, esp. 161.

the figures as universals, before one applies them in the specific situation intended.[9]

That suggests that art in the twentieth century, whether modernist or postmodernist, functions significantly differently from how it did in the past. If so, at least two issues of major importance are raised. The first is that the decline in art as narrative may all too easily lead us to misread the functions of art in Christian believing in past centuries. The temptation is to suppose a universal image, and not see the image as a means of invoking a particular story. At all events, such a contrast does suggest to me that the rejection of some images from the past may be because they have been wrongly conceived within what is in effect a contemporary framework. So, for instance, it is surely one thing to suppose that a picture of Mary Magdalene represents a sinner; quite another to say that the intention is to allude to a story of a sinner forgiven. Again, hell as an image of pain or punishment is one thing; as a story of connections between a life lived and its consequences quite another. Much of Parts One and Two of my companion volume will be devoted to such issues, for the imaginative practice of discipleship will scarcely be possible if the images upon which it could be based are consistently misappropriated or misunderstood. We need to be on our guard against attempts to impose modern assumptions about the role of images on to their past usage. The relation between universal and particular needs to be properly understood. But if that can lead to a different estimate of Christianity's past visual history from that currently given,[10] there is also another, perhaps less welcome, second issue that needs to be faced, and that is the tensions inevitably thrown up by the inherent limitations of any particular narrative to which appeal is made, including the biblical.

Tensions in story

It has recently been persuasively argued that film is the modern equivalent of painting, not only in the kind of role it exercises in

---

[9] The series was installed during 1995 in the late eighteenth-century Roman Catholic church of St Mary's in Manchester's city centre.

[10] Though not always. More attention will be devoted in that volume than in this to cases where tradition went wrong, and produced images that mislead rather than help in the pursuit of discipleship.

society but also, more profoundly, in there being obvious anticipations of types of camera shot, forms of lighting and so forth, particularly in the more emotionally charged version of the Renaissance that took place in northern Europe.[11] Certainly, as noted above, modern art that has a religious dimension seldom now begins with narrative, whereas film does, and indeed went through a period when narratives either of Christ's life itself or interconnecting with that life achieved great box-office success.[12] It has also been a period when quite a number of novelists have sought to tell the story of Jesus in their own terms. So it is worth considering whether painting has been displaced by film and novel as means of engaging with the story at a more imaginative level, or whether we are now in a period when neither the original narratives nor these more modern forms are particularly successful at securing an appropriation that goes beyond intellectual and emotional interest and becomes a real commitment to certain beliefs and practices.

It is fascinating to observe that the retelling of our own day continues past patterns. For, after some initial reserve over any direct portrayal of Christ on the screen,[13] soon one was finding modifications to the story no less significant than what earlier chapters suggested happened in the visual arts. Admittedly, part of the motivation can be seen as historical. Directors and novelists alike show signs of background reading, and sometimes explicitly advert to the fact.[14] Sometimes, though, even when historical, these changes can be otherwise motivated. So, for instance, the anti-Jewish thrust of aspects of the Gospel accounts disappears, but

[11] A. Hollander, *Moving Pictures* (Cambridge, Mass.: Harvard University Press, 1991). Her suggestion is that, whereas in the Italian Renaissance one is required to respond through the cleverness of the artist, in the north the impact is immediate, with tilted floors to accommodate our perspective (22, 57), figures growing as we watch (54–6) and so forth, with 'total engagement' the result (51).

[12] The 1959 *Ben-Hur* made forty million dollars, while in 1973 *Jesus Christ, Superstar* grossed twenty million. For a complete catalogue of the genre, R. Kinnard and T. Davis, *Divine Images* (New York: Citadel Press, 1992).

[13] It is hard for us to imagine the extent of initial public hostility even as late as 1941, when Christ was first portrayed on the radio in Dorothy Sayers' play, *The Man Born to Be King*.

[14] For some examples, W. R. Telford, 'The depiction of Jesus in the cinema', in C. Marsh and G. Ortiz (eds.), *Explorations in Theology and Film* (Oxford: Blackwell, 1997), 115–39, esp. 125.

this probably had more to do with the nature of American society and of the film industry in particular than with historical considerations, not least because in some films it is replaced by a no less implausible entirely negative portrayal of the Roman imperial government or (more worryingly) by Arab corruption.[15] Other alterations find their rationale in the desire for a more integrated narrative, and in this objective they often succeed remarkably well. A minor example would be Peter being told the parable of the prodigal son when he objects to the inclusion of Matthew among the disciples; a major, a prime role given to Barabbas as competitor for Judas's loyalty.[16] These are modifications that could have happened in any century. Others are more characteristic of our own. The downplaying of miracles would be one; references to Jesus' sexuality another. Both indicate a desire to make Jesus' life more immediately relevant to our own experience. So too does the attempt to plot some notion of psychological development in Jesus' responses.[17] Yet within such a frame the inclusion of divine elements inevitably generates new strains and tensions. This is particularly obvious in Martin Scorsese's film *The Last Temptation of Christ*, in which the two natures seem almost at war with one another.[18]

That potential for conflict is by no means, though, the only

[15] It was apparently under Jewish pressure that Cecil B. De Mille added an opening title to his 1927 version of *King of Kings* that exculpated the Jews of the time. In Nicholas Ray's version of 1961 Herod the Great is specifically identified as 'an Arab of the Bedouin tribe'. For the former, B. Babington and P. W. Evans, *Biblical Epics* (Manchester: Manchester University Press, 1993), 121.

[16] The first example comes from Zeffirelli's *Jesus of Nazareth* (1977), the second from Ray's *King of Kings* (1961).

[17] This is major feature of Norman Mailer's novel *The Gospel According To The Son* (New York: Random House, 1997). The result is sometimes intriguing explanatory hypotheses. Jesus does not act with Jairus' daughter as Elisha did in similar circumstances because any failure would then have been all the greater (98). Again, he delays going to Lazarus because he himself is in a state of feverish anxiety (142).

[18] Jesus' confrontation with a talking lion, and him pulling out his own heart to demonstrate the commitment of his 'sacred heart' are particularly unconvincing. Yet there is no doubt about the sincerity of Scorsese's desire to 'force people to take Jesus seriously', though he might have been better advised to follow his instincts and 'stress the human side' which he found 'the most accessible': D. Thompson and I. Christie (eds.), *Scorsese on Scorsese* (London: Faber & Faber, 1989), 116–45, esp. 116, 124.

source of difficulty. No less acute are the problems generated by the tension between the desire for a humanity relevant to our own day and the precise nature of Jesus' humanity, so far as this is recoverable. We have already noted the invention of a sexual history, but relevant too is the suppression of other features which, though they added to Jesus' effectiveness in first-century Palestine, are now almost inaccessible to contemporary culture, such as his visionary experience or desire to deepen observance of the Law. The reason why such problems have become so acute in our own day, I suggest, has less to do with the features in themselves and more with the way in which almost the whole burden of the significance of Christ is now placed on imitating Jesus' life.

Earlier generations approached the matter rather differently, not least because their primary focus was on his divine nature. That forced a search for various forms of mediation, as in the exploration of how his disciples or imaginary disciples responded to him, or even how later generations attempted an imitation, in lives more like the believer's own, even if declared 'saintly'. Investigation of how such mediation worked might well have lessons for today. Certainly, what we can say is that the burden of Jesus' life as at present conceived is too great. To make Jesus a homosexual in order to speak to homosexuals or to require of him belief in the equality of the sexes to speak to women suggests to me an agenda wrongly conceived. This is not because Jesus must have been heterosexual or because he believed in male hierarchy, though both are possibilities (and indeed, in my view, probabilities). Rather, it is because the question needs to be put differently, and with less exclusive a focus. The imaginative mediation of Christ's life available in earlier generations may not be the means we would now choose, but the question still needs to be raised. Must the example of the historical Jesus always be directly appropriated, if at all, or are there ways of feeding his life imaginatively through the lives of others that will then allow issues to be faced that either he himself did not face (for example, motherhood) or else faced very differently (for example, sexuality)?

In other words, instead of simply assuming immediate universal applicability, we need to face honestly the problem of what kind of role might reasonably be expected of the biblical narratives in the matter of discipleship. Must they really bear every burden or only certain kinds, and, if so, which? Might there be a legitimate task for derivative narratives that seek to apply the example of Christ in quite different social circumstances? Or are there any imaginative resources which could help deepen our involvement with the existing biblical narratives? Is there, for example, any way in which we might be enabled to place ourselves, as it were, within the story, as a means of deepening our relationship with Christ as Lord and Saviour? Or do we need a combination of such approaches? It is such issues as these that will be the other main focus of Parts One and Two of *Discipleship and Imagination*.

The authority of revelation

Because I have stressed so frequently the importance of cultural context, a hostile or more casual reader might possibly have gained the impression that I see the working of revelation as something essentially passive, as responding to cultural context rather than transcending it. That has certainly not been my intention. My point is rather that new contexts can give the necessary spur to new ways of thinking, but the latter are by no means solely the product of those contexts. Because a religion has an already existing tradition it has the resource to interact with its context, and produce in the process something that is quite different. I suggested that sometimes we should use the image of a trajectory, at other times the more radical notion of the tradition, as it were, turning back on itself to offer a critique of earlier views. That does not make it a purely human enterprise, though it does make it more difficult to identify precisely where God is at work. To locate divine activity only within the tradition would be to ignore what is sometimes an indispensable contribution from the wider cultural context. Equally, though, to leave the final say with the present would also seem a mistake, since tradition gains its power not only through its capacity for change but also sometimes from its past returning to haunt it, requiring a return to earlier views. In other words, God defies our desire for tidy categories, and so in trying to tell the revelatory story we need to recognize a God at work everywhere in his world in helping to shape our comprehension of his purposes. That of course does not mean that he is at work equally everywhere, but it should mean our readiness to listen even where he seems most distant. As I sought to indicate in Chapter 3, even biblical passages that we would not wish to describe as revelatory in themselves can still serve a function, in helping us to comprehend the fallibility of the revelatory process, and thus also of our own judgements.[19]

There is an obvious need for a more careful analysis both of how changing cultural contexts prompt changes in perception, and of what criteria might be used in judging one development revelatory and another not. In answering such questions greater clarity could be given both to the issue of how truth is being understood, and to the role envisaged for the community in coming to such decisions. Those are the major tasks reserved, primarily, for the final Part of the companion volume.[20] In this book, though, I have had to be content with more moderate aims, in illustrating specific cases in operation. Even so, the necessity for a wider conception of truth than currently prevails in much theological thinking should now be clear. The Enlightenment urged us to concentrate on truths of reason and questions of fact, and that at least has been corrected by the rise of postmodernism. But postmodernism too has its limitations. The text can become a tyrant, for ever deferring its meaning rather than liberating the reader to go beyond it.

The Authorised Version of the Bible and the Book of Common Prayer did much to shape English thinking on religion. Despite the brilliance of the authors' efforts at translation, they were clearly afraid of the imagination. Though this was not required by the original ancient languages, the word is found overwhelmingly in a negative sense.[21] Yet it was as a Christian that Wordsworth owned

> Imagination, which, in truth
> Is but another name for absolute power
> And clearest insight, amplitude of mind
> And Reason in her most exalted mood.[22]

[19] The danger otherwise is that the meaning of Scripture will constantly be distorted, in order to produce acceptable meanings.

[20] Primarily, not exclusively, because throughout the volume attention will be devoted to the implications of discipleship being pursued as part of a community, as also to providing examples where tradition failed to generate the 'right' results.

[21] e.g. Gen. 8: 21: 'the imagination of man's heart is evil' (AV). There is a similar usage in the Prayer Book's version of the Psalms, as also in the *Magnificat*: 'the proud in the imagination of their hearts'. In most modern translations the reference to the imagination disappears.

[22] *The Prelude*, Book 14, 190. The poem was rewritten several times over Wordsworth's life, and only published posthumously in 1850.

The imagination too needs its critics. But just as Wordworth here corrects his classical religious inheritance, so we too need to acknowledge how much religion flourishes, and thus the revelation that God seeks to address to humanity, by the reader in each generation being set free to appropriate what the imagination can discover in the interstices of the 'moving' texts that are a religion's story. For that to be possible truth cannot be narrowly confined to 'fact'; nor can the biblical text be allowed the final say. Image, text and truth need to work together, not in opposition.

Plate 1: In common with many others, Correggio transforms the story of the young Ganymede's violent abduction and rape by Zeus into a spiritual allegory. Whereas at roughly the same time Michelangelo chose to retain the element of homo-erotic violence as a metaphor, and a century later Rubens to supplement it with extensive use of heterosexual imagery, in this version of 1532 by Correggio it seems to have disappeared altogether. Instead, the attentive dog indicates the need for a simple faith like the child-like Ganymede, drawn by God beyond the sensuality of the painting's companion piece (the story of Io). In a similar way Pieter de Hooch was later to use the incident (in the form of a painting within a painting) to provide a critique of worldly behaviour portrayed in the main body of the canvas. For other developments, pp. 205-7.

Plate 2: There is a long history in art and literature of the story of Iphigenia being treated as the pagan equivalent of the sacrifice of Isaac. This painting is a variant on the fresco that Giambattista Tiepolo did for the Villa Valmarana at Vicenza in 1757. As here, her father Agamemnon, is placed at the edge of the painting, his head buried in his cloak and unable to look at the impending sacrifice. Likewise, in both Iphigenia is an adult and unbound, ready for her task. Here, though, she is so overwhelmed by it that she fails to notice the divine response to her commitment in the arrival of the goddess Artemis and the substitute stag. By contrast, at Vicenza she looks confidently towards the goddess who is only just appearing in the distance. The close paralleling of the two stories can be observed in the way in which his son, Giandomenico, makes the intervening angel in his *Sacrifice of Isaac* (in the Metropolitan Museum, New York) resemble his father's Artemis. For related developments, pp. 200-2, 242.

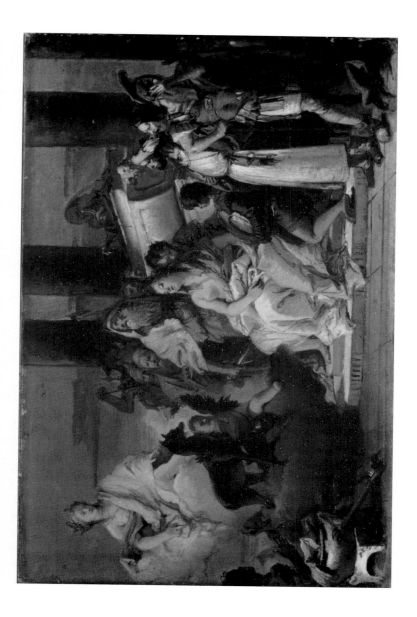

Plate 3: Although the authenticity of this painting has been challenged, it seems likely that both it and the closely related version now in Leningrad both stem from the hand of Rembrandt. In this version Abraham is clearly the main focus, a fact which could be used to argue for the view that the artist has returned to a more biblical presentation. Yet Isaac, though bound, is an apparently willing youth and not a boy, while the substitute ram is prominent on the left. In the Leningrad version (probably painted about the same time) the ram disappears and the focus definitively moves to Isaac, towards whom the angel looks instead of at Abraham (cf. pp. 237-60).

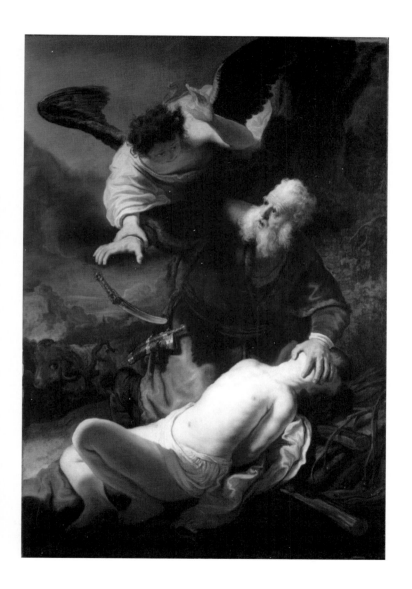

Plate 4: Probably made for the translation of Cuthbert's body in 698, the work has been described as exhibiting 'quiet simplicity' and 'homeliness' (Greenwell). Note, though, the way in which, in common with the Mediterranean models from which it ultimately derives, the child is presented not as a child but as a mini-adult, with the book of its authority (a roll) already held in its hand. For related attitudes, pp. 77-80.

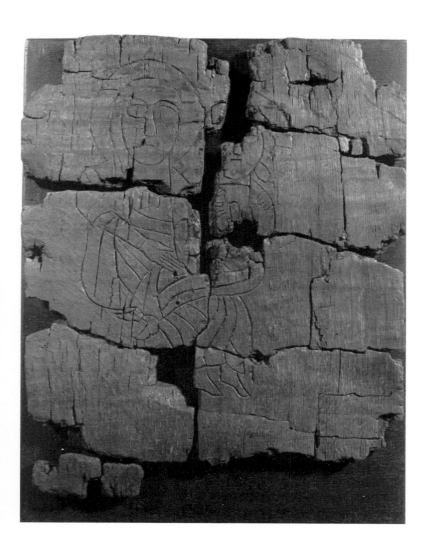

Plate 5: Although the move in art of the shepherds from their vision in the field to adoration in the stable is surprisingly late, thanks to the invention of the story of the two midwives women make an early appearance at the scene. Here the women who secure front place as worshippers are more likely to be farmers' wives since they present the child with a freshly laid egg. As symbol of the resurrection, incarnation and resurrection are thus united, with the means of their union indicated to the observers on the edge of van Dyck's painting by the sacrificial lamb before them. For shepherds, pp. 93-8, for women, pp. 75, 96.

Plate 6: In this crowded canvas, in theory devoted to the Adoration of the Kings, Jordaens seeks to indicate the participation of not only all of humanity but also of the animal world as well. Thus the identity of the kings hovers between that of state and church, while soldiers and peasants, the elderly and children, all make their appearance. Then, in addition to the usual ox and ass we also find camels, horses, and even a parrot. Perhaps recalling the cosmopolitan character of his native Antwerp (ruined by the treaty of Münster in 1648), he gives central place to the young black king. For animals, pp. 98–102.

Plate 7: In almost all first millennium portrayals of the crucifixion, the element of victory and of triumph over suffering and death is very much to the fore. But even here where the lower figures direct sponge and lance towards Christ, and Christ's own face scarcely exhibits joy, the mood is still one of interrogation of the spectator rather than of fellow-suffering. It is a stern judge who directs his gaze upon us, supported by seraphim above him, and he remains indifferent to the sponge close by his mouth (cf. pp.348–51).

Plate 8: Sutherland, reflecting on the work of Grünewald, once commented: ' I respect him, perhaps more than any other, and rank him among the greatest painters of all time'. Unlike Francis Bacon, however, who was similarly influenced and found in such tortured depictions only evidence of the meaninglessness of life, for Sutherland they contain 'an innate promise of salvation,' here hinted at in the 'aliveness' of the thorn bush at Christ's head and feet (in the latter case also acting like an altar rail). Whether the new image comes at too high a price is discussed on pp. 333-4, 351-2, 368-70.

INDEX

history   18;0923 c.csope

H. Bloom as suggesting Harnack's demand 28

80-81 foilozy - lose medieval imagination
54   230

c 279   p 295 n 54

339 Anton Catholot -> model
        open to Xp

346 origins (?) of societal imagination?
350 Durkheim as picture of the worshipper

Barnes   182